New Directions in Sexual Violence Scholarship

This edited collection brings together leading and emerging scholars in the important field of sexual violence scholarship.

The last ten years have witnessed an international reckoning on sexual violence, typified in the mainstream imagination by the #MeToo movement, acknowledgement of the violence of university campus life, and the overdue recognition of the enduring harms of child sexual abuse. While the state has been forced to respond through law and other political processes, at times revealing its agility and at other times its archaic investment in the past, much of the real work responding to sexual violence and abuse has taken place within communities, and in the personal responses of the individuals writing the scripts of their experiences. This volume explores the nuances of these individual experiences and considers how they are shaped and reflected by intersecting axes of power including gender, race, class, age and able-bodied status. It reflects on law and law reform in the area and suggests new modes and frames through which to explain and understand sexual violence and institutional responses to it. Debates within this contested personal and political arena do not map onto long-standing binaries of liberal and radical feminism, nor conservative and progressive politics. This interdisciplinary volume traces that murky terrain and features some of the leading international scholars writing on sexual violence in English today.

This book will appeal to scholars and students across the broad disciplines of law and legal studies; criminology; gender studies; political science and sociology.

Kate Gleeson is Associate Professor of Politics and Law at Macquarie University, Sydney, Australia.

Yvette Russell is Associate Professor of Law and Feminist Theory at the University of Bristol, UK.

New Directions in Sexual Violence Scholarship

Law, Power and Change

Edited by Kate Gleeson and Yvette Russell

Routledge
Taylor & Francis Group
a GlassHouse Book

First published 2023
by Routledge
4 Park Square, Milton Park, Abingdon, Oxon OX14 4RN

and by Routledge
605 Third Avenue, New York, NY 10158

Routledge is an imprint of the Taylor & Francis Group, an informa business

A Glasshouse book

British Library Cataloguing-in-Publication Data
A catalogue record for this book is available from the British Library

ISBN: 978-1-032-05146-8 (hbk)
ISBN: 978-1-032-45937-0 (pbk)
ISBN: 978-1-003-37933-1 (ebk)

DOI: 10.4324/9781003379331

Typeset in Bembo
by Deanta Global Publishing Services, Chennai, India

Contents

Contributors

Hilary Caldwell's research focus is on clients of the sex industry. Her masters at the University of Sydney explored themes such as intimacy in the commercial engagements of men who had been buying sexual services for extended periods. Her PhD at the UNSW Centre for Social Research in Health examined an emerging phenomenon of women buying sexual services. Underpinning her research, Hilary has completed masters in Health Science (Sexual Health) at the University of Sydney and works in private practice as a sex therapist seeing a broad range of clients with sex and relationship issues.

Anna Carline is a Professor of Law at the University of Liverpool. Her main areas of expertise are criminal law and criminal justice (in particular, violence against women and sexual offences), family law and feminist/gender theory, with a particular focus on New Materialism. Professor Carline has published extensively on the issues of rape, sexual violence, sex work and trafficking. Her research is socio-legal, comparative and interdisciplinary in nature, examining legal developments by drawing upon a range of social science and legal methodologies and different theoretical approaches. She is the co-author of *Rape and the Criminal Trial: Reconceptualising the Courtroom as an Affective Assemblage* with Drs Gunby and Murray.

Joanne Conaghan is a Professor of Law at the University of Bristol. She has written extensively on issues relating to law and gender, including in the areas of tort, labour law and criminal justice. She is the author of *Law and Gender.*

Sharon Cowan is Professor of Feminist and Queer Legal Studies at the University of Edinburgh. Sharon has wide academic interests and has written extensively on rape law in Scotland. Her current research is a comparative socio-legal project looking at the impact of law on transgender people.

Eithne Dowds is a Senior Lecturer in Law at Queen's University, Belfast. Her research intersects the areas of international and domestic criminal law. She is particularly interested in social and legal constructions of consent within the framework of sexual offences. Eithne's monograph, *Feminist Engagement with International Criminal Law: Norm Transfer, Complementarity, Rape and Consent*, was published in 2019. To date she has published work in a number of peer-reviewed journals including *The Modern Law Review, Feminist Legal Studies, Journal of International Criminal Justice, International Feminist Journal of Politics* and *Children & Society*.

Louise du Toit is Professor of Philosophy at Stellenbosch University in South Africa. She published *A Philosophical Investigation of Rape: The Making and Unmaking of the Feminine Self* (Routledge, 2009). She is a member of the Sexual Violence in Armed Conflict international research group based at the Institute for Social Research in Hamburg.

Nizma Fadila is the Indonesia Business Coalition for Women's Empowerment (IBCWE)'s MEL Coordinator and Research Manager who is responsible for the analysis of Gender Equality Assessment, Result, and Strategy (GEARS) at the workplace. She completed a master's degree in public health with a focus on health information at The University of Indonesia, and has been working as a professional practitioner in monitoring, evaluation and learning in various international development programs and institutions for more than ten years.

Kate Gleeson is an Associate Professor of Politics and Law at Macquarie University, Sydney, Australia. She has published widely on the legal and political regulation of sex and harm in Australia, Ireland and the UK.

Clare Gunby is a Senior Lecturer in gender based violence at Manchester Metropolitan University. Her research interests focus on sexual violence, justice, mental health and emotional labour. Clare works across disciplines and has examined legal, public health and voluntary sector responses to sexual violence (and gender-based violence more broadly) and how these can be used, typically in tandem, to reduce, prevent and recover from victimisation. Her co-authored monograph (with Drs Anna Carline and Jamie Murray), *Rape and the Criminal Trial: Reconceptualising the Courtroom as an Affective Assemblage*, was published in 2020. She has also published in a range of peer-reviewed journals including the *British Journal of Criminology* and *Feminist Criminology*. She is committed to the adoption of participatory research methods and the co-production of knowledge.

Lany Harijanti has more than 20 years of working experience in the development sector. She assisted the Ministry of Women Empowerment in establishing the minimum service standards for a multisectoral approach in handling victims of violence against women and children. In another role, she worked with Indonesia's Ministry of Planning and Development in setting up the coordination mechanisms to localise Sustainable Development

Goals in the Indonesian context. Since 2018, with the Global Reporting Initiative (GRI), she has been raising corporate awareness and provides a series of capacity building on sustainability reporting.

Anna Hush completed her PhD at the University of New South Wales Faculty of Law and Justice in 2022. Her PhD explored the institutional politics of sexual violence in the Australian neoliberal university, critically examining the role of student feminist movements and the challenges that they face within contemporary university settings. Her thesis and other peer-reviewed research lie at the intersection of feminist theory, political economy and education policy. Anna now works as a Senior Researcher in the NSW Department of Education.

Maya Juwita is the Executive Director of Indonesia Business Coalition for Women's Empowerment (IBCWE). She completed her master's degree in Business Law at The University of Gajah Mada, Indonesia, with more than 20 years of working experience as a human resources practitioner in both the private and development sector. Specifically, she has more than ten years of experience in handling sexual harassment issues in the workplace, and served as one of the workplace dignity advisors at the World Agroforestry Centre in 2011. Currently, she continues promoting the concept of workplace dignity advisory teams for companies in Indonesia.

Zelda Lupsita is the Program Manager at the Indonesia Business Coalition for Women's Empowerment (IBCWE). She held a Bachelor of Arts (BA) in Psychology from the University of Nebraska – Lincoln, a Master of Science (MS) in Human Capital Management from Bellevue University, Nebraska in 2011 and CHRP from Unika Atmajaya in 2017. She has more than ten years of experience in Social Work, Management Consultant, and Human Resources roles in several companies.

Luke McNamara is a Professor in the Faculty of Law and Justice, and co-director of the Centre for Crime, Law and Justice, at the University of New South Wales. Together with Julia Quilter he is completing the first Australian multi-jurisdictional study of sexual assault trials and how evidence of intoxication operates in trials (funded by an Australian Research Council Discovery Project Grant – DP200100101).

Vanessa E. Munro is Professor of Law at the University of Warwick, UK. She has published widely on legal and social responses to sexual violence and domestic abuse. She has been involved in several projects exploring jury decision-making in rape cases. Most recently, she has worked with colleagues on projects that explore the use and impact of the not proven verdict in Scottish rape cases; the use and impact of sexual history and private data in Scottish rape cases; the implementation of coercive control offences in England & Wales and Scotland; the use and outcomes of Domestic Homicide Reviews in cases of domestic abuse suicide; and the handling of complaints of sexual misconduct within University disciplinary processes. In the past, she has been a visiting scholar at the Universities of North Carolina and Auckland, Victoria University Wellington and Australian National University.

Julia Quilter is a Professor of Law at the University of Wollongong and has published widely in the area of sexual assault law reform.

Yvette Russell is an Associate Professor of Law and Feminist Theory at the University of Bristol. She has published widely on law, sexual violence, and feminist philosophy.

Tess Ryan is an Aboriginal woman of Biripai country, originating from Taree, New South Wales. Dr Ryan was awarded the University of Canberra Medal in 2013 for her Honours thesis regarding Indigenous political engagement. She then completed a PhD at The University of Canberra on Indigenous women's leadership in Australia. Dr Ryan has held a Postdoctoral position with The Poche Centre for Indigenous Health at The University of Melbourne which involved the facilitation of a leadership program with King's College, London, research collection and data dissemination relating to Indigenous health. Her multi-disciplinary work involves Indigenous women, media representation, Indigenous research, health, leadership and diversity. Dr Ryan has previously worked with the Australian Catholic University across curriculum, research building and leadership roles. She also works as a freelance writer, consultant and contributing editor for Croakey Health Media.

Tanya Serisier is a Reader in Feminist Theory at the School of Law, Birkbeck College. She has published widely on cultural politics of sex, sexuality and sexual violence with a particular focus on feminism, survivor discourse and speaking out. Her 2018 book, *Speaking Out: Rape, Feminism and Narrative Politics* is the only scholarly monograph to offer both a historical and a critical account of 'speaking out' as a central theme of feminist politics around sexual violence.

Zahra Stardust is a socio-legal scholar working at the intersections of sexual health, queer criminology and human rights. She is currently a Postdoctoral Research Fellow at the ARC Centre of Excellence for Automated Decision-Making and Society at Queensland University of Technology, and works on projects relating to sexual surveillance, algorithmic sexual profiling and the political economy of sextech. Her forthcoming monograph *Indie Porn: Revolutionary Promises, Regulatory Fantasies, Resistance Politics* explores the regulation of queer and feminist pornographies.

Hendri Yulius Wijaya is an Indonesian writer and the author of *Intimate Assemblages: The Politics of Queer Identities and Sexualities in Indonesia* (2020). He is also the co-editor of *Queer Southeast Asia* (Routledge 2022). He completed a research master's degree in Gender and Cultural Studies at The University of Sydney and a master's degree in Public Policy at Lee Kuan Yew School of Public Policy, National University of Singapore.

New Directions in Sexual Violence Scholarship

Law, Power and Change

Kate Gleeson and Yvette Russell

How to generate meaningful change in response to sexual violence is a perennial problem for feminist scholars. The legal and policy environments in which we conduct research give the impression of simultaneous movement and stasis in which a great deal is said, planned and even implemented but very little seems to change; a veritable "review-go-round," in Jan Jordan's words (2011). In an academic environment that prioritises fast and tangible 'impactful' research, with this volume we (the interlocutors) sought the space to think together with a view to opening up new, and repurposing 'old' and established, avenues of enquiry. We hope that what has resulted will assist all those working on sexual violence to seek out new directions for their scholarship and, ultimately, for what we demand as 'justice' in the crowded fields of sexual violence research, law and policy.

Sexual violence research and activism has always been a fast-moving field. The pace of research and of law reform has arguably accelerated in the last ten years, during which many countries witnessed a public reckoning with sexual violence, typified in the mainstream imagination by the #MeToo movement. At the same time, revered institutions were forced to confront the ubiquity of sexual assault and harassment on university campuses and governments were compelled to acknowledge the enduring harms of institutional child sexual abuse.[1] While state responses of law and other political processes have at times revealed their agility, and at other times their archaic investment in the past, much of the real work responding to sexual violence has taken place within communities and in the personal responses of individuals writing the scripts of their own experiences. This volume explores the nuances of these individual and collective experiences and how they are reflected in, and are shaped by, intersecting axes of power including gender, race and the material conditions

1 See, for example, Lewis 2022, revealing a significant number of post-18 students across the UK have experienced sexual harassment and violence during their time in further or higher education. In the Australian context, see AHRC 2017.

DOI: 10.4324/9781003379331-1

of economic class. It also reflects on processes and experiences of domestic and international law and suggests new modes and frames by which to explain and understand sexual violence and institutional responses to it: both the ways through, and the obstacles to, the realisation of justice.

The original interdisciplinary research presented in this volume was generated in two workshops that took place in Bristol, UK and Sydney, Australia in 2019.[2] These workshops brought together leading and emerging scholars along with activists and campaigners to discuss the myriad of challenges in this thorny area and to think together about the future of sexual violence research. As each workshop soon demonstrated, contemporary debates within this contested personal and political arena do not map onto long-standing binaries of liberal or radical feminism, conservative or progressive politics. Nor can our approach to sexual violence research be limited by artificial disciplinary boundaries which can have the consequence of unnecessarily restricting the scope of our thinking. For these reasons, this volume attempts to illustrate the breadth of current work being done in this area and to put different types of scholars and scholarship into conversation with each other. The volume features some of the leading international scholars writing on sexual violence in the English language today alongside the insights of a new class of emerging scholars working within law and other disciplines, as well as activists leading campaigns for a world free from sexual violence.

The volume begins with three essays that return to the nexus of an old problem identified by feminists in relation to sexual violence: The relationship between power and consent. In part one, *Reconsidering Power and Consent*, the authors re-evaluate much that is taken for granted about the nature of sexual violence and the axiomatic power of consent to act as the arbiter of ethical and lawful sexual behaviours. In the first essay, Anna Hush provides a challenge to contemporary sexual violence prevention doctrine centred on 'changing the culture' of sexist and misogynist attitudes and beliefs. Hush charts the ascendancy of cultural understandings of sexual violence in tandem with that of neoliberalism and the linguistic turn of academia since the 1990s. She instead exhorts a materialist analysis of sexual violence informed by Black and Marxist feminists to inform the dismantling of the power structures that maintain the conditions of inequality in which sexual violence takes place.

The second essay in part one is authored by Eithne Dowds, who turns to international criminal law to examine the working nature of 'consent' as a legal and common-sense construct that functions to demarcate lawful sexual

2 *New Directions in Sexual Violence Scholarship*, 16 May 2019, University of Bristol, funded by the University of Bristol Law School; *Sex and Consent in the Age of #MeToo*, 8–9 November 2019, Macquarie University, Sydney, funded by the Macquarie University Research Centre for Agency, Values and Ethics.

behaviours as those that do not entail the power relationship of coercion. Through examining sexual coercion trials conducted at the International Criminal Court (ICC) and the International Criminal Tribunal for Rwanda, Dowds highlights the relative limitations of consent in domestic criminal law, which is founded on abstracted notions of autonomy. Dowds argues for new consideration of the potential for a 'norm transfer' from international to domestic law, as one way to capture the structural, material and interpersonal pressures that impact on individuals' abilities to exercise free choice in respect of sex. In the third essay, and continuing to scrutinise consent, Zahra Stardust and Hilary Caldwell examine recent changes to Australian criminal law in respect of sexual violence perpetrated against sex workers through consent induced by fraudulent representations. Through an analysis of court cases and legislative reforms the authors demonstrate law's belated acknowledgement of the harm of consent that is vitiated by the power of fraud rather than force, the rights of sex workers to bodily integrity and their professional boundaries. Even so, this inclusive recasting of consent is defied by the state's upholding of the ultimate hierarchy of power in the form of police immunity for fraudulent representations made to sex workers in the course of their investigations. Recognising the spectrum of carceral power in which the law and police operate, Stardust and Caldwell ultimately call for the development of more just and equitable sexual societies that support sex workers' decision making and heighten their clients' communication skills, respect and capacities for consent and, therefore, the kinds of materialist social transformations envisaged by Hush and the legal evolution of consent imagined by Dowds.

In part two of the book, *Challenging the Colonial Order*, the authors reflect on the colonial origins of international and domestic laws and how these origins continue to shape the lived experiences of populations of the Global South and First Nations communities. In the first essay in this part, Louise du Toit advances a Global South critique of international law through an examination of the jurisprudence of the ICC response to rape in war. Du Toit reveals the historical contingency of the ICC's jurisprudence on European wars and its uneven infringement upon national sovereignty in countries of the North and the South. Despite welcome advances in the recognition of rape as a war crime, Du Toit identifies within the ICC a tactic of 'spectacularising' sexual violence in non-Western states that implicates international criminal law in enduring structures of coloniality based on long-standing legal and social constructs of racial and sexual difference.

In her essay in part two, Tess Ryan notes how in Australia, Aboriginal and Torres Strait Islander women have been at the fore of resisting power and advocating against the violence perpetrated against them under conditions of colonialism, and yet the political and legal regimes they are subject to are such that many of their experiences of oppression and resistance remains undocumented. Ryan highlights the paucity of statistical data concerning Aboriginal and Torres Strait Islander Australians' experiences of sexual violence and how this wilful distortion of national knowledge intersects with other power dynamics, including those within white feminism and the coercive power of the state. She contrasts these forms of malign power with the resources drawn on by Indigenous communities, including of lived experience in narrative stories and trauma-informed practices that provide self-determined approaches to healing.

Continuing in Australia, in her essay Kate Gleeson illustrates the complex ways in which sexual violence becomes a touchstone through which the state inflicts violence on colonised communities through the criminal law. Through the example of the recent abolition of the Homosexual Advance Defence, Gleeson demonstrates the limitations of law reform in combatting racism and homophobia, the vestiges of which endure long after the decriminalisation of men's same-sex desire in Australia and the passage of racial equality laws. She positions this legacy of homophobia alongside the related aftermath of colonial sexual violence enacted on the bodies and nations of First Peoples as a form of occupation, to highlight the enduring coloniality of law that cannot simply be absolved in the course of its amendment. All three essays in part two note the continuing power of the state and institutions to write the scripts of the lives of colonised peoples and the tireless resistance required to identify the workings of this regime by reading from the South and from First Nations perspectives.

In part three of the book, *Reforming the Rape Trial*, the authors tackle one of the key sites where sexual violence is mediated, proscribed and delineated by the state: The domestic courtroom and its arcane rules and procedures. Reflecting on several common law jurisdictions, the authors analyse and account for outcomes for those victims of sexual violence who choose to engage with the criminal justice system. Despite the distinct trajectories of law reform in different jurisdictions throughout the past 40 years, the authors reach chillingly similar conclusions about the limitations of procedural and evidentiary reforms. In their essay, Joanne Conaghan and Yvette Russell engage in a jurisdictional review of several similar common law countries focusing on the development and critical reception of laws concerning the admissibility of 'sexual history' evidence. Despite the recognition of the need for reform in the area, Conaghan and Russell demonstrate that in many of the jurisdictions considered, the conceptual and practical problems of evidentiary procedures around sexual history are remarkably similar, and that a deep mistrust of women's claims of sexual violation persists at the heart of the common law. Conaghan and Russell draw together some key recurring trends in the law and policy of these disparate jurisdictions concluding with a call for feminist scholars to prioritise the important and difficult work of reckoning with the underlying logic that continues to support the use and relevance of sexual history evidence in the rape trial.

Writing from Scotland, Sharon Cowan continues this theme in the second essay in this part, through her analysis of the failures of 'rape shield' laws designed to protect complainer from inappropriate questions about their sexual history and character in court. In a contemporary legal and political climate characterised by much fanfare about reforms and attention paid to sexual violence, Cowan documents the repeated failures of Scottish rape shield laws that work to sustain a 'justice gap' for victims, and she identifies the deeper changes required at substantive, procedural and societal levels.

Julia Quilter and Luke McNamara present an original empirical study of Australian higher court decisions considering evidence about a complainant's level of intoxication in sexual assault trials. Much like the preceding essays, the authors point to the failure of reforms when they observe that across all Australian states and territories complainant intoxication evidence continues to impede conviction, despite legislative efforts to the contrary. Persistent myths about women, alcohol, inhibition and the capacity for accurate recall continue to sway both judges and juries. In all these essays the authors reckon with the paradox presented by academic and activist engagement with legal reforms, which often fail to achieve the change it purports to be enacting while remaining the primary gateway for change in liberal society.

Finally, for part three, in her essay Vanessa Munro provides an original empirical study of complainers' experiences of the unique Scots verdict of 'not proven,' by which jurors can elect to acquit accused persons without determining they are not guilty. Munro draws on interviews and focus groups to understand complainers' experiences of this troubling verdict, including its long-term impacts on their sense of closure and justice, to reflect on how those challenges are likely to be echoed in the experiences of other victim-survivors, regardless of individual case progressions and outcomes.

In part four of the book, *Speaking Truth to Power*, the authors examine how individuals respond to sexual violence, politically, collectively and personally. They also attempt to think-through the implications of different modes of resistance to sexual violence and harassment. In the first essay in this part, Tanya Serisier provides a compelling account of the aftermath of the international #MeToo movement, situating it in the context of the long history of feminists 'speaking out' about sexual violence and identifying the continued obstacles for grassroots movements driving systemic change in the face of powerful opposition of the state. For revolutionary change to occur, Serisier argues that sexual violence must be understood as part of a nexus of power relations, including race and class, and for greater strategic precision to be applied to the 'politics of speech' as one arm of activism in campaigns against oppression.

In their essay, Anna Carline and Clare Gunby report on an empirical study of individuals who attended the evocative *Let's Talk About Sexual Violence* art exhibition the authors conducted at the University of Leicester, UK, to challenge misconceptions about sexual violence and educate students and the public about the limits of the law. Reflecting on affect theory and New Materialism, Carline and Gunby bring to life the extraordinary power of art to evoke empathy and other emotions through aesthetics, and thereby transform attitudes including stereotypes about sexual violence – work which goes to the core of violence prevention initiatives.

Finally for this volume, in their essay Hendri Yulius Wijaya, Lany Harijanti, Maya Juwita, Nizma Fadila and Zelda Lupsita provide unique insights from activists working on the ground to combat sexual harassment in Indonesian workplaces, in the form of the Indonesia Business Coalition for Women's Empowerment (IBCWE). In the context of heightened political attention paid to sexual and morality offences in Indonesia, the authors draw on academic insights about governance feminism to characterise the work of the IBCWE challenging sexist stereotypes and predatory workplace behaviours, through voluntary initiatives that lie beyond the scope of legal regimes. Through their work with individual businesses, the authors provide original and convincing arguments for the power of activists to drive social and cultural change, potentially years in advance of state responses, if they are to ever eventuate. Perhaps most of all, each of the essays in this part inspires us to consider new directions in sexual violence scholarship which, although it is often conducted in the shadow of the law, may realise its ultimate potential when considering the work of victim-survivors, grassroots activists and professional practitioners whose day-to-day work embodies the ethos of speaking truth to power and holding the state to account for its endemic failures in this area.

As editors we want to extend our thanks to the contributors to this volume and to the other participants of our workshops in 2019, from which this remarkable work originated. We consistently benefit from the solidarity and nourishment of the community of scholars, activists and thinkers working on sexual violence, whose desire for justice, in its many guises, drives our work forward. Moreover, it is an immense privilege to 'think together' in spaces in which we feel supported and inspired and in which we can do our best work. It is our hope that readers of the volume will be similarly inspired and the conversation can continue.

References

Australian Human Rights Commission. 2017. "Change the Course: National Report on Sexual Assault and Sexual Harassment at Australian Universities." *Redress* 26 (2): 27–29.

Jordan, Jan. 2011. "Here We Go Round the Review-Go-Round: Rape Investigation and Prosecution—Are Things Getting Worse Not Better?" *Journal of Sexual Aggression* 17, no. 3: 234–249.

Lewis, Joe. 2022. *Sexual Harassment and Violence in Further and Higher Education*. House of Commons Library. Accessed August 17, 2022. https://researchbriefings.files.parliament.uk/documents/CBP-9438/CBP-9438.pdf.

Part One

Reconsidering Power and Consent

Chapter 1

Thinking beyond 'Cultural Change'

Towards a Materialist Theory of Sexual Violence Prevention

Anna Hush

The mainstream contemporary feminist movement overwhelmingly conceptualises the problem of sexual violence as a cultural issue, perpetuated by gendered attitudes, beliefs and norms. This dominant paradigm produces a widespread impetus towards 'cultural change' as a means of addressing sexual violence. The term is splashed across the cover of publications from UN Women (Sen 2019) and the World Health Organization (2009); it is also particularly prominent in literature on campus sexual violence, such as the Universities UK Taskforce report *Changing the Culture* (2016), and is a buzzword in popular media coverage of sexual violence in workplaces and in the broader public. But, despite its popularity, this rhetoric of 'cultural change' is broad, vague, and rarely critically interrogated. If 'culture' is standing in for norms, values, and beliefs, then the cultural paradigm suggests that this is the level on which sexual violence primarily ought to be challenged: That is, the level of ideas, representation and attitudes. This touches on deep and persistent theoretical questions about the relationship of culture to social structure on which feminists have significant disagreements. Some feminist traditions focus on how demeaning representations of marginalised groups create a socio-cultural environment in which sexual violence is more likely to take place, and correspondingly concentrate on the potential for transforming cultural norms and representations in order to reduce the prevalence of sexual violence.

Yet there are other feminist traditions which foreground instead how the structural conditions of a particular society create the grounds for sexual violence to occur. Marxist feminists have worked to highlight the interconnections between the structural inequality produced by the capitalist mode of production and the prevalence of sexual violence. This theoretical tradition understands culture as inherently connected with social *structure*, rather than something free-floating that can be changed by fiat, independently of social structures. In this sense, Marxist feminists envision a much deeper and wider social transformation than merely changing ideas and beliefs, suggesting that any transformation of culture must go hand-in-hand with transformations in the gendered and racialised capitalist mode of production. Here, I draw on Black and Marxist feminist theory to critically appraise widespread calls for cultural change, to consider how culture relates to social structure, and thus

DOI: 10.4324/9781003379331-3

to follow pathways for thinking differently about sexual violence prevention, against the dominant injunction to 'change the culture.'

In this chapter, I first explore the dominance of the concept of cultural change in mainstream sexual violence policy and prevention work, analysing Australia's national primary prevention framework to demonstrate the influence of this cultural paradigm. I link the rise of this particular way of thinking about sexual violence to the postmodernist 'cultural turn' in academic feminist theory, as well as the broader effects of neoliberalism on radical political theory. I argue that while the transformation of norms, values and attitudes is of critical importance to social change, the cultural paradigm has displaced analysis of the relationship between culture and social structure, and thus that mainstream sexual violence prevention focuses too narrowly on intervening in the former. Then, I turn to Black and Marxist feminist theory to consider alternative ways of understanding the roots of sexual violence and the strategies for resisting it. Focusing particularly on the seminal work of Angela Davis and Silvia Federici, I argue that these theoretical traditions offer critical insights for conceptualising the historical and material contexts of sexual violence. These interventions reveal how sexual violence functions as a tool of white supremacist, patriarchal capitalism, situating sexual violence within broader patterns of conflict and antagonism within society. In the conclusion, I consider the implications of a materialist theory of sexual violence for praxis – that is, the strategies that movements and communities adopt to challenge sexual violence – highlighting transnational struggles against sexual violence that mobilise a materialist understanding of sexual violence and its prevention.

'Rape Culture' and Cultural Change in Australian Primary Prevention Work

Thinking about rape through a cultural lens (what I call the 'cultural paradigm') has a significant history in feminist theory. Its main roots lie in 1970s radical feminism, which sought to show that sexual violence was not a series of isolated, individual incidents, but a systemic phenomenon that permeated many or all aspects of patriarchal societies. The popular concept of *rape culture* has since come to signify the extensive and culturally entrenched nature of sexual violence as "a complex of beliefs that encourages male aggression and supports violence against women" (Buchwald, Fletcher and Roth 2005, xi).[1] Conceiving of rape culture in this way has a number of putative benefits and strategic aims. First, it aims to highlight the socialised nature of sexual violence.

1 It is noteworthy that early radical feminists put forward a somewhat different understanding of rape culture than the more recent one cited here. As Ellen Willis reflects, "we argued that male supremacy was in itself a systemic form of domination - a set of material, institutionalized relations, not just bad attitudes" (Willis 1984, 93).

This paradigm suggests that in a culture where men are expected to be more dominant, assertive and physical, and women more passive, self-effacing and emotional, sexual violence is more likely to be tolerated and excused (Gavey 2005, 79–101). Thus, rather than being biological or inevitable, sexual violence is culturally instantiated through gendered norms and expectations. This exposes both the historical contingency of rape culture and its potential for transformation. Second, the cultural change paradigm draws connections between seemingly harmless or small acts such as sexist jokes or micro-aggressions, and the prevalence of sexual violence and other more extreme forms of gendered violence. According to this paradigm, small acts like jokes create a cultural climate in which sexual violence is more likely to be tolerated or normalised. This paradigm is often visually summarised in a pyramid shape, with acts such as "offensive jokes," "slut-shaming," "objectification," or "catcalling" at the base, and rape and murder at the apex (see, for example, 11th Principle: Consent! 2017). This pyramid structure posits cultural norms and discursive acts as the enabling foundation for sexual violence. In this way, the cultural paradigm suggests a clear strategy for addressing sexual violence. If norms are what enable sexual violence, then these same norms can act as a lever for reducing the incidence of sexual violence; remove the foundations, and the building collapses.

The concept of rape culture has also faced some critique. A monolithic understanding of rape culture might suggest that all women within such a culture (and the term 'culture' is, usually, employed in the singular) are equally at risk of experiencing sexual violence or victim blaming, or that these experiences are homogeneous, when evidence shows that they are in fact highly stratified along lines of class, disability, race and so on. As Alison Phipps et al. (2018, 5) note, populist discourses of rape culture can betray "a tendency to essentialize the male body *as violence*" – perhaps a legacy of the historical roots of these discourses in 1970s radical feminism, as noted above.[2] Further, writing specifically about university policies that presume a "universally experienced 'campus rape culture,'" Grace Kyungwon Hong (2018) argues that such a perspective is "inadequate because it flattens out the very different hierarchies of power that are animated by and contribute to sexual violence," such as racism, homophobia and transphobia. In this way, popular understandings of rape culture can reinscribe a universalising meta-narrative that "rape can happen to anyone" (Hall 2004). This paradigm also, as I will go on to argue in this chapter, runs the risk of over-emphasising the cultural and discursive aspects of sexual violence, in doing so overlooking the structural and institutional

2 For an analysis of how public discourses on rape prevention reinforce an essentialist understanding of women's "vulnerability" and rely on fear to enlist women into risk management practices, see Hall 2004.

conditions that enable sexual violence to occur, a shift in emphasis that has significant implications for prevention work.

These critiques notwithstanding, the concept of rape culture has had an immense influence on popular understandings of sexual violence, bringing to the foreground the normative and attitudinal patterns that are associated with high rates of sexual violence. This influence is evident in mainstream sexual violence prevention work, in which norms and attitudes are conceptualised as being the key drivers of sexual violence and thus constitute the key targets for prevention efforts. This trend is visible at the level of international governmental organisations (such as UN Women and the World Health Organization, as indicated above), as well as at national and local levels. Given my positionality as an Australian researcher and practitioner, I focus here on an example from the Australian context (the national primary prevention framework) to demonstrate the influence and effects of this way of thinking. Released in 2015, *Change the Story* is Australia's national framework for the primary prevention of gendered violence. This framework puts forward an explanatory model of violence against women that posits a causal relationship between four primary "gendered drivers of violence against women" and the prevalence of gendered violence in Australia. These drivers are:

1. Condoning of violence against women;
2. Men's control of decision making and limits to women's independence in public and private life;
3. Rigid gender roles and stereotyped constructions of masculinity and femininity;
4. Male peer relations that emphasise aggression and disrespect towards women (Our Watch et al. 2015, 23–26).

The *Change the Story* framework places its emphasis primarily on individual beliefs, behaviours and attitudes and collective norms as the drivers of gendered violence, especially in points 1 (*condoning*), 3 (*stereotyped constructions*) and 4 (*male peer relations*). While the second driver might seem to hold more promise for analysis of the institutional and material conditions that distribute power, the framework goes on to articulate this driver as "men who adhere to notions of masculinity that involve male control and dominance" (Our Watch et al. 2015, 24), rather than any specific institutional structures that afford men power and control in public and private life. Further, while the framework does note that these four drivers occur in the broader context of "gender inequality in public and private life" (Our Watch et al. 2015, 24), it largely omits analysis of any specific social structures (such as legislation, policy, institutional structure and the distribution of resources) that shape the prevalence of gendered violence. There is no sustained attention given to how poverty, homelessness, or other forms of economic disadvantage place certain people at a heightened risk of experiencing sexual violence – any structures other than gender are considered to be of secondary importance.[3] The framework states, "other factors [such as economic inequality] interact with or reinforce gender inequality to contribute to increased frequency and severity of violence against women, but *do not drive violence in and of themselves*" (Our Watch et al. 2015, 6, emphasis added). Correspondingly, the need to address structural discrimination and disadvantage is placed last in the list of recommended actions in the report, under the category "supporting actions" rather than "essential actions" (Our Watch et al. 2015, 34). In his analysis of this document and its approach, criminologist Michael Salter (2016, 466) concludes that *Change the Story* "sustains the prioritisation of gender norms over structural gender inequality at the macro-level and indeed at all levels of the social ecology, with the exception of 'systems, institutions and policies'."

Flowing on from this conceptual focus on gender norms as the 'story' behind sexual violence, the practice of primary prevention in Australia is organised around education. A report published by the National Association of Services Against Sexual Violence noted that education programs, especially those based in schools, "are now recognised as the most prevalent form of doing sexual and domestic violence prevention in Australia" (Carmody et al. 2009, 14). In some instances, primary prevention is treated as functionally synonymous with education; for example, Australian sexual violence researchers Nicola Henry and Anastasia Powell describe primary prevention as "commonly directed towards addressing the key underlying causes of sexual violence, including cultural *attitudes, values, beliefs and norms* about masculinity, sexuality, gender and violence" (Powell and Henry 2014, 3, emphasis added). Similarly, the Women NSW strategy for preventing sexual violence (2017–2021) conceptualises prevention as "*increasing knowledge, awareness and understanding* of the nature and causes of domestic and family violence; and *influencing attitudes* to bring about behavioural change" (Women NSW 2016, 3, emphasis added). Financial support for educational activities under 'Respectful Relationships' funding streams reinforce the centrality of education to primary prevention activity in Australia (Walden and Wall 2014, 11).

I do not want to undermine the important efforts by primary prevention practitioners in challenging damaging gender norms, nor underestimate the potential for education to meaningfully contribute to political change. My concern, rather, is that this focus on culture has eclipsed analysis of the range of structural and material conditions that give rise to sexual violence (as seen, for example, in the *Change the Story* framework, in which socioeconomic inequality, racism, homophobia, and colonialism are relegated to being secondary factors that 'do not drive violence'). My contention here is that the predominantly cultural approach taken in mainstream sexual violence policy and prevention

3 This particular deficiency is acknowledged in the interim review and reflection on *Change the Story*, released three years after the original report's publication (Our Watch 2019, 36–37).

is practically and conceptually deficient due to its delinking of culture from the structural contexts that are mutually constitutive with cultures of violence.

Feminist Theory's 'Cultural Turn' and the Advent of Neoliberalism

How did this understanding of sexual violence as a cultural problem, constituted predominantly by beliefs, attitudes and behaviours, reach a position of hegemony? After all, it is not the only way of thinking about sexual violence; there are a number of alternative traditions that frame the problem rather differently, as I will explore in the next section. Here, I argue that there are two major, and interrelated, trends that have underpinned the dominance of a cultural understanding of rape. The first is a shift in feminist theory during the 1980s that is commonly referred to as the 'cultural turn.' Michèle Barrett (1992, 204) describes this decade in feminist theory as being characterised by "a marked interest in analysing processes of symbolization and representation — the field of 'culture' — and attempts to develop a better understanding of subjectivity, psyche and the self." At a time where Marxist and socialist feminism were declining in popularity (particularly after the end of the Cold War) and liberal feminism was in ascendance, the structural analysis and historical materialist methods of Marxist feminism, and indeed the more systematic critiques of the patriarchy put forward by radical feminists, were eclipsed by a cultural approach. This new form of analysis focused primarily on language, psychology and identity in a search to understand how identities and practices were discursively constituted in the cultural field. Nancy Fraser describes this movement as one from a focus on *redistribution* of resources and power, to a focus on the *recognition* of maligned identities through, for example, better representation in the media and in organisational hierarchies. While claims for recognition are of central importance to feminist, anti-racist and other progressive struggles, Fraser (2000, 108) argues that they take on a particular tenor and prominence in the context of neoliberal globalisation: "in this context, questions of recognition are serving less to supplement, complicate and enrich redistributive struggles than to marginalize, eclipse and displace them." When this movement of displacement occurs, "the roots of injustice are located in demeaning representations, but these are not seen as socially grounded. For this current, the nub of the problem is free-floating discourses, not institutionalized significations and norms" (Fraser 2000, 110).

This cultural turn, of course, is not confined to feminist theory. It occurred alongside a much broader shift towards postmodernist and poststructuralist approaches in social and political theory, as has been widely analysed by critical theorists and Marxist philosophers (see, for example, Jameson 1991; Callinicos 1990). As Fraser (2000) notes, it is no coincidence that this shift occurred simultaneously with major transformations in the global political economy from the 1970s onwards. During a period in which capital accumulation was facing a number of crises and worker organisation and militancy were at a relative high, the capitalist class sought "to open up new fields for capital accumulation in domains hitherto regarded off-limits to the calculus of profitability" through financialisation, privatisation and commodification (Harvey 2005, 160). At the same time, postmodernist theory was on the rise in the academies of the Global North. Its focus on subjectivity, perception and affect, and the differences and fractures not only between individuals but within the "schizoid" subject itself (Deleuze and Guattari 2014) called into question notions of solidarity and collective identity that underpinned working-class and anti-colonial movements, which were simultaneously under assault by neoliberal shifts in the global political economy. Encapsulating the decline of institutional and systemic analysis in the postmodern intellectual era, Jean-François Lyotard (1984, xxiv) famously defined postmodernism as "incredulity towards meta-narratives." Structural accounts of social phenomena, such as those posited by anti-colonial and Marxist theorists, were now to be treated with suspicion – hence Chandra Talpade Mohanty's claim that postmodernism "depoliticizes radical theory" through "the privatization of social divisions and the individualization of experience" (Mohanty 2013, 970, 986). It is true that feminist theorists have more recently shifted away from a hegemonic adherence to postmodernism, as is evident in the rising popularity of 'new materialist' feminisms, though as Joanne Conaghan (2016, 43) argues, little work in this field has engaged in depth with "the diversity and sophistication of positions within the existing historical materialist tradition." In this sense, the hostility of much mainstream feminist theory towards Marxist analysis endures, explaining in part the marginalisation of structural concerns within theories of sexual violence prevention.

Analysing the concept of cultural change within this political, economic and theoretical context allows us to consider the conceptual baggage that the concept carries by virtue of this lineage. While radical feminists who initially proposed the concept of 'rape culture' did so to highlight the systemic and structured nature of sexual violence, the contemporary paradigm of sexual violence as a cultural problem is vulnerable to an individualising tendency, and risks regressing to a 'bad apples' approach (for example, the focus in *Change the Story* on "men who adhere to notions of masculinity that involve male control and dominance").[4] Ironically, given the aversion of postmodern theorists to meta narratives, this cultural turn has in some ways reinscripted its own meta-narrative in which all men are potential rapists and all women potential victims. The cultural paradigm also motivates particular responses to sexual violence.

4 This is not to say that all social constructionist accounts are necessarily individualistic – Nicola Gavey, for example, uses Foucault to "think beyond reductive individualistic ways of understanding human behaviour" and to consider "how culturally shared patterns of meaning and normative practices limit us in various ways" (Gavey 2005, 7).

Instead of participating in collective movements to smash the patriarchy, the onus of the prevention of sexual violence has shifted to an interpersonal level, where the focus is on calling out micro-aggressions and educating individuals into the correct form of sexual politics. In some cases, as Tanya Serisier (2021, 15) notes, such an approach to sex education may implicitly position middle-class white women (and feminists) as those with "respectable" knowledge about consent, and those without such knowledge as unsophisticated, ignorant, and in need of instruction. As Salter (2016, 466) summarises,

> the proposition that [violence against women] is a cultural problem to be prevented and treated largely by improved education and changes to attitudes dovetail[s] with neoliberal characterisations of social problems in terms of individual maladjustment and 'bad' family and community cultures.

While the concept of cultural change can resonate with the disciplinary individualism of neoliberalism, it may also evoke associations between culture and race that are present in populist and neo-conservative discourses. There is, I would argue, an association between emphasising the cultural dimensions of sexual violence, and the tendency of politicians, conservatives and some feminists to blame sexual violence on "other cultures," a tendency that is heightened in a climate of anti-immigrant sentiment, Islamophobia and anti-Black racism (Phipps 2020, 12–34). In such a climate, the existence of sexual and family violence within migrant, Indigenous and non-white communities tends to be treated as a symptom of inherent cultural difference or 'tradition,' rather than as an effect of poverty, displacement, colonialism and/or structural oppression.[5] In her analysis of *femonationalism* – the mobilisation of notions of women's rights in the service of Western empires – Sara Farris (2017) examines European integration policies to show how the formulation of gender equality as a 'Western value' to which migrants must assimilate relies on an imaginary of migrants as culturally backwards and sexually devious, with violence embedded in 'Islamic culture.' The concept of 'cultural change' in this context takes on a more sinister tone, with the imperative of cultural integration (imagined as a route towards gender equality and freedom) linked to forced assimilation policies, surveillance and threats of deportation. While this connotation certainly may not be intended by mainstream feminists who promote 'cultural change' as a remedy for sexual violence, it is nonetheless important to be attentive to the conceptual baggage that the notion of 'culture' carries in a context where

5 Examples of this in the Australian conservative media include frequent fear-mongering about "sexual assault by young migrants from cultures with deeply ingrained hostility towards Western women" (Oriel 2019), as well as about "African gangs" with a "pattern of contempt for police and pitiless violence against outnumbered victims" (The Australian 2018).

'culture' is frequently deployed as a softer, or more socially acceptable, synonym for race.

Idealism and Materialism

So far, I have argued that there is a tendency in mainstream sexual violence prevention work to think of sexual violence in predominantly cultural terms, foreclosing opportunities for structural and institutional analysis. I now consider more closely the conceptual relationship between culture and social structure from a historical materialist perspective, proposing that the materialist method provides critical insights for conceptualising the relationship between cultural formations, social structure and social change. Within the cultural paradigm, the dominant focus on attitudinal change, and the relegation of structural disadvantage to a factor of relatively minor importance, is reliant on an implicit theory of change that understands ideas and thought as the primary levers of social change, an orientation that can be described as *idealist* in the philosophical sense (Marx and Engels 1977, 39–41). As I argued above, this is linked to the postmodernist and social constructionist foundations of the cultural change paradigm, which foreground the discursive construction of subjects, identities and practices. As a result, the cultural change approach begins at the individual level, seeking to change hearts and minds through education, in order to "shift social support for attitudes, beliefs, behaviours, systems and practices that justify, excuse, trivialise or downplay violence against women and their children" (Our Watch, VicHealth, and ANROWS 2015, 33). Once these phenomena no longer have attitudinal support among the population, it is posited, they will no longer occur.

A materialist approach, in contrast, seeks to place ideologies within the context of specific social structures that uphold, and are upheld by, these ideologies. Materialism as method begins not with the consideration of thought and concepts, but with the historical conditions of social life: "the real individuals, their activity and the material conditions under which they live, both those which they find already existing and those produced by their activity" (Marx and Engels 1977, 42). For Marx, the capitalist mode of production is therefore treated as the substrate upon which thoughts and representations emerge within any particular social context: "as individuals express their life, so they are. What they are, therefore, coincides with their production, both with *what* they produce and with *how* they produce" (Marx and Engels 1977, 42). Human thought, under this model, stands in a dialectical relationship to the material conditions that produce it. In the context of sexual violence, this approach suggests that what enables the occurrence of sexual violence is not *only* the mindset of certain people (for example, their feeling of entitlement to sex or their flawed understandings of consent) but *also* the social conditions that they find themselves in, and the distribution of power and resources within these conditions. As cultural norms and material conditions stand in a dialectical relationship, the latter shape and reinforce the former, and vice-versa. To give a more concrete example, the widespread sexual harassment of women in subordinate positions in the workplace is partially due to the misogynistic attitudes of individual men in positions of power, but also partially due to the gendered relations of production that concentrate women in lower-paid and more precarious working conditions. These labour relations have a double effect: they can justify and reinforce the attitudes of those in power that treat these women as expendable or as objects for their own gratification, and they also constrain the ability of women workers to challenge this harassment, at the risk of losing their jobs. So, while educating these men about treating women with respect is important, it only addresses part of the equation. It leaves untouched the social relations that are mutually constitutive with the ideology in question, failing to draw links between the violence of sexual harassment and the exploitation that women face *as workers* within the patriarchal capitalist mode of production. Drawing these links, as I will argue in the final section, has significant implications for anti-rape praxis.

Materialist Theories of Sexual Violence

In this section, I turn to Black and Marxist feminist theory to consider alternative ways of understanding the roots of sexual violence. These approaches use the tools of political economy to understand the historical emergence of sexual violence as a widespread social phenomenon, and its function within the social relations of white supremacist, patriarchal capitalism. Broadly, this tradition "locates sexuality within a broader set of social relations through which people make lives, specifically the organization of production and social reproduction" (Sears 2017, 172). My account of this alternative tradition, which I group under the broad umbrella of 'materialist theories of sexual violence,' is just a sketch; my aim in this section is to highlight some scholarship that thinks differently about sexual violence, provides alternatives to the 'cultural change' paradigm, and might open up new directions for prevention practice by broadening the horizon of what sexual violence prevention looks like.

The first contention of a materialist account of sexual violence is that this phenomenon has not always existed in the same way – the dynamics of sexual violence have shifted over time to serve somewhat different social functions, attendant to historical shifts in the social relations of production and reproduction. Marxist feminists understand gender relations, within the capitalist mode of production, to represent a means of ordering production and reproduction. Gender roles act, in part, to segregate unpaid reproductive work in the domestic sphere from waged labour in the sphere of production, and to naturalise this division. Through this lens, sexual violence can be understood as one form of violence that reinforces this gender order, securing both the social power of men and the profits of the capitalist class. Clearly, these social relations between genders and economic classes are not static, with the distinction between production and reproduction varying across time and space (Bakker 2007). A materialist account, then, seeks to situate the shifting prevalence and state regulation of sexual violence within these social relations – not to argue that sexual violence is simply determined by these macro-social forces, but to understand whose interests are served by its prevalence.

In *Caliban and the Witch*, Silvia Federici (2014) puts forward a historical analysis of the privatisation of social reproduction, unearthing the bloody history of the transition from feudalism to capitalism in Europe. Federici argues that the witch hunts carried out in the 16th and 17th centuries were primarily an attempt to stifle the erotic, reproductive and social power that women held, to entrench the new sexual division of labour that the capitalist mode of production necessitated, and in doing so to forcibly confine women to unwaged, domestic reproductive labour. As Federici shows, though, proletarian women and men did not accept their fate within this new order easily, staging rebellions and revolts to defend the commons, looting property, and becoming vagabonds. The constant resistance of peasants and serfs motivated new forms of social discipline on the part of capital and the state, including the strategic and selective authorisation of sexual violence against proletarian women. Federici posits that rape was effectively *de*-criminalised in 14th-century Venice, as long as its victims were lower-class women (Federici 2014, 47). The effect of this, Federici argues, was that "the state-backed raping of poor women undermined the class solidarity that had been achieved in the anti-feudal struggle" (Federici 2014, 48). At the same time, the normalisation and legalisation of sexual violence "desensitized the population to the perpetration of violence against women, preparing the ground for the witch-hunt which began in this same period" (Federici 2014, 48–49). New modes of sexual politics emerged, in other words, that were directly beneficial to the political and economic projects of the church, the state and the emergent capitalist classes, serving to undermine the organised power of proletarian women and to justify and normalise the brutal and deadly witch hunts that were to follow.

While Federici's account is largely confined to Western European history, Black Marxist theorists such as Angela Davis offer further insights into how sexual violence has functioned as a tool of racial capitalism, particularly in the context of the institution of slavery. Davis explores how the institutionalisation of property rights, held by slaveowners over Black slaves, enabled sexual violence against Black women, whose bodies were assumed to be "accessible to the slavemaster at all times as well as to his surrogates" (Davis 1985, 8).[6] She argues that rape was used as a "routine arm of repression" while slavery

6 Similarly, in the Australian context, Aileen Moreton-Robinson (2000, 168) describes sexual contact between Indigenous women and white men as "a social practice which reinscribes white racial superiority into identities of white masculinity, because for over 200 years the Indigenous woman's body has been positioned within white society as being accessible, available, deviant and expendable."

was legal, but also that this institutionalised sexual abuse was carried on and expanded after the formal abolition of slavery as a tool of social control used against Black people (Davis 1983, 175–176). *Accusations* of rape, Davis points out, also served another social function: as lynching emerged as a strategy for white people to maintain their ongoing domination of Black people, claims of rape made by white women against Black men were increasingly used to justify lynching. Here Davis draws on Frederick Douglass, who characterises such rape charges as products of shifting social relations after the American Civil War: "the altered times and circumstances have made necessary a sterner, stronger, and more effective justification of Southern barbarism" (Douglass 2021). Davis' careful historical analysis of the dynamics and social function of sexual violence reveal it as inextricable from the dynamics of racial capitalism, which reinforces and exploits racialised hierarchies of power in part through fostering antagonistic gender relations.

Marital rape provides another example of how sexual violence is authorised and enabled by property relations. Marital rape is still not explicitly criminalised in more than half the world's countries (Randall and Vankatesh 2015), and even in jurisdictions where it is criminalised, marital rape remains common and conviction rates low. The prevalence of marital rape, in the broader spectrum of domestic and family violence, functions to reinforce hierarchies of power within domestic spaces, animated by the history of rape as a property crime. There is also a tension between the formal criminalisation of marital rape (for example, in Australia and the US) alongside the emergence of neoliberal political economies which serve to restore and reinforce patriarchal family structures (Cooper 2017). As Juanita Elias and Shirin Rai write, the result is "a social welfare system that serves to trap women in situations of domestic violence and invisibilises the harms that they experience" (Elias and Rai 2019, 216). In this sense, while state regulation can in some cases selectively authorise sexual violence in ways that underpin gendered hierarchies of power, in other cases regulations prohibiting sexual violence may fail to have an effect against the enduring power of capitalist, patriarchal, and racialised social relations.

Finally, a materialist account of sexual violence highlights that the vulnerability of certain groups of people to sexual violence is conditioned by the exploitation they face as workers, and thus cannot be understood simply as a function of gender inequality. Davis (1983, 200) considers how sexual violence, amongst other forms of domination over women, may offer working-class men "a bribe, an illusory compensation for their powerlessness" as workers. Rather than treating sexual violence as an expression of the domination of all men over all women (and thus solely or primarily an effect of gender inequality), Davis suggests that this phenomenon is linked to the exploitation and domination that working-class men themselves face through the wage relation. Similarly, women's role within production renders them vulnerable to gendered violence in their capacity as workers. This is particularly the case for women of colour in global labour chains that are unregulated and un-unionised, as Jessica

Livingston (2004) shows in her analysis of the murders of women in the export processing zone of Ciudad Juárez. This highlights the interconnection between experiences of violence and the structural inequalities that are underpinned by racialised and gendered stratifications within the capitalist mode of production. This point is summarised by bell hooks (1984, 122), who writes:

> Unlike many feminist activists writing about male violence against women, black women and men emphasize a 'cycle of violence' that begins in the workplace because we are aware that systematic abuse is not confined to the domestic sphere, even though violent abuse is more commonly acted out in the home.

The work of Federici and Davis, amongst others, cautions against an ahistorical, universal understanding of sexual violence or rape culture. The traditions of radical Black and Marxist feminism suggest that to grasp the dynamics of sexual violence, we must understand its concrete functions within the totality of white supremacist capitalist social relations, including within the sexual division of labour. Such functions include undermining solidarity between working people, creating or heightening division and conflict between and within social groups, justifying racial oppression and criminal punishment, and stabilising existing power relations. Sexual violence, therefore, is understood within this paradigm as a structural phenomenon that functions to benefit those at the helm of the interlocking systems of capitalism, imperialism and patriarchy. Like the rape culture approach described above, it mitigates against an individualistic understanding of sexual violence as a series of individual acts perpetrated by bad apples; but, unlike the rape culture approach, this materialist analysis is grounded in a broader historical understanding of racism, class struggle, and gender as historical processes. A materialist approach does not deny that cultural norms and significations are important in legitimising and conditioning the occurrence of sexual violence, but rather seeks to place these cultural norms in relation to the systemic distributions of power and resources that they assist in upholding. If, then, sexual violence is inextricably linked to "a system of hierarchical power that fuses gender, race, and class" (Arruzza, Bhattacharya and Fraser 2019, 28), it would seem that what is needed to combat this violence and its pre-conditions is something *more than* education and awareness-raising. In the conclusion, I turn towards contemporary emancipatory movements that are challenging the social relations that enable sexual violence, and argue that struggles against racist policing, state power, and capitalist exploitation should be considered as radical, collective, and transformative practices of sexual violence prevention.

Conclusion: Implications for Praxis – Broadening the Scope of Sexual Violence Prevention Work

Locating sexual violence within the social relations of white supremacist patriarchal capitalism offers a nuanced understanding of how and why sexual violence occurs. In doing so, it also opens up new ways of conceptualising sexual violence prevention. While tackling white supremacist patriarchal capitalism may seem a daunting task, there are a multitude of movements already undertaking this work, highlighting the connections between sexual violence, racism, and capitalism that I have discussed above, and using strikes and mass mobilisations to transform the structures that underpin sexual violence. In their recent manifesto *Feminism for the 99%: A Manifesto*, Cinzia Arruzza, Tithi Bhattacharya and Nancy Fraser (2019, 6) argue that "a new feminist wave is reinventing the strike." They trace a transnational wave of feminist struggles over production, social reproduction, sexual violence and state power, arguing that these movements have "invented *new ways to strike* and infused the strike form itself with a *new kind of politics*" (Arruzza et al. 2019, 8, original italics).

This can be seen, to give one example, in the 'Ni Una Menos' movement, which began with an uprising of 200,000 people in Buenos Aires in 2015 protesting against the abuse and murder of women, and later spread around Latin America. Organisers of the Ni Una Menos movement have described it as a struggle "against racism, discrimination and xenophobia against indigenous women, black afro-descendants and afro-indigenous women [...] against the genocide and the femicide of women, which has its origins in the slave trade and colonial violence," and draw particular attention to the role of the state in reproducing these relations (Langlois 2020). In the US, low-wage workers involved with the #Fightfor15 campaign to raise the minimum wage, and emboldened by the #MeToo movement, have drawn attention to the prevalence of sexual harassment and violence to which casualised workers are subjected, with McDonald's workers walking off the job in protest and demanding not only better institutional procedures for responding to sexual violence, but also higher wages and better protections on their right to unionise (Ryzik 2019). Also in the US, the Black Lives Matter movement has led to "renewed conversations about how sexual violence and sexual intimidation are part of how black women experience racist policing" (Chatelain and Asoka 2015). Mass mobilisations and riots against police brutality have reinvigorated abolitionist movements against sexual violence, which look beyond the state and the criminal justice system to imagine and build transformative, community-based responses to sexual violence (INCITE! Women of Color Against Violence 2016; Law 2011). In Australia, grassroots organisations like Sisters Inside are explicitly organising towards "abolition of the carceral state," recognising the state itself as a perpetrator of sexual violence through acts such as strip searching (Kilroy and Quixley 2021, 21).

These movements transcend a simplistic understanding of sexual violence as a symptom of gender inequality that can be ameliorated through cultural change. They are, I suggest, examples of a materialist understanding of sexual violence put into motion. These movements use the tactics of the strike, the mass demonstration and the riot in order to render explicit the connections between sexual violence, racism, capitalism and imperialism, and to demand not just awareness but the redistribution of power and resources. They complement and extend the work of educators who challenge the cultural significations that support gendered violence, by seeking to transform the structural conditions that underpin sexual violence. These protestors and organisers put forward what Kathi Weeks describes as the "utopian demand": "a political demand that takes the form not of a narrowly pragmatic reform but of a more substantial transformation of the present configuration of social relations [...] a demand that raises eyebrows" (Weeks 2011, 176).

Materialist approaches to sexual violence and abuse, policing and incarceration, and exploitation at work, then, present a provocation to mainstream sexual violence prevention work. They challenge the view that "other factors [such as economic inequality] interact with or reinforce gender inequality to contribute to increased frequency and severity of violence against women, but *do not drive violence in and of themselves*" (Our Watch, VicHealth, and ANROWS 2015, 6, emphasis added). They propose, instead, that there are deep internal connections between the violent dynamics of racism, economic exploitation, and sexism. A materialist approach fills in the gaps of the cultural change approach by showing how culture is grounded in, and reinforced by, the structural distribution of power and resources. In tracing these links, materialist approaches to sexual violence reveal a complex and expansive web of social relations that require transformation. The utopian demands of grassroots feminist struggles can thus enrich the conception of culture in mainstream sexual violence prevention work and expand the horizon of sexual violence prevention, to encompass not just education workshops and awareness-raising, but also the collective struggles of everyday people against structures of domination, exploitation and violence.

References

11th Principle: Consent! 2017. "Rape Culture Pyramid." Accessed May 2, 2021. https://www.11thprincipleconsent.org/consent-propaganda/rape-culture-pyramid/https://www.11thprincipleconsent.org/consent-propaganda/rape-culture-pyramid/.

Arruzza, Cinzia, Tithi Bhattacharya, and Nancy Fraser. 2019. *Feminism for the 99%: A Manifesto*. London and Brooklyn: Verso.

Bakker, Isabella. 2007. "Social Reproduction and the Constitution of a Gendered Political Economy." *New Political Economy* 12 (4): 541–556.

Barrett, Michele. 1992. Words and Things: Materialism and Method in Contemporary Feminist Analysis. In *Destabilizing Theory: Contemporary Feminist Debates*, edited by Michele Barrett and Anne Phillips, 201–219. Stanford: Stanford University Press.

Buchwald, Emilie, Pamela Fletcher, and Martha Roth. 2005. *Transforming a Rape Culture*. Minneapolis: Milkweed Editions.

Callinicos, Alex. 1990. *Against Postmodernism*. New York: St. Martin's Press.

Carmody, Moira, Susan Evans, Chris Krogh, Michael Flood, Melanie Heenan, and Georgia Ovendon. 2009. *Framing Best Practice: National Standards for the Primary Prevention of Sexual Assault through Education*. University of Western Sydney. Accessed June 10, 2021. http://www.nasasv.org.au/PDFs/Standards_Full_Report.pdf.

Chatelain, Marcia, and Kaavya Asoka. 2015. "Women and Black Lives Matter: An Interview with Marcia Chatelain." *Dissent Magazine*. Accessed June 15, 2021. https://www.dissentmagazine.org/article/women-black-lives-matter-interview-marcia-chatelain.

Conaghan, Joanne. 2016. "Feminism, Law and Materialism: Reclaiming the 'Tainted' Realm." In *The Ashgate Companion to Feminist Legal Theory*, edited by Margaret Davies and Vanessa. E. Munro, 31–50. Oxon and New York: Routledge.

Cooper, Melinda. 2017. *Family Values: Between Neoliberalism and the New Social Conservatism*. Brooklyn: Zone Books.

Davis, Angela. 1983. *Women, Race & Class*. New York: Vintage Books.

Davis, Angela. 1985. *Violence against Women and the Ongoing Challenge to Racism*. Freedom Organizing Series, #5. New York: Kitchen Table: Women of Color Press.

Deleuze, Gilles, and Félix Guattari. 2014. *Anti-Oedipus*. London: Bloomsbury.

Douglass, Frederick. 2021. *'The Lessons of the Hour' Speech by Frederick Douglass, January 9, 1894*. State Historical Society of Iowa. Accessed May 22, 2021. https://iowaculture.gov/history/education/educator-resources/primary-source-sets/reconstruction-and-its-impact/lessons-hour.

Elias, Juanita, and Shirin M. Rai. 2019. "Feminist Everyday Political Economy: Space, Time, and Violence." *Review of International Studies* 45 (2): 201–220.

Farris, Sara. 2017. *In the Name of Women's Rights: The Rise of Femonationalism*. Durham: Duke University Press.

Federici, Silvia. 2014. *Caliban and the Witch: Women, the Body and Primitive Accumulation*. Brooklyn: Autonomedia.

Fraser, Nancy. 2000. "Rethinking Recognition." *New Left Review* 3: 107–20.

Gavey, Nicola. 2005. *Just Sex? The Cultural Scaffolding of Rape*. East Sussex: Routledge.

Hall, Rebecca. 2004. "'It Can Happen to You': Rape Prevention in the Age of Risk Management." *Hypatia* 19 (3): 1–19.

Harvey, David. 2005. *A Brief History of Neoliberalism*. New York: Oxford University Press.

Hong, Grace Kyungwong. 2018. *Intersectional and Anticarceral Approaches to Sexual Violence in the Academy: Rethinking Campus Policies*. American Association of University Professors. Accessed May 2, 2021. https://www.aaup.org/article/intersectional-and-anticarceral-approaches-sexual-violence-academy#.X82GKBMzaqB.

hooks, bell. 1984. *Feminist Theory: From Margin to Centre*. Boston: South End Press.

INCITE! Women of Color Against Violence. 2016. *Color of Violence: The INCITE! Anthology*. Durham: Duke University Press.

Jameson, Fredric. 1991. *Postmodernism, or, the Cultural Logic of Late Capitalism*. Durham: Duke University Press.

Kilroy, Debbie, and Suzi Quixley. 2021. "A Word Waiting to Happen: Sisters Inside's Abolition Journey." In *The Routledge International Handbook of Penal Abolition*, edited by Michael J. Coyle and David Scott, 21–31. London: Routledge.

Langlois, Aude. 2020. *#NiUnaMenos: Countering Hegemonies in Argentina. Engenderings: LSE Department of Gender Studies*. Accessed June 15, 2021. https://blogs.lse.ac.uk/gender/2020/02/10/niunamenos-countering-hegemonies-in-argentina/.

Law, Vikki. 2011. "Where Abolition Meets Action: Women Organizing against Gender Violence." *Contemporary Justice Review* 14 (1): 85–94.

Livingston, Jessica. 2004. "Murder in Juárez: Gender, Sexual Violence, and the Global Assembly Line." *Frontiers: A Journal of Women Studies* 25 (1): 59–76.

Lyotard, Jean-François. 1984. *The Postmodern Condition: A Report on Knowledge*, translated by Geoff Bennington and Brian Massumi. Minneapolis: University of Minnesota Press.

Marx, Karl, and Friedrich Engels. 1977. *The German Ideology*, edited by C.J. Arthur. London: Lawrence and Wishart.

Mohanty, Chandra Talpade. 2013. "Transnational Feminist Crossings: On Neoliberalism and Radical Critique." *Signs: Journal of Women in Culture and Society* 38 (4): 967–91.

Moreton-Robinson, Aileen. 2000. *Talkin' up to the White Woman: Aboriginal Women and Feminism*. Brisbane: University of Queensland Press.

Oriel, Jennifer. 2019. "We Still Need to Decide Who Comes Here, and How." *The Australian*, July 22, 2018, 12.

Our Watch. 2019. *Change the Story Three Years On: Reflections on Uptake and Impact, Lessons Learned and Our Watch's Ongoing Work to Embed and Expand the Evidence on Prevention*. Melbourne: Our Watch.

Our Watch, VicHealth, and ANROWS. 2015. *Change the Story: A Shared Framework for the Primary Prevention of Violence against Women and Their Children in Australia*. Melbourne: Our Watch.

Phipps, Alison. 2020. *Me, Not You: The Trouble with Mainstream Feminism*. Manchester: Manchester University Press.

Phipps, Alison, Jessica Ringrose, Emma Renold, and Carolyn Jackson. "Rape Culture, Lad Culture and Everyday Sexism: Researching, Conceptualizing and Politicizing New Mediations of Gender and Sexual Violence." *Journal of Gender Studies* 27 (1):1–8.

Powell, Anastasia, and Nicola Henry. 2014. "Framing Sexual Violence Prevention." In *Preventing Sexual Violence: Interdisciplinary Approaches to Overcoming a Rape Culture*, edited by Nicola Henry and Anastasia Powell, 1–21. London: Palgrave Macmillan UK.

Randall, Melanie, and Vasanthi Venkatesh. 2015. "The Right to No: The Crime of Marital Rape, Women's Human Rights, and International Law." *Brooklyn Journal of International Law* 41 (1): 153–202.

Ryzik, Melena. 2019. "In a Test of Their Power, #MeToo's Legal Forces Take on McDonald's." *The New York Times*, May 19. https://www.nytimes.com/2019/05/21/business/mcdonalds-female-employees-sexual-harassment.html.

Salter, Michael. 2016. "'Real Men Don't Hit Women': Constructing Masculinity in the Prevention of Violence against Women." *Australian & New Zealand Journal of Criminology* 49 (4): 463–79.

Sears, Alan. 2017. "Body Politics: The Social Reproduction of Sexualities." In *Social Reproduction Theory: Remapping Class, Recentering Oppression*, edited by Tithi Bhattacharya, 171–191. London: Pluto Press.

Sen, Purna. 2019. *What Will It Take? Promoting Cultural Change to End Sexual Harassment*. New York: UN Women. Accessed May 2, 2021. https://www.unwomen.org/-/media/headquarters/attachments/sections/library/publications/2019/discussion-paper-what-will-it-take-promoting-cultural-change-to-end-sexual-harassment-en.pdf?la=en&vs=1714.

Serisier, Tanya. 2021. "From Date Rape Jeopardy to (Not) Drinking Tea: Consent Humour, Ridicule and Cultural Change." *Australian Feminist Law Journal*, published online. Accessed May 11 2021. doi:10.1080/13200968.2021.1885200.

The Australian. 2018. "Editorial: Melbourne's African Gangs." *The Australian*, December 31, 11.

Universities UK. 2016. *Changing the Culture: Report of the Universities UK Taskforce Examining Violence against Women, Harassment and Hate Crime Affecting University Students*. London: Universities UK. Accessed May 2, 2021. https://www.universitiesuk.ac.uk/policy-and-analysis/reports/Documents/2016/changing-the-culture.pdf.

Walden, Inara, and Liz Wall. 2014. *Reflecting on Primary Prevention of Violence against Women: The Public Health Approach*. ACSSA Issues, 19. Melbourne: Australian Centre for the Study of Sexual Assault.

Weeks, Kathi. 2011. *The Problem with Work: Feminism, Marxism, Antiwork Politics, and Postwork Imaginaries*. Durham: Duke University Press.

Willis, Ellen. 1984. Radical Feminism and Feminist Radicalism. *Social Text* 9/10: 91–118.

Women NSW. 2016. *NSW Domestic and Family Violence Prevention and Early Intervention Strategy 2017–2021*. North Sydney: NSW Ministry of Health. Accessed May 2, 2021. https://www.women.nsw.gov.au/__data/assets/pdf_file/0010/388846/dfv-prevention-intervention-strategy.pdf.

World Health Organization. 2009. *Changing Cultural and Social Norms That Support Violence*. Geneva: World Health Organization. Accessed May 2, 2021. https://www.who.int/violence_injury_prevention/violence/norms.pdf.

Chapter 2

Consent, Coercive Circumstances and (Imbalances of) Power

Lessons from International Criminal Law

Eithne Dowds

Introduction

Debates on whether the legal definition of rape should focus on the presence of coercion or the absence of consent have featured in both international and domestic criminal legal contexts. Although international human rights law has sought to clarify the relationship between the two approaches, by emphasising the central role of consent within each,[1] often the literature presents these approaches in oppositional terms (e.g., MacKinnon 2006; O'Byrne 2011). Such opposition is set against a backdrop of extensive feminist and philosophical investigations into the harm or wrong of rape (e.g., Du Toit 2011; Burgess Jackson 1999), generating what Conaghan (2019, 152) has described as "a series of parallel, often discordant, narratives," that inform social, cultural and legal constructions of rape. For instance, those who favour definitions of rape based on coercion often view rape as a crime of inequality and an abuse of power (MacKinnon 2016; Anderson 2016), whereas those who favour consent view rape as a violation of sexual autonomy, understood as the right to sexual self-determination (Grewal 2012; Munro 2010a). Yet both conceptualisations have fallen foul to critiques of over and under-inclusion (Conaghan 2019; Munro 2010b) giving rise to discussions around the extent to which more "plural" conceptions of rape, encompassing elements of consent and coercion or, to borrow language from international criminal law, "coercive environments/circumstances" can be developed (see Dowds 2020a; Munro 2010a).

Discussions around the interrelationship between consent and coercion that draw from both international and domestic criminal law are complicated by the distinctiveness of both contexts; the former operating during peacetime and the latter operating in the oppressive context of war or mass violence (see Dowds 2020a). In this respect, it has been claimed that there are qualitative differences between rape committed in war and peace. For example, it has

1 *M.C. v Bulgaria* (Application no 39272/98) 4 December 2003, at 164–66; *Vertido v The Philippines* (Communication No. 18/2008) Committee on the Elimination of Discrimination against Women July 2010, at 2.9.

DOI: 10.4324/9781003379331-4

been suggested that rape in war is often committed in public, involves multiple perpetrators and the use of weapons, whereas rape in peacetime occurs in private settings, usually between people known to one another, thus rendering developments in either domain "untranslatable" to the other (see Grewal 2010, 68; Dowds 2020a, 122–123). Yet, there is appetite for what I have described elsewhere as "norm transfer" between international and domestic criminal law (Dowds 2020a), particularly in respect of the "more intersectional and complex approach" (McGlynn and Munro 2010, 2) offered by the explicit attention to coercive environments in some international criminal definitions of rape. As Chinkin (2014, 491) notes: "A coercive environment does not only exist in armed conflict; gang rape, social and economic circumstances which are exacerbated by gendered expectations can also be coercive and the international criminal law approach provides a model for domestic legislation." This chapter explores the potential of 'coercive environments/circumstances' by engaging with cases from international criminal law that have sought to delineate the parameters of the concept.

The chapter proceeds as follows: First, it sets out the current legal landscape on consent and coercion in domestic and international criminal contexts. Second, it engages with the wide-ranging debate in respect of how the wrong of rape should be conceptualised within legal frameworks. Third, it sets out the approach to coercive circumstances in international criminal law. The final section concludes by underlining the importance of thinking beyond dichotomies and connecting conversations on rape and sexual violence across international and domestic contexts to draw out shared challenges as well as lessons that can be learned.

Consent and Coercion in Domestic and International Contexts

Recent domestic rape law reform efforts have positioned consent, or lack thereof, as opposed to force and resistance, as the determining factor in distinguishing legal from illegal sexual conduct (see Dowds 2020b). Although variation exists across jurisdictions, one example of a consent-based definition can be found in the Sexual Offences Act 2003 for England and Wales (mirrored in Northern Ireland).[2] According to section 1 of the 2003 Act, to establish rape the prosecution must prove that the sexual activity took place without the complainant's consent and that the defendant did not reasonably believe that person consented. The Act also provides that reasonableness will be determined with reference to the surrounding circumstances, including any steps taken by the accused to ascertain consent.[3] Consent is defined as agree-

2 Article 5 Sexual Offences NI Order 2008.

3 Section 1(2) Sexual Offences Act 2003; article 5(2) 2008 Order ibid.

ment by choice and having the freedom and capacity to make that choice.[4] The meaning of consent, or absence thereof, is further illuminated by the inclusion of a number of rebuttable and irrebuttable presumptions as to consent and the defendant's reasonable belief, including, for example, where violence is used against the complainant.[5] Similar constructions of consent can be found in Canada and across parts of Australia,[6] with jurisdictions such as California, Sweden and Iceland adopting more affirmative or communicative conceptions of consent e.g., expressed through words or conduct[7] (for overview see Dowds 2020a, 116).

Although a clear trend towards consent is evident, it is not without controversary. Research has demonstrated that even though requirements of force and resistance have been formally removed from many definitions, these factors continue to dominate contestations over consent (see e.g., Burgin 2019) and that the complainant's behaviour before, during and after the encounter, is routinely drawn upon to imply consent or attach reasonableness to the defendant's belief in consent (see Finch and Munro 2006; Burgin and Flynn 2019). Reliance on these circumstantial factors can be situated within problematic sex scripts that blur the boundaries between rape and "normal" sexual interactions (Frith 2009). In this respect, cases that fall outside what has been described as "real rape" (Estrich 1987), that is a violent rape perpetrated by a stranger against a physically resisting victim, are less likely to be recognised as non-consensual sexual encounters and thus less 'deserving' of the label rape. While the 'real rape' stereotype is socially constructed, it has been argued that such a stereotype is reinforced through the law, with the presumptions against consent contained in the Sexual Offences Act 2003, for example, inviting narrow temporal assessments of sexual encounters that ignore more subtle and prolonged notions of coercion (Carline and Gunby 2011; Palmer 2020).

Within this context scholars have questioned whether the challenges associated with criminal legal responses to rape are the product of bad laws or bad attitudes (Leahy 2014a; Russell 2016). While the two are entwined due to the male gaze upon which the law is constructed, interpreted and applied (see Naffine 2019; MacKinnon 1987), the law is also a site of struggle wherein careful feminist intervention can challenge the privilege, power and patriarchy that currently sets the social and legal parameters of rape (see Conaghan 2019). Thus, efforts continue to be directed towards rethinking rape law (McGlynn and Munro 2010), whether that be refining the definition of consent or, as will

4 Section 74 2003 Act ibid, article 3 2008 Order ibid.

5 Sections 75 and 76 2003 Act ibid; article 9 and 10 2008 Order ibid.

6 See section 273.1 and 273.2 Criminal Code of Canada 1985; section 61HE New South Wales Crimes Act 1900

7 Section 261.6. The Penal Code of California; Iceland: Act on the amendment of the Criminal Code, no. 19/1940, with subsequent changes (sexual offenses) 2018; Criminal Code (Sweden) Brottsbalk (1962: 700) as amended in 2018, chapter 6, section 1.

be discussed further below, redefining rape based on alternative models such as coercion.

At the level of international criminal law, parallel debates on the role of consent in defining rape came to the fore following the establishment of the International Criminal Tribunal for the former Yugoslavia (ICTY) and the International Criminal Tribunal for Rwanda (ICTR). Following the wars in the former Yugoslavia and the genocide in Rwanda, reports of grave crimes in both sites emerged, including widespread and systematic rape and sexual violence (see Haddad 2011). As no definition of rape existed in international criminal law, the ICTR developed the first definition in the 1998 case of *Akayesu*.[8] While it was observed that domestic definitions are often based on non-consent to specific physical acts, the Trial Chamber in *Akayesu* opted for a more conceptual definition due to the cultural sensitives involved in speaking about sexual violence[9] and as a result of the circumstances described in the case – involving rape by many perpetrators, the insertion of weapons and mutilations – that meant "there was no place whatsoever for the consideration of consent" (Pillay 2010, 849). Rape was defined as "a physical invasion of a sexual nature, committed on a person under circumstances that are coercive."[10] Three months later, while acknowledging the *Akayesu* definition the ICTY asserted that most legal systems frame rape around forcible penetration and opted for a force/coercion based definition.[11] In 2001 the ICTY revisited the definition of rape again, this time adopting a consent-based definition due to the need to capture additional factors that "would render an act of sexual penetration non-consensual or non-voluntary on the part of the victim."[12] Although both of these subsequent formulations were the result of extensive surveys of national law to identify shared principles,[13] the primacy given to one element over the other in each case reflects the situatedness of rape (Conaghan 2019, 162), which, in the context of international criminal law gives rise to a tension between recognising rape as an individual crime or as part of collective violence (Dowds 2020a; Grewal 2010).

8 *Prosecutor v Akayesu,* No. ICTR-96-4-T, Judgment (2 September 1998).

9 Ibid, at 687.

10 Ibid, at 598.

11 *Prosecutor v Furundžija,* No. IT-95-17/1, Judgment (10 December 1998), at 184–185: (i) The sexual penetration, however slight: (a) of the vagina or anus of the victim by the penis of the perpetrator or any other object used by the perpetrator; or (b) of the mouth of the victim by the penis of the perpetrator; (ii) by coercion or force or threat of force against the victim or a third person.

12 *Prosecutor v Kunarac, Kovac, Vukovic,* No IT-96-23 and 23/1, Judgment (22 February 2001), at 438: The sexual penetration, however slight: (a) of the vagina or anus of the victim by the penis of the perpetrator or any other object used by the perpetrator; or (b) of the mouth of the victim by the penis of the perpetrator; where such sexual penetration occurs without the consent of the victim. Consent for this purpose must be consent given voluntarily, as a result of the victim's free will, assessed in the context of the surrounding circumstances.

13 See *Furundžija* n 11, at 181; *Kunarac* ibid, at 438.

A fourth definition of rape was advanced following the establishment of a permanent International Criminal Court (ICC). The definition for the ICC, as set out in the courts Elements of Crimes (2002) document, provides four circumstances within which the crime of rape can occur: By force; by threat of force or coercion, such as that caused by fear of violence, duress, detention, psychological oppression or abuse of power, against such person or another person; by taking advantage of a coercive environment; or against a person incapable of giving genuine consent.[14] While the ICC has declared that, save in the very specific situation of a person whose "incapacity" was "taken advantage of," the Elements of Crimes definition does not refer to the victim's lack of consent, and therefore this need not be proven,[15] other international criminal judicial bodies have combined the ICC definition and the consent-based *Kunarac* definition, developing a more comprehensive account of rape.[16] Such an approach is aligned with international human rights standards that have emphasised the central role of consent and held that even where consent is not included as an explicit element, definitions of rape should be interpreted in a way that encompasses the notion of a lack of freely given consent.[17] Although there has been resistance to including consent in international criminal definitions of rape (see e.g., O'Byrne 2011), my research has shown that, in a manner similar to domestic definitions that removed consent (Temkin 2002, 176), consent continues to feature within trial narratives at the ICC and may, in limited circumstances, be raised as defence (Dowds 2020a, 173–175).

The debates around consent and coercion in international criminal law have filtered into scholarship on rape and consent in domestic settings. For instance, MacKinnon, who has previously labelled consent a meaningless concept under conditions of patriarchy, asserted that the *Akayesu* definition represents the first time rape has been "defined in law as what it is in life" (2006, 944). While for MacKinnon, as will be discussed in the next section, a definition based on a range of coercive factors is preferrable to consent, others have recognised the potential of supplementing domestic consent-based definitions with the categories of coercion included in international criminal definitions (Munro 2010a; Dowds 2020). In this respect, it has been recognised that while definitions constructed solely on the basis of absence of consent or the presence of coercion can be interpreted narrowly, when combined they have the potential to contribute to a more contextual framework within which allegations of rape can be considered (Dowds 2020a, 190–195).

14 See e.g., art 7(1)(g)-1 International Criminal Court (ICC), Elements of Crimes, 2002.

15 *Prosecutor v Germain Katanga* ICC-01/04-01/07-3436 (7 March 2014), at 965.

16 See e.g., *Prosecutor v Sesay et al* 2009 Case No SCSL- 04-15-T, Judgment, (2 March 2009).

17 See *M.C.* v *Bulgaria* 2003 n 1; Council of Europe Treaty Series. 2010. Explanatory Report to the Council of Europe Convention on preventing and combating violence against women and domestic violence. No. 210, at 193).

Significantly, some jurisdictions have begun to expand their consent-based frameworks in a way that aligns with these broader notions of coercion. By way of example, a recent review in Northern Ireland recommended legislative reforms to the list of presumptions against consent within articles 9 and 10 of the Sexual Offences (NI) Order 2008 to take account of situations where "C submits to the act because of a threat or fear of violence or other serious detriment, such as intimidating or coercive conduct or psychological oppression" (Gillen 2019, 377). Similarily, in New South Wales, the Law Reform Commission (2020, 101) recommended the adoption of a provision within the Crimes Act to provide that:

> a person does not consent to sexual activity if the person participates because of coercion, blackmail or intimidation, regardless of when the coercion, blackmail or intimidation occurs, or whether it occurs in a single instance or as part of an ongoing pattern.

While the inclusion of such provisions are to be welcomed, their progressive application is complicated by the perennial problem of agreeing on the exact level of oppression or coercion that must be exerted over another person to warrant criminal sanction. Indeed, existing definitions framed around coercion have a tendency to be narrowly interpreted due to lingering associations with physical force (see Dowds 2020b). These challenges maps onto a wider process of evolution in terms of the very idea of rape, what the crime entails and the harm or wrong involved. The following section considers these issues in more detail.

What is Wrong with Rape: Contesting the Conceptual and Legal Boundaries

Rape has been described as an "essentially contested concept" (Reiten 2001), open to differing and conflicting interpretations. Such concepts often have clear paradigmatic cases, such as the real-rape scenario outlined earlier, which everyone would agree fall within the concept, and borderline cases, for example, those involving non-physical force or certain forms of deception, which may fall within some but not all interpretations. These different interpretations are influenced by the underlying conceptualisations of what rape is and the laws role in regulating sexual encounters. For instance, historical conceptualisations of rape, and the resulting legal frameworks, were closely tied to the social status of men and women, with a woman's status and worth determined by her virginity and chastity (Bennice and Resick 2003). As women were deemed the property of the dominant male family member, men benefitted socially and materially from the intact "honour" of their women (see Burgin 2019). Within this context, rape was understood as a wrong against male property as opposed to a wrong against the woman herself. Moreover, there was a deep suspicion of female sexuality, as infamously noted by English Lord Chief Justice Matthew Hale, rape accusations are easily made but difficult to dispute (Hale 1736). This problematic assumption has pervaded the practice of rape law, and sexual offence laws more broadly, for centuries, contributing to a tendency to disbelieve victims as well as the adoption of high evidentiary standards, including the need to prove physical force and resistance to establish the offence (see Kirkland Gillespie and King 2015; Ehrlich 2002).

The early women's movement, however, spearheaded legislative reform across many jurisdictions to reflect the understanding of sexual offences as crimes against self-determination and sexual autonomy, rather than family honour or male property, resulting in a doctrinal shift towards consent (see West 2020). Indeed, according to Fletcher (1996, 109), "no idea testifies more powerfully to individuals as a source of value than the principle of consent." It thus provides the legal paradigm within which sexual choices are evaluated: It is not the presence of force that renders sexual activity wrong, it is the absence of freely given consent. Yet, the move to sexual autonomy and consent has not been without controversary. Roberts (1993) for instance, cautions that sexual autonomy relies on a baseline of choice and conceals the subtle ways society works to constrain women's freedom. Similarily, Du Toit (2012) argues that modern rape law has retained the idea of women as property, concerned primarily with the unsanctioned use of the body property, most obviously identified through the presence of physical trauma, obscuring the violation of an individual's sense of sexual integrity and security.

The extent to which these different conceptualisations adequately capture the harm of rape can be situated within the long-running debate on the nature of rape: As a crime of sex or violence. Within this debate, Brownmiller (1975, 378) called for a "gender free, non-activity specific law" on rape. Brownmiller rejected the distinction between rape and other crimes, arguing that this distinction reinforces the perception that rape is less important. She argued that rape should be recognised as "an injury to the victim's bodily integrity and not as an injury to the purity or chastity of man's estate" (Brownmiller 1975, 378). Therefore, she sought to separate rape from sex with a view to exposing the violent nature of the subordination of women by men. From a radical feminist perspective, MacKinnon (1987, 174) rejects the sex or violence dichotomy arguing that sex and violence are mutually definitive rather than mutually exclusive. In drawing attention to the dominant social script in sexual relations, which condones a certain level of force, MacKinnon argues that calling rape violence fails "to criticize what has been made of sex, what has been done to us through sex" (MacKinnon 1987, 86 87). Thus, in MacKinnon's view, recognising the sexual aspect of rape is not to undermine its violence, but rather to expose the way sexuality has been used as the medium of power and violence by the perpetrator – a fundamental difference between rape and assault.

In conceptualising rape as crime of gender inequality, MacKinnon advocates a move away from consent and towards coercion on the basis that:

> [C]oercion definitions of rape see power – domination and violence – nonconsent definitions envision love or passion gone wrong. Consent definitions accordingly have proof of rape turn on victim and perpetrator mental state: who wanted what, who knew what when. This crime basically occurs in individual psychic space. Coercion definitions by distinction turn on proof of physical acts, surrounding context, or exploitation of relative position: who did what to whom and sometimes why.
>
> (MacKinnon 2006, 941)

Relatedly, Anderson (2016, 58) argues that reconceptualising rape as coerced sex has the potential to capture the "use of asymmetric power that one sort of agent may hold over another." Anderson's account chimes with earlier investigations of coercion that sought to expose situations where the perpetrator created or took advantage of the vulnerability of the victim (Burgess-Jackson 1999, 99–103), as well as contemporary accounts tracking the "sexual abuse of power" by those using their authority, dominance, and influence to compel another's submission to unwanted sex (Buchhandler-Raphael 2011, 151). The common thread running through these investigations is an attempt to focus attention on the interpersonal, as well as structural, conditions that construct and constrain individual sexual freedom, and to attend to these violations with the same level of condemnation as those that involve explicit violence.

The sentiments expressed by these scholars are evident in the more demanding accounts of sexual autonomy that have developed. Although still privileging consent, or lack thereof, consent is situated within the broader circumstances within which sexual decisions are made to determine whether the conditions necessary for meaningful choice were present (Dowds 2020b; Munro 2010a). However, concern has been raised that an over-contextualisation of autonomy may blur the boundaries between constraint and coercion, resulting in paternalism and disempowering interventions. For instance, Halley (2016, 266) cautions that:

> [R]adical feminists mean a lot more by coercive circumstances than the threat to maim or kill made by a man holding a knife. They mean the coercive circumstances of male domination, a pervasive cultural condition. Where there is no force or threat of force to render subjective consent morally problematic, should we supply in its place a general cultural condition of domination in which women operate all the time?

While it is important to be sensitive to the conditions of patriarchy and acknowledge that the inducements and pressures that derive from it, as well as the ensuing sexual activity, may indeed be harmful (see West 2020), it has been suggested that to equate them with rape is to:

> […] trivialise what rape is and what it does to a woman […] Women are not helpless in lovemaking, or even in the going-along-with-it instance

> where sexual desire may not exist but affection does; whereas women experience total helplessness and obliteration during rape. When a woman's existence just does not matter, intercourse becomes rape.
>
> (Henderson 1987, 226)

However, this does not mean that a contextual approach should be abandoned. Rather, as Munro has argued, we should engage with the "the messiness and complexity of the middle ground" (2010b, 68). Such engagement would allow us to think outside of narrow paradigms of rape, expose the "continuum of coercion" (McGregor 2011, 70) within which the crime occurs, and promote dialogue and debate on the parameters of this crime.

The importance of such an approach is illuminated when situated within research on the nature and extent of sexual coercion, broadly defined as the persuasion of an unwilling partner to comply with non-consensual sex through nonviolent means (Mitchell and Raghavan 2019, 3). For instance, studies in the context of intimate relationships have identified eight specific tactics of sexual coercion: threats of/physical force, exploitation, humiliation/intimidation, pressure, relational threats, bullying, hopelessness and helplessness (Raghavan et al. 2015). While the first few tactics might be used at the time of the sexual interaction, the last two refer to historical pressures: Hopelessness referring to situations where the victim feels that the consequences of refusing sex are more aversive than suffering through unwanted sex; and helplessness referring to a learned response where resistance to sex has been futile and ignored in the past. An early study exploring reasons for engaging in unwanted sex found that 27% of participants did so as a means of avoiding coercion, and 20% to avoid physical abuse that they had previously experienced at the hands of their partner (Basile 1999). A more recent study similarly found that women who experienced past coercion from their partners were 7.25 times more likely to comply with unwanted sex in the future (Katz and Tirone 2010). Beyond compliance, victims may also respond to prolonged abuse by becoming an active, rather than passive, participant and even initiate sexual relations as a means to manage and control risk (Lembert 1996, 281; Palmer 2017, 19).

When these sexually coercive tactics, as well as the possible victim responses, are exposed, they paint a more complex picture of sexual violation than the dominant stereotypes of rape perpetration and victimhood normally allow. Due to social and cultural expectations around what constitutes 'real rape' as noted earlier, passivity, compliance or sexual initiative on the part of the victim might be interpreted by an outsider, and even by the victim themselves (see Jeffrey and Barata 2017), as them "not doing enough" to stop the abuse, thus rendering them complicit in their own victimisation or as having consented (Mitchell and Raghavan 2019, 13). This brings into sharp focus the need to distinguish between real consent, expressed in circumstances of free choice, and apparent consent, expressed in circumstances where the conditions for autonomous choice have been breached. Attention to this broader picture may help to expose subtle forms of power and oppression, such as that found in relationships categorised by coercive control (see Stark 2007; Bettinson 2017). Indeed, in recent times legislation on domestic abuse and coercive control has been adopted by the Council of Europe, the United Kingdom and some Australian territories, recognising wider patterns of abuse, including psychological or economic harms.[18] More robust legal frameworks on rape, such as those proposed in Northern Ireland and New South Wales that explicitly recognise intimidation, coercive conduct, psychological oppression and patterns of abuse, are thus significant and may help to align rape offences with the offence of coercive control.[19] As noted earlier, however, much will depend on how any new provisions within rape law are interpreted and applied. So, in returning to the words of Chinkin (2014, 491) as set out in the introduction to this chapter, might the approach taken in international criminal law and the notion of coercive circumstances developed therein provide "a model for domestic legislation." The following section considers this approach in more detail.

Coercion and Coercive Environments: Lessons from International Criminal Law?

An important development in international criminal law is the recognition that consent can only be free and voluntary where the parties are not overpowered by coercive circumstances. This notion was first developed in *Akayesu*, a case heralded for its innovative construction of rape (see Dowds 2020, 91). In elaborating on the meaning of coercive circumstances, *Akayesu* explained that physical force is not necessary: "[T]hreats, intimidation, extortion and other forms of duress which prey on fear or desperation may constitute coercion, and coercion may be inherent in certain circumstances"; such as, in this case, military presence among displaced persons.[20] However the case itself mainly recounts rapes that fit within the narrow lens of force, as evidenced in references to women having been "beaten," "taken by force," "threatened," "locked up" and raped with objects.[21]

18 The Council of Europe Convention on preventing and combating violence against women and domestic violence (Istanbul Convention) 2011; Section 76 Serious Crimes Act 2015; The Domestic Abuse (Scotland) Bill 2017; Domestic Abuse and Civil Proceedings Bill 2021 (Northern Ireland); G. Wilson and N. Tognini, *Australia's approach to domestic violence: Focus on coercive control* (HopgoodGanim February 2014).

19 See discussion of coercive control in a rape case in the CPS, Violence against Women and Girls Report 2017–18, pg. 9; For an insight into the potential challenges around aligning sexual offences and coercive control legislation, including the extent to which evidence in respect of coercive control could be used to corroborate incidents of alleged rape see *Mark William Duthie v. Her Majesty's Advocate* [2021] HCJAC 23.

20 *Akayesu* n 8, at 688.

21 Ibid, at 419–436.

The ICC adopted a similar term under its categories of coercion, that of someone "taking advantage of a coercive environment."[22] In the *Bemba* case, the court drew primarily on the *Akayesu* description of coercive circumstances to define this term,[23] but in a similar manner to *Akayesu,* the court refers only to penetration by force in their legal findings as opposed to taking the opportunity to build on the broader coercive factors contained in the definition.[24] The failure to engage with these factors has been described as a "missed opportunity" (Sankey 2017, 156):

> [T]aking a broad approach to coercion would enable recognition of some of the structural and gendered aspects of coercion that would highlight some of the continuities of violence. It is therefore hoped that future cases will more fully outline the elements of coercion, and enable some acknowledgment of the interrelationships between rape in situations of conflict or mass atrocity and everyday sexual violence.
>
> (Sankey 2017, 156–157)

The more recent *Ongwen* case is noteworthy in this regard, as it provides further insight into how the court determines a coercive environment and the perpetrators use of this environment to undermine the complainant's freedom of choice.[25] Ongwen, a former commander of the Ugandan rebel group, the Lord's Resistance Army (LRA), was convicted of a number of crimes including rape and sexual violence against women who were abducted and given to him as "wives." The Court explained that the "wives" existed in a coercive environment that was a "microcosm" of the broader coercive environment of the LRA; an environment characterised by extreme violence used to instil obedience and discipline among abductees and soldiers.[26] It was noted that while there was evidence that the "wives" would be beaten so as they would submit to sexual intercourse, it was clear that the soldiers relied on the fact that the women were held captive and that they would use the organisation and its rules as a form of coercion. The chamber also noted that "the use of threatened or actual physical violence on the abductees for a protracted period of time… caused severe psychological suffering."[27]

In *Ongwen* the court had to address contradictory statements made by two witnesses that had the potential to complicate the assessment of the sexual interactions and their non-consensual nature. For instance, in response to a question about whether the witness wanted to sleep with Ongwen, she explained

22 See n 14.

23 *Prosecutor v Jean-Pierre Bemba Gombo* ICC-01/0501/08 (22 March 2016), at 103.

24 Ibid, at 633.

25 *Prosecutor v Dominic Ongwen* ICC-02/04-01/15 (4 February 2021).

26 Ibid, at 2028.

27 Ibid, at 2309.

"Yes, I was – I had become of age"[28] and another witness stated that "during the eight years, he [Ongwen] did not force me. I was with him as husband and wife."[29] In taking a contextual approach, the chamber explained that the coercive nature of the relationship was clear from the "totality" of the evidence, which included evidence of threats, fear and beatings upon refusal.[30] In teasing out the issue of real consent versus apparent consent, the court also drew on evidence from other women who had been abducted by the LRA, including Evelyn Amony, who was forced to marry the leader of the LRA, Joseph Kony: "I had no choice…You know, when you are there, you stay with somebody, not out of love, but you stay with somebody because you need to protect your own life."[31]

Additional insights in relation to coercive environments can be drawn from the *Nikačević* case before the Court of Bosnia and Herzegovina.[32] This case included the rape, among other crimes, of two Muslim women by a Serb police officer in territory of the Foča Municipality at a time when non-Serb civilians were subject to a widespread and systematic attack. During this time, some of the Muslim women in the area gathered together in an apartment building for safety. The accused, who was a neighbour of the victims and thus vaguely known to them, would come to the building armed and in uniform. He would tell the women of the "horrific rapes and violence occurring in Foča," information he characterised as helpful but that the court found to be a method of "fear and psychological oppression to coerce the victim."[33] The court explained that while both of the witnesses in the case had sought protection from the accused when paramilitaries entered the building looking for women, the "[A]ccused used fear and intimidation cloaked as protection to control these women."[34] The rapes perpetrated by the accused occurred when he ordered one victim to accompany him to her apartment to retrieve her appliances in an effort to save them from pillaging, and when he ordered another victim to clean his apartment. While the evidence demonstrates that both victims initially tried to refuse to go with the accused, they both accompanied him as asked and were subsequently raped. With respect to one of the victims, the court addressed claims by the defence that the victim, at some time following the rape, had been driven from Foča to Montenegro by the accused.

28 T-14 Trial Transcript, *The Prosecutor v Dominic Ongwen* 10 November 2015 ICC-02/04-01/15-T-14-CONF-ENG, 33.
29 T-13 Trial Transcript, *The Prosecutor v Dominic Ongwen* 9 November 2015. ICC-02/04-01/15-T-13-CONF-ENG, 20.
30 *Ongwen* n 25, 2044 and 2047.
31 Ibid, at 2218.
32 *Prosecutor v. Nikačević,* No. X-KR-08/500, Trial. Verdict, 40, 42 (Court of Bosn. & Herz. February 19, 2009)
33 Ibid, 32–33.
34 Ibid, 34.

The court explained that the defence was raising this evidence in an attempt to undermine the complainant's credibility:

> Why after all would any reasonable woman go anywhere with her rapist? To ask this question points to the ignorance of this crime. Rape is a crime of power and there is no one way a reasonable woman responds to an unreasonable crime. This was a time of war and chaos. The Panel believes that the issues of the trip, the car…are all part of the will to survive and no more meaning than that should be attached to these details.[35]

The court's acknowledgement that there is "no one way" to respond to rape is important, however the reference to "war and chaos" seems to qualify the statement in a way that limits its application to this particular context. Nonetheless, the court also explained that while "certain facts, when viewed in isolation, are subject to multiple interpretations" the evidence proves beyond reasonable doubt that there was an absence of free and voluntary consent.[36] The Court drew particular attention to the actions of the accused stating that he "created an atmosphere of extreme violence, fear, and psychological oppression, and further that he took advantage of a violent and coercive environment, to break the victim's will."[37]

While the cases of *Nikačević* and *Ongwen* occurred against a backdrop of widescale violence thus making the coerciveness of the situation more pronounced, the contextualisation of the different incidents provide a useful frame. For instance, the *Ongwen* case draws attention to the continuity of abuse experienced by the women and the environment of control within which they lived, ensuring that any statements of willingness or of a lack of force were assessed within the 'totality' of that context and centring the issue of choice or lack thereof. Similarly, in *Nikačević* the court describes very clearly how the accused was able to create an environment of fear and control by recounting stories of abuse faced by other women and positioning himself as a protector. His position as protector was reinforced by his formal role as a police officer who therefore occupied a position of trust in the community; trust he manipulated and abused. It is within this context that the court challenges simplistic accounts of subsequent interactions between the victim and perpetrator by emphasising the role of power and the broader relationship of the parties. While the relationship between victims and alleged perpetrators is often used problematically to imply consent (see McGregor 2005), both these cases illuminate how attention to the relationship between the parties can uncover coercion either as a product of a formal relationship and/or due

35 Ibid, 37.
36 Ibid, 32.
37 Ibid.

to dominance or control exerted by one party over another. In this respect, there are similarities with the sexually coercive tactics used by perpetrators in domestic contexts who assert control over their victims by inducing feelings of helplessness and hopelessness, limiting the victim's options and ability to express their will.

So, in thinking through what we might learn from international criminal law, the cases of *Nikačević* and *Ongwen* in particular highlight the need to concentrate on the background environment and relationship between the parties, whether that be an existing environment/relationship or one that has been strategically created; to consider the options (or lack of options) open to the victim and the victim's perception of these; and to consider the victim/perpetrator interactions holistically and not as one-off incidents. Indeed, a significant finding in both cases was the role of psychological oppression in breaking the victims will. Such oppression occurs over time and would require a shift in the current narrow temporal frames through which sexual offences are normally viewed (Palmer 2020). As Amnesty International (2011, 22) have explained, psychological oppression can be more easily used by perpetrators where there is a pre-existing relationship or psychological bonds between the victim and the perpetrator. Where such a relationship exists, abuse may be more insidious, and the victim may respond in ways that are difficult to understand. For example, Jokila and Niemi (2020) applied a coercive circumstances approach to domestic cases in Finland, highlighting how such circumstances undermine the autonomy and trust of victims. One case involved intimate partner abuse where the complainant allowed her estranged spouse into the apartment where she was subsequently raped, and another involved rape between acquainted youths where the complainant stayed and smoked a cigarette with the perpetrator following the rape. Emphasising the coerciveness of the situations – including the long-term abuse in the former case and the defendant's persistent sexual advances in the face of verbal refusals in the latter – and the difficulties faced by courts in understanding the actions or inactions of victims, Jokila and Niemi (2020, 131) explain:

> Such complainants do not fit in with the idea of the autonomous rational decision-maker who assertively expresses her non-consent and fights against her attacker. But if trust is taken into account in the interpretation of events, then some of these behaviours can be understood. For example, girls are traditionally brought up to behave nicely and to negotiate themselves out of difficult situations. When in the company of someone whom the girl trusts, these tactics should succeed. When confused by the breach of trust, however, the girl might behave, from a judge's perspective, in a strange manner.

Taking a coercive circumstances approach can therefore help to overcome two core barriers of prosecuting rape: Recognising non-physical coercion and reating a space within which victim reactions that may, on first impression, eem counter-intuitive, can be understood.

Conclusion

This chapter has engaged with a core controversary in international and domestic criminal law on rape: The relationship between consent and coercion. Building on literature emphasising the supplementary nature of these two elements, this chapter highlighted the need to move beyond minimalist understandings of consent and sexual autonomy, while being cognisant of the ability for individuals to have agency even within the structural constraints of patriarchy. In this way, the law is tasked with striking the appropriate balance between respecting sexual expression while guarding against violations of sexual autonomy. A very real challenge, however, is that our current social, cultural and legal imaginaries struggle to recognise the various forms of non-physical coercion that are used to facilitate rape (Leahy 2014b; Dowds 2020b; Palmer 2020). In this respect, feminist scholars have sought to reformulate rape in a way that "enables it to take greater account of the peculiarities of context, constraint and construction, and to operate with renewed vigour in the pursuit of social justice" (Munro 2008). Within this context, the coercive circumstances approach in international criminal law is noteworthy, as it has the potential to capture the structural, material and interpersonal pressures that impact the ability to exercise free choice.

Yet, on a closer inspection of international criminal cases, it would seem there were missed opportunities, at least in the early cases at the ICTR and ICC, to thoroughly develop the concept of coercive circumstances and associated categories of coercion. Thus, we have a parallel between rape in conflict and rape in peace, at least in terms of responses: What might be perceived as the most dramatic examples continue to be reinscribed in criminal justice processes. As noted by Kelly (2010, 122), "legal systems are incapable of understanding, and therefore adjudicating, on all but the most extreme forms of coerced heterosex and … despite out best efforts we are left with [only] 'real rapes' being prosecuted effectively whatever the context." The recent case of *Ongwen* at the ICC, as well as the case of *Nikačević* before the Court of Bosnia and Herzegovina, are more promising. As this chapter demonstrated, even though the background conditions to the rapes committed in these cases might be substantially different to what we associate with rape during peacetime i.e., the women were held captive or in hiding while hostilities were ongoing, they have illuminated how attention to the totality of the circumstances can reveal environments of control and fear, abuses of trust and psychological oppression that undermine free choice. Such an approach can be of benefit beyond the narrow confines of international criminal law and applied in domestic cases where non-physical sexually coercive tactics are used to facilitate rape. This chapter thus underscores the importance of thinking beyond dichotomies and connecting conversations on rape and sex ual violence to draw out shared challenges as well as the lessons that can b learned.

Bibliography

Amnesty International. 2011. Rape and Sexual Violence: Human Rights Law and Standards in the International Criminal Court, March 1, 2011, Index number: IOR 53/001/2011.

Anderson, S. 2016. "Conceptualising Rape as Coerced Sex." *Ethics* 127 (1): 50–87.

Basile, K.C. 1999. "Rape by Acquiescence: The Ways in Which Women 'Give In' to Unwanted Sex with Their Husbands." *Violence Against Women* 5: 1036–1058.

Bennice, J.A., and A. Resick. 2003. "Marital Rape: History, Research, and Practice." *Trauma, Violence, & Abuse* 4: 228–246.

Bettinson, V. 2017. "Coercive Control: In the Commission of Sexual Violence and Domestic Violence." *Contemporary Issues in Law* 14 (2): 85.

Brownmiller, S. 1975. *Against Our Will: Men, Women and Rape.* New York: Bantam Books.

Buchhandler-Raphael, M. 2011. "The Failure of Consent: Reconceptualizing Rape as Sexual Abuse of Power." *Michigan Journal of Gender and Law* 18 (1): 147–228.

Burgess-Jackson, K. (ed.). 1999. *A Most Detestable Crime: New Philosophical Essays on Rape.* New York: Oxford University Press.

Burgin, R. 2019. "Persistent Narratives of Force and Resistance: Affirmative Consent as Law Reform." *The British Journal of Criminology* 59 (2): 296–314.

Burgin, R., and A. Flynn. 2021. "Women's Behavior as Implied Consent: Male 'Reasonableness' in Australian Rape Law." *Criminology and Criminal Justice* 21(3): 334–352.

Carline, A., and C. Gunby. 2011. "How an Ordinary Jury Makes Sense of it is a Mystery': Barristers' Perspectives on Rape, Consent and the Sexual Offences Act 2003." *Liverpool Law Review* 32: 237–250.

Chinkin, C. 2014. "Addressing Violence Against Women in the Commonwealth Within States' Obligations Under International Law." *Commonwealth Law Bulletin* 40 (13): 471–501.

Conaghan, J. 2019. "The Essence of Rape." *Oxford Legal Studies* 39 (1): 151–182.

Dowds, E. 2020a. *Feminist Engagement with International Criminal Law: Norm Transfer, Complementary and Consent.* Oxford: Hart.

Dowds, E. 2020b. "Towards a Contextual Definition of Rape: Consent, Coercion and Constructive Force." *The Modern Law Review* 83 (1): 35–63.

Du Toit, L. 2011. "Introduction: Meaning/s of Rape in War and Peace." *Philosophical Papers* 38 (3): 285–305.

Du Toit, L. 2012. "From Consent to Coercive Circumstances: Rape Reform on Trial." *South African Journal of Human Rights* 28 (3): 380–404.

Ehrlich, S. 2002. *Representing Rape: Language and Sexual Consent.* London: Taylor & Francis.

Estrich, S. 1987. *Real Rape: How the Legal System Victimizes Women Who Say no.* Cambridge, MA: Harvard University Press.

Finch, E., and Munro, V. 2006. "Breaking Boundaries? Sexual Consent in the Jury Room." *Legal Studies* 26 (3): 303–320.

Fletcher, G.P. 1996. *Basic Concepts of Legal Thought.* New York: Oxford University Press.

Frith, H. 2009. "Sexual Scripts, Sexual Refusals and Rape." In *Rape: Challenging Contemporary Thinking*, edited by M. Horvath and J. Brown, 99–122. Cullompton: Willan Publishing.

Grewal, K. 2010. "Rape in Conflict, Rape in Peace: Questioning the Revolutionary Potential of International Criminal Justice for Women's Human Rights." *Australian Feminist Law Journal* 33 (1): 57–79.

Grewal, K. 2012. "The Protection of Sexual Autonomy Under International Criminal Law: The International Criminal Court and the Challenge of Defining Rape." *Journal of International Criminal Justice* 10 (2): 373–396.

Haddad, H. 2011. "Mobilizing the Will to Prosecute: Crimes of Rape at the Yugoslav and Rwandan Tribunals." *Human Rights Review* 12: 109–132.

Hale, M. 1736. *Historia Placitorum Coronae*. London: Professional Books Limited.

Halley, J. 2016. "The Move to Affirmative Consent." *Signs* 42 (1): 257–279.

Henderson, L. 1987. "What Makes Rape a Crime?" *Berkeley Journal of Gender, Law & Justice* 3 (1): 193–230.

Jeffrey, N.K., and P.C. Barata. (2017). "'He Didn't Necessarily Force Himself Upon me, but . . .': Women's Lived Experiences of Sexual Coercion in Intimate Relationships With Men." *Violence Against Women* 23 (8). 911 933.

Jokila, H., and J. Niemi. 2020. "Rape Law and Coercive Circumstances." In *Rape the Nordic Countries: Continuity and Change*, edited by M. Heinsjou, M.L. Skilbrei, and K. Stefansen, 120–136. London: Routledge.

Katz, J., and V. Tirone. 2010. "Going Along with it: Sexually Coercive Partner Behavior Predicts Dating Women's Compliance with Unwanted Sex." *Violence Against Women* 16 (7): 730–742.

Kelly, L. 2010. "The Everyday/Everynightness of Rape: Is it Different in War?" In *Gender, War and Militarism: Feminist Perspectives*, edited by L. Sjoberg and S. Via, 114–123. Santa Barbara: Praeger.

Kirkland Gillespie, L., and L. King. 2015. "Legislative Origins, Reforms, and Future Directions." In *Sexual Victimization: Then and Now*, edited by T.N. Richards and C.D. Marcum, 15–32. Thousand Oaks: Sage.

Leahy, S. 2014a. "Bad Laws or Bad attitudes? Assessing the Impact of Societal Attitudes Upon the Conviction Rate for Rape in Ireland." *Irish Journal of Applied Social Studies* 14 (1): 18–29.

Leahy, S. 2014b. "'No Means No', But Where's the Force? Addressing the Challenges of Formally Recognising Non-Violent Sexual Coercion as a Serious Sexual Offence." *The Journal of Criminal Law* 78 (4): 309–325.

Lembert, L. 1996. "Women's Strategies for Survival: Developing Agency in Abusive Relationships." *Journal of Family Violence* 11: 269–289.

MacKinnon, C. 1987. *Feminism Unmodified*. Cambridge, MA: Harvard University Press.

MacKinnon, C. 2006. "Defining Rape Internationally: A Comment on *Akayesu*." *Columbia Journal of Transnational Law* 44 (3): 940–958.

MacKinnon, C. 2016. "Rape redefined." *Harvard Law and Policy Review* 10: 431–477.

McGlynn, C., and V. Munro. 2010 "Rethinking Rape Law. An Introduction." In *Rethinking Rape Law: International and Comparative Perspectives*, edited by C. McGlynn and V. Munro, 1–14. London: Routledge.

McGregor, J. 2005. *Is it Rape?: On Acquaintance Rape and Taking Women's Consent Seriously*. London: Routledge.

McGregor, J. 2011. "The Legal Heritage of Rape." In *Handbook on Sexual Violence*, edited by J.M. Brown and S.L. Walklate, 69–89. Abingdon: Routledge.

Mitchell, J.E., and C. Raghavan. 2021. "The Impact of Coercive Control on Use of Specific Sexual Coercion Tactics." *Violence Against Women* 27 (2): 187–206.
Munro, V. 2008. "Constructing Consent: Legislating Freedom and Legitimating Constraint in the Expression of Sexual Autonomy." *Akron Law Review* 41 (4): 923–956.
Munro, V. 2010a. "From Consent to Coercion: Evaluating International and Domestic Frameworks for the Criminalization of Rape." In *Rethinking Rape Law: International and Comparative Perspectives*, edited by C. McGlynn and V. Munro, 15–29. London: Routledge.
Munro, V. 2010b. "An Unholy Trinity? Non-Consent, Coercion and Exploitation in Contemporary Legal Responses to Sexual Violence in England and Wales." *Current Legal Problems* 63 (1): 45–71.
Naffine, N. 2019. *Criminal Law and the Man Problem*. Oxford: Hart Publishing.
New South Wales Law Reform Commission. 2020. *Consent to Sexual Offences*. Report 148. September 2020.
O' Byrne, K. 2011. "Beyond Consent: Conceptualising Sexual Assault in International Criminal Law." *International Criminal Law Review* 11 (3): 495–514.
Palmer, T. 2017. "Distinguishing Sex from Sexual Violation: Consent, Negotiation and Freedom to Negotiate." In *Consent: Domestic and Comparative Perspectives*, edited by A. Reed and M. Bohlander, 9–24. London: Routledge.
Palmer, T. 2020. "Failing to See the Wood for the Trees: Chronic Sexual Violation and Criminal Law." *The Journal of Criminal Law* 84 (6): 573–595.
Pillay, N. 2010. "Address-Interdisciplinary Colloquium on Sexual Violence as International Crime: Sexual Violence: Standing by the Victim." *Law and Social Inquiry* 35 (4): 847–853.
Raghavan, C., S. Cohen, and T. Tamborra. 2015. "Development and Preliminary Validation of the Multidimensional Sexual Coercion Questionnaire (MSCQ)." *Journal of Sexual Aggression* 21 (3): 271–289.
Reiten, E. 2001. "Rape as an Essentially Contested Concept." *Hypatia* 16 (2): 43–66.
Roberts, D. 1993. "Rape, Violence and Women's Autonomy." *Chicago-Kent Law Review* 69 (2): 359–388.
Russell, Y. 2016. "Woman's Voice/Law's *Logos*: The Rape Trial and the Limits of Liberal Reform." *Australian Feminist Law Journal* 42 (2): 273–296.
Sankey, D. 2017. "From *Lubanga* to *Bemba*: Towards the Recognition of Sexual Violence and Gendered Harms at the International Criminal Court?" *Contemporary Issues in Law* 14 (2): 141.
Stark, E. 2007. *Coercive Control: How Men Entrap Women in Personal Life*. Oxford: Oxford University Press.
Temkin, J. 2002. *Rape and the Legal Process*. Oxford: Oxford University Press.
The Gillen Review. 2019. *Report into the Law and Procedures in Serious Sexual Offences in Northern Ireland*.
West, R. 2020. "Consent, Legitimation and Dysphoria." *Modern Law Review* 83 (1): 1–34.

Chapter 3

Archetypal Sluts

Payment of Sex Workers as a Condition of Consent

Zahra Stardust and Hilary Caldwell

In October 2010, Akis Livas texted a sex worker in the Australian Capital Territory (ACT) to make a booking. He made an arrangement to pay her $850 for services including sexual intercourse. Upon arrival, Livas gave the sex worker a sealed envelope and told her that it contained the fee. However, he insisted that the envelope must not be opened before the service because it was part of his fantasy. During the session, Livas psychologically and physically blocked the sex worker from opening the envelope, using his body to herd her into the shower and onto the bed. After intercourse, and while Livas was still in the room, the sex worker opened the envelope only to find folded pieces of paper and a romantic rose card.

Realising that she had been tricked, the worker became visibly upset. A scuffle broke out when she tried to call for help on her phone. She managed to grab a folder of paperwork belonging to Livas and pushed it under the bed, out of reach. Livas tried to buy time in the shower and dressing, however by that point the sex worker was shaking and sobbing loudly. She eventually convinced Livas that a security guard was on the way, and he left without his paperwork. The paperwork contained details of his legal name, previous violent offences, and established that he was on bail. The sex worker reported the incident to the police.

Upon arrest, Livas initially pleaded guilty to sexual intercourse without consent, on the basis that consent was negated by his fraudulent misrepresentation of payment. Later, he unsuccessfully contested the appropriateness of the charge, changed his plea to not guilty, and left the Territory in breach of bail. The sentencing occurred in February 2015, almost five years after the event, and Livas made a last-minute guilty plea. He was sentenced to 25 months imprisonment, (reduced from 30 months for his guilty plea). Taking into account his suspended sentence, his period already served, and his non-parole period, his penalty amounted to a total of eight months. In her Victim Impact Statement, the sex worker asserted that payment was a prerequisite for her consent. Her statement reinforced the labour sex workers perform in maintaining

DOI: 10.4324/9781003379331-5

their personal boundaries and reflected upon the fraudulent misrepresentation as a breach of her trust (*R v Livas*)[1]

> In my work, I do not simply allow clients access to my body. For a short time, I give them the opportunity to feel loved. In a world that values romantic fantasy, I offer a commercialised version. The care and affection that I showed Mr Livas during what I thought to be an honest service was completely devalued when I realised that I had been deceived.

The case of *R v Livas* represents a symbolic shift in how the law conceives of sex work and consent. At the time, it sparked controversy in the media about how the law ought to respond to the non-payment of sex workers, including debate over the appropriate charges and whether the sex worker was a survivor of fraud, theft, procurement, sexual assault or something else. In her judgment, Penfold J made it clear that "no one should doubt that fraudulently achieving sexual intercourse by this kind of activity constitutes rape, rather than a dishonesty offence, although of course dishonesty is a major element of this fact situation".[2] The decision stands out in contrast to judicial commentary in Australia about the perceived 'rapeability' of sex workers, including historical sentencing decisions that have assumed the psychological impact upon sex workers to be less than that for 'chaste' women (Fisher and Ammett 1992). In *Livas*, Penfold J determined that "[s]ex workers clearly fall into the category of vulnerable workers in general and may be particularly vulnerable to abuse of this kind".[3]

This chapter explores how the law conceptualises sex, money and consent through an analysis of select case law and recent law reform. As 'archetypal sluts,' how the law treats sex workers has broad implications for survivors of sexual violence who are impacted by myths and stereotypes of the "ideal victim" (Christie 1986) and what constitutes "real rape" (Estrich 1988). These recent shifts demonstrate that rape itself does not have a static and universal "essence" but rather is "politically contested and contextually bound" (Conaghan 2019, 151). As a result of long-standing sex worker interventions in the public discourse, the law (in these narrow instances) belatedly acknowledges sex workers' bodily integrity, recognising the labour of sex work, acknowledging payment as a condition of consent, and taking seriously fraud committed against sex workers. Numerous states in Australia are now reviewing their sexual consent laws with a particular focus on the fraudulent non-payment of sex workers.

However, the chapter remains suspicious of the selective expansion of the criminal law, which has broadened to encapsulate sex workers' clients but not

1 [2015] ACTSC 50, at 22.
2 *R v Livas* [2015] ACTSC 50, at 34.
3 *R v Livas* [2015] ACTSC 50, at 34.

police. Sex worker organisations have argued that fraud ought not to be limited to clients who misrepresent payment, but ought to capture those who surreptitiously record sessions or stealthily remove condoms. Further, they state that consent should be vitiated on occasions where police and private investigators misrepresent themselves by posing as clients (Scarlet Alliance and Vixen Collective 2020). Such arguments highlight the dual status of sex workers as survivors of both sexual and state violence. They underscore the paradoxical position whereby sex workers continue to be targeted as 'criminals,' even and especially when they attempt to report rape and sexual assault. Indeed, there remain systemic barriers to reporting for sex workers, who face legal, cultural and social narratives that they are either (a) in a perpetual state of consent or (b) victims without agency to consent. Sex workers report police not treating their claims seriously or expecting free services in return for not charging them for sex work offences (Stardust et al. 2021).

While criminal law is beginning to recognise sex worker agency in terms of consent (for the purpose of prosecution and incarceration), the tandem project of decriminalising sex work (one that will reduce the state violence, harassment and targeting of sex workers and improve sex workers' capacity to negotiate consent) receives less state investment. 'Progress' in consent law reform therefore ought to be considered critically in light of these unevenly-weighted objectives. Finally, because sexual violence is a space in which narratives of white victimhood are often mobilised to justify the expansion of a prison industrial complex that disproportionately impacts people of colour, we do not accept that carceral solutions will create a safer sexual culture. Instead, we argue that far more is necessary to build just and equitable sexual societies that support sex workers' sexual decision making and up-skill client skills in communication, respect and consent.

Inherent Victims, Paid Rape and Perpetual States of Consent

At the heart of many rape myths is the figure of the sex worker. Stereotypes that are frequently deployed against survivors of sexual assault – about sexual availability, provocative dress, sexually suggestive behaviour and sexual history – rely not only upon slut-shaming, but upon whorephobia. As former president of Scarlet Alliance Elena Jeffreys claimed at Slutwalk, sex workers "live the life of the archetypal slut" (Jeffreys and Automony 2011). Media representations commonly reinforce cultural narratives that the sexual assault of sex workers is not "real rape" (Miller and Schwartz 1995, Associated Press 2007) and that raping sex workers will result in impunity (Elks 2019). A lack of credibility assigned to 'prostitutes' and an expectation that sex workers are 'commonly available' have historically contributed to legal and conceptual frameworks that position sex workers as unable to be raped (Mac and Smith 2018, 44–45). Indeed, "the 'ideal victim' myth often works to undermine the credibility of those women who are seen to deviate too far from stereotyp cal notions of 'authentic' victims" (Randall 2010, 398). And yet sex worke of diverse genders continue to call out their experiences of sexual violence media, reports, policy briefs, journal articles and anthologies, from *Whores ar Other Feminists* (Nagle 1997) to *We Too: Essays on Sex Work and Survival* (We and Horn 2021).

At the same time, sex workers have historically been positioned in radica feminist thinking as inherent victims, unable to consent. Some have arguec that all sex work is effectively "paid rape" (Raymond 1995) or that womer cannot freely consent to sex with men because desire is fundamentally shapec by patriarchy (Pateman 1988). Many of these readings are founded in fixed and essentialist gender stereotypes about sex workers and their clients. In assuming that sex workers can neither consent nor refuse sex, they have reinforced cultural attitudes which result in violence against sex workers and operated to threaten sex workers' consensual capacity. It was not until the 1980s and 1990s that sex workers were first legally considered individuals able to give and withhold sexual consent (Sullivan 2016, 127).

In her analysis of Australian legal judgements between 1829 and 2004, Barbara Sullivan found that although some rape cases against sex workers were successfully prosecuted, sex workers faced barriers to reporting, including shame and powerlessness, risk of disbelief by police and prosecutors, fears of being charged with offences, low likelihood of convictions and the traumatic experience of trial. However, Sullivan found that

> sex workers engage, as a matter of routine, in detailed stipulation with clients and others over the nature of the sex acts they will (and will not) engage in… [and are] more actively involved in communication about consent, and nonconsent, than most other adults involved in sexual activity. (2016, 137)

Subsequent research supports the fact that sex workers often operate as consent educators among their clients. In Caldwell's research into women who buy sexual services, participants spoke about the lack of adequate consent education they had received in school and remarked that teaching women to say 'yes' or 'no' to sex reinforced women's passivity and receptivity to men's advances. Instead, the act of paying for sexual services was a teaching moment to learn skills to initiate and negotiate consent from experts (2018, 177).

Feminist debates continue to shape regulatory responses to both sex work and consent, including how discourses of innocence, guilt and blame "shape and inform respective hierarchies of victimhood and offending" (McAlinden 2014, 182). For decades, sex workers have argued that the solution to sexual violence is not the abolition of sex work but the removal of legislative frameworks that jeopardise sex workers' safety, agency and rights (Alexander 1994). The abolitionist model has now been replaced by binary distinctions between forced" and "voluntary" sex work (Kempadoo and Doezema 2018, 46). This false distinction operates to justify an international criminal justice approach to trafficking that controls who can consent to travel for work (Doezema, 2010) and puts migrant sex workers in danger of targeted policing, arrest and deportation, as well as creating new iterations of the "ideal victim" (O'Brien 2013). Like other workers under capitalism, sex worker decision-making is shaped by a myriad of social and cultural forces that cannot be "magicked away with liberal or carceral solutions" (Mac and Smith 2018, 39). Recent case law in Australia considers how the law can play a role in understanding payment of sex workers, not as evidence of rape, but as a condition of consent.

Chastity, Revulsion and Whorephobic Rape Myths

Judicial attitudes towards sex work were publicly contested in Australia following a series of cases in Victoria during the 1980s and 1990s where sex workers were victims of crime. These unreported cases were analysed in detail by feminist legal scholars (Fisher and Ammett 1992; Cass 1993; Graycar and Morgan 2002). In the 1981 case of *Attorney-General v Harris*.[4] Starke J stated that sexual assault "when committed against prostitutes … is not as heinous as when committed, say, on a happily married woman living in a flat in the absence of her husband when the miscreant breaks in and commits rape on her"[5] because "the forcible sexual act itself would not cause a reaction of revulsion" in a sex worker "which it might cause in a chaste woman".[6] In applying this decision a decade later, Jones J commented in *The Queen v Hakopian*[7] that a sex worker would experience less psychological harm because they "would have been involved in sexual activities on many occasions with men she had not met before, in a wide range of situations." The case of *Hakopian* involved rape with aggravating circumstances, indecent assault with aggravating circumstances and kidnapping.

Such decisions were also informed by the Victorian Sentencing Manual, which, at the time, suggested that sex workers would not experience the same level of psychological impact as other survivors. In a section listing victim details relevant to the seriousness of the offence, the manual in 1991 provided that although "prostitutes" and others "of dubious moral standards" are entitled to protection of "their right to determine for themselves when and in what circumstances they will permit access to their bodies by men," the guide assumed that the psychological trauma experienced by a sex worker would be less (Fisher and Ammett 1992, 684). The (il)logical implication of these

4 Unreported, Victorian Court of Criminal Appeal, 11 August 1981.

5 *Attorney-General v Harris* unreported, Victorian Court of Criminal Appeal, 11 August 1981, at 7.

6 *Attorney-General v Harris* unreported, Victorian Court of Criminal Appeal, 11 August 1981, at 6.

7 Unreported, County Court of Victoria, 8 August 1991.

decisions was, as Graycar and Morgan phrased it, that "all victim/survivors of convicted rapists should be asked how active a (consensual) sex life they have had: if they have had an active sex life, then presumably the sentence of their rapist should be reduced?" (2002, 347). Despite many subsequent reforms to procedural and evidentiary rules (including restrictions on the use of sexual reputation evidence) the Victorian Sentencing Manual was not updated to remove the reference to sex work until 2016.

Serial Offending and Impunity

One of the most high-profile Australian cases involving the rape of sex workers provides an indication of how treating sex workers as inferior, blameworthy victims operates to harm women more broadly. In June 2013 Adrian Bayley was sentenced to life imprisonment for the rape and murder of Jill Meagher (not a sex worker) when she was walking home from a pub in Melbourne. The case received widespread media attention because Bayley was on parole following conviction for a series of offences against sex workers. Bayley had previously been imprisoned for five years in 1991 for raping a teenager and the attempted rape of two further women, and then imprisoned again for 11 years in 2002 for 16 charges of rape against five street-based sex workers in St Kilda, Melbourne. In a submission to the NSWLRC, the Sex Workers Outreach Project NSW argued that "[l]enient sentencing relating to these offences against sex workers ensured Bayley remained at large to sexually assault and murder Jill Meagher" (2018, 3). Indeed, Meagher's husband had stated publicly (ABC 2013):

> I'm aware his previous victims in previous cases before Jill were sex workers, and I'll never be convinced that doesn't have something to do with the lenience of his sentence… Put it like this: if he'd raped five people like Jill that many times in that brutal a fashion, I don't think he would have served eight years in prison.

In 2013, Bayley was again convicted by juries in the Victorian County Court for the rapes of three more sex workers, including one in 2000 and two in 2012 while he was on parole. County Court Judge Pullen described his attacks as "chilling," stating "[e]ach in their own way was prey, and you … were an experienced hunter" (Australian Associated Press 2015) and sentenced him to 18 years imprisonment, with a new non-parole period of 43 years. Although Bayley successfully appealed his conviction in respect of one of those sex workers in 2016, the Court of Appeal noted that "Over many years, the applicant has shown a depraved predilection to attach, degrade and humiliate women." (Cooper 2016). This case sparked intense media debate about the ways in which sex workers are treated as disposable victims whose lives, bodies and decisions are seen as less valuable.

Vulnerable Workers and Psychological Impact

More recent cases on sex work in Australia are characterised by a very different sentiment that focus largely on sex workers' vulnerability to assault and the breach of trust by the defendants. In *Livas*, the sex worker specifically wrote in her Victim Impact Statement about her sense of powerlessness, shame and hurt at her client's deception:[8]

> My retrospective regret focused mainly upon my naivety.... My desire to give clients a service that I think they deserve was used to goad me into not checking the payment...I did have a sense of powerlessness after being thwarted in my attempts. In the days following the incident, I was unable to think clearly, eat or sleep properly and I felt continuously tired. I was confused and hurt in a deeply emotional way, feeling shame about my gullibility.

Penfold J made it clear that this kind of fraudulent activity ought to be classified as rape rather than as part of a continuum of dishonesty offences such as theft. She made note of the fact that the offence was "clearly premeditated," remarking that this was a case in which the defendant had "abused the trust that the complainant had placed in him".[9] It was evident that the offence was not simply about the commercial transaction. The Judge paid specific attention to the defendants' deception of the complainant and his violation of her personal integrity. She remarked:[10]

> It seems that Mr Livas is still focused on the event as a commercial transaction that he says he always intended to make good. While he may be genuinely regretful that he was not able to pay the money, it is hard to see this as remorse for the deliberate deception, and the violation of the complainant's personal integrity that he achieved by it.

Upon appeal, the court noted the seriousness of the offence, and remarked that a sentence involving full-time custody was "inevitable." They found that the period that Livas had been ordered to serve was "modest".[11]

Cultures of Entitlement

The cases involving deliberate non-payment of sex workers reveal much about cultures of entitlement among clients. In the subsequent case of *R v Mynott*

8 *R v Livas* [2015] ACTSC 50, at 22.
9 *R v Livas* [2015] ACTSC 50, at 23.
10 *R v Livas* [2015] ACTSC 50, at 25.
11 *Livas v The Queen* [2015] ACTCA 54.

No 2,[12] the defendant pled guilty to two counts of sexual intercourse without consent. On the first count, the complainants were male escorts. They were booked by the defendant using a pseudonym, who paid their flights to Canberra using a credit card that he had fraudulently obtained. Despite the escorts repeatedly asking when they would be paid, the defendant insisted he would go to an automatic teller machine following the booking. In the taxi on the way to the airport, the defendant asked the taxi to stop at an ATM so he could withdraw money, however, when he left the car he did not return. On the second count, the defendant booked another male escort for an overnight stay using a prepaid mobile in a false name. The escort booked his own flights on the promise that the defendant would repay him. The defendant brought a third person to join them despite that this was not part of their agreement, and offered the escort additional money. The escort repeatedly raised the issue of payment in his text messages, however following the booking, the defendant left, saying he was taking the other man back to his apartment, and never returned. In these cases, consent to sex was negated because it was caused by his fraudulent misrepresentation of payment.

In *Mynott*, the issue of breach of trust was again relevant to the sentencing. In that case, the defendant was sentenced to three years and four months' imprisonment. Chief Justice Murrell noted at 33 that according to the Victim Impact Statement, "The loss of trust associated with the incident affected the [complainants'] ability to engage in escort work and he had to change his line of work." She stated:[13]

> Each offence was of significant objective seriousness. Each was associated with significant planning. The offender did not reveal his real name to the complainants, and he financed or attempted to finance their expenses using the credit card details of a third party. Each offence encompassed several episodes of sexual activity. Because of the nature of sex work, sex workers are vulnerable to sexual offences of this kind.

Arguably, sex workers' vulnerability to sexual offences is not necessarily due to 'the nature of sex work' at all, but rather a consequence of the legal frameworks and regimes of stigma that cultivate attitudes of entitlement, expectations of impunity and barriers to justice. However, what is striking about these cases, when compared to earlier sentencing decisions, is their acknowledgement of the psychological impact of sexual assault upon sex workers and their exposing of the defendants' inability or refusal to grasp the meaning of consent. In *Livas*, for example, the Pre-Sentence Report detailed that while Livas was "able to articulate the seriousness of the offence that is before the Court, it appears that

12 [2020] ACTSC 232.
13 *R v Mynott No 2* [2020] ACTSC 232, at 35.

he has limited ability to accept personal responsibility or to demonstrate a full understanding of consent".[14] Livas fixated on the issue as a commercial transaction or debt without appreciating the psychological implications of his breach of trust.

These cases reflect problematic trends in client behaviour, including expectations of free sexual services, minimising of their own culpability, assumptions that sex workers are easy victims, and practices of time-wasting. These practices of trickery, bargaining and calculation indicate a lack of respect for the role, labour and bodily integrity of sex workers. They position sex workers as constant gatekeepers, performing the hyper-vigilant labour of boundary maintenance. In one case in Queensland, discussed below, a sex worker reported that her client told her that it was his first session, that he was running late and that he was nervous – tactics that served to delay, dismiss, stall and deny payment. As the worker reported, "I was just trying to make him feel comfortable" (McGowan and Knaus 2018).

Prosecutions, Penalties and Appropriate Charges

Not all instances of fraudulent non-payment of sex workers have been charged as rape. In 2018, two sex workers in Queensland reported a similar factual scenario to *Livas*. On one occasion, the client had left an envelope on a table in the sex worker's apartment. Instead of being stuffed with paper, it was empty; on another occasion, the client retrieved his wallet following the booking and remarked that he had "forgotten to go to the bank" (McGowan and Knaus 2018). However, this client was charged not with rape but with fraud. He was ordered by the Brisbane Magistrates court to pay $350 in restitution to each woman and was fined $750 for each offence (McGowan and Knaus 2018).

When sex workers report clients who misrepresent payment, the relevant charge will be determined by the police officer responsible for the matter. Each jurisdiction has different levels of criminal liability regarding fraudulent sex, with the most permissive in NSW and the most restrictive in the ACT (see Chen 2020). In addition, each state has prosecutorial guidelines that set out distinct criteria for charging and prosecution. For example, in the Queensland *Director's Guidelines* (Department of Justice and Attorney General 2016, currently under review), the decision to prosecute is based on a two-tiered test of whether there is sufficient evidence (including a reasonable prospect of conviction) and whether a prosecution is required by the public interest. Sometimes, the prosecution will choose between a number of overlapping alternative charges and have an obligation to avoid overcharging. This means that similar sets of factual circumstances may lead to different charges, penalties and outcomes. The Queensland Law Reform Commission has remarked that the

14 *R v Livas* [2015] ACTSC 50, at 24.

fraudulent non-payment of sex workers could be charged as fraud or stealing, if they adequately covered the total criminality of offending, or alternately as procuring a person to engage in a sex act on false pretences (2020, 125–126).

The politics and practices of charging depend in part on individual officers' understanding of sex work, however they also reflect what kind of behaviours the law takes seriously. In response to the Queensland case being charged as fraud, Estelle Lucas notes that by comparison, under the Queensland's *Prostitution Act 1999*, if a sex worker "causes unreasonable annoyance to another person," they can be fined $1,958 (Lucas 2018). The Queensland Police Service's own 2016–17 statistics show a 450% increase in police entrapment of sex workers and a 126% increase in charging sex workers for the offence of "knowingly participat[ing] in the provision of prostitution" (Jeffreys, O'Brien and Fawkes 2019). In Queensland's Public Hearing, the Chief Executive Officer of Scarlet Alliance, Jules Kim, noted that the Queensland Criminal Code itself "criminalise[s] the safety strategies that sex workers use in order to reduce the risk of sexual violence" (Legal Affairs and Safety Committee 2021, 26):

> This include such things as working in pairs, hiring a receptionist, even making a call or sending a text to another sex worker when they are going into a booking or when a booking is finished … Sex workers in Queensland are effectively forced to work either safely or legally. This is obviously an untenable situation that significantly exacerbates the risk of sexual violence for sex workers

Despite shifts in case law to recognise sex worker agency in the ACT, the ongoing legacy of criminal and licensing laws in other jurisdictions maintains sex workers' risk of sexual violence.

Consent Law Reform

Criminal law in Australia is currently undergoing a substantial review of sexual consent, and some state law reform commissions have cited *Livas*, specifically noting opportunities for the law to respond (Queensland Law Reform Commission 2020, 131). In 2020, three states undertook a consent law reform process: the Queensland Law Reform Commission issued a report into their *Review of Consent Laws and the Excuse of Mistake of Fact*, while NSW Law Reform Commission tabled their report on *Consent in Relation to Sexual Offences* and the Victorian Law Reform Commission invited public submissions on their Issues Paper on *Improving the Response of the Justice System to Sexual Offences*. In their report, the New South Wales Law Reform made particular note of the lack of protection afforded to sex workers in that state (2020, 6.177):

> The absence of a specific fraud provision also creates gaps in legal protection. For instance, a range of submissions, survey responses and researchers

> express concern about the lack of protection afforded to sex workers who are fraudulently promised payment for sexual services. Submissions argue that this should be considered sexual assault, as this reflects the experiences of complainants.

In Queensland, some submissions recommended clarification that non-payment of sex workers would amount to rape in order to impact the attitudes of police officers towards sex workers reporting such offences, while others argued that this scenario was already addressed in case law, that a distinct offence was unnecessary because the list of circumstances negating consent is already non-exhaustive (QLRC 2020, 131–133). At the public hearing of the Legal Affairs and Safety Committee, Elena Jeffreys, the State Coordinator of Respect Inc. reported that in practice sex workers reporting rape in Queensland were being belittled by police (2021, 24):

> Even sex workers who surmount the significant barriers to reporting rape or sexual assault are being told by police, 'I don't see the crime,' or 'It is a civil, not a criminal, matter.' This happens regularly, and our organisation has progressed formal complaints about this behaviour, as well as bringing it to the attention of the Minister for Police and the Police Commissioner.

In part, sex worker organisations have pushed for recognition that sex workers can indeed experience sexual assault (both in the workplace and outside it). They have urged legislators to clarify that sex workers have capacity to refuse sexual activity and place conditions on their consent. The Inner City Legal Centre (ICLC), which run a Sex Worker Legal Service in NSW, advocated in its submission that "the law ought to clarify that payment for sex (whether it be in money or in kind) does not equate to consent" (ICLC 2019). This is reflected in recent law reform in the Northern Territory, where the *Sex Industry Act 2019 NT* states in s9(1) that "Despite anything in a contract for sex work, a person may, at any time, refuse to perform or continue to perform sex work."[15] In addition, the Act specifies in s9(2) that "The fact that a person has entered into a contract for sex work does not of itself constitute consent for the purposes of the criminal law if the person does not consent, or withdraws the person's consent, to performing sex work."[16] This clause positions sex workers as agentic and distinguishes sex work from sexual assault.

In addition, the submissions of sex worker organisations to these public inquiries commented on the incidence of fraudulent behaviour ought to vitiate consent. For example, Scarlet Alliance, Australian Sex Workers

15 *Sex Industry Act 2019 NT* s9(1).
16 *Sex Industry Act 2019 NT* s9(2).

Association, and Vixen Collective, Victoria's peer sex worker organisation, noted the lack of redress when clients stealthily removed condoms during a booking or secretly recorded footage of sex workers (2020). Legal scholars have debated whether the practice of 'stealthing' is already sufficiently covered under various sexual assault provisions (see Chesser and Zahra 2019). The ICLC reported seeing sex workers whose clients had deliberately reversed payments following their session or provided falsified proof of payment in advance of the session (2019).

Government-funded Rape

Significantly, the submissions of sex workers to these inquiries went further than clients, turning to the role of private companies and state agencies. Scarlet Alliance and Vixen Collective argued that police officers and private investigators who dishonestly and deceptively misrepresent themselves by posing as clients in order to entrap sex workers or collect evidence for their compliance investigations ought to be captured by the offence of sexual assault, primarily because the consent was induced by fraud (2020). Police and private investigators – who are hired by local councils to prove that massage parlours and brothels are operating in ways that are not council approved – betray the trust of sex workers and ought to vitiate consent. In a specific position paper on obtaining sex under a false pretence for the purposes of investigation, SWOP NSW (2019) write:

> It is SWOP's view that consent is negated when private investigators, police, prison officers, and immigration and border control officers, initiate sexual contact under the false pretense that said sexual contact is not undertaken on the course of their employment or engage in sexual intercourse with people, either in the process of investigating them, investigating their employer, arresting or detaining them, or while they are in custody or detention.

In their paper, SWOP set out a series of incidents between 2013–2019 where local councils had hired private investigators (termed 'brothel busters') to have undercover sex with sex workers as part of their surveillance and compliance activities, including one sustained practice over the course of 10 years responsible for 60 brothel closure orders across 16 different local government areas. SWOP cite quotes from individual sex workers noting their distress at the prevalence of such practices and specifically stating that they would not give their consent if they knew the 'client' was police or an investigator. One of the sex workers cited refers to this practice as "government/council-funded rape" (2019, 4). Existing jurisprudence on sex and deception is yet to consider whether such private and state activities would constitute sanctioned, funded, organised and calculated form of rape.

Sexual Fraud and Criminal Overreach

Exactly at what point deceptive sex ought to be subject to criminal liability is the source of much contention. Legal scholars have offered various frameworks that seek to distinguish different circumstances and discern codified principles, with attention to issues of power, authority, exploitation, trust, vulnerability, dignity, autonomy and identity (Kennedy 2021). It is worth noting that historically, the spectacle of deception has been used *against* sex workers, who themselves are frequently painted in the socio-cultural imaginary as misleading, dishonest, fake, illusory or fraudulent. Trans sex workers have been portrayed through both media scripts and legal narratives as deceptive in order to excuse violent and sometimes lethal responses to non-violent sexual advances (the 'homosexual advance defence' remained present in NSW until 2014). Sex workers living with HIV are pictured as deceptive when they do not disclose their serostatus and continue to be criminalised, regardless of the services they offer or whether they have undetectable viral load, practice safer sex, employ risk reduction strategies or cater to HIV positive clients (Jeffreys, Matthews and Thomas 2010). Sexual offence provisions on fraud therefore have the potential to be weaponised against marginalised communities, susceptible to misuse by police, disgruntled clients and former sexual partners who are struggling with their own transphobia, whorephobia or fear of HIV.

As Alex Sharpe points out, the expansion of criminal liability for sexual fraud is vulnerable to "criminal law overreach" (Sharpe 2016). Sharpe discusses nine cases of "gender fraud," all instigated by cisgender women against against transgender men, genderqueer people or lesbians, where all convicted defendants were placed on sex offender registers for life (Sharpe 2016). Sharpe notes that "transgender operates as a synonym for deception in a ciscentric society" (39) and argues that "There is a real danger here that cissexist understandings of gender, identity and authenticity will expand the net of criminalisation beyond the example of transgender" to capture genderqueer people, gender flux or playfulness (2016, 42). The submissions of Vixen Collective, Scarlet Alliance and the Inner City Legal Centre were all concerned that fraud provisions may be misused in this way, and specified that a person's gender experience, history and identity should not be read as a dishonest or deceptive misrepresentation, regardless of whether their gender has been legally or medically affirmed. Similarly, they expressed concern that fraud provisions could be used to charge people with HIV who have not disclosed their serostatus and noted the cases in which HIV positive sex workers had been prosecuted and imprisoned in the ACT and Western Australia. The requirement to disclose HIV status was removed from the *Public Health Act 2010 NSW* in 2017[17] because of the seri-

17 Section 79 of the *Public Health Act 2010 NSW* was amended by the *Public Health Amendment (Review) Act 2017 No 43*.

ous risks of stigma, discrimination and violence facing people with HIV upon disclosure.

Unpaid Debts and Civil Alternatives

The *Livas* proceedings generated a substantial amount of Australian media at the time, including news articles reported by the *Australian Broadcasting Corporation*, *The Canberra Times* and *The Guardian*. Some disputed that this type of deception ought to constitute rape at all. One article claimed that "A recent conviction in the ACT makes rapists of us all" (O'Neill 2015), while others claimed that treating the incident as rape would make a mockery of 'real rape' victims. These complaints were largely made by men's rights activists, some of whom expressed disbelief that lying to obtain sex would constitute rape because it was so commonplace. One of the tensions that arose within the sex worker rights movement itself was how to best conceptualise this kind of conduct and the most appropriate means of redress. If sex work is to be treated like other forms of work, and if sex is not to be exceptionalised simply because it involves sex, then arguably non-payment would amount to a breach of contract, and these circumstances could simply be understood as a case of fraud (obtaining financial advantage by dishonest deception) rather than rape.

In some cases, sex workers can use civil law to recover unpaid debts such as these. Claims for unpaid debts are a common practice for the Inner City Legal Centre in NSW as part of their free state-wide Sex Worker Legal Service. In these instances, sex workers can issue letters of demand asserting the amount owing and a payment deadline, and if this is not forthcoming, sex workers can commence legal proceedings in court to recover the debt plus interest. One of the challenges in these scenarios is correctly identifying the defendant, especially where they have provided false or no identification. Another is the likelihood that the defendant will simply not respond to the plaintiff's Statement of Claim. On these occasions, sex workers can obtain a default judgment in the absence of the defendant, and have a judgment entered against the defendant without a hearing. This process can be lengthy, because if the client fails to comply with the default judgment and does not pay the amount requested, sex workers will need to take a series of further steps to enforce the debt. These include issuing an examination notice to investigate the client's financial status (their income, assets and debts) and then taking enforcement action such as a garnishee order (through which banks, employers or other third parties can withhold money to pay the debt), issuing writs for the seizure of the client's property, or, in some cases, instigating bankruptcy proceedings.

Civil avenues to recover unpaid debts can be a validating means for sex workers to recover money from services provided, because they recognise the existence of a contractual relationship. They can also be effective in reinforcing to clients their contractual obligations in a context where they might not otherwise take them seriously. Civil proceedings can also be brought simultaneously in tandem with criminal proceedings, and so regardless of the outcome of a criminal case, sex workers may be able to recover their debt. These options ought to be available to sex workers in all states and territories for free through their local community legal centre, and yet such projects remain largely unfunded. Community legal centres have different policies relating to eligibility (based on income and residence) and may not have lawyers that are culturally competent in dealing with sex workers. Furthermore, stigma, lack of resources, and the threat of retaliation or repercussion may pose barriers to sex workers accessing civil mechanisms, especially because of the need to bring proceedings under one's legal name. By contrast, criminal proceedings offer the opportunity for survivor's names to be suppressed and proceed with the survivor as a witness rather than a plaintiff.

In jurisdictions where sex work is criminalised or licenced, it may not be legally possible to enter or enforce a contract for sexual services, and civil remedies may not be available. The major problem for sex workers is that courts are unlikely to enforce contracts for unlawful activities and may consider such contracts void. Where sex work is directly prohibited by statute, or where a contract has been entered into for an illegal purpose (such as to provide a service that is criminalised), or even if the performance of the contract is considered to be against public policy, the contract may be void. Because of the obstacles to accessing civil remedies, it is important for sex workers to have multiple options for redress. While civil law has potential to recognise the existence of a legally enforceable contract (acknowledging sex work as work), the availability of criminal law as a means of redress can recognise the serious psychological impact for sex workers experiencing fraudulent non-payment.

State Violence, Carceral Politics and Sexual Justice

While it may appear to be a progressive step that consent law in Australia is now shifting to recognise sex workers' agency, we ought to be suspicious that the criminal law is *selectively* expanding to capture more behaviour whilst failing to address forms of sexual violence that are enacted by police and the state. The law already lags behind community standards in its understandings of consent and bondage/discipline, dominance/submission, sadism/masochism (BSDM) (where practitioners risk being prosecuted for assault or actual or grievous bodily harm). It lags behind epidemiological and scientific evidence on HIV transmission and relies on cisnormative concepts of gender authenticity. There are plenty of ways that sex positive legal thinking could improve sex work regulation (see Bennett and Stardust 2022), however we ought to pay attention to the irony (and injustice) of the situation whereby the criminal law is widening its net to capture the clients of sex workers, whilst continuing the criminalisation and licensing of sex work and ignoring the complicity of law enforcement.

In some countries, steps have been taken to encourage sex workers to report as victims of crime. For example, in 2019 'immunity from arrest' legislation

(SB-233 2019–2020) was proposed in California to protect sex workers from prosecution when they report serious crimes such as assault, extortion, sexual battery domestic violence or human trafficking (NSWP 2019). The legislation makes evidence of sex work at or around the time of the crime inadmissible for the purposes of proving criminal liability for sex work. Respect Inc. recommend a similar amnesty clause in their submission to the Queensland Law Reform Commission (Respect Inc. 2021, 2). While this may serve to reduce barriers for sex workers in accessing the criminal legal system, the risk is that, where such offers are not coupled with decriminalisation, sex workers can become pawns in a carceral system. Instead of concern over sex worker industrial rights, health or safety, the law remains disproportionately fixated upon sex workers' experiences of violence and criminalising clients as part of a broader carceral expansion. This has been a critique of simply including sex workers in hate crimes legislation, without addressing the structures that cause vulnerability (Holt and Gott 2022).

Sex worker activism, in Australia and internationally, has a long history of advocating against police targeting, state violence and criminal justice approaches to labour and migration. It recognises that carceral approaches to sexual violence do not necessarily result in justice for survivors, nor does imprisonment result in proactive cultures of sexual consent for offenders. By contrast, transformative justice approaches seek to achieve a broader transformation of sexual relations that does not simply restore the status quo but transforms the systems which enable and facilitate these kinds of abuse. Judith Levine and Erica R. Meiners urge us to aim for radical change rather than reformism to confront sexual harm and end state violence whilst also transforming communities and cultures. Their recommendations include investing in radical and free sex education, building a robust welfare - not a carceral - state, practising transformative justice and embracing abolition feminism, and complicating consent (Levine and Meiners, 2020). Part of complicating consent means understanding that sex workers have "personal criteria for what kind of sex they have" and that criteria can include payment (2020, 170).

Soliciting for Change

As the archetypal sluts, the treatment of sex workers under the law matters. How criminal law understands sex work has a significant flow on effect for other survivors in the criminal legal system. Sex worker complainants, litigants and advocates are changing the course of consent law in Australia, opposing cultures of entitlement and impunity and reinscribing systems of value. Challenging the historical assumptions that sex for money equals rape, recent cases instead treat the fraudulent non-payment of sex workers as rape. Rejecting the popular assumptions that sex workers are in a perpetual state of consent, sex workers position themselves as agents who request money as a *condition* of consent. But further, sex workers are intervening into public discourse on consent to redirect it towards not only interpersonal violence but state violence. If sex workers are expected to come forward as victims, the law must stop treating sex workers as criminals. A long-term transformative justice approach to sexual violence relies not only on consent education but on decriminalisation, destigmatisation and decarceration.

References

ABC. 2013. "Jill Meagher's Husband Tom Meagher Says Justice System Failed Her and Adrian Bayley's Sentence is a Disgrace." June 19. https://www.abc.net.au/news/2013-06-19/tom-meagher-says-justice-system-failed-his-wife/4766620.

Alexander, Priscilla. 1994. "Prostitutes Are People Too." *Off Our Backs* 24 (9): 26–28.

Associated Press. 2007. "Judge Criticized for Considering Gang Rape on Prostitute 'Theft of Services'." November 1. https://www.foxnews.com/story/judge-criticized-for-considering-gang-rape-on-prostitute-theft-of-services.

Australian Associated Press. 2015. "Adrian Bayley, Jill Meagher's Killer, has Jail Term Increased to 43 Years Non-Parole." *The Guardian*, May 28.

Bennett, Theodore and Zahra Stardust. 2022. "Positive Potential: The Benefits of Sex Positivity for Legal Thinking and Sex Work Regulation in Australia." *Monash University Law Review* 48 : 1–42.

Caldwell, Hilary. 2018. *Women Who Buy Sex in Australia: From Social Representations to Lived Experiences*. PhD Dissertation. Centre for Social Research in Health, University of NSW.

Cass, Deborah Z. 1993. "R v Hakopian." *Feminist Legal Studies* 1: 203.

Chen, Jianlin. 2020. "Fraudulent Sex Criminalisation in Australia: Disparity, Disarray and the Underrated Procurement Offence." *University of New South Wales Law Journal*, 43 (2): 581–614.

Chesser, Brianna and April Zahra. 2019. "Stealthing: A Criminal Offence?" *Current Issues in Criminal Justice* 31 (2): 217–235.

Christie, N. 1986. The Ideal Victim. In Ezzat A. Fattah (ed.) *From Crime Policy to Victim Policy*. 17–30. London: Palgrave Macmillan.

Conaghan, Joanne. 2019. "The Essence of Rape." *Oxford Journal of Legal Studies* 39 (1): 151–182.

Cooper, A. 2016. "Court of Appeal Cuts Adrian Bayley's Sentence by Three Years" *Sydney Morning Herald*. 13 July

Doezema, Jo. 2010. "Who Gets to Choose? Coercion, Consent, and the UN Trafficking Protocol." *Gender and Development* 10 (1): 20–27.

Elks, Sonia. 2019. "Sex Workers Denied Justice Over Rapes, Says UK Prostitutes' Collective." *Thomson Reuters Foundation*, November 6. https://www.reuters.com/article/us-britain-women-rape-trfn-idUSKBN1XF1QE.

Estrich, S. 1988. *Real Rape*. Cambridge (US): Harvard University Press.

Fisher, Michelle, and Fahma Annett. 1992. "Sentencing of Sexual Offenders when their Victims are Prostitutes and Other Issues Arising out of Hakopian." *Melbourne University Law Review* 18: 683–691.

Graycar, Regina, and Jenny Morgan. 2002. *The Hidden Gender of Law*. Sydney: The Federation Press.

Holt, Victoria, and Chloe Gott. 2022. "The Limits of Vulnerability: Arguments Against the Inclusion of Sex Workers Within Hate Crime Policy in England and Wales." *International Journal of Gender, Sexuality and Law* 2 (1): 360–393.

ICLC 2019 Inner City Legal Centre, Submission to the NSW Law Reform Commission inquiry into Consent in Relation to Sexual Offences, https://www.lawreform.justice.nsw.gov.au/Documents/Current-projects/Consent/Submissions/CO82.pdf

Jeffreys, Elena, and Audry Automony. 2011. *Speech for Melbourne Slutwalk*. https://www.youtube.com/watch?v=zkssSK-Pnnk.

Jeffreys, E., K. Matthews, and A. Thomas. 2010. "HIV Criminalisation and Sex Work in Australia." *Reproductive Health Matters* 18 (35): 129–136.

Jeffreys, Elena, Erin O'Brien, and Janelle Fawkes. 2019. "The Case for Decriminalisation: Sex Work and the Law in Queensland." Crime and Justice Briefing Paper. Queensland University of Technology. Issue 1.

Kempadoo, Kamala, and Jo Doezema (eds.). 2018. *Global Sex Workers: Rights, Resistance, and Redefinition*. New York and London: Routledge.

Kennedy, Chloe. 2021. "Criminalising Deceptive Sex: Sex, Identity and Recognition." *Legal Studies* 41 (1): 91–110.

Legal Affairs and Safety Committee. 2021. "Public Hearing – Inquiry into the *Criminal Code (Consent and Mistake of Fact) and Other Legislation Amendment Bill 2020*." *Transcript of Proceedings*, January 21.

Levine, Judith, and Erica R. Meiners. 2020. *The Feminist and the Sex Offender: Confronting Sexual Harm, Ending State Violence*. London and New York: Verso Books.

Lucas, Estelle. 2018. "Abused by the System: The Unfair Stigma Surrounding Sex Work." *Independent Australia*, November 15. https://independentaustralia.net/life/life-display/the-unfair-stigma-surrounding-sex-workers,12100#.X6jDm7he1Q8.link.

McAlinden, A.-M. 2014. "Deconstructing Victim and Offender Identities in Discourses on Child Sexual Abuse: Hierarchies, Blame and the Good/Evil Dialectic." *British Journal of Criminology* 54 (2): 180–198. https://doi.org/10.1093/bjc/azt070.

McGowan, Michael, and Christopher Knaus. 2018. "'It Absolutely Should be Seen as Rape': When Sex Workers Are Conned." *The Guardian*, October 13. https://www.theguardian.com/australia-news/2018/oct/13/it-absolutely-should-be-seen-as-when-sex-workers-are-conned.

Miller, Jody, and Martin D. Schwartz. 1995. "Rape Myths and Violence Against Street Prostitutes." *Deviant Behavior* 16 (1): 1–23.

Nagle, Jill (ed), 1997. *Whores and Other Feminists*. New York and London: Routledge.

NSWP. 2019. "New Legislation in San Francisco to Protect Sex Workers When Reporting Serious Crime." *Global Network of Sex Work Projects*. https://www.nswp.org/news/new-legislation-san-francisco-protect-sex-workers-when-reporting-serious-crime.

O'Brien, Erin. 2013. "Ideal Victims in Trafficking Awareness Campaigns." In *Crime, Justice and Social Democracy*, 315–326. London: Palgrave Macmillan.

O'Neill, Brendon. 2015. "Sex, Lies and, er, Rape: A Recent Conviction in the ACT Makes Rapists of us All." *Spectator*, February 28. https://spectator.com.au/2015/02/sex-lies-and-er-rape/.

Pateman, Carole. 1988. *The Sexual Contract*. Stanford: Stanford University Press.

Queensland Law Reform Commission. 2020. *Review of Consent Laws and the Excuse of Mistake of Fact*. Report No. 78. June. https://www.parliament.qld.gov.au/Documents/TableOffice/TabledPapers/2020/5620T1217.pdf.

Randall, Melanie. 2010. "Sexual Assault Law, Credibility, and 'Ideal Victims': Consent, Resistance, and Victim Blaming." *Canadian Journal of Women and the Law* 22 (2): 397–433.

Raymond, Janice. 1995. "Perspective on Human Rights: Prostitution Is Rape That's Paid For." *Los Angeles Times*, December 11. https://www.latimes.com/archives/la-xpm-1995-12-11-me-12813-story.html.

Respect Inc. 2021. *Submission to the Queensland Law Reform Commission in Response to the Discussion Paper: Review of Consent Laws and the Excuse of Mistake of Fact.* January 31.
Scarlet Alliance and Vixen Collective. 2020. *Submission to the Victorian Law Reform Commission on Improving the Response of the Justice System to Sexual Offences.*
Sex Workers Outreach Project NSW. 2018. *Submission to the NSW Law Reform Commission Review of Consent in Relation to Sexual Offences.* July 11.
Sex Workers Outreach Project NSW. 2019. *Position Paper: Obtaining Sex Under a False Pretencefor the Purpose of Investigation or Obtaining Information is Rape.*
Sharpe, A. 2016. "Expanding Liability for Sexual Fraud Through the Concept of 'Active Deception': A Flawed Approach." *The Journal of Criminal Law* 80: 1.
Smith, M., and J. Mac. 2018. *Revolting Prostitutes: The Fight for Sex Workers' Rights.* London: Verso.
Stardust, Zahra, Carla Treloar, Elena Cama, and Jules Kim. 2021. "'I Wouldn't Call the Cops if I was Being Bashed to Death': Sex Work, Whore Stigma and the Criminal Legal System." *International Journal for Crime, Justice and Social Democracy* 10 (2): 142–157.
Sullivan, B. 2016. "Prostitution and Consent: Beyond the Liberal Dichotomy of 'Free or Forced'." In *Making Sense of Sexual Consent*, edited by Mark Cowling and Paul Reynolds, 127–139. New York and London: . Routledge.
West, Natalie, and Tina Horn (eds.). 2021. *We Too: Essays on Sex Work and Survival.* New York: Feminist Press.

Part Two

Challenging the Colonial Order

Chapter 4

Reading International Rape Law from the South

Louise du Toit

Introduction

Western modernity does not stand over against the non-West, or global South, associated as the latter is with the pre-enlightenment, pre-modern categories of tradition, religion, and ethnicity. Instead, the very distinction between the West and its others, the so-called 'colonial difference,' is a product of modernity itself and is moreover its hidden and seemingly unstoppable engine. Without the systemic material and epistemic exploitation that this artificial hierarchical distinction legitimises, neither Western modernity nor its others would exist. To develop a perspective 'from the South,' means to confront this machinery which drives what some authors call 'coloniality'; namely, the ongoing exploitation of former colonies (roughly equivalent to the 'global South') after political decolonisation, as I show in the section 'Reading from the South.' I apply this lens throughout the rest of the argument, and specifically to a consideration of the jurisprudence of the international criminal courts in their[1] response to rape and sexual violence[2] during war. In the section 'International Law's Complicity in Coloniality,' the complicity of international law in the creation and maintenance of this engine is discussed, *inter alia* international criminal law's (ICL's) historical roots in European wars and its uneven infringement upon different states' national sovereignty.

In the section 'ICL's Focus on Sexual Violence and "War Rape,"' I show that the ongoing tension between the concepts of 'consent' and 'coercion' noticeable in rape trials before the international criminal courts and tribunals,

1 I refer here broadly to all the courts and tribunals that apply international criminal law, including the ICTR and ICTY, the Special Court for Sierra Leone, as well as the International Criminal Court (ICC), which was established in 2002 as the first permanent international court with jurisdiction to prosecute individuals for international crimes.

2 Although at times I will speak more broadly of SVAC, or 'sexual violence in armed conflict,' thus indicating many different forms of sexual violation and including forms of armed conflict that might not accede to the level of formally declared war, my focus in this article is on 'war rape,' which is narrowly circumscribed in ICL. Moreover, there is much evidence for significant numbers of male victims of SVAC (Carpenter 2006; Ferrales, Nyseth Brehm and McElrath 2016; Gorris 2015; Žarkov 2007) and although I have written on this important topic elsewhere (Du Toit and Le Roux 2021 and Du Toit 2022), this is not my focus in the current chapter.

DOI: 10.4324/9781003379331-7

is indicative of the tension that exists within the heart of what international criminal law aims to do, namely, to address *systemic violence* through the trial and punishment of *individuals* who had acted in unique events. Since these trials are haunted by the same problems experienced in domestic and peace-time rape trials, most saliently the issue of consent, there is a growing and unrealistic inflation by these courts of the harms of so-called 'war rape' as compared to other rape. I argue that the need for ICL to spectacularise the sexual violence that accompanies war in those mostly far-off, non-Western places where its focus lies, feeds directly into the colonial difference and implicates ICL in coloniality. I argue that this approach reinscribes the 'stranger rape' myth with racist undertones on a global scale. These effects of the ICL's work thus far – which might be distinguished from its intention – become clearer when one considers the inseparability of race and sex in the production of colonial difference, and the special place of abjection that is reserved for the hypersexualised Black female body in this system of signification. Understanding these criticisms from the South against how ICL operates, has far-reaching implications for how we think about feminist activism in relation to 'war rape,' as well as for trans-national feminist solidarity, as I show in the section 'Some Implications for International Feminist Solidarity.'

Reading from the South

Jean and John Comaroff[3] (2016, 1) write in *Theory from the South*,

> Western enlightenment thought has, from the first, posited itself as the wellspring of universal learning, of Science and Philosophy, uppercase; concomitantly, it has regarded the non-West—variously known as the ancient world, the orient, the primitive world, the third world, the under-developed world, the developing world, and now the global south—primarily as a place of parochial wisdom, of antiquarian traditions, of exotic ways and means. Above all, of unprocessed data.[4]

At the heart of modern enlightenment thought (myth) one finds the notion of Western exceptionality. Just as enlightened 'Man' is deluded into supreme, cerebral, and disembodied detachment from the material world and formative relations that produced him in fact, the Western world of this myth sprang into existence as "the wellspring … of Science and Philosophy," generated purely

3 Fifteen Harvard Anthropology Professors Call on Comaroff to Resign Over Sexual Harassment Allegations | News | The Harvard Crimson (thecrimson.com). John Comaroff has been accused of sexual harassment by three of his students. If the allegations are true, his actions must be condemned. At the same time, however, these developments do not imply he should be ignored as a scholar.

4 To "unprocessed data" one might add of course 'unprocessed raw materials,' both of which passively await the European imprint of form and meaning.

from internal power and brilliance. Unaided by any other region or culture, ideas or resources, it gave birth to itself. In the mind-matter dichotomy of the Platonic and Cartesian traditions, the West represents animating mind, and the non-West is pure, inert matter. It is therefore just as natural for the West to impose 'universal' meaning upon the formless and meaningless matter of the non-West as it is for the mind of 'Man' to project meaning onto the senseless material world around him. Resources extracted from the "non-West," "human and physical, moral and medical, mineral and man-made, cultural and agricultural," have therefore been routinely regarded as 'raw materials' and "unprocessed data," to which the West subsequently added all possible "value and refinement" (Comaroff and Comaroff 2016). Recall the so-called 'wastelands' of colonial interiors that the colonisers felt they had the right, indeed the duty, to subdue through cultivation, extraction and production for the benefit of 'civilisation.' Plunder and subjugation were justified as universal progress, since it placed unprecedented concentrations of wealth and power in the hands of the 'civilised.'

To read from the South means first to highlight and then to trouble this dominant understanding of the 'colonial difference' that the idealogues of modernity construe(d) between West and non-West. Like Walter Mignolo (Mignolo 2000, quoted in Alcoff 2007, 83), who coined the term "colonial difference," the Comaroffs (2016, 2) also urge us to "move beyond the north-south binary" viewed as a neutral and static descriptor of two separate entities, and to "lay bare the larger *dialectical processes* that have produced [past tense] and sustain [present tense] it" (emphasis and additions mine – LdT).[5] Mignolo describes the same dynamic dialectic by recalling that Western modernity "emerged from colonialism, not after it or simply alongside" (see Alcoff 2007, 83). Colonialism and slavery, exploitation, and subjugation, of the so-called non-West, are therefore not anomalies within Western modernity but are instead some of its key products and symptoms. Similarly, Antony Anghie uses the term "the dynamic of difference," to refer more pointedly to the strategy of some jurists in international law to use the tools of positivism, to continuously reproduce "a gap ... between the civilized European and the uncivilized non-European world" – a distance finally to be bridged by "civilizing the uncivilized" (Anghie 1999). We[6] will return to this illusory 'distance,' 'gap' or 'separation,' at once (covertly) created and sustained, *and* supposedly (overtly) bridged, by international law. We should thus remain vigilant about how the colonial imagination has inaugurated, and still maintains as justificatory strategy, the very process of differentiation between the

5 I show at the hand of a missionary hearing elsewhere (Du Toit 2019: 38) how the production of the 'colonial difference' was in fact an erasure of actual difference. Missionaries equated a lack of (especially sexual) self-restraint with 'going native' or falling back into indigenous ways. In this manner, Xhosa precolonial sexual mores were effectively erased and in fact equated with a pre-social state of nature, and thus with the complete *absence* of norm and restraint.

6 'We' here means you (reader of the text) and I (writer and narrator of the text).

West and (its) rest. What Mignolo labels "the evaluative binary structure" that serves empire and "nourishes western modernity" (quoted in Alcoff 2007, 87), situates the colony (and former colony) spatially at modernity's periphery ('far-off and exotic'), and temporally in modernity's past ('backward, traditional, savage, tribal and ethnic'). As a first attitude, then, readers 'from the South' expose the workings of colonial difference, nowadays also called 'coloniality.'

Reminiscent of feminist standpoint theory (Patricia Hill Collins 1990, 2019; Sandra Harding 1991; Nancy Hartsock 1998), Jean and John Comaroff point to a long line of anti-colonial thinkers (e.g., Bhabha 1997, Chakrabarty 2000, Coetzee 2003) who have urged us by way of a second Southern reading attitude, to move the location of theory-making to an "ex-centric site," to deliberately take up a perspective on the global order, which is situated in its margins. From those places that can ostensibly only be included in "the grand human story" or "the international community," if they visibly transform themselves into versions of (and try to "catch up" with) Western capitalist modernity (Comaroff and Comaroff 2016, 3). But self-consciously situating our theorising selves in these marginalised spaces, they contend, leads to a surprising discovery: the epistemological schema is turned upside down, because we discover that modernity was, "almost from the start, a north-south collaboration—indeed, a world-historical production—albeit a sharply asymmetrical one" (2016, 6). While colonies served as "critical sources of surplus value and cultural innovation" for the emerging Northern states, the colonised were excluded from full humanity and "colonial polities were sustained by acts of violence that flew in the face of the vaunted tenets of liberal European law and civility" (Comaroffs 2016, 5). One stark example of this duality is how the wealth of North America was built on slave labour. Thus, to read from the South is to read from modernity's dark underbelly.

We then also discover, as a third dimension of reading from the South, that "the history of the present" reveals itself more starkly in the margins, than in the centres, because the system sustaining the centre cannot be properly understood without witnessing its actions in and on the peripheries. Stein et al. (2021) describe the situation thus: "the house modernity built" can only be sustained by unjustly extracting value (energy, knowledge and labour) from the margins and by also dumping its toxic waste and its surplus populations and products there. And these injustices can only be sustained through the creation of an "illusion of separation" between modernity's house (and its inhabitants) and those 'far-off' places, peoples, 'resources,' and extractive and poisoning practices that sustain capitalist modernity from the outside. These latter peoples and places are included in the system through their exploitation but excluded from its benefits. The best way to cover over these contradictions is to insist on the great ontological divide between modern and pre-modern peoples and countries. Against this ideological illusion[7] of separation, the Comaroffs (2016, 11) emphasise the one-system view:

7 I use 'ideology' here in the sense of John Thompson (1990), as "meaning in the service of relations of domination."

> while modernization as Western ideology might have represented non-Western worlds as just so many not-yet-modern outsides, the capitalist imperium *has* no exteriors, although it has many peripheries. Its exclusions and its margins, as critical theorists of various stripes have stressed, are a requisite condition for the growth of its centers.

One of the key machineries for creating this illusion of separation – and denying the centre's dependency on the peripheries – is the sexual-racist nexus, which sets its recipients apart from normative humanity, as I will show. But the reader from the South knows that the supposedly far-off and 'lagging' places are not in fact 'outside' or 'non-Western'; there is only one system. In this way, the tensions produced by modernity, e.g., increasing global wealth plus increasing inequality and poverty, are often evident earlier, and in a more concentrated manner, in the marginal territories than in the centres.[8] However, by portraying the populations of those places as abject beings, their poverty and suffering are attributed to their own inherent flaws, and thus de linked from the processes of amassing wealth in the global North. What is relegated to the outskirts and violently oppressed in the (former) colonies, is as integral a part of European modernity as are technological advances and human rights. European modernity's workings can therefore be more clearly deciphered from a perspective situated from within those margins that are in fact integral to its existence yet occluded or erased from its self-understanding. Or, more clearly: reading from the South means reading from those margins that serve as the very foil or counterpart of European self-understanding – everything that the West is not – and which reinforces the latter's superiority. Reading from the South is therefore at once also a critique of ideology, an exposure of denied interdependencies and asymmetrical, exploitative power relations. To summarise this discussion of reading from the South: it (i) exposes the machinery that perpetually produces 'the colonial difference,' (ii) insists that the global neo-colonial order is one system, dependent for its functioning on unjust exclusions and (iii) holds that viewing the whole from the margins has an epistemological advantage that can provide a powerful critique of those ideological manoeuvres that serve to justify global relations of domination.

International Law's Complicity in Coloniality

Scholars reading from the South, including the TWAIL (Third World Approaches to International Law) network (see Chimni 2006), have started to identify international law's complicity in reinforcing the 'colonial difference' ideological construct explained above. This criticism has not been limited to international criminal law. For example, in a powerful 2021 article, Kotzé,

8 In this regard, the subtitle of *Theory from the South* is telling: 'How Euro-America Is Evolving Toward Africa.' Compare also Mbembe's (2017) phrase "the becoming Black of the world," to refer to the extension of capital's dehumanising labour practices from the African slave to the global population.

Du Toit and French discuss the structural complicity of international environmental law (IEL) in the Anthropocene's climate injustices. Apart from its "neoliberal anthropocentrism" and its "entrenchment of the sovereign right [of nation-states] to exploit energy resources," they also investigate IEL's "entanglement with (neo)colonialism." They show the historical roots of IEL in events such as the London Convention of 1900, which attempted to preserve environmental resources in "their possessions in Africa" for their financial exploitation by "a small number of powerful European states" (Kotzé et al. 2021, 189). Providing environmental protection for either the non-human or human lives inhabiting these colonised places – especially protection against colonial extraction and labour exploitation – clearly did not feature in these early conventions. Moreover, IEL has historically allowed colonial powers to gain "uninterrupted supply and access to a range of environmental resources that were critically important for sustaining their domestic economies," under the guise of "conservation" enterprises in the colonies (Kotzé et al. 2021, 192). Since Earth is indeed a single, interdependent life system, the uneven distributions of environmental harms can only be concealed for a limited period before they come back to haunt the health of the system as a whole.

IEL has furthermore been structurally linked with colonial laws "which promoted the appropriation of foreign lands, the exploitation through the slave trade, and resource extraction" (see Alam et al. 2015). Fully commensurate with the colonial difference described above, Gonzales (2015, 411) further shows how the division between "civilised" and "uncivilised" nations designated the latter as in need of modernisation and development, which justified unimpeded access of Northern/European states and companies into lands where they could and still today can "objectify and monetize the non-human world and human labour" alike. Kotzé et al. (2021, 193) further state that IEL persists in ignoring the Southern perspectives and concerns, e.g., it has "consistently resisted providing a global right to a clean, healthy and safe environment;[9] a provision that could have gone … a long way in confronting the Anthropocene's climate injustices." These injustices are mostly visited upon poor and racialised peoples of the global South (see Nixon 2011).[10] Moreover, IEL fails dramatically to rein in "neoliberal corporate globalization," a "highly uneven process still exhibiting pathological patterns of domination" (Grear 2015, 233), and a continuation of the original colonial logic, which had been pioneered by multinational companies such as the Dutch East India Company (VOIC).[11] My choice of international environmental law as another example of historical and

9 It should however be noted that in 2021, the UN Human Rights Council finally recognised this right and there is now a push for this right to be included in a UN General Assembly resolution.

10 It is interesting that the right to (a decent, safe or clean) environment is explicitly recognised in the African and Inter-American regional human rights systems. See African Charter on Human and Peoples' Rights Article 24 and San Salvadore Protocol, Article 11.

11 The Dutch-origin "Vereenigde Oostindische Compagnie," 1602 – 1800.

structural complicity in coloniality is not random. It helps to demonstrate how the ideological positioning of the non-West as lagging behind the West and standing in need of the latter's interventions, perpetually justifies the West's parasitism on, and control of, the non-West or global South, also in other branches of international law. Moreover, it shows the necessary entanglement of meaning-making, interpretation, framing and symbolisation (of the colonial difference) with material exploitation. And indeed, even the way in which the prosecution of SVAC (sexual violence in armed conflict) has played out on the stage of ICL, as I will show, surreptitiously facilitates neo-colonial, corporate exploitation of bodies, labour, and resources in those territories.

When it comes to International Criminal Law, Michelle Burgis-Kasthala (2016) criticises ICL's self-understanding as liberal, universal, neutral and progressive. As an example of this limited and naive understanding, she quotes David Luban (2013, 509) who writes:

> Speaking law to power ... is the major point of ICJ (international criminal justice). Its ... aim is norm projection, the dissemination through trials, punishments and jurisprudence of a set of norms very different from the Machiavellian brutality of the past. The radical goal of ICJ is a moral transformation of how ordinary men and women regard political violence against civilians.

This supposedly apolitical and progressive project of saving humanity and working "against power" and "for global justice" is described by Burgis-Kasthala as not nearly self-aware enough. Like IEL, ICL also has its roots firmly in modern-colonial European history. These can be traced back to a thinker like Immanuel Kant, who published his famous essay 'Towards Perpetual Peace' in 1795, just as the French revolutionary wars started. Kant's concern about European wars is that "the depravity of human nature appears nakedly in the unrestrained relations of nations to each other." His immediate focus was therefore the lawlessness that characterised the treatment of enemy soldiers, enemy civilians, refugees and displaced persons and so on. A "law of nations" should therefore be established that would regulate the excesses of war. Even between enemies, some form of minimalist social contract is needed, so that wars between (European) nations might be fought "in accordance with principles which leave states with the possibility of entering a 'state of right' after the war." Thus, war must be fought in such a manner that the enemies can re-enter a civil coexistence (a social contract of non-enmity and cooperation) afterwards (Article 6 of the essay). The alternative is "a war of extermination," which for Kant leaves no opening for peace afterwards. "Dishonourable stratagems" such as the use of assassins and poisoners, incitement to treason and "breach of capitulation" cannot be allowed.

Historically, Kant's listed concerns came to be best captured under International Humanitarian Law (IHL), the law governing the conduct of hostilities (jus in bello), which seeks to limit the suffering caused by war. At the same time, under the banners of IHL but also of International Human Rights Law and later under International Criminal Law, the 'law of nations' was expanded considerably. Where Kant's focus was on the treatment of enemies or non-citizens during war, the field expanded to include international legal concern with the treatment of civilians during war, the treatment of a state's own citizens, internal or civic conflicts, and even the conduct of state-analogous organisations such as rebel groups. The different strands of international law moreover have different foci and jurisdictions, entail different fields of law, which nevertheless overlap with one another (Melzer 2019), with state conduct falling under IHL and IHRL, and individual conduct under ICL. The youngest branch of public international law, ICL, draws greatly upon IHL's definition of war crimes and IHRL's definitions of genocide and crimes against humanity when prosecuting 'international crimes' committed by individuals rather than states. In general, we see how a higher or international concern with human dignity and with the ability of enemy states to re-enter a 'state of right' after war, necessarily implied a weakening of the principle of state sovereignty, and along with that, even of the very distinction between war and peace. This is the case even though the assumption is that only states that have signed up to these laws of nations can be held accountable to them, in line with Kant's moral principle that one gives the law to oneself, based on the demands of reason.

ICL and the related fields of law therefore clearly have their roots in European history, concerns and concepts, and its internationality initially was conceived of as an agreement among 'civilised' nations. This version of the colonial difference is particularly noticeable in Kant's essay, where he draws upon the notion of social contract. Kant mentions among the vulnerable populations of war such as refugees and captured enemies also colonised people, who similarly find themselves in a precarious position beyond the legal protection of a nation-state. The result, as he writes, is "the inhospitable actions of the civilised and especially of the commercial states of our part of the world," the "injustice" meted out "to the lands and people they visit (which is equivalent to conquering them)." This is moreover an injustice, Kant acknowledges, that is "carried to terrifying lengths" because these "civilised intruders count the inhabitants as nothing."[12] However, instead of allowing these terrifyingly unjust behaviours and attitudes of the civilised nations to call into question their supposed civilised status, Kant allows for the supposed uncivilised state of the colonised to leave them permanently outside the protection of the national or international law. This he does through the evocation of social contract logic: he reads the colonised territories as

12 Drucilla Cornell (2008: 129) rightly calls the colonial encounter "the [total] collapse of the ethical," in that the humanity of the other party is fundamentally denied. She means this primarily in phenomenological terms, but I would argue that one should extend this insight to the international legal domain during the colonial period.

inherently lawless, because trapped in a state of nature and therefore as pre-civil. He regards the lawlessness of the colonised territories not as the result of the colonisation and conquest as such, but rather of the inherent lawlessness of the natives. He writes, "savages ... are attached to their lawless freedom," which entails "a brutish degradation of humanity." The treatment of colonised people is therefore, by implication, also not of 'international' concern, because there is no anticipated 'state of right' to be entered into between 'nations' after the war-like situation characterising the colonies. Colonies and the colonised are therefore treated as a permanent exception to civil order, in contrast with the civilised nation-states, where the potential or partial collapse of the social contract that we call 'war' is seen as always strictly temporary and exceptional.

Thus, not only does public international law have firm roots in modern-European history and philosophy, and historically excluded the colonised from the conceptualisation of the 'internationality' of its agreements, authors are showing that still today its Eurocentrism and coloniality endure. Burgis Kasthala (2016) as we have seen, criticises Luban's (2013) rather naïve and a-historical view of ICL as neutral and innocent. Too often, she says, what he described in the quote above as "the Machiavellian brutality of the past" (Luban 2013, 509), is projected onto current global South countries and territories, with international law supposedly representing a definitive break with the irrational and oppressive past that characterises their present (Burgis-Kasthala 2016, 927-928). We see here ICL simultaneously instituting, maintaining, and claiming to bridge the colonial divide. The apolitical harbingers of a brand-new set of universally emancipatory norms to "ordinary men and women" who ostensibly regard political violence against civilians as normal, are distinctly Western-dominated, supposedly 'enlightened' institutions and individuals. In contrast, reading from the South, TWAIL scholars[13] try to "understand, deconstruct, and unpack the uses of international law as a medium for the creation and perpetuation of a racialized hierarchy of international norms and institutions that subordinate non-Europeans to Europeans" (Mutua and Anghie 2000). One way in which Elizabeth Philipose (2009, 183) for one sees this role of international criminal law playing out, is in the grossly uneven way in which it is enforced across the globe, with the result that two types of national sovereignty emerged after the Second World War: (i) the "sovereignty inherent to European powers, thought to reflect their essential civilized nature" and (ii) the "second-tier and contingent sovereignty granted to non-European states after decolonization and the decline of the European imperial order." In terms of this two-pronged logic, second-tier states in the global South must continually demonstrate their 'civilized nature' to a European audience, failing which, all kinds of Northern (labelled 'international') interventions and external

13 TWAIL refers to a network of scholars developing Third World Approaches to International Law.

structuring (including economic, military, and social) are seen as justified. In this manner, the old colonial difference between war as a state of exception *in* the North and of war (or social collapse, or instability) as a permanent state *of* the South, is held in place and perpetuated.

The upshot is that this two-tiered structure, still structured around the colonial divide between the civilised and the un(der)civilised, is maintained by the way in which ICL functions. It is telling, against this backdrop, that "before 2016, the ICC [International Criminal Court, established in 2002] had never opened an investigation outside of Africa and the Court had never issued an arrest warrant for a non-African"[14] (Dowds 2020, 42–43). This is a key example of the "illusion of separation" Stein et al. discuss, and of colonial difference – a gap that is produced and reproduced, between the global North and its others in such a way as to rationalise ongoing access and control of the former over the latter.

It is then against this backdrop of a wider complicity of international law and ICL in coloniality and the reinforcement of colonial difference, that one needs to engage its courts' and tribunals' specific focus on SVAC. The sexual nature of sexual violence in conflict and war adds another layer or dimension to this complicity.

ICL's Focus on Sexual Violence and 'War Rape'

After a long battle to get SVAC recognised as a war crime by ICL, many feminist scholars were greatly encouraged by the trials in the International Criminal Tribunal for Rwanda (e.g., the Akayesu trial), and the International Criminal Tribunal for the former Yugoslavia (e.g., the Kunarac trial) in which war time rape, for instance, was included under war crimes and crimes against humanity. This decisive stance on sexual violence in war was further enforced and expanded with the Rome Statute of 1998 and the establishment of the permanent International Criminal Court in 2002. The point of the critical argument presented here is not to give up on these efforts associated with ICL. At least two great benefits flowed from these developments since the 1990s war tribunals: (i) the inclusion of women's sexual integrity into the concept of human dignity to be protected by human rights and enforced by ICL mechanisms; and (ii) the recognition of the multiple and enduring harms, including interpersonal and social harms, that rape (in war) might cause. At the very least,

14 This fact remains worrying, even if one acknowledges that many of the cases brought before the ICC were referred there by the concerned African states themselves, saying they do not have the capacity to prosecute. Viewed from this perspective, the African continent benefited most from the ICC's existence over this period, and in turn played a key role in strengthening its legitimacy. But that is not the whole story.

ICL has demonstrated a grasp of the different context-specific ways in which women's bodies are harmed with the aim to spread terror amongst populations.

The Rome Statute's classification of so-called 'war rape' as war crimes, genocide, torture, and crimes against humanity constitutes on the face of it a clear recognition of the harms these crimes inflict. These 'symbolic' developments are not insignificant, and should be acknowledged and furthered by feminists. As Debra Bergoffen states (2003, 118), ICL now recognises that "women's humanity can be criminally abused even if they have not been subjected to physical violence or injury," because, quoting from the Kunarac verdict (ICTY), "severe pain and suffering, as required by the definition of the crime of torture, can … be said to be established once rape has been proved, since the act of rape necessarily implies such pain or suffering." A feminist activist can immediately spot the potential for transferring these milestone recognitions emerging in international law, to domestic jurisdictions and peace time rape. In her 2020 book, Eithne Dowds discusses how the principle of legal complementarity allows for the transfer of criminal legal norms between international and domestic criminal law (p. 9), and this avenue must be explored and further developed through feminist scholarship and activism.

And yet, one must *also* ask critically about the specific context/s in which this new openness towards the prosecution of sexual crimes as war crimes was carved out within ICL over the past thirty years. We must also ask at what price these developments came about. Elizabeth Philipose's concern is mine also, when she writes that, reading from the South, feminists should become more aware of the extent to which

> … the contemporary practice of naming war crimes and spectacular violence is both *a racialized and a racializing enterprise* that reflects gendered and sexualised assumptions about the perverse sexuality of the Other.
>
> (Philipose 2009, 198; emphasis added)

As such, I argue that ICL repeats the colonial difference with a racialised inflection. It would serve us well to heed Judith Butler's (2020, 5) caution that we be alert to "the power to attribute violence" to others, which operates within schemes that are often used to justify state violence or international violence such as military interventions, occupations, and other forms of "legalist civilizing missions" (Philipose's formulation). Similarly, Linda Martín Alcoff (2018, 21) alerts us to the fact that generally speaking, "there is less policing of rape than of rape victims' speech." These authors point us to the very politics and power of naming and framing violence, sexual violence in particular.

When first the ICTR, then the ICTY, and then the ICC, under pressure from feminist activists worldwide, started to include instances of SVAC as free-standing crimes prosecutable under ICL, they elevated sexual violence to a matter of potential international concern. For feminists who have long worked against the privatisation of sexual violence and insisted upon its instrumentality for the unequal distribution of power between the sexes, this was a very promising move indeed. However, the courts and tribunals were immediately faced with the problem of 'rape culture,' or the extent to which sexual violence is normalised and treated with impunity in every patriarchal culture, nation, and institution. International criminal interference with the prosecution of sexual violence simpliciter seems to imply an impossible overreach of these legal instruments into the 'private business' of states and nations. As Catharine MacKinnon (1994, 15) wrote during and in response to the war in the former Yugoslavia: "each state's lack of protection of women's human rights is internationally protected, and that is called protecting state sovereignty." Since she wrote this, international criminal instruments have started to interfere in states' and other bodies' sexual violation of women, and thereby to threaten state sovereignty, but the point is that this was only allowed to happen under very specific and very narrow circumstances and that we must carefully investigate the nature of these.

Since states are normally held responsible for the prosecution of international crimes, international courts and tribunals only come into play when two conditions are met: (i) the crimes involve a severe breaching of human rights, and are systematic and (ii) the domestic courts are unable or unwilling to prosecute them. There are different mechanisms for referring cases to the international bodies. In whichever way they may be constituted, courts that attempt to prosecute SVAC must first distinguish in a meaningful way between those instances of sexual violence that constitute, and those that do not constitute, an international crime such as genocide, a crime against humanity or a war crime. For sexual violence to qualify as a war crime, it must happen 'in war,' but we have seen – in Sierra Leone, for instance – many victims of rape during war whose injury was not considered a war crime, technically speaking, and thus was treated as a "normal" crime, to be tried by the domestic courts (Grewal 2010, 66, 71). Similarly, even though a crime against humanity does not require that it take place during war, it is hard to believe that any international tribunal will be willing to declare even the world record figures of sexual violence against women and children in contemporary South Africa a crime against humanity. Unwilling to acknowledge the extent of harm caused by everyday, peacetime, domestic sexual violence, instruments of ICL must elevate SVAC somehow, in order to justify its being of international concern and to justify its interference in a sovereign state's criminal justice system. When and how and why does one instance of rape but not another become a crime of international concern?

For sexual violence to become prosecutable as an international crime, it must be elevated high above the kind of sexual violence that forms part of the everyday maintenance of patriarchy. Against the insights of many feminists who emphasise the continuities between pre-conflict, conflict, and post-conflict sexual violence (e.g., Buss 2007), ICL is more likely to treat SVAC as exceptional, extreme, spectacular and crisis-related, as the result of social collapse (Burgis-Kasthala 2016, 935). One anti-feminist implication of such a framing of SVAC is that it (further) trivialises or even normalises 'everyday' or 'private' sexual violence in comparison; it does this by denying and erasing continuities between rape inside and outside of armed conflict. Moreover, this trivialisation of the everyday crime and comparative elevation of the 'crisis' crime are respectively tied to a primary injury to the victim and to primary injury to the group to which she belongs. Simply put: raped outside of conflict, she might be raped as a woman, but inside of conflict, she is raped as a Hutu in the Rwandan genocide, for example, and the injury is amplified to include the whole Hutu nation. Put differently: peace time rape is not political and war time rape is not gendered. Buss (2007, 11) makes a similar point, saying,

> while sexual violence may be visible in the decision [regarding the rape of the witness TAS, a Hutu woman], gender inequality is not, and nor are the other systemic variables that produced a situation in which the mass sexual violation of women was made possible in the first place.

To clearly distinguish one rape (even within the same war theatre) from another, the gender of the victim must necessarily be downplayed, and another identity marker emphasised. In the Gacumbitsi trial (before the ICTR) discussed here by Buss, however, the Tribunal struggles with this attempt to substitute the victim's ethnic identity for her gender identity, precisely because she is raped by two men from the same ethnicity, by two Hutu men. The problem is subsequently 'solved' when the Tribunal discovers that the victim was married to a Tutsi man, so that when he becomes the main or real target of the rape, the crime is once again rescued from being unexceptional. The injury done to the victim garners international attention because it was not done to her alone, but metaphorically or in a transferred manner, to her (husband's) Tutsi group and *their* ethnic identity. At this point, even her true ethnic identity has been erased, alongside her gender, in order to fit the crime into the parameters of the Tribunal.

I thus see what Philipose (2009, 198) describes as the naming of certain crimes as both a racialised and racialising enterprise as playing out in at least two main ways in the war tribunals. First, there is the emphasis on ethnic and tribal identities, which are distinctly pre-modern identities, and which thus reinforces the framing of these instances of sexual violence within the colonial difference. Neither the perpetrators nor the victims are 'civilised like us' and therefore there can be no continuity between the sexual violence observed and tried in the ICTR, for instance, and that observed and tried within Western domestic settings. The ethnic identities of the parties involved is already a way of stamping them with colonial difference and innate lawlessness. In the second place, through the lens of colonial difference, although the sexual violence is spectacularised and framed as exceptional, in another sense, it is equated with ethnic difference, with the figure of the "stranger" (see Ahmed 2000). This means that once it was established that a perpetrator and victim belonged to different ethnic (or religious, in the case of the ICTY) groupings, no further explanation for sexual violence was required. As Buss (2007, 12) states: "The text [of the *Gacumbitsi* decision], the words, the outcome are a story about the attacks by Hutu against Tutsi in which the widespread and systemic sexual violence against women *as women* is strangely absent." Such a strategy served the colonial difference as follows: the genocidal violence itself was at once ruptured from all international dynamics (and Western involvement and culpability) and from more complex internal dynamics, including the use of sexual violence to impose ethnic boundaries. As Burgis-Kasthala (2016, 936) points out, ICL tends to focus on "indigenous causes of violence," especially categories of ethnic (premodern) identity as drivers, while other contributing contextual factors, like colonialism, poverty, and gender dynamics, are suppressed. "By framing the causes" of Third World violence as indigenous [and I would add, ethnic, thus 'uncivilized,' 'premodern,' 'state of nature'']," she argues, "the justice/violence binary [deployed by ICL practitioners] can then serve as a powerful rhetorical device in affirming the need for ICL deliverance in the Global South."

In her book, Dowds (2020) discusses in detail the tension between the absence of consent and the presence of coercion in the evidentiary approaches of the different courts and tribunals of ICL. As we know, in the *Akayesu* decision of Trial Chamber I of the ICTR (1998), where rape was for the first time defined under international law, and charged as a crime against humanity, it was defined as "a physical invasion of a sexual nature, committed on a person under circumstances which are coercive."[15] This definition was not narrowly interpreted, for example by stating that "coercive circumstances need not be evidenced by a show of physical force, but may be inherent in certain circumstances," such as armed conflict. This approach caused Catharine MacKinnon to rejoice: "arguably for the first time, rape was defined in law as what it is in life" (MacKinnon 2006, 944), and to include under inherently coercive circumstances "the military presence of threatening forces *on an ethnic basis*" (p. 943; emphasis added). Apparently, the presence of 'ethnic' conflict renders it unnecessary even to ask about the possibility of consent. However, as Dowds shows, by the time of the *Kunarac* trial of the ICTY, consent returns to the definition of rape under international law (because of the closer geographical and 'racial' proximity of this war to Europe?). And thus, predictably, during this trial, the accused claimed consent, even where the women were raped under conditions of imprisonment. MacKinnon (2006, 953) rightly criticises this trial, arguing that rape thereby became the only crime against humanity where, even after all the other evidentiary standards for the crime had been met, non-consent still had to be proven by the complainant. Vesna Nikolić-Ristanović (2005) remarks,

15 *Prosecutor v Akayesu*, Case No. ICTR 96-4-T, Judgment, 688 (September 2, 1998).

> ...by finding evidence of rape camps and yet finding that individual women are not to be believed in their accounts of rape and violence at those same camps, the Yugoslav Tribunal reproduces many of the same problematic aspects of the rape trial found in Western domestic legal systems were reproduced in the ICTY.

The way in which the courts tried to solve these problems and tried to prevent all the problems associated with consent in domestic rape trials from derailing the prosecution of the exceptional 'war rape,' was to emphasise, even hypostatise, the role of ethnic identities in these conflicts. My claim is that this 'solution' played right into the hands of colonial difference, second-tier or weakened national sovereignty, and a racist resurrection of the 'stranger rape' myth. In short: it is only by racializing SVAC that the artificial and severe hierarchy between 'war rape' and 'normal rape' could be upheld.

In conclusion: ICL needs to insert a dramatic distinction between 'normal' or 'everyday' sexual violence and SVAC, to justify its own interference in the criminal justice systems of sovereign states. It must, in short, justify why some instances of sexual violence and rape but not others, are of international concern. I have argued that historically the instruments of SVAC have done so by spectacularising these instances of violence, presenting them as especially severe and damaging to a whole (ethnic or religious) collective, instead of 'only' to the direct victim (and her direct relations and dependents, for instance). In the process, continuities between sexual violence phenomena before, during and after conflict have had to be downplayed, and the gender dimension of the crime largely erased, except in as far as it may be harnessed to amplify the indirect harm done to the collective. I think of the example of the argument that states that the men of a particular collective are 'emasculated' because of being proven incapable of 'protecting' 'their' women. Moreover, in order to dispel the problems associated with evidentiary proof of the absence of consent and to convey the irrelevance of the very question of consent, these legal bodies have tended to couch SVAC in ethnic terms, which aims to naturalise the absence of consent under the covertly racist figure of the stranger who pollutes the collective identity. Moreover, I claim that such an ethnic framing of SVAC serves to erase larger, also external, and international, causes of conflict, by sketching sexual violence as a purely internal, natural problem. Here, the process of colonial differentiation plays an important role, when the parties to the conflict are portrayed as racialised and thus as relatively uncivilised.

In this respect, it is important to recall that Kant and other Enlightenment thinkers equated the "lawless freedom" of the "savages" with "a brutish degradation" of their own humanity. The incapacity for civilisation (social contract) of the colonised peoples is the result of their inherent incapacity to obtain self-mastery. This is why the figure of the racialised inhabitant of the colony cannot be meaningfully detached from his supposed animal appetites for sex and violence. As Coetzee and I have argued elsewhere, racist-colonial abjection cannot be properly understood without its sexual dimension. We wrote there:

> The two pseudo-biological categories of race and sex … mutually imply and reinforce each other: the racial 'backwardness' of the 'native' (masculinised) is rooted in his biology as expressed most pertinently in his 'unruly' sexual practices. By locating his inferiority in his very body as sexual depravity epitomised, colonial logic justifies violent external control over the native.
>
> (Coetzee and Du Toit 2018, 220)

I refer to this phenomenon as the sexual-racist nexus of coloniality. It is then against this backdrop of a wider complicity of international law and ICL in coloniality and the reinforcement of colonial difference, that one needs to critically investigate its courts' and tribunals' specific focus on SVAC.

Some Implications for International Feminist Solidarity

John D Haskell (2009, 35) similarly sees the international criminal tribunals not so much as heralding unprecedented inclusion for rape victims from armed conflicts, as instead constituting "a renewed rhetorical and institutional legitimisation of colonialism." Like the point made by Kotzé et al about IEL, Haskell argues that the recent promise of ICL to include (especially formerly colonised and Black) women into the international legal framework, must be read against the backdrop of the history of an international law that justified "the continued exclusion of non-European peoples from international law" (Haskell 2009, 38) and its demands for the realisation of human rights. International law is historically implicated in the subordination of non-European peoples to European powers. The colonial logic is repeated by ICL when it presents itself as the means to "civilize the uncivilized," or put differently, to bestow a new identity on the female "other" – as a new "member within civilization, and hence [as if for the first time] entitled to human dignity, self-determination, and justice" (Haskell 2009, 39). However, like the criticism of Buss above, Haskell (2009, 39) also claims that ultimately, and despite this promise, "the conceptual identities and practical realities of raped women are subordinated, and sometimes excluded completely, in the … dialogue among international scholars concerning rape in armed conflict…"[16] Haskell goes further than Buss

16 Of course, criminal law in the Western punitive paradigm is not focused on remedies for victims of crime. In a way, every criminal investigation of sexual violence instrumentalises the victim to put away a criminal who is threatening society as a whole. The price of giving testimony regarding sexual violence, whether in war or peace, is typically high for the victim-survivor – it comes at the cost of public shame, disbelief, reliving of the trauma, etc. One might argue this is part of the inevitable cost of ICL justice, or one might insist that ICL take more seriously victims' own

and Burgis-Kasthala, however, by describing the creation of the ICTY and the ICTR as a feeble *substitute* for effective international (military) intervention in these regions while the genocidal conflicts were raging.

ICL, thus in a sense, steps in where realpolitik failed to protect the human rights of victims of war. Haskell shows how the European community was historically directly implicated in the conflict that erupted in the former Yugoslavia; even worse, UN peacekeepers and troops were reported to have participated in the mass rapes and trafficking of women and girls (Robson 2002). With China, Russia, and the USA against the use of military force, the UN Security Council in 1993 "decided against military intervention and in favour of establishing the ICTY" (Haskell 2009, 49). Similarly, Belgian colonisers encouraged "a historical myth of differences between Hutu and Tutsi to control the majority Hutu and institutionalise minority rule" in Rwanda early in the twentieth century (Miller, quoted in Haskell, 50). Although there was "ample evidence of an imminent genocide" at least since late 1990, the international community did not intervene; in fact, the UN "reduced its presence in Rwanda from 2500 to 270 peacekeepers during the first three weeks of the genocide" (Haskell, 52). From April to November 1994, the genocide raged, still characterised by the US Ambassador to Rwanda, David Rawson, as 'tribal killings' rather than genocide, in a typical move of colonial differentiation. "Finally," says Haskell, "on November 8, 1994, the UN acted; pursuant to Resolution 955, the Security Council created the ICTR."

By styling itself as an 'unprecedented' solution to sexual violence in armed conflict, ICL as a *symbolic substitute* for effective international peacekeeping, deflects attention away from the international community's *implication in its causes*; it internalises the problem as one of insufficient civilisation. It is against this self-justifying and self-purifying backdrop that one should then place the discussion above, which showed how ICL tends to frame human rights violations in armed conflict (including sexual violence) as purely internally generated. The ICL's successes in prosecuting sexual crimes in non-Western theatres of war represent the kind of civilising mission which possibly does more harm than good, when viewed more holistically, even from the perspective of the (majority of) SVAC victims. If the trade-off for symbolically acknowledging 'indigenous' women's sexual integrity as a human right is a reinforced racist-colonial difference – the difference which placed Indigenous women's sexual dignity beyond the concerns of civilised law in the first place – then one must wonder if it is really an improvement. This, I contend, is the critical view from the South that is opened upon the ICL's apparently progressive and feminist focus on SVAC, if one foregrounds the colonial difference and its global effects.

need for justice. For that, it might have to turn to more restorative models of justice, such as those represented by the Gacaca courts in Rwanda.

Haskell unambiguously sees ICL as reproducing the power disparities between European and non-European states "in the name of extending benevolent protection and guidance to less stable territories" (Haskell 2009, 64). Interestingly, the gap is no longer labelled 'civilized' versus 'uncivilized' nations, but is now rather recreated on the axis of the euphemism of peace versus war or low-level armed conflict, or 'instability,' which Western interests are often complicit in creating. As argued, the ICC and other international bodies style themselves as the opposite of war and social breakdown, and as the restorers of (international) peace and security, but then only along the lines of the status quo and reigning international (and national) interests within a grossly unequal global order. Moreover, Western conceptions of justice and more material interests determine what count as threats to international peace and security. This means that the five permanent nation-state members of the UN Security Council can effectively decide "what constitutes a legitimate threat to international peace and security, which territories are included within the international order, and how disturbances should be addressed" (Haskell, 64). This has a devastating impact on the promise of ICL to deliver justice to SVAC victims.

This leads us to the question how feminist scholars and activists should respond to these failures of international law, inclusive of international criminal law. It is salutary here to recall María Lugones' (2007, 188) insistence, "I do not believe any solidarity or homoerotic loving is possible among females who affirm the colonial/modern gender system and the coloniality of power." An instructive example of the breakdown in feminist solidarity precisely around on this issue happened during the very high-profile conference, the June 2014 Global Summit to End Sexual Violence in Conflict. This summit was held in London and chaired by UN special envoy for refugees Angelina Jolie and the UK Foreign Secretary William Hague (see www.gov.uk/government/topical-events/ sexual-violence-in-conflict). While 123 country delegations and 79 ministers were attending the official event, an envoy of Congolese rape survivors and Rape Crisis activists were *barred by the security company* from entering the *public fringe event*, ostensibly because they were carrying posters saying: "No end to rape without an end to war" and were calling upon the UK and other Western powers to own up to their involvement in "the economic war for illegal exploitation of [the DRC's] wealth" (Westmarland 2014). In other words, the rape survivors were pointing to the systemic 'power of coloniality,' which is continually destabilising the region and arming the rebels in order to get African natural wealth into the hands of Western capitalists. The many militias often use rape to terrorise populations and clear them off their lands if they get in the way of the private companies' extractive aims. The supply lines to large Western-based corporations are deliberately obscured to hide their complicities in these atrocities, and to uphold the colonial difference. The women's activism highlighted the parallels between the colonial rape of the continent and the rape of women's and girls' bodies and the centrality of sexual exploitation in the larger context of continued colonial aggression.

Neither African pre-modern backwardness nor depravity lay at the root of the Congolese women's sexual exploitation and abandonment by the law, but rather Western greed. But Western greed is of course enabled: by an apparent indifference from the side of white and Western feminists towards 'heteropatriarchal colonialism,' as well as the same apparent indifference of the racialised men who make up the militias and government in the Congo, all of which taken together set up the Congolese women for ongoing sexual violation. A global network of complicities, it seems, is necessary to keep up this astounding hypocrisy leading to so much destruction. This is the larger picture occluded when ICL zooms in on the individual perpetrator and individual victim of sexual violence in armed conflict, and often in the process spectacularises such instances of violence in ways that stabilise the colonial difference. Africans are portrayed as finally responsible for their own suffering due to their own backwardness, which makes it impossible for them to be unconditionally included in the small fraternity that constitutes the 'civilised' international community. In this way, then, ICL interventions in a place like the DRC repeat and help to justify ongoing neo-colonial relations and the exploitation of non-Western peoples and their lands.

Conclusion

As Burgis-Kasthala said about the importance for ICL scholars to engage with TWAIL scholars, I would in the light of my argument above urge all feminists excited about the prospects for the prosecution of sexual violence by the developments within ICL, to enter urgent conversation with the critical perspective 'from the South' offered here. Feminist activists, scholars and legal practitioners must work harder to establish ways of vindicating all victims of sexual violence through innovative processes and procedures of international criminal justice, even while equally steadfastly refusing to repeat the colonial logic.

Bibliography

Ahmed, Sara. 2000. *Strange Encounters: Embodied Others in Post-coloniality*. London and New York: Routledge.

Alam, S., et al., eds., 2015. *International Environmental Law and the Global South*. New York: Cambridge University Press.

Alcoff, Linda Martín. 2007. "Mignolo's Epistemology of Coloniality." *CR: The New Centennial Review* 7/3: 79–101.

Alcoff, Linda Martín. 2018. *Rape and Resistance: Understanding the Complexities of Sexual Violation*. Cambridge: Polity Press.

Anghie, Antony. 1999. "Finding the Peripheries: Sovereignty and Colonialism in Nineteenth-Century International Law." *Harvard International Law Journal* 40 (1): 1–80.

Bergoffen, Debra. 2003. "February 22, 2001: Toward a Politics of the Vulnerable Body." *Hypatia* 18 (1): 116–134.

Bhabha, Homi K. 1997. "Editor's Introduction: Minority Maneuvers and Unsettled Negotiations." *Critical Inquiry* 23 (3) Front Lines/Border Posts: 431–459.

Burgis-Kasthala, Michelle. 2016. "Scholarship as Dialogue? TWAIL and the Politics of Methodology." *Journal of International Criminal Justice* 14 (4): 921–937.

Buss, Doris E. 2007. "The Curious Visibility of Wartime Rape: Gender and Ethnicity in International Criminal Law." *Windsor Yearbook of Access to Justice* 25: 3–22.

Butler, Judith. 2020. *The Force of Nonviolence: An Ethico-Political Bind*. London: Verso.

Carpenter, R. Charli. 2006. "Recognizing Gender-Based Violence Against Civilian Men and Boys in Conflict Situations." *Security Dialogue* 37 (1): 83–103.

Chakrabarty, Dipesh. 2000. *Provincializing Europe: Postcolonial Thought and Historical Difference*. Princeton: Princeton University Press.

Chimni, B.S. 2006. "Third World Approaches to International Law: Manifesto." *International Community Law Review* 8: 3–27.

Coetzee, Azille and Louise du Toit. 2018. "Facing the Sexual Demon of Colonial Power: Decolonising Sexual Violence in South Africa." *European Journal of Women's Studies* 25 (2): 214–227.

Coetzee, J.M. 2003. *Elizabeth Costello*. London: Secker and Warburg.

Collins, Patricia Hill. 1990. *Black Feminist Thought: Knowledge, Consciousness, and the Politics of Empowerment*. New York: Hyman.

Collins, Patricia Hill. 2019. *Intersectionality as Critical Social Theory*. Durham: Duke University Press.

Comaroff, Jean and John L Comaroff. 2016. *Theory from the South. Or, how Euro-America is Evolving Toward Africa*. London and New York: Routledge.

Cornell, Drucilla. 2008. *Moral Images of Freedom: A Future for Critical Theory*. Boulder and New York: Rowman and Littlefield.

Dowds, Eithne. 2020. *Feminist Engagement with International Criminal Law: Norm Transfer, Complementarity, Rape and Consent*. Oxford: Hart.

Du Toit, Louise. 2019. "Towards a Slow Decolonisation of Sexual Violence." *The Philosophical Journal of Conflict and Violence* 3 (1): 35–54.

Du Toit, Louise. 2022. "Contesting the Meaning/s of Sexual Violence in the South African Postcolony: Where are the Male Victims?" In *Intimacy and Injury: In the Wake of #MeToo in India and South Africa*, edited by Nicky Falkof, Shilpa Phadke, and Srila Roy, 152–173. Manchester: Manchester University Press.

Du Toit, Louise and Le Roux Elisabet. 2021. "A Feminist Reflection on Male Victims of Conflict-Related Sexual Violence." *European Journal of Women's Studies* 28 (2): 115–128.

Gabrielle, Ferrales, Nyseth Brehm Hollie, and McElrath Suzy. 2016. "Gender-Based Violence Against Men and Boys in Darfur: The Gender-Genocide Nexus." *Gender and Society* 30 (4): 565–589.

Gonzalez, Carmen G. 2015. "Bridging the North-South Divide: International Environmental Law in the Anthropocene." *Pace Environmental Law Review* 32 (2): 407–434. Accessed May 25, 2022. https://digitalcommons.pace.edu/pelr/vol32/iss2/3/.

Gorris, Ellen Anna Philo. 2015. "Invisible Victims? Where are Male Victims of Conflict-Related Sexual Violence in International Law and Policy?" *European Journal of Women's Studies* 22 (4): 412–427.

Grear, Anna. 2015. "Deconstructing Anthropos: A Critical Legal Reflection on 'Anthropocentric' Law and Anthropocene 'Humanity'." *Law and Critique* [online] 26 (3): 225–249. Accessed May 25, 2022. https://doi.org/10.1007/s10978-015-9161-0.

Grewal, Kiran. 2010. "Rape in Conflict, Rape in Peace: Questioning the Revolutionary Potential of International Criminal Justice For Women's Human Rights." *The Australia Feminist Law Journal* 33: 57–79.

Harding, Sandra. 1991. *Whose Science? Whose Knowledge? Thinking from Women's Lives.* Ithaca: Cornell University Press.

Hartsock, Nancy. 1998. *The Feminist Standpoint Revisited and Other Essays.* Boulder: Westview Press.

Haskell, John D. 2009. "The Complicity and Limits of International Law in Armed Conflict Rape." *Boston College Third World Law Journal* 29 (1): 35–84.

Kant, Immanuel. 2006. (1795). "Toward Perpetual Peace: A Philosophical Sketch." In *Toward Perpetual Peace and Other Writings on Politics, Peace and History*, edited and with an Introduction by Pauline Kleingeld. Translated by David L. Colclasure. New Haven and London: Yale University Press.

Kotzé, Louis Jacobus, Louise Du Toit, and Duncan French. 2021. "Friend or Foe? International Environmental Law and its Structural Complicity in the Anthropocene's Climate Injustices." *Oñati Socio-Legal Series* 11 (1): 180–206: Climate Justice in The Anthropocene.

Luban, David. 2013. "After the Honeymoon: Reflections on the Current State of International Criminal Justice." *Journal of International Criminal Justice* 11: 505–515.

Lugones, María. 2007. "Heterosexualism and the Colonial / Modern Gender System." *Hypatia* 22 (1), Writing Against Heterosexism: 186–209.

MacKinnon, Catharine A. 1994. "Rape, Genocide, and Women's Human Rights." *Harvard Women's Law Journal* 17: 5–16.

MacKinnon, Catharine A. 2006. "Defining Rape Internationally: A Comment on Akayesu." *Columbia Journal of Transnational Law* 44 (3): 940–958. HeinOnline.

Mbembe, Achille. 2017. *Critique of Black Reason*, translated by Laurent Dubois. Durham: Duke University Press.

Melzer, Nils. 2019. *International Humanitarian Law: A Comprehensive Introduction.* Geneva: International Committee of the Red Cross.

Mignolo, Walter D. 2000. "The Geopolitics of Knowledge and the Colonial Difference." *South Atlantic Quarterly* 101 (1): 57–97.

Miller, Alexandra A. 2004. "Comment, *From the International Criminal Tribunal for Rwanda to the International Criminal Court: Expanding the Definition of Genocide to Include Rape*." *Pennsylvania State Dickenson Law Review* 108 (1): 349–373.

Mutua, Makau, and Antony Anghie. 2000. "What is TWAIL?" *Proceedings of the Annual Meeting (American Society of International Law)*, April 5-8, 94: 31–40.

Nikolić-Ristanović, Vesna. 2005. "Sexual Violence, International Law and Restorative Justice." In *International Law: Modern Feminist Approaches*, edited by Doris E. Buss and Ambreena Manji. Oxford and Portland: Hart Publishing, 273–293.

Nixon, Rob. 2011. *Slow Violence and the Environmentalism of the Poor.* Cambridge, MA and London: Harvard University Press.

Philipose, Elizabeth. 2009. "Feminism, International Law, and the Spectacular Violence of the Other': Decolonizing the Laws of War." In *Theorizing Sexual Violence*, edited by Renée J. Heberle and Victoria Grace, 176–204. Abingdon: Routledge.

Robson, Tony. 2002. *Human Trafficking and Prostitution - World Socialist Web Site*. Bosnia: The United Nations. Accessed July 22, 2022. wsws.org.

Stein, Sharon, Andreotti Vanessa, Hunt Dallas, and Ahenakew Cash. 2021 "Complexities and Challenges of Decolonising Higher Education: Lessons from Canada." In *Decolonisation as Democratisation: Global Insights into the South Africa Experience*, edited by S.H. Kumalo. Cape town: UKZN Press, 48-65.

Thompson, John B. 1990. *Ideology and Modern Culture: Critical Social Theory in the Era of Mass Communication*. Stanford: Stanford University Press.

Westmarland, Nicole. 2014. "Not All Messages About Rape Were Welcome at Hague and Jolie's Sexual Violence Summit." *Durham University News*, June 16. Accessed July 22, 2022. http://www.dur.ac.uk/news/allnews/thoughtleadership/?itemno=21476.

Žarkov, Dubravka. 2007. *The Body of War: Media, Ethnicity, and Gender in the Breakup of Yugoslavia*. Durham and London: Duke University Press.

Chapter 5

No Consent and No Disclosure

Black Australian Women and Sexual Violence

Tess Ryan

Aboriginal and Torres Strait Islander women have been at the forefront of resisting power and advocating against numerous modes of violence perpetrated against them in Australia. From oppressive acts of the state, societal issues relating to racism and discrimination and interpersonal acts of physical, verbal and sexual violence, these women have responded in various ways. Yet there are still gaps in the research relating to violence (and in particular, sexual offences against women) that must be addressed in order to unpack its interplay with Aboriginal and Torres Strait Islander women. How do we begin to deal with sexual violence for Indigenous women in Australia when we haven't even begun to deal with oppressive power structures that ignore racism in this country?

This chapter considers what is missing in our understanding of sexual violence and the push/pull of power that interacts between Australian society and Aboriginal and Torres Strait Islander women. It will examine the structural reinforcement of power discrepancies that exist, including that of institutional domains, white feminist discourse, and gaps in the data that are just part of the story in discussing violence against Black Australian women that is historical and has endured in different ways over time. Aboriginal and Torres Strait Islander women's experiences of sexual violence has long been documented throughout historical and contemporary commentary. Yet, the documentation appears fragmented; statistics contain gaps that must be understood in the context of the overpowering matter relating to powered acts between the state, Australian society and Aboriginal and Torres Strait Islander women. These women have long had to endure various elements of violence placed upon them since Colonisation in Australia. The reinforcement of power through structural elements in society is a place of primacy within discussions on sexual violence. Power relations and its intersection with this population of women is an important point of discussion relating to violence, and in particular sexual violence against this marginalised group.

Within numerous institutional domains, these power dynamics do impact on women overall. Yet for Aboriginal and Torres Strait Islander women, the overriding element of power within institutions determines policy, behaviour

DOI: 10.4324/9781003379331-8

and actions that further perpetrate numerous forms of violence upon them. Aboriginal and Torres Strait Islander Australians have been largely omitted from histories of the Colonial period through to contemporary times and when they have been included, they have usually been misrepresented under the gaze on the Black body overall. This pattern of omission and misrepresentation has been particularly pronounced in relation to Aboriginal and Torres Strait Islander women. Gaps in the data for Aboriginal and Torres Strait Islander women are symptomatic of this broader pattern of omission and misrepresentation. The most pertinent gaps are exacerbated by a lack of willingness to disclose sexual violence, as underpinned by Colonialism, racism and cultural difference, as well as a lack of appreciation of data, research, its importance in knowledge translation and its contribution to society as a whole. There also exist issues relating to data design and defined consistent ethical frameworks, along with appropriate processes in dealing with data sovereignty for many Aboriginal and Torres Strait Islander populations.

This chapter will articulate new levels of discourse surrounding Aboriginal and Torres Strait Islander Australians and knowledge about the sexual violence perpetrated on them. It will consider historical connections to power dynamics, coercive control, data gaps in research, the power of lived experience in narrative stories and trauma-informed practices that provide self-determined approaches to healing. Through this analysis it will demonstrate the issues that ultimately impact on the gaps found in statistical data on sexual violence that tells only part of the story for Aboriginal and Torres Strait Islander women.

Gaps and Problems with Existing Data

For further clarification on the issues relating to this chapter, some definitions must be made. The term "Family Violence" has been used to include not just physical, sexual, psychological, social and economic abuse (Memmott et al., 2006), but also forms of coercive control (Longbottom 2021). The terms Indigenous, Aboriginal and Torres Strait Islander and Black will be used to define the population in question for this chapter. Colloquially, many within an Australian context use the term Black (Heiss, 2012, n.p.), regardless of skin colour as it determines a strength of identity. The term Indigenous has largely come into the lexicon from the 1990s and has been used by the Australian government in many policy initiatives. Aboriginal and Torres Strait Islander people as a term incorporates the cultural lands within Australia, and the Torres Strait Islands that are off the north of the continent.

The issue of sexual violence is one that touches all ethnicities and socio-economic groups and much has been documented concerning diverse spaces where women and non-binary peoples have been most impacted (Tarczon and Quadara 2012; Tayton, Kaspiew, Moore and Campo 2014). One cannot ignore the issue of discrimination when discussing any violence against all people of colour, ethnicity or people who are gender diverse in their identity.

The term gender diverse is defined as "An umbrella term that acknowledges the many ways people may identify their gender; examples include Nonbinary, Agender, Gender fluid and Genderqueer" (University of New South Wales, 2019). It also imperative in this context, to include Aboriginal and Torres Strait Islander gender diverse and non-binary individuals in the space to avoid further exclusionary practices, as this population group are even more ignored and neglected in the discourse and the statistics relating to sexual violence.

There are also data gaps related to the intersections of Indigeneity and disability, and experiences of sexual assault. The Australian Institute of Health and Welfare (AHIW 2019) has stated that approximately 45% of Aboriginal and Torres Strait Islander peoples over the age of 15 report having a disability. The ABS has also reported that over 50% of the Aboriginal and Torres Strait Islander population that have experienced family violence are listed as having a disability (AIHW 2019)

The Statistical Landscape

Sexual assault in Australia is under-reported by all victims and when it is reported, the data collected is often incomplete. These reporting and data gaps are most pronounced among Aboriginal and Torres Strait Islander women and women from culturally and linguistically diverse (CALD) backgrounds. Considering the sparse data related to Black women and sexual violence, an understanding of why some gaps exist in the data is required. The landscape of statistics and research for many Indigenous, Black, people of colour, minority groups and ethnic groups globally that do not have a share in political power is a complex measure of power and control of these populations. There is a long history of distrust within global Indigenous society of scientific research domains, stemming from inappropriate studies performed with the 'native' used as the disposable object, rather than the subject of research. The impact of this history has modern-day implications for the gathering and the uses of data in relation to Aboriginal and Torres Strait Islander peoples. This creates gaps in data collection across many different societal issues connected to Indigenous populations, including who is permitted to tell their story and how their story is told. Regarding sexual and family violence, the gathering of research is becoming more focused on elements previously overlooked and information on the differing narratives surrounding sexual violence is emerging.

The history of exploitation in data is an important aspect of sexual violence research for Aboriginal and Torres Strait Islander women and non-binary peoples in Australia. The Eugenics movement from 1910 through to the 1930s (Cawte 1986) is one example of the dehumanisation that occurred for Indigenous populations. This dark scientific history that focused on improving race ultimately by sterilisation and institutionalisation of those seen as deficient included the Aboriginal population. Research performed on these populations is wrought with fear and distrust. While the history of research is littered with these negative stories, there appears to be a gradual shift underway in the ways ethical research is undertaken within these communities, such as the Code of Ethics framework developed by the Australian Institute of Aboriginal and Torres Strait Islander Studies (AIATSIS). More Black, Indigenous people of colour entering higher education and research roles appears to have had a positive impact on the shift in research involving Indigenous peoples, and better ethics, rules and protocols for research are being developed and applied.

Due in part to the legacy of objectification in research, limited data on the experiences of violence within diverse groups in Australia has been published (Lievore 2004; Phillips and Vandenbroek 2014; Tarczon and Quadara 2012; Tayton, Kaspiew, Moore and Campo 2014). On closer inspection of some of the statistics, the gaps denote a level of underreporting and unreliable recording (Olsen and Lovett 2016; Queensland Centre for Domestic and Family Violence Research [QCDFVR] 2019). The focus on sexual violence within Aboriginal and Torres Strait Islander communities has fallen under some sub-categories. Firstly, there has been research examining sexual violence and communities which includes sexual abuse of Aboriginal and Torres Strait Islander children, such as the *Little Children are Sacred Report* (2007) and subsequent Northern Territory Emergency Response, in which a flawed interpretation of the Report led to the Australian Federal Government enacting policy to bring the Australian Defence Force into communities in the Northern Territory under the guise of "protecting" children from sexual abuse (Ghezelbash and Newhouse 2009). However, this also enabled a level of institutional power to dominate the communities involved, as the suspension of the Racial Discrimination Act 1975 to enter those communities protected the state and further demonised whole townships of people. This "weapon of race" (Moreton-Robinson 2009, 68) simultaneously removed self-determination for those communities to deal with the issue and created the notion that Aboriginal people were the only perpetrators of such violence. The misuse of research pertaining to Black bodies can have long lasting societal and political impacts for those who are the subjects of the data.

There needs to be a greater understanding that sexual violence does not sit alone and therefore the data around sexual violence for Aboriginal and Torres Strait Islander women will include the term 'family violence' to encapsulate the lived realities and broader contexts. Sexual violence regarding an intimate partner can be the escalation of domestic disputes, verbalisations and other forms of control in some circumstances. In research undertaken by Cripps, there are factors which can contribute to violent acts including sexual violence, suggesting:

> Colonisation: policies and practices; dispossession and cultural dislocation; and dislocation of families through removal, marginalisation as a minority; direct and indirect racism; unemployment; welfare dependency; past

> history of abuse; poverty; destructive coping behaviours; addictions; health and mental health issues; and low self-esteem and a sense of powerlessness. (Cripps 2007, 7–18)

A 2013 Our Watch report stated that Aboriginal and Torres Strait Islander women were five times more likely to experience physical violence and three times more likely to experience sexual abuse than other Australian women (Our Watch 2014). It is suggested that up to 90 percent of incidents of violence against Aboriginal women go undisclosed (DSS 2016; Willis 2011). There are a multitude of reasons for this, including shame; fear of reprisals from the perpetrator or from within the community; fear of ramifications from the justice system and other government services; a perception that abuse is normal and must be endured; the difficulty of keeping something private in a close-knit community; poverty and isolation; and a lack of culturally appropriate services (Braybrook 2015; Cripps and Adams 2014; Lowitja Institute 2019; QCDFVR 2019).

Data related to Aboriginal and Torres Strait Islander women and forms of violence appears at times conflated, with such terms as 'greater proportions' or 'at a higher rate than that of' used frequently, showing there is an obvious missing element in the gathering of this data. These points of research appear to lay a veneer of dysfunction in Aboriginal and Torres Strait Islander communities, once again obfuscating and demonising all Aboriginal and Torres Strait Islander people. Without demonstrating the nuances within this broad-brush stroke, data (and deeper understanding) has slipped through the sieve.

Yet one cannot ignore that violence within some of these communities exist, and numerous reports have demonstrated this (Gordon, Hallahan and Henry 2002; New South Wales Aboriginal Child Sexual Assault Taskforce 2007; Victorian Indigenous Family Violence Taskforce 2003; Wild and Anderson 2007). The reports into Indigenous family violence, child abuse and sexual assault over the past decade including the 2007 Social Justice Report have contained a wealth of information about the context and experience of violence and its aftermath for all those affected. These reports have also provided suggestions on pathways forward, many of which have been based on international examples (Cripps and McGlade 2008). Yet some statistical gaps will remain, as Ahmat has stated, "Our statistics are never going to be really known because our women aren't going to report at all" (2021).

Viewing the Whole Picture

It appears only part of the story is appropriately collected in matters of data, Black women and sexual violence, and significantly more is needed to understand the true diversity of statistics involved in the research. Aboriginal and Torres Strait Islander women are regularly placed in the same group as others of diverse cultures and ethnicities, while also being treated in a binary gendered way which aggregates specific elements of data that denotes a form of homogeneity that should not be present when discussing First Nations people on their own unceded land. There are also the issues of 'diversity within diversity' – the intersections of identity and disadvantage: Identity as an Aboriginal and/or Torres Strait Islander, as well as disability and cultural and linguistic diversity are experienced among other identities including gender. While there is a growing body of evidence on the diverse experiences of family violence and sexual assault in Australia, the experiences of women with multiple identities (e.g., culturally and linguistically diverse women with a disability) and the experience of compounded disadvantage is under-researched.

This is an issue for all of society as the gaps in data covering diversity appear to be extensive. This is an ongoing issue in Australian data collection ignoring societal diversity, as evidenced by the Australian Census data of 2021 which did not give adequate attention to non-binary peoples within their gathering of gender information (Stephenson and Hayes 2021). Excluding the true diversity that may exist within all populations, including Aboriginal and Torres Strait Islander peoples, means data, and people, fall through the cracks. Not only are there limited statistics on Aboriginal and Torres Strait Islander populations who are disabled and working through Family Violence issues, but also for those of the population who identify themselves as LGBTIQ. Social epidemiologist and advocate Vanessa Ahmat has stated:

> There is actually no data by the ABS or the AIHW collected on Aboriginal and Torres Strait Islander LGBTIQ. Being LGBTIQ and Aboriginal and Torres Strait Islander puts you at the bottom of the whole diversity level and that whole area of making policies. Because without those policies, without the data, without statistics, we have no services.
>
> (Ahmat 2021)

There also needs to be stronger distinctions between data that has been collated from specific geographical locations, as Indigenous communities are not homogenous, and differentiations must be made statistically between what is meant by a 'rural' and 'remote' community. Both of these subcategories need further exploration in the data in terms of economic and social systems employed within these areas, and how they differ from 'urban' populations of Aboriginal and Torres Strait Islander people overall. Regarding sexual violence in these communities, all three terms ethnographically can suggest different perpetrators, different services, and different levels of ramifications for survivors of violence and police, legal or social intervention.

In these statistical gaps, people's lives are entangled, and the absence of data suggests a lack of evidence, thereby creating a gap in government policy and funding. Research and regulation appear to be lagging in the gathering of diversity in data which creates ongoing problems for society. If diverse peoples are not recorded in data, they essentially disappear from addressing issues that arise within that diversity such as domestic, sexual and family violence. This cycle of denial or invisibility creates problems containing no support and no solutions. A 'one size fits all' approach to addressing these issues appears to negate lived cultural experience and results in approaches that further marginalise those in diverse spaces. In missing these 'others' in our otherness, we are further perpetuating a silence.

The Need to Think About Sexual Violence in Relation to Colonialism and Racial Power

The Long History of Colonial Violence in Australia

The multifaceted historical elements of power, oppression and consent require interrogation to fully comprehend what occurs regarding Aboriginal and Torres Strait Islander women's representations and sexual violence. This is ever present when considering the overriding structures that have been utilised since Colonisation, and the power exhibited within structures that still remain and which further reinforce that for Aboriginal and Torres Strait Islander women, consent has never been truly given.

The representation of Black Aboriginal women in sexual violence data has connections with other representations of Aboriginal and Torres Strait Islander women in a dominant white Australian society. These depictions that have worked since Colonisation to demonise and fetishise the Black body have adapted themselves into the modern age and impact on the way these women are perceived within media stories and the legal system in a modern-day context.

State based violence, institutional violence and person-to-person violence have been historically prevalent and regularly used as tools to assimilate Aboriginal and Torres Strait Islander families into compliance to the notion of 'one Australia.' This forced contract on these families suggest they have no choice in being subjected to racist tropes and stereotyping of Black bodies as savage, untamed, sullied and promiscuous. The "Colonial project" is a term used to describe efforts from the British Empire to eliminate Aboriginal and Torres Strait Islander people from "Terra Nullius" (Short 2016). These efforts include dispossession of lands, placing families and communities into missions and reserves, removal of children from their families, introduction of alcohol and criminalisation of peoples for such crimes as speaking in their own language or being in areas without permission. Within the Colonial project, there was a component of sexualising Black women and a perpetuation of denying their humanity as a Peoples throughout Australia (Watson 2009).

Colonisation and its connection to violence have been corroborated by the ABS research (2006 as cited in Healing Foundation et al. 2017), stating that Aboriginal and Torres Strait Islander peoples who were forcibly removed from their family were almost twice as likely to be victims of violence.

Within modern Colonial discourse is the notion that the practice of removing Aboriginal and Torres Strait Islander children from their families ceased as a practice in the 1970s. However, the rates of children removed from Aboriginal and Torres Strait Islander families today are still at rates much higher than for other Australian families. This ongoing programme of institutional state sanctioned child removal perpetuates generational cycles of violence.

The negative representations of Black women can be found with the "Black Velvet" paintings depicting naked Aboriginal women and in colloquial terms used in Australia's early history (Ryan 2019; Conor 2013). These depictions demonised, sexualised and exoticised Black women's bodies. The colloquial usage of names to categorise Black bodies also demonstrates that for Aboriginal and Torres Strait Islander women, they were considered last in a delineation of who deserves to be treated humanely. In discussing these terms, Connor has stated, "the presence as much as the absence of 'Black Velvet' in print demonstrates how colloquial language was a means for White colonisers to boast ownership over Aboriginal women's bodies" (Conor 2013, 52).

But what is more evidential, are the ways in which Black women's bodies were viewed as disposable by 'The Colony' and its inhabitants. However, there was also an interplay of agency in connection with Aboriginal women and sexual behaviours, possibly used as a tool for survival. These women were "given" to sealers and whalers in the early 1820s (Russell, 2007). In discussing two individuals, Russell posits that these individuals may have utilised their bodies as a form of agency, and highlights the contestation between Black women as vulnerable victims or engaging in acts of survival:

> The assumption that the men 'shared' the women tends to privilege the sexual relationships, which I suggest is problematic on two fronts. First, we do not know how these people themselves articulated the prominence or otherwise of their sexual relationships; and second, the understandings of sexual relationships asserted by previous researchers tend to use contemporary monogamous (heterosexual) and romantic marriage as a normative, and historically accurate, model.
>
> (Russell 2007, 30)

Aboriginal and Torres Strait Islander women were also used heavily in domestic servitude after being forcibly removed from their families, and there are numerous narratives of those women being used for the sexual favours of white pastoralists (Haskins, 2007). In Quandamooka, academic Aileen Moreton-Robinson's seminal book, *Talking up to the White Woman* (2000), clear and succinct statements are made relating to power imbalances brought on by white Colonial rule. The perception of Black women's bodies through this lens demonstrates the power interplay within that of the British Empire, its settler society and Indigenous women:

> The rape and sexual abuse between Indigenous women and white men is a social practice which reinscribes white racial superiority into identities of white masculinity, because for over 200 years the Indigenous woman's body has been positioned within white society as being accessible, available, deviant and expendable.
>
> (2009 p 168)

"Broader Australian society remains deaf and blind to the numerous behaviours contributing to Black Women's oppression" (Ryan 2019, 118). Since European arrival, these women have been viewed as "lascivious and manipulative beasts, erotic curios, and domicile victims at the whims of men" (Ryan 2019, 120). The fascination with Black women's bodies has led to Aboriginal and Torres Strait Islander women being placed in power dynamics where choice was not an option.

The denial of voices permitted to speak to the realities of Black Australian lives lies at the heart of what Australia represents since Colonisation. There is a lack of understanding beyond simplistic realms of modernity that impact on issues of family violence in Australia, and without comprehending these issues, dominant society will continue to see dysfunction and trauma within diverse ways of being for Indigenous peoples. These experiences sit within a shared history of global Indigenous women that includes dominance, removal and subjugation (Baily and Shayan 2021; Nagy 2015; Kuokkanen 2008). The Colonial project's past and current use of structural power is often not considered when attempting to understand sexual violence as it relates to Aboriginal and Torres Strait Islanders, despite it being a significant part of the story.

Stories, Narratives, Power and Overpower

One aspect that can be missing from the data on sexual violence is the contexts behind these incidents and from the perspective of the lived experiences of Aboriginal and Torres Strait Islander peoples. When discussing Sexual, Domestic and Family violence concerns, there is a deeper conversation required not only of the historical connections to consent and trauma, but also the ongoing ways that violence manifests and reproduces through the systems in our society. These stories contain empowering narratives of overcoming forms of violence, and stories that move from the personal reflection towards a collective advocacy for survivors. It is in the collective power of voice that healing for survivors of such events begin to advocate for better policy, more government funding, and more holistic approaches. While statistics tell a portion of the story of Aboriginal and Torres Strait Islander peoples, they also contain a rendering which removes the relationality, the long enduring years of pushing for a degree of sovereignty and humanity within a country whose sovereignty was never ceded. The undermining of narratives in this area is once again a denial of Black voices and a further perpetuation of Western ideas of data being numbers and not a humanities issue relating to social justice and equality.

Lived experience and narrative enquiry has been long established as a form of qualitative evidence in knowledge production, and the act of storytelling in safe, cultural space is an aspect of many Indigenous cultures globally (Wesley-Esquimaux 2010; Bessarab and NgÁndu 2010). Yet the quantitative substance of research relating to Black bodies overall steers away from that of lived experience, choosing to prefer snapshots rather than testimony in context.

Why would an Aboriginal and Torres Strait Islander person feel safe to disclose any violent act to the authorities, when those in power are seen as consistently enacting violence upon them? When consent has not been given since British arrival, and there remains structural reinforcements of power discrepancies between those whose ancestors arrived or invaded, and those whose ancestors were always here, why would you wish to disclose that violence to the structure that introduced such violence to your land? The comprehension required in low levels of disclosure of violent behaviours and sexually violent incidents begins in defining what degrees of control Aboriginal and Torres Strait Islander women, and Indigenous non-binary people feel over their own bodies and existence, and the levels of consent to which they can give to the incidents around them.

Media Representations of Aboriginal and Torres Strait Islander Bodies

Representations of women through media outlets have a pervasive impact on how we view women's bodies, and our understanding of power dynamics relating to subjugation and subservience. The discourse around Black women's bodies may have stemmed from historical elements of power and oppression, yet they still remain today in altered ways from those of the past. An example of this found in modernity is the case of Aboriginal woman Lynette Daley in 2011. Her death following a brutal rape by two men was reported by News .com with the headline "Campaign for justice over death of Lynette Daley, left to bleed after 'wild sex'," (Burke, 2016). After complaints were made to the Australian Press Council, this article was found to have breached its standards of practice (Australian Press Council. Media representations of Aboriginal and Torres Strait Islander women in Australia). As Cripps has stated, "For Indigenous women, the framing of victimhood through an ideal 'good woman' type immediately sets them apart as to fit this type inevitably means one must be a member or be reflective of the dominant hegemonic group" (2021, 304).

Media representation of women's lives and public scrutiny can have impacts on the ways other institutional domains react to such cases. The legal system determines through biased legislative interpretation, what should be seen as criminal and what is not. Structural abuses exercised through Australian government institutions regarding Aboriginal and Torres Strait Islander women can have huge ramifications for an individual. For those women experiencing sexual or family violence, those ramifications can include child removal (Gorrie 2021), criminalisation (Watego et al. 2021) and death (Atkinson 1990).

The levels of structural abuses that Aboriginal and Torres Strait Islander women and non-binary peoples can encounter, which stem from historical views creating a gaze of sexualisation and subjugation and have been further perpetuated through political decision making and representations within the media, have enabled a system of power to dominate these women's lived experiences. Sexual violence is but one form of that domination.

Feminism Only Works for White Women.

White feminism still works to reinforce a non-diverse space and a middle-class understanding of what it means to be a woman. This has occurred historically and is regularly called out in the modern era by Black and Indigenous feminists. As O'Shane has stated "The myth of the sexually promiscuous and deviant Indigenous woman meant that middle-class white women positioned her as competition" (O'Shane 1976, 33, cited in Moreton-Robinson 2000, 168).

While there has been a steady increase in discussions within the Feminist movement/s on African American academic Kimberlie Crenshaw's concept of "Intersectionality" (1991), this construction has become entwined with dynamics of power and the imbalance seen in who gets to share discourse on what it means to be a feminist in the modern era. Intersectionality is not an entirely new concept and has been in the zeitgeist for many years, yet it is currently facing a concern of "appropriation" from white feminists who assert that they have an understanding and can speak to the many intersections that can occur for Black and Indigenous women (Davis 2020).

In this instance, the lived experiences of Aboriginal and Torres Strait Islander women and non-binary peoples is once again erased or examined from a gaze of white feminism such as what bell hooks described in "Feminist theory from margin to center" (1984). The ownership of your own story and the sovereignty of your own data is imperative for all, and for Black and Indigenous women, having the power of one's story be appropriated or propagated by anyone else can trigger feelings of disempowerment. One cannot look at sexual violence and control without looking at other social issues that impact on women in society. For Black, native, and Aboriginal and Torres Strait Islander women, these issues form a multi-layered level of oppression when combined with that of sexual dominance and violence, which can seem overwhelming. The larger discussion on power imbalance and a denial of Black bodies demonstrates that a lack of consent regarding Indigenous people of colour has long been accepted by mainstream society. Aboriginal and Torres Strait Islander women are placed at the lowest end of priorities when considering feminist rights and beliefs.

Ways Forward

New Directions in Research and Discourse

In recent years, new developments regarding our understanding of sexual violence and First Nations populations have been emerging. These include some discursive elements that provide more nuanced understanding and more self-determined responsive solutions to broaden societies' comprehension of what requires further investigation for all differing identities when discussing violence, filling in some of the gaps in the larger story.

The emergence of discussion on coercive control has become an important moment for all survivors of sexual violence incidents. Black Academic Dr Marlene Longbottom has stated:

> In my work as a researcher, I have spoken to Indigenous women who have disclosed coercive control early in the relationship and over time this progressively became physical or of a sexual nature. I have also heard from Indigenous women who have stated that at the commencement of a relationship they experienced sexual violence or were raped.
>
> (Longbottom 2019)

There have been moves within Australian law to bring coercive control into a space of criminal behaviour, thereby seemingly enabling more convictions of offenders of sexual violence to take place. However, within an Indigenous context, there are issues within coercive control laws that can devastatingly impact on Aboriginal and Torres Strait Islander populations. Longbottom also highlights:

> #FDV data is skewed in identifying when Indigenous women come forward to report. Police use their discretion to intervene, which also includes police making AVO/DVO applications. This is not differentiated in current data extraction & reporting processes.
>
> (Longbottom July 2, 2021, Twitter)

Coercive control legislation would ultimately involve more policing of communities who already have a devasting history with policing and over incarceration. Many First Nations people believe that law reform provides more power to the authorities that use policing powers against First Nations people as a means of control. Culturally appropriate, intersectional responses are needed in determining such control through these communities, and the concern over this legislation has highlighted once again the intersectional divide that can occur between white feminism and Black feminism.

The diversity of encounters with law enforcement can regularly be neglected and disregarded. Due to Indigenous women being unlikely to report violence, as a result of intergenerational trauma and previous negative interactions with police, patterns of coercive control are unlikely to be identified until the situation becomes fatal, or the severity of the violence escalates. In dealings with the police, Indigenous women are at times being misidentified as the perpetrator rather than the victim. Years of coercive control can manifest in the victim of such control perpetuating a violent act as a self-defence mechanism. This is why patterns of abuse must be documented in partner-perpetrated violence. But this becomes challenging when there is fear or distrust involved in disclosing to authorities and when authorities exhibiting bias, respond to these disclosures.

Self-determined Responses

Mainstream service responses to domestic, family and sexual violence includes urgent removal from the circumstance the survivor of abuse finds themselves in (Olsen and Lovett 2016, 4), a punitive response in prosecuting and punishing the perpetrator (Cripps and Davis 2012), and many unintended consequences for the family that may be involved, such as children being removed from both the perpetrator and the survivor of the violent incident.

Much has been reported on the lack of appropriate services and funding to address domestic, family and sexual violence in Australia overall. Both State, Territory and Federal governments have suggested in the epidemic that they will do the political work to address this. Yet, in analysis of the state government allocation of funds towards domestic violence (2018–2019, News South Wales), Domestic Violence NSW discovered there was no significant new allocation for the domestic and family violence sector. It was also reported:

- No new funding or an evidence-based strategy for violence prevention across NSW (the small-scale Domestic Violence Innovation Fund only received $2.7m. This fund includes early intervention and crisis responses).
- No additional funding for specialist women's services to meet the current demand.
- No funding to implement the yet-to-be-released Sexual Assault Strategy. (2019, n.p., cited in Langton et al. 2020).

These mainstream services do not provide appropriate service delivery for First Nations Peoples due to their lack of diversity and cultural competence regarding how different family groups and individuals may approach circumstances of violence. The added component of various cultural aspects relating to shame and community recognition of personal events associated with violence appears lacking within mainstream approaches to healing also (Carlson et al. 2021).

For Aboriginal and Torres Strait Islander women and non-binary peoples, understanding trauma-informed work and practice as it aligns with sovereignty is an important aspect of the healing process, and enables survivors' opportunities to become further enriched in a holistic approach to healing beyond the incidents of personal violence, towards comprehending the intergenerational traumas that may lie behind these incidents occurring. More work has been occurring recently with extended family and men's mentoring programmes to assist in a family and community-oriented healing process which aims to change behaviours and attitudes amongst varied levels of society (McCalman et al. 2006). The Healing Foundation has found with the evaluation of three pilot programmes addressing healing that they are "creating significant and sustained change at the community, family and individual levels at each site" (The Healing Foundation 2015b).

Within these trauma-informed practices one is required to see the structural barriers that impact on violent incidents. Addressing these structural barriers in areas of mental health, drug and alcohol usage, housing and so on, assists the perpetrator to understand what lies behind the violence. The holistic approach to understanding levels of violence has been suggested by Longbottom stating, "We can't look at violence in our communities without addressing housing. We can't look at it without addressing the child protection issues or the over-incarceration issues. We have to look at trauma in its entirety" (Longbottom July 2, 2021, Twitter). Government responses, however, fall short in addressing these matters. Therefore, the approach from government appears to be reactive rather than proactive in assisting in eliminating multiple barriers which may contribute to the prevalence of those in crisis and at risk of experiencing a violent act.

Gaining more understanding of the ways in which masculinity is posited within society is another element that can positively impact on domestic and sexual violence occurrences. Seeing the issue of violence (sexual, domestic or family) as purely an issue regarding women once again denotes a lack of diversity as well as a lack of identifying the genuine pre-cursors that may occur for the perpetrator. Aboriginal and Torres Strait Islander organisations work to impact on the statistics and help to change their communities. Although this is regularly neglected in the reporting around sexual, domestic and family violence, the strength in these organisations should be noted and acknowledged. Such programmes as a Townsville based Cultural Mentoring Program providing cultural and spiritual support to Aboriginal and Torres Strait Islander sexual offenders once they are released from incarceration and back into their communities (Richards, Death and McCartan 2020) is one such initiative that demonstrates one possible solution to addressing a complex issue. Including perpetrators within the process has been long called for from Aboriginal and Torres Strait Islander women to promote a whole of community response (McCalman et al. 2006; Willis 2010). The Healing Foundation also positions that addressing men in the issue of violence can be beneficial:

> While communities should collectively be engaged to identify their healing needs and aspirations, the many strong Aboriginal and Torres Strait Islander men must be supported to lead healing work with men and boys.

> As Aboriginal and Torres Strait Islander women in some communities live with significant levels of violence, they cannot continue to be burdened with responsibility for improving safety for themselves and children.
> (2017, 4)

Conclusion

Aboriginal and Torres Strait Islander women and non-binary peoples are regularly rendered invisible in the statistics and in the media reportage of sexual and family violence. The history of Colonisation in Australia has contributed to this rendering, in as much as it has perpetuated stereotyped notions of First Nations people as being untamed savages, subjugated and manipulative beings not deemed good enough. Statistically, issues remain in the reporting of sexual and family violence regarding conflation, obfuscation, and the level of distrust from this population towards authoritative measures and data collection purposes. Furthermore, Aboriginal and Torres Strait Islander women are seen as the lowest priority within feminist discourse, often relegated as an afterthought of white feminists when discussing the rights of women.

The concept of institutional power and a lack of consent also demonstrates that Aboriginal and Torres Strait Islander peoples have long endured having forms of power over them and are loathe to disclose to a system that continues to ignore the truth of the structural barriers that can envelop First Nations societies. Yet many communities are contributing to solving these issues; from more First Nations people entering research domains to Indigenous-led and self-determined programmes assisting survivors of sexual and family violence. The anecdotal evidence strongly indicates that empowered communities with their own agency have far stronger outcomes in addressing family, domestic and sexual violence than external governmental/institutional controlling interventions, showing a way forward out of the perpetual Colonial inflicted hurt. Statistics are already showing this in small initiatives and are expected to be proven with wider adoption if support, finances, and ethical inclusive intersectional research and data gathering is further grown in this area.

References

Anderson, Patricia, and Rex Wild. 2007. "Ampe Akelyernemane Meke Mekarle 'Little Children are Sacred': Report of the NT Board of Inquiry Into the Protection of Aboriginal Children From Sexual Abuse."

Atkinson, Judy. 1990. "Violence Against Aboriginal Women: Reconstitution Of Community Law: The Way Forward." *Aboriginal Law Bulletin* 2 (46): 6–9.

Australian Institute of Health and Welfare. 2019. "Aboriginal and Torres Strait Islander Health Performance Framework" (ABS). https://www.indigenoushpf.gov.au/measures/1-14-disability#:~:text=Psychiatric%20and%20intellectual%20disabilities%20were

%20the%20most%20common,perform%20activities%20in%20different%20areas%20of%20their%20lives.

Bailey, Jane, and Sara Shayan. 2021. "The Missing and Murdered Indigenous Women Crisis: Technological Dimensions." In 125–144. *The Emerald International Handbook of Technology Facilitated Violence and Abuse*. Emerald Publishing Limited.

Bessarab, Dawn, and Bridget Ng'Andu. 2010. "Yarning About Yarning as a Legitimate Method in Indigenous Research." *International Journal of Critical Indigenous Studies* 3 (1): 37–50.

Braybrook, Antoinette. 2015. "Family Violence in Aboriginal Communities." *DVRCV Advocate* 2 (Spring/Summer): 18–21.

Burke, Liz. 2016. "Campaign for Justice Over Death of Lynette Daley, Left to Bleed After 'Wild Sex'." *News.com*, May 13. Accessed August 10, 2021. https://www.news.com.au/national/nsw-act/courts-law/campaign-for-justice-over-death-of-lynette-daley-left-to-bleed-after-wild-sex/news-story/e088b64b79d2706bcc5cafcc476d1fbe.

Campo, Monica, Rae Kaspiew, Sharnee Moore, and Sarah Tayton. 2014. "Children Affected by Domestic and Family Violence." A Review of Domestic and Family Violence Prevention, Early Intervention and Response Services. Melbourne: Australian Institute of Family Studies.

Carlson, Bronwyn, Madi Day, and Terry Farrelly. 2021. *What Works? Exploring the Literature on Aboriginal and Torres Strait Islander Healing Programs That Respond to Family Violence* (Research report, 01/2021). ANROWS.

Cawte, Mary. 1986. "Craniometry and Eugenics in Australia: RJA Berry and the Quest for Social Efficiency." *Australian Historical Studies* 22 (86): 35–53.

Conor, Liz. 2013. "'Black Velvet "and" Purple Indignation': Print Responses to Japanese' Poaching' of Aboriginal Women." *Aboriginal History Journal* 37: 51–76.

Crenshaw, Kimberlé. 1991. "Mapping the Margins: Identity Politics, Intersectionality, and Violence Against Women." *Stanford Law Review* 43 (6): 1241–1299.

Cripps, Kyllie. 2007. "Indigenous Family Violence: From Emergency Measures to Committ ed Long-Term Action." *Australian Indigenous Law Review* 11 (2): 6–18.

Cripps, Kyllie. 2021. "Media Constructions of Indigenous Women in Sexual Assault Cases: Reflections From Australia and Canada." *Current Issues In Criminal Justice* 33(3): 1–22.

Cripps, Kylie, & Hannah McGlade. 2008. Indigenous Family Violence and Sexual Abuse: Considering Pathways Forward. *Journal of Family Studies* 14(2–3): 240–253.

Cripps, Kyllie, and Mick Adams. 2014 "Indigenous Family Violence: Pathways Forward." in R. Walker, P. Dudgeon and H. Milroy (Eds) *Working Together: Aboriginal and Torres Strait Islander Mental Health and Wellbeing Principles and Practice*. Canberra: Department of Prime Minister and Cabinet.

Cripps, Kyllie, and Megan Davis. 2012. "Communities Working to Reduce Indigenous Family Violence." Indigenous Justice Clearinghouse, Australian Institute of Criminology. Analysis & Policy Observatory. https://apo.org.au/sites/default/files/resource-files/2012-06/apo-nid30379.pdf.

Davis, K. 2020. "Who Owns Intersectionality? Some Reflections on Feminist Debates on how Theories Travel." *European Journal of Women's Studies* 27 (2): 113–127.

Department of Social Services. 2016. *Third Action Plan 2016–2019 of the National Plan to Reduce Violence Against Women and Their Children 2010–2022*. Canberra: DSS.

Ghezelbash, Daniel, and George Newhouse. 2009. "Calling the Northern Territory Intervention Laws to Account: Complaint to the UN Committee on the Elimination of

All Forms of Racial Discrimination." *Law Society Journal: The Official Journal of the Law Society of New South Wales* 47 (9): 56–59.

Gordon, Sue, Kay Hallahan, and Darrell Henry. 2002. *Interim Report: Inquiry Into Response by Government Agencies to Complaints of Family Violence and Child Abuse in Aboriginal Communities*. Government of Western Australia.

Gorrie, Ronnie. 2021. *Twitter Comment*. May 19. Accessed August 12, 2021. https://twitter.com/RonnieGorrie/status/1394936242979016704.

Government of Victoria. 2003. Victorian Indigenous Family Violence Task Force Final Report. Melbourne: Department for Victorian Communities-Aboriginal Affairs Victoria.

Haskins, Victoria. 2007. "Domestic Service and Frontier Feminism: The Call for a Woman Visitor to" Half-caste" Girls and Women in Domestic Service, Adelaide, 1925–1928." *Frontiers: A Journal of Women Studies* 28 (1/2): 124–164.

Healing Foundation. 2015. *Our men our Healing - Creating Hope, Respect and Reconnection: Evaluation Report*. Canberra: Healing Foundation.https://healingfoundation.org.au//app/uploads/2017/03/OMOH-60-pg-report-small-SCREEN-singles.pdf.

Healing Foundation. 2017. *Annual Report 2017-2018*. Canberra: Healing Foundation. HF-AR-2018-digital.pdf (healingfoundation.org.au)

Heiss, Anita. 2012. "Am I Black Enough for You?" North Sydney: Random House Publishers.

hooks, b. 1984. *From Margin to Center*. Boston: South End.

Kuokkanen, Rauna. 2008. "Globalization as Racialized, Sexualized Violence: The Case of Indigenous Women." *International Feminist Journal Of Politics* 10 (2): 216–233.

Langton, M., K. Smith, T. Eastman, L. O'Neill, E. Cheesman, and M. Rose. 2020. *Improving Family Violence Legal and Support Services for Aboriginal and Torres Strait Islander Women*. Sydney: Australia's National Research Organisation for Women's Safety. ANROWS. .

Lee-Ahmat, Vanessa. 2021. *We say no More Broadcast. Special Broadcasting Service*. Accessed August 7, 2021. https://www.sbs.com.au/ondemand/watch/1888140355857.

Lievore, Denise. 2004. *Recidivism of Sexual Assault Offenders: Rates, Risk Factors and Treatment Efficacy*, Vol. 80. Canberra: Australian Institute of Criminology.

Longbottom, Marlene. 2019. "National Data set Misses the Important Factors Relating to Indigenous Women and Violence." *Croakey Health Media*, February 22. Accessed July 7, 2021. https://www.croakey.org/national-data-set-misses-the-important-factors-relating-to-indigenous-women-and-violence/.

Longbottom, Marlene. 2021. Indigenous experts respond to SBS' 'See What You Made Me Do' in a must-watch panel discussion. Special Broadcasting Service (SBS). Sydney, 2021. https://www.sbs.com.au/nitv/article/indigenous-experts-respond-to-sbs-see-what-you-made-me-do-in-a-must-watch-panel-discussion/m1k6un52w

Lowitja Institute. 2019. *The First Response Project: Trauma and Culturally Informed Approaches to Primary Health Care for Women who Experience Violence: Summary Report*. Melbourne: Lowitja Institute.

McCalman, Janya, Komla Tsey, Mark Wenitong, Mary Whiteside, Melissa Haswell, Yvonne Cadet-James, and Andrew Wilson. 2006. Indigenous Men's Groups: What the Literature Says. *Aboriginal and Islander Health Worker Journal* 30(3).

Memmott, Paul, Catherine Chambers, Carroll Go-Sam, and Linda Thomson. 2006. "Good Practice in Indigenous Family Violence Prevention: Designing and Evaluating Successful Programs." 1–36. Issues paper 11. University of NSW, Sydney: Australian Domestic and Family Violence Clearinghouse. Sydney.

Moreton-Robinson, Aileen. 2000. *Talkin' up to the White Woman: Aboriginal Women and Feminism*. Brisbane: University of Queensland Press.

Moreton-Robinson, Aileen. 2009. "Imagining the Good Indigenous Citizen: Race war and the Pathology of Patriarchal White Sovereignty." *Cultural Studies Review* 15 (2): 61–79.

Nagy, Rosemary. 2015. "Combatting Violence Against Indigenous Women." In A. Powell, N. Henry, A. Flynn. *Rape Justice*, 182–199. London: Palgrave Macmillan.

New South Wales Government. 2007. NSW Interagency Plan to Tackle Child Sexual Assault in Aboriginal Communities: 2006-2011. Sydney: New South Wales Government.

Olsen, Anna, and Ray Lovett. 2016. *Existing Knowledge, Practice and Responses to Violence Against Women in Australian Indigenous Communities*, Vol. 2. Landscapes State of Knowledge paper. Sydney: ANROWS. media.aomx.com/anrows.org.au/s3fs-public/FINAL.

O'Shane, Pat. 1976. "Is There any Relevance in the Women's Movement for Aboriginal Women?" *Refractory Girl*, September. Cited in Moreton-Robinson, Aileen. 2000. *Talkin' up to the White Woman: Aboriginal Women and Feminism*. Brisbane: University of Queensland Press.

Our Watch. 2014. *Reporting on Family Violence in Aboriginal and Torres Strait Islander Communities*. Melbourne: Our Watch.

Phillips, Janet, and Penny Vandenbroek. 2014. "Domestic, Family and Sexual Violence in Australia: An Overview of the Issues." Parliament of Australia Parliamentary Library Research Paper Violence iseries, 2014-2015. https://apo.org.au/sites/default/files/resource-files/2014-10/apo-nid41752.pdf

Queensland Centre for Domestic and Family Violence Research. 2019. *Prevention, Early Intervention and Support for Aboriginal and Torres Strait Islander People who Have Experienced Sexual Violence*, Practice paper, February. QCDFVR.

Richards, Kelly, Jodi Death, and Kieran McCartan. 2020. *Community-based Approaches to Sexual Offender Reintegration. No. ANROWS Research Report 07/2020.* Australia's National Research Organisation for Women's Safety.

Russell, Lynette. 2007. "'Dirty Domestics and Worse Cooks': Aboriginal Women's Agency and Domestic Frontiers, Southern Australia, 1800–1850." *Frontiers: A Journal of Women Studies* 28 (1/2): 18–46.

Ryan, Tess. 2019. "This Black Body is not Yours for the Taking." In B. Fileborn, R. Loney-Howes *# MeToo and the Politics of Social Change*, 117–132. Cham: Palgrave Macmillan.

Short, Damien. 2016. *Reconciliation and Colonial Power: Indigenous Rights in Australia*. London: Routledge.

Stephenson, Elise, and Jack Hayes. 2021. "LGBTIQ+ People are Being Ignored in the Census Again. Not Only is This Discriminatory, it's bad Public Policy." *The Conversation*, August. Accessed August 14, 2021. https://theconversation.com/lgbtiq-people-are-being-ignored-in-the-census-again-not-only-is-this-discriminatory-its-bad-public-policy-165800.

Tarczon, Cindy, and Antonia Quadara. 2012. *The Nature and Extent of Sexual Assault and Abuse in Australia*. Melbourne: Australian Institute of Family Studies.

University of New South Wales. 2019. Student Life. Working with Staff and Students who are Transgender, non-binary or gender diverse. https://www.arc.unsw.edu.au.

Watego, Chelsea, Alissa Maccoun, David Singh, and Elizabeth Strakosch. 2021. "Carceral Feminism and Coercive Control: When Indigenous Women Aren't Seen as Ideal Victims, Witnesses or Women." *The Conversation*, May. Accessed August 12, 2021. https://theconversation.com/carceral-feminism-and-coercive-control-when-indigenous-women-arent-seen-as-ideal-victims-witnesses-or-women-161091.

Watson, Irene. 2009. "'Aboriginality and the Violence of Colonialism.' Watson, Irene (2009) 'Aboriginality and the Violence of Colonialism'." *Borderlands E-Journal* 8 (1): 1–8.
Wesley-Esquimaux, Cynthia. 2010. "Narrative as Lived Experience." *First Peoples Child & Family Review: An Interdisciplinary Journal Honouring the Voices, Perspectives, and Knowledges of First Peoples Through Research, Critical Analyses, Stories, Standpoints and Media Reviews* 5 (2): 53–65.
Willis, Matthew. 2010. *Community Safety in Australian Indigenous Communities: Service Providers' Perceptions.* Canberra: Australian Institute of Criminology.
Willis, Mathew. 2011. Non-disclosure of Violence in Australian Indigenous Communities. *Trends and issues in crime and criminal justice*, (405): 1–11.

Chapter 6

After Provocation

Reconciling the Legacy of the Homosexual Advance Defence in Occupied Australia

Kate Gleeson

In 2020, South Australia (SA) became the last Australian jurisdiction to overturn the Homosexual Advance Defence (HAD) when it reformed the law of provocation,[1] a puzzlingly overdue move in the first Australian state to have decriminalised men's gay sex in 1975 and passed anti-discrimination legislation in 1976. In response to recommendations of the SA Law Reform Institute (SALRI), the reforms abolished the plea of provocation to murder in its entirety (including HAD) and made changes to defences of self defence, necessity and duress to accommodate family violence victims who may no longer plead provocation[2]. The *Sentencing Act* was also amended to provide for consideration of family violence as "exceptional circumstances" in murder sentencing, which is otherwise governed by mandatory life sentences.[3] The "landmark" package was passed with bipartisan support to bring SA in line with the other Australian states and territories, which had all abolished HAD and reformed provocation in recent years (Dayman 2020).

The SALRI review was prompted by the 2015 High Court of Australia appellate case of *Lindsay*, which ruled that because the SA parliament had failed to legislate to overturn HAD, the courts must entertain it (*Lindsay v R*[4]). Centring on an Indigenous accused person, Michael Lindsay, who killed in the aftermath of a white man's so-called 'homosexual advance,' the judgment considered intersectional factors that might inform judicial assessments of provocation to kill as experienced by an Aboriginal man. Australian courts have considered so-called 'cultural factors' such as ethnicity in cases of provocation where men kill women (*Stingel v R*; *Masciantonio v R*[5]), and one jurisdiction, the Northern Territory, made special provision for Aboriginal identity in provocation, but did not have cause to adjudicate HAD (Douglas 2006). *Lindsay* represented the first time the High Court brought discourses of racism

1 Statutes Amendment (Abolition of Provocation and Related Matters) Act 2020.
2 (s.14B, s.15B).
3 Sentencing Act 2017 SA s.48(3a).
4 [2015] HCA 16.
5 [1990] HCA 61; [1995] HCA 67.

DOI: 10.4324/9781003379331-9

and homophobia into dialogue in the context of Aboriginal identity intersecting with homosexual sex and homicide.

When SA reformed the law, much thoughtful consideration was given to the gendered doctrine of provocation and the special needs of women as family violence victims. And yet, despite the impetus of *Lindsay*, structural factors of race, colonialism and Indigeneity were all but absented from the political debate and associated commentary justifying reform of the law.[6] Within the SALRI review and elsewhere, HAD was portrayed as an outdated ruling on men's *individual* expressions of homophobia and anger with little consideration of where these states of mind might originate. There is a paradox at the heart of progressive law reform that aims to present a tale of whiggish progress away from past discriminatory regimes that are conveniently no longer the responsibility of the state. Legalistic progress narratives confoundingly position the law as an agent of social change whilst also relying on the justification of extant social change for its reform. Evidence of the failure of this progress can be marginalised for political ends, especially complex intersectional evidence. In the 21st century, Western gay progressive narratives have been imbued with strategic significance in neo-colonial campaigns of homonationalism (Puar 2018); they are neither incidental nor organic, but instrumental. In settler-colonial societies like Australia in particular, such progress narratives are liable to invest in the demarcation of the past and the present in ways that politically annihilate representation of experiences of intergenerational colonisation. In this respect, *Lindsay* provided a brief inconvenient interjection to the predominant master narrative of modern Australia, which the SALRI and SA government appeared keen to correct.

Informed by Carol Smart's formative analysis of the power of law laying in its "claim to speak the truth, to 'know' and therefore control" (in Morgan 1993, 748) this chapter considers the political legacy of *Lindsay* in the context of the entrenched violence of a country characterised by ruthless colonial relationships to both homosexuality and the sexual exploitation of First Peoples. It aims to extend our understandings of what sexual violence entails – epistemically and physically – to consider lethal outcomes of the state-sponsored violence of homophobia, the vestiges of which endure long since the intense criminalisation of men's same-sex desire throughout the 20th century. And it seeks to position this legacy alongside the related aftermath of colonial sexual violence enacted on the bodies and nations of First Peoples as a form of occupation. Specifically, by analysing *Lindsay* and the political purposes it served, the chapter seeks to illuminate the white-washing of social relationships, historical and contemporary, that occurs when structural forces (factors of colonialism) are politically marginalised in favour of personal and individualistic

6 For an exception see Blore 2018.

explanations of human behaviour (emotions such as anger) in representations of the common law and arguments for its progressive reform.

Far from being atomised or separate concerns, legislated racism and homophobia in any country's history reflect complex structures of normative domination when considering law as a set of "hierarchical and authoritarian" textual practices systematically implemented to "impose a particular and exclusive meaning on the world" (Moran 2002, 8). Indeed, Eve Kosofsky Sedgwick had long established that uniquely modern forms of violence such as "race and colonisation" can be starkly illuminated from the vantage point of "antihomophobic inquiry" (in Warner 1993, xiv). It is my argument that the afterlife of each expression of legalised structural violence – racism and homophobia – cannot simply be legislated away by acts of parliament and wishful thinking that the discriminatory social power of law will be absolved in the course of its amendments. My aim is not to defend the law of provocation. Not in the least. But it is to remind of the importance of our remaining vigilant and relentless in remembering the "institutional responsibility for violence and subordination" that informs individual expressions of homophobia and racism at their inception (Morgan 1993, 748).

This chapter is structured as follows. First, it outlines the doctrine of HAD as a subset of provocation and its use in Australian courtrooms since the 1990s. Second, it explains *Lindsay* and the landmark consideration the High Court case gave to the subjective elements of provocation in terms of Aboriginal identity. Third, it explains the incoherence of HAD centred on the legal construct 'loss of self-control,' as derived from archaic common law rulings about the acceptable context for men's violence. Fourth it gives a brief overview of the colonial legal environment informing contemporary homophobia and race relations in Australia. Finally, it explains the political representation of HAD in the SA law reform process, which skirted discussion of structural factors in provocation, in favour of an emphasis on individualistic drivers such as emotions. It concludes by situating the modernising law reform project underway in SA in the broader context of a political movement invested in absenting the state from debates about homophobia and racism in 21st-century Australia.

Provocation and HAD

Provocation is a plea that, when successfully argued, reduces a potential murder conviction to one of manslaughter through the doctrine of justification. Although it is commonly described as a "partial defence," the correct position is that unlawful intentional killing under provocation is not murder (*Lindsay v R*[7]). Provocation came to feature in 17th-century common law in an era of

7 [2015] HCA 16, at 15.

duelling and "pistols at dawn" dispute settlement between honourable men, to provide leniency in sentencing in light of mandatory capital punishment for murder (SALRI 2017, 10). Typical scenarios were gendered and heteronormative, concerning transgressions of sexual norms and defences to sexual violence, such as a man 'discovering' his wife's adultery and killing her lover or a man fending off a "grossly indecent assault" with lethal force (SALRI 2017, 10). Central to provocation is the idea of 'loss of self-control' provoked by the deceased's behaviour, which militates against the possibility of the malice and *mens rea* required for murder (*Lindsay v R*[8]). Even in the absence of capital punishment, provocation is raised by men who kill their female partners for reasons of separation or suspected infidelity (*R v Butay*[9]) and, sometimes, by women who kill abusive men in the context of domestic violence (*R v Chhay*[10]).

Despite historical consideration of "grossly indecent assaults," provocation seems not to have been raised in the context of so-called 'homosexual advances' until the late 20th century in Australia. HAD was first pleaded in the New South Wales (NSW) courts in 1992, at a time of unchecked violent homophobia in response to the AIDS crisis that was only subdued with the onset of triple combination antiretroviral therapy in 1996, the current and effective standard of HIV care (Albion Centre 2012, 30). When gay men most needed protection, their killings were diminished if not sanctioned by the state.[11] The essence of HAD is that the implicitly straight defendant 'lost control' when confronted by a sexual advance by an assumedly gay man. However, the straight man's subjective state of mind alone is not sufficient to establish diminished culpability. Provocation involves a two-limbed subjective-objective test to be considered by the jury which, in the context of HAD, necessarily involves the extrapolation of homophobia to 'ordinary' people in the community, perhaps the most odious aspect of the law.

A jury is asked to appraise "highly complex and artificial" distinctions between subjective and objective elements (SALRI 2017, 19) when considering (subjective) circumstances of the accused's experiences including their "age, race, ethnicity, physical features, personal attributes, personal relationships or past history" in gauging the degree to which they were provoked (*Masciantonio v R*[12]); and then determining if an "ordinary person" provoked to that degree in the accused's situation could (objectively) have lost control and killed. The latter test, appraised against the standard of the "power of self-control of a truly hypothetical 'ordinary person' relative to the age of the

8 [2015] HCA 16, at 284.
9 [2001] VSC 417.
10 (1994) 72 A Crim R 1.
11 The use of HAD bears some relationship to the contemporaneous use of the "gay panic" defence in the US, which pleads a form of temporary insanity sparked by latent homosexuality manifesting as deranged homophobia (Howe 1997, 339).
12 [1995] HCA 67, at 66.

accused" (the *Stingel* test, in Douglas 2006, 201), is meant to enforce the idea that "equality before the law can only be achieved through all members of the community observing a minimum level of self-control" (De Pasquale 2002, 121). But legal academics describe the test as a "nonsensical nightmare" for juries (SALRI 2017, 20) and as providing a perverse disincentive for all men to learn self-control (Howe 1997, 360).

The spate of 13 NSW HAD cases heard from 1993–1997 was troubling even to the government as it involved acquittals for murder, including a defendant who allegedly boasted of "rolling a fag" and convictions of manslaughter for men who perpetrated frenzied lethal violence with weapons (Howe 1997).[13] By the time the High Court in *Green* in 1997 ordered a retrial for a man convicted of murder for repeatedly stabbing and bashing his gay friend to death, disfiguring his face to the point of unrecognisability, there was pronounced public concern about the ratio that rewarded violent homophobia as typical of the "ordinary person" and implicated gay men in having provoked "their own demise" (Howe 1997[14]). The protracted reform process commenced in Tasmania in 2003. NSW, where HAD was most frequently deployed, took until 2014 to reform the law to recognise only "extreme provocation" in the context of the commission of a serious indictable offence, and explicitly not in response to a non-violent sexual advance.[15] By 2017 all states had reformed the law except SA, a curious (non)response given that the state's historic decriminalisation of homosexual sex in 1975 was prompted by a gay hate killing. Under the common law, even when provocation is not pleaded, the trial judge must put it to the jury if there is evidence that it might be relevant. The prosecution then carries the onus of negativing provocation by excluding the reasonable possibility that the accused was acting under it. And so, when 28-year-old Michael Lindsay – also known as Sun Sun – was brought before the SA courts in 2013 charged with the murder of 37-year-old Andrew Negre, the jury was directed to consider HAD. The facts of the case are summarised as follows.

The Case of *Lindsay*

Aboriginal man Michael Lindsay met Caucasian man Andrew Negre while out drinking with others at a pub and invited him back to his home for further drinks. Present at Lindsay's home were his female partner and two younger sisters, Lindsay's friend Luke Hutchings and his female partner, and another male friend. Lindsay's young son was also at home. Negre is said to have made

13 In the early NSW cases, juries were instructed to consider both provocation and self-defence. In *McKinnon* (unreported) self-defence was accepted by the jury, allowing for acquittal. See Howe 1997.

14 *Green v R* [1997] 191 CLR 344.

15 Crimes Act 1900 (NSW) s.23.

a 'homosexual advance' on Lindsay when he straddled Lindsay's legs and made a thrusting motion with his hips. Lindsay's girlfriend admonished Negre saying "don't go doing stuff like that" while Lindsay stated that he was not gay and warned, "don't go doing that sort of shit or I'll hit you." Negre apologised and Lindsay told him, "That's okay, just don't go doing stuff like that." Eventually, Lindsay invited Negre to sleep in his guest room. Negre then propositioned Lindsay by saying he did not want to sleep alone and "I'll pay you for sex then," to which Lindsay replied, "What the fuck did you say, cunt?" Negre repeated his proposition, offering to pay Lindsay several hundred dollars. A witness then heard "a terrible thud." Negre, on the ground with Lindsay on top of him, continued to offer Lindsay money. Lindsay stabbed Negre to death with some assistance from Hutchings. Negre's body was located a week later in bushland. Negre's family described Andrew as, "easy to get along with and make new friends regardless of who they were or where they came from. He was very much a ladies' man and would quite often hand his phone number out to someone he just met" (Akerman 2013). They believed the murder was pre-meditated.

At committal, Lindsay argued he was unfit to plead due to cognitive impairment suffered as the result of two incidents when he was hit by cars in his infancy and childhood. The trial judge accepted that Lindsay had brain damage, was of low intelligence and illiterate and had difficulty processing information, especially complex information, but compelled him to stand trial (*R v Lindsay*[16]). At trial, Lindsay's defence was that it could not be proven beyond reasonable doubt it was he who fatally stabbed Negre (co-accused Hutchings was charged with and acquitted of murder and convicted of assisting an offender, Lindsay). The judge directed the jury to consider provocation: That if it were a reasonable possibility that Lindsay, as a consequence of the deceased's conduct that amounted to provocation, "suffered a sudden and temporary loss of self-control and killed Mr Negre whilst out of control, then Mr Lindsay would be not guilty of murder but guilty of manslaughter" (*R v Lindsay*[17]). But the judge erred when explaining the subjective-objective test by directing the jury to "put themselves in the appellant's position" and consider what they would have done (*R v Lindsay*[18]). First, the objective test turns not on what the ordinary person *would have done* in response to the provocation, but on what the ordinary person "*could have been induced to intend*" including grievous bodily harm or death (*Green v R*[19]. Original emphasis). Second, the judge's direction "created a risk that jurors might substitute their own personal standards for those of the 'ordinary person'" (*R v Lindsay*[20]).

16 [2013] SASC 104.
17 [2014] SASCFC 56, at 25.
18 [2014] SASCFC 56, at 131.
19 [1997] HCA 50, at 660.
20 [2014] SASCFC 56, at 2.

Lindsay was convicted of murder and sentenced to life imprisonment with a non-parole period of 23 years. He appealed *inter alia* on the misdirection as to provocation and severity of sentence (the non-parole period). The SA Court of Appeal found that despite the judge's error, no "reasonable jury could have failed to find that an 'ordinary person' could not have lost self-control so as to attack the deceased in the way the appellant did" (*R v Lindsay*[21]). The objective limb was portrayed as "an instrument of policy employed to keep the partial defence of provocation within bounds acceptable to contemporary society," as compared to the past when gay sex constituted serious crime and "men were accustomed to resort to weapons and violence to defend their honour" (*R v Lindsay*[22]). Lindsay's appeal was dismissed on all grounds. He was then granted leave to appeal to the High Court, which noted that because SA had failed to reform the law, the common law plea of HAD as upheld in *Green* remained the law in that state. Because neither counsel had argued for a manslaughter conviction to substitute for murder, the Court ruled that a retrial should be conducted for the following reasons.

The majority accepted Lindsay's appeal concerning the misdirection as to provocation with the reasoning that "it cannot be concluded that, if the jury had been correctly instructed on the issue of provocation, the appellant would inevitably have been convicted of murder" (*Lindsay v R*[23]). The High Court has previously considered whether so-called 'cultural factors' (ethnicity) should inform jury assessments of the objective limb of provocation, concluding that only age and not even gender can be taken into account when determining whether the hypothetical ordinary person could have lost control and killed when provoked to the degree of the accused (*Masciantonio v R*[24]). In *Lindsay*, the Court instead drew attention to the need to understand the subjective limb of the test – the degree to which the accused was provoked – in terms of personal characteristics including, in this case, the accused's gendered and racialised experiences as a First Nations Australian man. While the SA courts mentioned Lindsay's Aboriginal identity only in passing, concluding it "did not reveal any particular characteristic of Lindsay relevant to the issue of provocation" (*R v Lindsay*[25]), the High Court viewed this evidence differently. The majority considered the cultural context of Lindsay's loss of self-control in a framework that seemed to invoke the parameters of the colonial encounter of invasion if not occupation:[26]

21 [2014] SASCFC 56, at 4.
22 [2014] SASCFC 56, at 234.
23 [2015] HCA 16, at 4.
24 [1995] HCA 67.
25 [2014] SASCFC 56, at 29.
26 Many thanks to Dave McDonald for this insightful reading.

> *The appellant was hosting the deceased as a guest at the appellant's house*; had reacted with anguish and loathing when the deceased made his first advance of the evening; had threatened violence if anything of the kind were repeated; and was then insulted in the presence of his partner, sisters and friends with an offer of several hundred dollars to prostitute himself to the deceased's desires. Further, as counsel for the appellant suggested in the course of argument (although no such submission was advanced below), it is not impossible that a jury could reasonably infer that, because the appellant is Aboriginal, he perceived the deceased's conduct towards him to be racially based and for that reason especially insulting.
>
> (*Lindsay v R*[27]. Emphasis added)

In a separate concurring judgment Nettle J ruled that,

> It was open, as the appellant submits, for the jury to consider that the sting of the provocation lay in the suggestion that, despite his earlier firm rejection of the deceased's advance, the appellant was so lacking in integrity that he would have sex with the deceased in the presence of his family in his own home in return for money. And as the appellant submitted on the hearing of the appeal in this Court, it was open to a reasonable jury to consider that an offer of money for sex made by a Caucasian man to an Aboriginal man in the Aboriginal man's home and in the presence of his wife and family may have had a pungency that an uninvited invitation to have sex for money made by one man to another in other circumstances might not possess.
>
> (*Lindsay v R*[28])

As Blore emphasises, in ordering a retrial the High Court did not find that Lindsay was innocent of any crime but that, "as inexcusable as Sun Sun's crime was, there may well have been some white provocation" (2018, 169). The case was remitted to the SA courts and in 2016 Lindsay was again convicted of murder by a jury, after a mistrial. He appealed again based *inter alia* on the judge's directions as to provocation. The SA Court of Appeal again considered Lindsay's appeal. The three judges ruled *inter alia* that the most recent trial direction was adequate in that although it did not highlight the racial elements considered by the High Court, it did direct the jury to consider that "Negre was talking down to Michael Lindsay and that he was a bragger" and that he persisted "in asking Mr Lindsay to sleep with him and when his persistence was rejected Mr Negre then said 'I'll pay you for it then' and he also made reference to having $600 in his wallet." The appeals judges concluded, "It is hard

27 [2015] HCA 16, at 81.
28 [2015] HCA 16, at 37.

to see what more could have been done" in the jury direction (*R v Lindsay*[29]). Lindsay's murder conviction was affirmed and his life sentence reinstated.

Loss of Self-control in Provocation and HAD.

Feminists have long observed that provocation is heteronormative in its basis in men's honour and its implicit ideas about male proprietorship of women (Howe 1997). Less attention has been paid to the legal rationale of what provocation is believed to involve *experientially* for the accused (Sorial 2019). There is no statutory definition of 'loss of self-control' and the assumption that it naturally concerns emotions such as anger is taken for granted in much case law and academic literature focused on men killing women (*R v Butay*[30]; Sorial 2019). A 'homosexual advance' presents challenges to this doctrine because it does not map neatly onto 'common sense' (misogynist) ideas about men's anger at their loss of proprietorship of women, although HAD is founded in associated sexist values of heteronormativity. As such, HAD is extremely confused. In part it would appear to be informed by ideas about anger; in part by ideas about consciousness. In reality, there are few reported HAD cases to draw on.

In the leading Australian case of *Green*, the loss of self-control imagined by the High Court appeared to be informed primarily by lay understandings of altered consciousness affected by past trauma.[31] In this interpretation, it is not necessarily anger in the moment that causes an individual to lose their self-control; rather it is the *present self* that is momentarily lost when memories or past associations involuntarily intrude upon their consciousness manifesting in them 'losing it' in violence.

Green turned on what was termed the "sexual abuse factor" but without any specialist medical or psychiatric evidence to support its significance.[32] Witnesses reported to the police that the appellant, Malcolm Green, had told them he "intended to knock someone off," the night before he beat and stabbed to death his older gay friend, Don Gilles (*Green v R*[33]). But Green claimed the crime was not planned. He testified that he suddenly "lost it" when "gently" and then more "insistently" sexually approached by Gilles, after the pair had become "much affected by the alcohol they had consumed"[34]. While Green did testify to feeling "upset" and "angry" in response to Gilles, his primary claim was to have experienced involuntary images of his sisters' childhood sexual abuse by their father (which he had not witnessed but said he believed occurred): "when I tried to push Don away and that and I started hitting him

29 [2016] SASCFC 129, at 46.
30 [2001] VSC 417.
31 Green v R [1997] 191 CLR 334.
32 [1997] 191 CLR, at 342.
33 [1997] 191 CLR 334, at 347.
34 [1997] 191 CLR, at 389.

it's just – I saw the image of my father over two of my sisters, Cherie and Michelle, and they were crying and I just lost it.... I can't remember stuff after it" (*Green v R*[35]). Green's case was remitted for retrial, to consider "the sexual abuse factor," and he was convicted of manslaughter on grounds of provocation with a maximum ten-year sentence.[36] Similar quasi-medicalised arguments about intrusions on consciousness have been accepted from women in provocation defences, albeit not in the context of homosexuality. In 2012 a woman successfully pleaded provocation in NSW in respect of her lethal reaction to requests for the enactment of child sexual abuse fantasies including child pornography (child sexual abuse material) from a male client when she was working as a sex worker. The woman had been repeatedly sexually abused as a child and testified that the requests and child sexual abuse material caused her to "snap" and "black out" while she killed her client (Alexander 2012).

In *Lindsay*, the SA courts barely explored the basis for the 'loss of self-control' said to be generated by a 'homosexual advance,' perhaps because homophobia is thought to be self-explanatory. The judge was only able to direct the jury that it must involve "*more than* mere anger or panic. It must be such, as in a case like this, it causes the accused's blood to boil to the extent where reason has been temporarily suspended" (*R v Lindsay*[37] emphasis added). Perhaps in recognition of the ill-fit of much case law centred on men killing their female partners, the Court relied on incongruous precedents of different heterosexual encounters, including killings performed by women who had suffered domestic violence and for whom the provocation had built up over time (*R v Chhay*[38]). In this context, the judge clarified:

> Emotions such as hatred, resentment, fear, or the desire for revenge, which commonly follow ill-treatment, and sometimes provide a motive for killing, *do not of themselves involve a loss of self-control* although on some occasions, and in some circumstances, they may lead to it. What the law is concerned with is whether the killing was done whilst the accused was in an emotional state which the jury are prepared to accept as a loss of self-control.
>
> (*R v Lindsay*[39] emphasis added)

Lindsay did not give evidence in court, so his personal processes associated with loss of self-control were not scrutinised. Witnesses described the fatal attack in terms that seemed less focused on emotions than states of consciousness. For

35 [1997] 191 CLR 334, at 348.
36 R v Green [1999] NSWCCA 97.
37 [2014] SASCFC 56, at 209.
38 (1994) 72 A Crim R 1.
39 [2014] SASCFC 56, at 210.

example, "it just happened in an instant out of nowhere"; "Sun Sun just lost it"; and had "just gone off his head like a *lunatic*" (*R v Lindsay*[40] emphasis added). What loss of control does not concern, according to SA law, is intellectual capacity. Lindsay's cognitive impairment was not considered by any court in assessing his degree of provocation or his loss of self-control, which were appraised against the objective standard of the 'ordinary person,' despite the medically documented association between impairment and behaviour regulation (Shepherd et al. 2017, 2).

The Subjective Limb of Provocation: First Peoples

As explained above, the High Court's assessment of Lindsay's state did not consider anger at all. In lieu of his own testimony, it was inferred that Lindsay was *insulted* and that he experienced provocative emotions of *anguish* and *loathing* in the context of a racist-homophobic milieu, the product of distinct colonial encounters and structures and their aftermath. The ruling thereby offers rare if fleeting recognition of the sexually violent aspects of colonialism that might persist in intergenerational expressions of racism and homophobia. Just a few of these factors are outlined here.

Michael – Sun Sun – Lindsay represents one of the approximately 2% of South Australians who identify as Aboriginal or Torres Strait Islander (ABS 2021). He also represents one of the 11,652 male Aboriginal prisoners in Australia, constituting 4,338 men per 100,000 Aboriginal and Torres Strait Islander men (11 times the imprisonment rate of the general adult male population) (ABS 2021). Like all Australian colonies, SA was the site of massacres of First Peoples that proliferated unaccounted for until the turn of the 20th century. Aboriginal prisoners were executed without trial, authorised by the colonial Governor with the circular racist logic that it was impossible to apply the rule of law in the courts to "people of a wild and savage tribe whose country, although within the limits of the Province of South Australia, has never been occupied by Settlers, who have never submitted themselves to our dominion" (in Watson 2002, 262). Sexual violence against Australia's First Peoples was a technique of occupation, establishing enduring power relationships through the children born of sexual exploitation, some of whom would go on the constitute Stolen Generations.

Eualeyai/Kamilaroi woman, Professor Larissa Behrendt, has documented the centrality of rape to the settler-colonial project in which Aboriginal women were taken as "spoils of colonial conquest": "Just as the invading colonists saw Aboriginal land as theirs for the taking, so too they assumed they could do as they wished with Aboriginal women without fear of interference from British law" (2000, 364 and 353). Aboriginal men who tried to protect Aboriginal women were assaulted or killed in acts of violence that communities had to "tolerate when they refused to

40 [2014] SASCFC 56, at 113.

supply women for prostitution" (Behrendt 2000, 353). This was a period when the predominant colonial stereotype "implied that all Indigenous women were 'available' for prostitution under any circumstances" (McGrath in Sullivan 2018, 403). Paternalistic laws and policies followed, to damaging effect. In the 20th century, SA was named respondent in a Stolen Generations lawsuit claiming Aboriginal child removal policies constituted "misfeasance in public office, false imprisonment, breach of duty of care and breach of fiduciary and statutory duties" resulting in injury, loss and damage (*Trevorrow v SA*[41]). Approximately one in ten Stolen Generations children placed in institutions and foster care throughout Australia were sexually abused (Wilson 1997, Chapter 3).

Racial discrimination is associated with Post Traumatic Stress Disorder and cognitive and biological stress responses that "contribute to an individual's increased vulnerability to developing mental health difficulties" (Mekawi et al. 2021,154). Moreover, recent advances in social epigenetics demonstrate that "historical trauma" – an "exceptional form of social adversity, defined as being destructive, collective, cumulative" – can be transmitted to anterior generations (Dubois and Guaspare 2020, 146), manifesting in factors such as: "Marginalisation, disadvantage, intergenerational trauma, discrimination, family and community breakdown, unemployment and poor educational attainment" (Shepherd et al. 2017, 3). Combined, these conditions can contribute to poor health and wellbeing outcomes including accidents and situational afflictions. Empirical research suggests that the extreme over-representation of First Nations Australians in prison is associated with brain damage or injuries, with causes ranging from foetal alcohol spectrum disorder, to drug and alcohol use, to accidents and violence (SALRI 2018, 106). These factors all lead to a heightened likelihood of interaction with criminal justice due to difficulties in regulating behaviours, impaired decision making, poor communication, poor understanding of the law and immaturity (Shepherd et al. 2017, 2).

Given the nature of Australian settler-colonialism including systematic sexual violence and the continuing violations of 'historical trauma' among First Peoples, it is reasonable to surmise that an 'ordinary' Australian provoked in the circumstances of *Lindsay* might have 'lost it' for reasons different than Sun Sun's, if at all. If the ordinary Australian is indeed homophobic then the role of the common law in shaping that prejudice warrants our attention.

The Objective Limb of Provocation: Ordinary Homophobia

The common law was imposed on First Nations in SA by way of the *Colonisation Act 1834*[42] at a time when First Peoples understood themselves as co existing

41 [2007] 98 SASR 136.
42 *South Australia Act 1834*.

with Aboriginal lore (law), rather than being governed by it: A legal culture that Tanganekald/Meintangk woman, Professor Irene Watson, describes as when "our laws [were] lived as a way of life" (2002, 255). The prohibition on men's homosexual sex, punishable by death, was imported from Great Britain in the *Offences Against the Person Act 1828* replacing the *Buggery Act 1533*: "every person convicted of the abominable crime… shall suffer death as a felon" (s.15). In the 1830s, just as English courts were developing the "ordinary person" test (Blore 2018, 160), homosexuality among Australian prisoners was a key concern of governments in colonies where European men outnumbered European women by ratios of five to one and the "horrors of transportation" were understood to include sodomy practised with men and boys (Evans and Thorpe 1998, 18 and 21) including Indigenous men and boys (Blore 2018, 176). In 1838 the UK Select Committee Molesworth Report on transportation reported that the colonial capital of Sydney was dominated by "drunkenness and shameless profligacy" among convicts and free settlers alike who, acknowledging "no law, either human or divine," had created a "Sodom and Gomorrah" in the antipodes (Peart 2019, 266). Unique European-Australian hegemonic masculinities were forged in the context of Frontier Wars and convict uprisings, elevating homophobia to accompany entrenched homosexual practices in an unnaturally male-dominated world where homosocial domination was constituted in part by the ostentatious "repudiation of erotic bonds among men" (Sedgwick in Warner 1993, xiv).

In the 20th century, SA appreciated relatively early the homophobic power of law when compared to other states. The prompt for the country's first homosexual decriminalisation Act was the murder of 41-year-old legal academic Dr George Duncan, killed at a gay beat when he was bashed and thrown into a river with his lover in 1972. During the period of Duncan's inquest, a bill was put to the SA parliament to decriminalise gay sex because it was understood even by conservative politicians that law was the primary hegemonic instrument of homophobia. No one was ever convicted of Duncan's murder, and it took until 1975 for the *Criminal Law (Sexual Offences) Act*[43] to become law. For some time gay hate killings remained widespread in SA, with most unsolved today (Whittaker 2016). The LGBTIQ+ community had been demanding repeal of HAD since at least 1993 when hundreds of people staged a public protest against an acquittal for the brutal bashing of a gay man with an iron bar at a beat (OutRage 1993, 2). Incredibly, it was only *Lindsay* that prompted a political response, 32 years later.

Michael Lindsay's lethal attack, committed in response to a white man repeatedly offering him money for sex, was perpetrated in the fermented context of enduring homophobia in contemporary Australia and widespread racialised sexual narratives about Aboriginal men as both "objects of fetish" and "disposable resources," (Blore 2018, 169). It was perpetrated in a country

43 *Criminal Law (Sexual Offences) Amendment Act* (No 66 of 1975) (SA).

where all men engaged in sex work are stigmatised and suspected of performing "'recruitment' into homosexuality which has has been conflated with child sexual abuse of youth" (Sullivan 2021, 53); where Aboriginal sex workers obscure their racial identities which they know are under-valued; and where some First Nations communities minimise the sexual diversity among themselves "by the force of social and cultural taboos" imposed by the colonial order (Sullivan 2021, 5). Hence, whereas the SA Supreme Court in *Lindsay* instructed the jury to employ a measure of cognitive agility and "put themselves in the appellant's position" with very little context, the High Court argued his was an *intractable* position shaped by sexual exploitation and other characteristics of settler-colonialism unique to his subject status as an Aboriginal man.

The SALRI Review

Reform of provocation had been floated in SA since Lindsay's first trial in 2013 when the government initiated a Select Committee that was unable to agree on reform (Blore 2018, 180). The SALRI was then commissioned to review all aspects of provocation in a two-part report published in 2017 and 2018: *The Provoking Operation of Provocation* (the report). The report rejected the High Court's interpretation of the role of "anguish and loathing" in *Lindsay* and characterised HAD in terms of 17th-century common law ideas about 'male honour': HAD involves a man feeling "so *affronted* and provoked that they lost their self-control and killed the other person in response" (SALRI 2017, 29 emphasis added). Characterising HAD in these terms supported SALRI's positioning of it as necessarily out of step with contemporary Australia, which has no reason for such affront:

> By demonstrating that the homosexual advance defence is a product of certain past cultural values and attitudes, the corollary is that if those values and attitudes have changed, the criminal law too should evolve to reflect modern (and very different) values and attitudes, especially to acceptance of LGBTIQ issues.
>
> (2017, 29)

While the SALRI received many submissions supporting the abolition of HAD, Aboriginal Legal Services had been cautioning against reform of provocation since testifying to the Select Committee, because of the "risk of accentuating the disproportionate impact of the criminal justice system on Indigenous Australians" in a jurisdiction that mandates life sentences for murder (Blore 2018, 180[44]). The Aboriginal Legal Rights Movement (ALRM) requested that

44 For a thoughtful proposal about the intersection of provocation and mandatory life sentences see Hemming 2010.

a category of "extreme provocation" be retained, like in NSW; consideration be given to domestic violence victims; and, separately, that consideration be given to

> frontal lobe damage – cases where persons have lost, as it were, their emotional intelligence and their ability to plan and deal rationally with the consequences of their actions or other people's actions and where their ability to reason appropriately is compromised by an acquired brain injury. This is of particular concern to the Aboriginal Legal Rights Movement because, regrettably, we have many cases before the criminal courts of persons who appear to have suffered from the effects of Foetal Alcohol Spectrum Disorder and the effects of petrol sniffing.
> (Legislative Review Committee 2017, 60)

The ALRM also explicitly warned against overturning *Lindsay* in any respect:

> [We] would never recommend the abolition of any judicial recognition of the particular circumstances of Aboriginal people. We have to say that—I think it was Justice Nettle; I could be wrong on that—the decision of the High Court certainly referred to the significance of Aboriginal identity in relation to the subjective aspects of the law of provocation. We would certainly oppose the abolition or the removal of anything that revolved around the acknowledgement of the significance of Aboriginal identity.
> (Legislative Review Committee 2017, 61)

When similar arguments were raised with the SALRI, they were mostly relegated to a footnote of the 347-page report. Accepting that provocation was problematic, the ALRM submitted that, at the very least, there need to be ways of recognising reduced culpability in cases of cognitive impairment, such as in the partial defence of diminished responsibility, which is the law in many jurisdictions, but not in SA (SALRI 2017, 106). In response, the report footnoted substantial evidence about cognitive impairment among First Nations Australians and its relationship to incarceration (2018, 106) but concluded that diminished responsibility would be "problematic and inappropriate" to introduce in SA (2018, 107). Michael Lindsay's Aboriginality, on which the High Court judgment turned, was mentioned once in the body of the report and twice in one footnote (2017, 32 and 34). Perhaps most directly revealing of the SALRI's thinking was its characterisation of HAD as concerning only *anger*. It recommended that (SALRI 2017, 97 emphasis added):

> The homosexual advance aspect of the provocation defence should be removed. Its continued existence tends to indirectly legitimise and sanction lethal violence towards people demonstrating homosexual behaviour. In this regard, it is contrary to South Australia's obligations under both

> state and Commonwealth legislation not to discriminate on the basis of sexual orientation, gender and gender identity. There is an obvious need for legislative reform of the current South Australian law of provocation to ensure that it does not discriminate on the grounds of sexual orientation. It is fundamental that the law should operate in a fair and non-discriminatory manner. Also, as a basic issue of policy, the law should not accept that in the 21st century, a person might lose self-control and kill someone. '*Angry responses resulting in homicide are completely unacceptable to the community in the 21st century.*'
>
> (Citing Hemming, discussing provocation more broadly, 2010)

While the SALRI's recommendation to finally abolish HAD in SA was commendable and long overdue, it is arguable that its justification as presented in the report unnecessarily skirted the confronting ruling of the High Court in *Lindsay*. The Court had determined that what was at stake in the case was something different to or greater than anger, that it involved a lethal mix of homophobia and racism in the context of sexualised intergenerational trauma as experienced by First Nations men. Given the extraordinary legal incoherence of HAD justified by archaic, incoherent ideas about 'loss of self-control,' and the history of provocation as a gendered, homophobic judicial response to capital punishment, outlawed in Australia in the 1970s, there are numerous arguments to be made for the abolition or reform of both defences in today's society. There are arguments that need not rely on the simplification of what are complex, perhaps unknowable depths of the human psyche and its prompts to unacceptable violence. To recognise the complexity presented in *Lindsay* is not to excuse unlawful killing or to deny the agency of First Nations men. It is to be open to consideration of the diversity of uncomfortable truths, legal and social, that inform contemporary Australia. Alternatively, marginalising confronting truths in service of elevating others for political ends performs an epistemic injustice to both the victim and the perpetrator of this horrendous crime. The injustice is that the complexity of each of their stories risks being diminished if not forgotten in the public record. Such a political elision warrants extra scrutiny in a country such as Australia, which is already vulnerable to the political erasure of colonial and colonial-inspired abuses (Wilson 1997).

Conclusion

The *Statutes Amendment (Abolition of Provocation and Related Matters) Act 2020* (SA) was introduced to parliament as a vital measure representative of a community that no longer tolerates the homophobia of HAD, and which understands the complicated dynamics of family violence that should be considered in relevant trials of unlawful killing. The question of unsolved gay hate killings has received less political attention despite pressure to reinvestigate George Duncan's killing amid persistent rumours it involved the police. In other states, foremost NSW, victims' families and communities have recently forced governments to reckon with potentially hundreds of unsolved gay hate killings from the 1970s to the 1990s that might implicate police in homophobic cover-ups if not the perpetration of crime (Tomsen and Kirchengast 2019). SA has been almost entirely resistant to this movement for historical justice (Whittaker 2016). When abolishing HAD and provocation, the SA government promoted a whiggish narrative situating the state-sponsored violence of homophobia in the past: a past to which it is no longer answerable. As epigenetics and social theories demonstrate, however, for some groups more than others the past is not so easily escaped.

SA is one of three Australian jurisdictions to retain mandatory life sentences for murder in direct contradiction of findings of the United Nations Committee Against Torture, the Australian Law Reform Commission and other authorities that mandatory sentencing is discriminatory against First Nations Peoples and that, according to the National Aboriginal and Torres Strait Islander Legal Services, it particularly fails to "deter persons with mental impairment, alcohol or drug dependency or persons who are economically or socially disadvantaged" (in ALRC 2018). For so long as SA maintains this policy it will prove politically expedient for the government to diminish structural analyses of the violent behaviours of First Nations men in favour of highlighting individualistic emotional motivations centred on *anger*, despite a paucity of legal, psychological or medical evidence to support this interpretation in the context of HAD. The modernising law reform project underway in SA, including the abolition of HAD, will perhaps only be politically persuasive when attention is also paid to reconciling the past and present violence and discrimination enforced and authorised *by the state* against both LGBTIQ+ and First Nations communities since the time of colonial rule.

References

Akerman, Tessa. 2013. "Family of Murder Victim Andrew Negre Tells Supreme Court of Their Loss Ahead of Sentencing." *The Advertiser*, September 11.

Albion Centre. 2012. *A HIV/AIDS Timeline*. Accessed July 15, 2021. https://www.acon.org.au/wp-content/uploads/2015/04/History_of_HIV_5th-Edition.pdf.

Alexander, Harriet. 2012. "Kill Case Relied on Provocation." *Sydney Morning Herald*, October 19.

Australian Bureau of Statistics (ABS). 2021. *Corrective Services, Australia*. March. Accessed 15 July 2021. https://www.abs.gov.au/statistics/people/crime-and-justice/corrective-services-australia/latest-release.

Australian Law Reform Commission (ALRC). 2018. *Pathways to Justice. Inquiry into the Incarceration Rate of Aboriginal and Torres Strait Islander Peoples* (ALRC Report 133). Accessed 15 July 2021. https://www.alrc.gov.au/publication/pathways-to-justice-inquiry-into-the-incarceration-rate-of-aboriginal-and-torres-strait-islander-peoples-alrc-report-133/.

Behrendt, Larissa. 2000. "Consent in a (Neo)Colonial Society: Aboriginal Women as Sexual and Legal 'Other'." *Australian Feminist Studies* 15 (33): 353–367.

Blore, Kent. 2018. "*Lindsay v The Queen*: Homicide and the Ordinary Person at the Juncture of Race and Sexuality." *Adelaide Law Review* 39 (1): 159–201.

Dayman, Isabel. 2020. "South Australia Becomes Final State to Abolish 'Gay Panic' Murder Defence." *ABC News*, December 1. Accessed July 15, 2021. https://www.abc.net.au/news/2020-12-01/gay-panic-defence-abolished-by-sa-parliament/12940296.

De Pasquale, Santo. 2002. "Provocation and the Homosexual Advance Defence: The Deployment of Culture as a Defence Strategy." *Melbourne University Law Review* 26 (1): 110–143.

Douglas, Heather. 2006. "Assimilation and Authenticity: The 'Ordinary Aboriginal Person' and the Provocation Defence." *Adelaide Law Review* 27 (2): 199–226.

Dubois, Michel, and Catherine Guaspare. 2020. "From Cellular Memory to the Memory of Trauma: Social Epigenetics and Its Public Circulation." *Social Science Information* 59 (1): 144–183.

Evans, Raymond, and Bill Thorpe. 1998. "Commanding Men: Masculinities and the Convict System." *Journal of Australian Studies* 22 (56): 17–34.

Hemming, Andrew. 2010. "Provocation: A Totally Flawed Defence that has no Place in Australian Criminal Law Irrespective of Sentencing Regime". *University of Western Sydney Law Review* 14 (1): 1–44.

Howe, Adrian. 1997. "More Folk Provoke Their Own Demise: Homophobic Violence and Sexed Excuses - Rejoining the Provocation Law Debate, Courtesy of the Homosexual Advance Defence." *The Sydney Law Review* 19 (3): 336–365.

Legislative Review Committee. 2017. *Inquiry into the Partial Defence of Provocation*. Hansard, August 9.

Mekawi, Yara, Sierra Carter, Brittney Brown, Ana Martinez de Andino, Negar Fani, Vasiliki Michopoulos, and Abigail Powers. 2021. "Interpersonal Trauma and Posttraumatic Stress Disorder Among Black Women: Does Racial Discrimination Matter?" *Journal of Trauma & Dissociation* 22 (2): 154–169.

Moran, Leslie. 2002. *The Homosexual(ity) of Law*. London and New York: Routledge.

Morgan, Wayne. 1993. "Identifying Evil for What it is: Tasmania, Sexual Perversity and the United Nations." *Melbourne University Law Review* 19: 740–757.

OutRage. 1993. "Hundreds Protest Bashing Acquittal." *OutRage* 177: 2.

Peart, Mark. 2019. "Sodom Island: Pandemonium and the Botany Bay of Botany Bay." *Journal of the History of Sexuality* 28 (2): 263–296.

Puar, Jasbir. 2018. *Terrorist Assemblages*. Durham and London: Duke University Press.

Shepherd, Stephane, James Ogloff, Yin Paradies, and Jeffrey Pfeifer. 2017. "Aboriginal Prisoners with Cognitive Impairment: Is This the Highest Risk Group?" In *Trends and Issues in Crime and Criminal Justice*. October 23. Canberra: Australian Institute of Criminology. Accessed July 15 2021. https://www.aic.gov.au/publications/tandi/tandi536.

Sorial, Sarah. 2019. "Anger, Provocation and Loss of Self-Control: What Does 'Losing It' Really Mean?" *Criminal Law and Philosophy* 13 (2): 247–269.

South Australian Law Reform Institute (SALRI). 2017. *The Provoking Operation of Provocation: Stage 1*. Accessed July 15, 2021. https://law.adelaide.edu.au/system/files/media/documents/2019-01/provocation_stage_1_report.pdf.

South Australian Law Reform Institute (SALRI). 2018. *The Provoking Operation of Provocation: Stage 2*. Accessed July 15, 2021. https://law.adelaide.edu.au/system/files

/media/documents/2019-02/MASTER-VERSION-FINAL-with-Bibliography-070518.pdf.
Sullivan, Corrinne. 2018. "Indigenous Australian Women's Colonial Sexual Intimacies: Positioning Indigenous Women's Agency." *Culture, Health & Sexuality* 20 (4): 397–410.
Sullivan, Corrinne. 2021. "'Hot, Young, Buff': An Indigenous Australian Gay Male View of Sex Work." *Social Inclusion* 9 (2): 52–60.
Tomsen, Stephen, and Tyrone Kirchengast. 2019. "Victimhood, Truth and Criminal Justice Failure in Relation to Anti-Homosexual Violence and Killings in New South Wales." *Current Issues in Criminal Justice* 31 (2): 181–193.
Warner, Michael. 1993. *Fear of a Queer Planet: Queer Politics and Social Theory* Minneapolis: University of Minnesota Press.
Watson, Irene. 2002. "Buried Alive." *Law and Critique* 13 (3): 253–269.
Whittaker, Mark. 2016. *Out of Sight. The Untold Story of Adelaide's Gay Hate Murders.* Accessed July 15, 2021. https://www.sbs.com.au/topics/feature/out-sight-untold-story-adelaides-gay-hate-murders.
Wilson, Ronald. 1997. *Bringing Them Home: Report of the National Inquiry into the Separation of Aboriginal and Torres Strait Islander Children from Their Families.* Sydney: Human Rights and Equal Opportunity Commission.

Part Three

Reforming the Rape Trial

Chapter 7

Sexual History Evidence in Review

Stasis in Constant Change

Joanne Conaghan and Yvette Russell

Introduction

Sexual history evidence (hereafter 'SHE') is often cited as the clearest example that remains codified in law of the general wariness and distrust of claims of sexual violation made by women against men. As Katherine Angel puts it: "A woman's (presumed) desire – even just once, for one man – makes her vulnerable. … Once a woman is thought to have said yes to something, she can say no to nothing" (2021, 4). In this chapter, we explore the current state of law and policy in several similar jurisdictions that have sought to counter the association of SHE with the dire implications for women's sexuality against which Angel warns. We find that virtually every jurisdiction we consider is in the process of reviewing their existing regulatory framework and/or trialling new approaches. Moreover, while doctrinal and procedural structures may differ, reflecting the unique political, social, and historical realities in which they evolved, many of the problems, conceptual and practical, associated with the use of SHE, recur regardless of regulatory configuration. In the final section of the chapter, we draw together some common themes and reflect critically on the 'policy cycle' that drives so much legislative and policy movement in this area. We conclude with a call to resist the artificially imposed strictures of the policy cycle and return to the important and difficult work of reckoning with the underlying logic that continues to support the use and relevance of SHE in the rape trial.

Scanning the Juridic and Policy Landscape

We begin by reviewing the current juridic and policy landscape surrounding SHE in seven countries, encompassing six jurisdictions, namely England and Wales, Northern Ireland, the Republic of Ireland (ROI), Scotland, New Zealand and Canada.[1] These jurisdictions are comparable in that they are all

1 Space precludes us from including Australia and the United States in this review but see Conaghan and Russell (2023).

DOI: 10.4324/9781003379331-11

common law based, and each bears the legacy of a colonial connection to England and English law, albeit in different ways. Notwithstanding their distinct jurisdictional status, we consider England, Wales and Northern Ireland together as they share the same statutory framework in relation to SHE. Our aim is to present a 'snap-shot' of this fast-moving area at this current moment, highlighting new directions and initiatives, and distilling key themes and challenges.

England, Wales and Northern Ireland

In England and Wales, section 41 of the Youth Justice and Criminal Evidence Act 1999 (YJCEA) governs the introduction of evidence "about any sexual behaviour of the complainant." These provisions are mirrored exactly in the law of Northern Ireland in Articles 28 and 29 of the Criminal Evidence (Northern Ireland) Order 1999.[2] Section 41 establishes a general rule excluding SHE, whether relating to sexual behaviour with the defendant or third parties, subject to four exceptions. Even where these exceptions or "gateways" are met, leave to admit SHE cannot be given unless the court is satisfied that "a refusal ... might have the result of rendering unsafe a conclusion of the jury or ... the court on any relevant issue in the case" (s 41(2)(b)).

The first exception to the general rule is in section 41(3)(a) and permits evidence of sexual behaviour that relates to a relevant issue in the case which is "not an issue of consent." Under section 42(1)(a), "relevant issue in the case" means "any issue falling to be proved by the prosecution or defence in the trial of the accused." Therefore, section 41(3)(a) provides wide scope to admit SHE not relating to consent, but which otherwise satisfies the test of relevance. This might include evidence showing a complainant had a motive to lie[3] or supporting a defendant's claim that the complainant consented.[4] The second exception is in section 41(3)(b) and applies where the matter for which the evidence is sought *is* one of consent. In that circumstance, SHE may be adduced if it occurred *at or about the same time* as the sexual activity which is the subject matter of the charge. The vagueness of the temporal requirement in section 41(3)(b) invites interpretation. In *R v A (No 2)*,[5] which involved a legal challenge to section 41 on grounds of its alleged incompatibility with the defendant's right to a fair trial under Article 6 of the European Convention of Human Rights

2 For expediency we refer in the subsequent discussion only to the English and Welsh provisions.

3 Although see YJCEA 1999, section 41(4): "No evidence or question shall be regarded as relating to a relevant issue in the case if it appears to the court to be reasonable to assume that the purpose (or main purpose) for which it would be adduced or asked is to establish or elicit material for impugning the credibility of the complainant as a witness."

4 Section 42(1)(b) explicitly clarifies that belief in consent is not "an issue of consent" for purposes of section 41.

5 [2001] UKHL 25.

(ECHR), their Lordships agreed that sexual behaviour taking place one week prior to the disputed event fell outside the scope of "at or the same time," but otherwise diverged as to the precise scope of contemporaneity required.

The third exception in section 41(3)(c) we might call the 'similar fact' gateway, and applies, as with the second exception, where the matter for which the evidence is sought is one of consent, but "the sexual behaviour of the complainant to which the evidence or question relates is alleged to have been … so similar" to either: Any sexual behaviour of the complainant which took place *as part of the event* which is the subject matter of the charge; or, any other sexual behaviour of the complainant that took place *at or about the same time* as that event. Note again the reliance on vaguely worded temporal norms to set the limits of protection. There is also the additional question of the degree of similarity required to trigger this gateway. According to section 41(3)(c), the previous behaviour of the complainant must be "so similar … that the similarity cannot reasonably be explained as a coincidence." In *Evans* the Court of Appeal considered the operation of section 41(3)(c) in some detail, noting that its requirements were strict and compelled the defendant to "overcome [a] high hurdle of relevance and similarity."[6] At the same time, the Court cited with approval the comments of Lord Clyde in *R v A (No 2)* on the scope and meaning of section 41(3)(c) namely that: "It is only a similarity that is required, not an identity"[7] and that there was no need for the defendant to show that the conduct invoked was "rare or bizarre… so long as the particular conduct goes beyond the realm of what could reasonably be explained as a coincidence, it should suffice."[8]

The final exception to the rule of exclusion permits the defence to challenge any prosecution evidence about the complainant's sexual behaviour. Under sections 41(5) and (6) of the YJCEA, questioning by the defence must "go no further than is necessary to enable the evidence adduced by the prosecution to be rebutted or explained" and, as with the other exceptions, must "relate to a specific instance or instances of alleged sexual behaviour on the part of the complainant."

In 2019, the British Home Secretary, Lord Chancellor, and Attorney General, spurred on by a freefall in prosecution and conviction rates for sexual offences across England and Wales, made a joint commitment to "understand[ing] why we are letting down rape victims and … to build the confidence of victims to come forward and report these horrendous crimes" (MOJ 2021: Ministers' Foreword). The subsequent publication of the *End-to-End Rape Review Report on Findings and Actions* in June 2021 announced a long list of commitments to change at every point in the criminal justice response to sexual violence (MOJ

6 *R v Evans* [2016] EWCA Crim 452, at 48.
7 L Clyde in *R v A (No. 2)* [2001] UKHL 25, at 135.
8 Ibid.

2021). Linked to the *End-to-End Review*, the Law Commission of England and Wales was tasked with "examin[ing] law, guidance and practice relating to the use of evidence in prosecutions of serious sexual offences and consider the need for reform" (MOJ 2021, 114). This project was launched at the end of 2021 and a consultation paper was expected towards the end of 2022.[9] The project includes a commitment to reviewing the provisions restricting the use of sexual history evidence, alongside review of the rules governing the use of a complainant's medical and counselling records at trial, special measures for vulnerable witnesses, and strategies to counter the effect of rape myths in courtroom proceedings.

Meanwhile, Northern Irish law and procedure on sexual offences has also been reviewed in the aftermath of the 'rugby rape trial' in 2018.[10] The *Gillen Report into the Law and Procedures in Serious Sexual Offences in Northern Ireland* was published in 2019, generating a range of recommendations including limiting public access to rape trials (Recommendation 2), introducing pre-recorded cross-examination (Recommendation 3), "a measure" of publicly funded legal representation for rape victims (Recommendation 4) and the promotion of a "more robust judicial attitude and case management approach to prevent improper cross-examination about previous sexual history" (Recommendation 7).

During the review, Gillen and his team considered the myriad problems with the operation and implementation of SHE provisions in arts. 28–30 of the Criminal Evidence (Northern Ireland) Order 1999 (Gillen 2019, ch 8). They noted that "across the globe, research indicates that the problem is not so much the statutory regime adopted but the failure of the judiciary to apply the provisions correctly" (Gillen 2019, at 8.22). Having considered the relevant law and secondary literature in England, Wales and Northern Ireland, Gillen concluded that while tightening legal tests of relevance and giving greater weight to a complainant's privacy rights were important, the law in practice was where change was most required. The Review emphasised the need to prioritise the enforcement of procedural rules along with rigorous and continual training of judges and counsel. Gillen also recommended the introduction of independent legal representation (ILR),[11] *inter alia*, to support complainants when applications to introduce SHE were heard (Gillen 2019, ch 8).

9 'Law Commission to review the trial process for sexual offences' www.lawcom.gov.uk/law-commission-to-review-the-trial-process-for-sexual-offences/. Accessed August 24, 2022.

10 See generally, Killean, Dowds and McAlinden (2021).

11 Gillen (2019, ch 5) accepts the case for publicly-funded legal representation for complainants in serious sexual offences cases to oppose cross-examination in relation to previous sexual history or disclosure of a claimant's personal medical records, as well as from first report up to the commencement of (but not during) the trial, to explain the complexities of, and the legal developments occurring in, the legal process.

The use of ILR in sexual offence trials in adversarial systems is often held up as a way in which many of the ills associated with the prosecution of sexual offences may be cured (Smith and Daly 2020). As we shall see, limited access to ILR is available to complainants in the ROI, and there are examples of similar arrangements in other common law countries including Canada, Australia and the United States (Killean 2021). At the same time, as Killean among others points out, the formal logic of the adversarial trial as a two-sided contest between the state and the accused presents structural and ideological obstacles to the introduction of ILR for rape complainants whose standing in criminal trials is merely that of a witness. In inquisitorial systems, by contrast, the idea that victims have an independent interest in or, indeed, right to participate in criminal proceedings, is more easily accommodated (Killean 2021, 179–181).

In the aftermath of Gillen, Mary Iliadis and colleagues have revisited the arguments for using ILRs in sexual offence trials, arguing that the Gillen proposals do not go far enough (Iliadis et al. 2021, 255–257). Challenging the prevailing notion that ILR for complainants poses an inherent threat to defendants' right to a fair trial, the authors propose a "Gillen-plus framework" which would extend ILR beyond the parameters recommended by Gillen albeit without according formal party status to complainants (Iliadis et al. 2021, 267). Central to this argument is an insistence that complainants' rights and interests do not neatly align with the prosecution stance, particularly in relation to matters of privacy and, to some extent too, the trauma of secondary victimisation. These concerns, Iliadis et al. argue, make the case for ILR throughout the trial process albeit "confined to specific matters of evidence and procedure that touch on the interests and rights of complainants" (ibid):

> Representatives should be able to protect complainants' rights and interests by objecting to specific questions, especially in light of research evidence indicating that advocacy practice often departs from formal evidential and procedural rules, as well as from specific judicial instructions/guidance issued in the pre-trial phase.
>
> (Iliadis et al. 2021, 268)

In response to Gillen, the Northern Ireland Department of Justice released an *Implementation Plan* in June 2020 (NIDJ 2020). Although identifying (pre-trial) ILR as a 'strategic priority,' the plan did not follow through with concrete proposals other than to recommend a limited pilot study, the results of which are yet to emerge.[12]

12 Victim Support in Northern Ireland are currently piloting ILR in respect of a sample of sexual offence cases. Complainants are entitled to advice and information from report, and to specific advice and advocacy on disclosure of personal information, where that is requested as part of the

Republic of Ireland

The ROI is of particular interest as an early pioneer of ILR for complainants in relation to applications by defence counsel to introduce sexual history evidence. The relevant law governing SHE is in section 3 of the Criminal Law (Rape) Act 1981. Prior to the 1981 Act, the complainant's sexual past was freely admissible. The defence had unlimited powers to question complainants about their past sexual experience, whether with the defendant or third parties[13] (Leahy and Fitzgerald O'Reilly 2018, 137–138). Under section 3(1), evidence about the sexual experience of the rape[14] complainant with any person (other than the encounter to which the charge relates) is not to be admitted except with leave of the trial judge. Notice of an intention to make an application must be given to the prosecution by, or on behalf of, the accused at the earliest available opportunity, namely "before, or as soon as practicable after, the commencement of the trial."[15] The Courts have indicated a willingness to consider late applications, including after the commencement of the trial, where it is in the interests of justice to do so.[16]

Section 3(2)(a) prescribes that the judge cannot give leave unless the defence makes an application to the judge in the absence of the jury. Moreover, leave shall only be given if the court is satisfied that the exclusion of the evidence would be unfair to the defendant (section 3(2)(b)). The test of unfairness is a typical example of statutory linguistic contortion: Leave shall only be given

> if the judge is satisfied, on the assumption that if the evidence or question was not allowed the jury might reasonably be satisfied beyond reasonable doubt that the accused person is guilty, the effect of allowing the evidence or question might reasonably be that they would not be so satisfied.
>
> (section 3(2)(b))

---

investigative phase of a case, and where the defence applies for the introduction of SHE in the trial. See www.justice-ni.gov.uk/news/justice-minister-launches-scheme-provide-free-legal-advice-victims-sexual-offences; https://www.victimsupportni.com/help-for-victims/solas/. Accessed August 24, 2022.

13 The 1981 statute, as originally enacted, was modelled on the SHE provisions in the English Sexual Offences (Amendment) Act 1976 and, as with that Act, only covered sexual experience with persons other than the accused. The scope of protection was later expanded in the Criminal Law (Rape) Amendment Act 1990 to cover sexual experience with the defendant.

14 Section 3 applies to a range of sexual offences including rape, aggravated sexual assault, sexual assault, and associated offences such as attempts to commit these offences. See generally Leahy and Fitzgerald O'Reilly (2018, 139).

15 CL(R)A 1981 (IRE) section 4A2.

16 *People (DPP) v Walsh*, extempore, Court of Criminal Appeal, July 18, 2008.

Case law suggests that the threshold applied in section 3(2)(b) is a "high one, though … not an impossible or unattainable one."[17]

The granting of leave does not give defence lawyers *carte blanche* to ask any questions they like about the victim's sexual experience. Section 3(3) empowers the judge to disallow a question if it is not thought to be in accordance with the leave given. In *People (DPP) v GK*, the Court was clear that section 3 should be interpreted restrictively and that, in general, sexual history evidence should be more likely excluded than admitted.[18] The Court also stated that where questioning is allowed, it must be confined to what is strictly necessary and should never be used as a form of character assassination.[19]

According to section 4A of the Criminal Law (Rape) Act 1981 (amended in 2001), victims in certain sexual offence trials are entitled to ILR in respect of any application made to question them about past sexual experience. Section 28(5A) of the Civil Legal Aid Act 1995 (amended in 2001) requires legal aid to be provided to complainants to fund this legal representation.

The Irish legislation differs from the law in England, Wales and Northern Ireland in adopting a discretion-based approach rather than prescribing formal gateways through which the evidence in question must pass. Subject to the test of unfairness in section 3(3), the discretion is unrestricted, and several feminist commentators have criticised its breadth, arguing that it has led to an alarmingly high rate of admission of SHE in sexual offence trials (Leahy 2014; Rape Crisis Network of Ireland 2009). As Leahy and Fitzgerald O'Reilly point out, the only clear requirements are that the application for leave must take place in the absence of a jury and that the complainant is entitled to be present and have ILR for purposes of the application (2018, 145).[20]

While judicial guidance suggests that section 3 should be restrictively applied,[21] research suggests that, in practice, a broad approach to the admission of evidence is adopted (Rape Crisis Network of Ireland 2012, 8; Leahy and Fitzgerald O'Reilly 2018, 146–147). Further, the lack of a definition of "sexual experience" in the Act means the boundaries of what comes within the terms of the statute (and therefore qualifies for protection) remain unclear. For example, the statute provides no guidance as to the admissibility of "secondary"

17 *People (DPP) v F.H.* [2019] IECA 30, at 28.

18 [2007] 2 IR 92, 103–104.

19 Ibid. Section 21 of the Criminal Justice (Victims of Crimes) Act 2017 (IRE) provides additional protection to crime victims questioned in criminal proceedings by permitting the court to give directions as to the questions asked in cross-examination where they relate to the private life of the victim. These provisions apply to all criminal proceedings (not just sexual offences) and enshrine the concept of 'repeat/secondary victimisation' in legislation.

20 A further limitation (which applies to England and Wales also) is that the provisions apply only to SHE sought to be introduced by the defence. As Leahy and Fitzgerald (2018, 143–144) argue, the complainant can equally be distressed by the (often inadvertent) references to her sexual experience by prosecuting counsel, at the same time inviting the introduction of rebuttal by the defence.

21 See *GK*, supra n 18.

evidence of sexual experience such as that a complainant has had an abortion or taken oral contraceptives (Leahy and Fitzgerald O'Reilly 2018, 144). In her recent report on the *Realities of Rape Trials in Ireland*, Leahy (2021, 28–29) recommends that the definition of "sexual experience" be statutorily clarified.

In 2020, prompted by widespread public concern about the treatment of sexual offence victims, the Irish Minister for Justice and Equality constituted a working group tasked with "examin[ing] certain key aspects of the criminal justice process in so far as it relates to vulnerable witnesses, and to identify ways in which the treatment of such witnesses might be improved" (O'Malley 2020, 8). With respect to the law governing the introduction of SHE, the group concluding that the statutory scheme in section 3 struck "a fair balance between protecting the rights of accused persons and those of victims in sexual offence trials" (O'Malley 2020, 66). Consequently, they did not recommend any changes to the core legislative provisions. The group did independently recommend the introduction of preliminary hearings to reduce delays and allow matters such as section 3 applications to be considered at a much earlier stage (O'Malley 2020, ch 5).

In respect of ILR specifically, O'Malley recommended the extension of ILR to encompass a broader range of sexual offences, and the enhancement of the ILR's role in monitoring the cross-examination of sexual offence complainants. They proposed that ILRs should be allowed to object to a question, or at least, submit to the trial judge that a particular question did not come within the terms of the leave granted (O'Malley 2020, 69). As things stand, the complainant is only entitled to legal representation in the section 3 hearing and not in relation to other aspects of the trial process such as cross-examination, where, as has been noted, much depends on the willingness of the judge to enforce the terms of leave granted.

Feminists remains unconvinced that ILR has fulfilled its undertaking to improve rape victims' experience of the legal process. Iliadis (2020) highlights several issues including the submission of late applications for SHE admission and the unduly circumscribed role of the ILR. Other studies, in particular Leahy (2021), also highlight the tendency to appoint inexperienced junior counsel as ILRs, a problem exacerbated by late notice of applications to the Legal Aid Board (and therefore of the need to appoint a representative). As Iliadis concludes, ILR is only as effective as the regulatory system in which it operates allows, meaning that in practice, victims often remain "equally as vulnerable as they would be if the [SHE] legislation did not exist" (Iliadis 2020, 428). Indeed, she goes onto speculate that "the implementation of ILR has had a counter effect of retaining sexual history evidence in trials" (429).

Scotland

Sections 274 and 275 of the Criminal Procedure (Scotland) Act 1995 (CP(S)A) govern the law of SHE in Scotland, which was radically amended by the

Sexual Offences (Procedure and Evidence) (Scotland) Act 2002.[22] Sharon Cowan's excellent chapter in this volume gives a thorough explanation of their genealogy and operation which we will not repeat, save to say that the Scottish approach differs from that of England, Wales and Northern Ireland in combining regulation of evidence of a complainant's bad character and sexual history into the same regulatory framework.[23] Historically this makes some sense as the emergence of evidentiary rules around the use of a complainant's sexual history was partly driven by judicial concerns to protect complainants from unwarranted attacks on their character. However, concerns about the use of bad character evidence – whether relating to witnesses or the accused – extend well beyond the sphere of sexual offences and, in England and Wales, the interest in ensuring a defendant's right to a fair trial has led to a predominant doctrinal orientation with regulating evidence of a *defendant's* bad character, first through common law, and, since 2003, through a distinct statutory framework.[24]

Feminist analyses of the Scottish provisions draw attention to a dissonance between law in the books and law in action (Cowan 2020; Campbell and Cowan 2017). Early analysis of the current Scottish provisions found that, paradoxically, the 2002 amendments had led to an increase in applications for SHE to be admitted and a subsequent increase in the admission of this kind of evidence (Burman et al. 2007, 7; Burman 2009, 388). The requirement for detailed written applications to be submitted to the Court in section 275 appears to have stoked this phenomenon because the fulsome "scatter-gun approach" often employed by defence counsel has increased the likelihood that at least some of the questioning contemplated will be allowed (Burman 2009, 389). Burman's research is borne out by a more recent small-scale case study of section 275 applications in Scotland made between January and April 2016 showing an approval rate of up to 84% (Cowan 2020, 16). Another recurring criticism of the Scottish law relates to the balancing that courts must effectively undertake between complainers' rights to privacy and dignity and an accused's right to a fair trial. Research found that the balancing of these rights in applications under section 275 was usually weighed heavily in favour of defendants, increasing the likelihood that SHE will be admitted (Burman et al. 2007, 393).

A review of the management of sexual offence cases by the Lord Justice Clerk's Review Group in 2021 problematised the interpretation and application

22 Section 274 CP(S)A 1995 specifies the kind of evidence prohibited, including sexual history evidence; section 275 prescribes the circumstances in which section 274 prohibitions may be circumvented, establishing a staged approach requiring that (i) the evidence is specific and relevant, (ii) its probative value significantly outweighs any risk of prejudice to the administration of justice. See Cowan in this volume; Campbell and Cowan (2017).

23 For proposals to combine sexual history evidence and bad character evidence in sexual offences cases in the same regulatory framework in England and Wales, see Brewis and Jackson (2020).

24 Criminal Justice Act 2003 (CJA), sections 98–113.

of the rape shield provisions contained in sections 274 and 275, criticising their effectiveness and implementation in practice (LJCRG 2021, 44–46). The report argues in favour of specialised sexual offences courts where all judges, lawyers, clerks and other staff are appropriately, uniformly and specifically trained (LJCRG 2021, 46–47).[25] In addition, a Scottish government-funded empirical project is currently being undertaken, observing rape and attempted rape trials, and scrutinising the content of section 275 applications, to investigate how the rape shield legislation and associated procedures are understood and applied during court proceedings. *The Use of Sexual History, Bad Character and Private Data Evidence in Scottish Sexual Offences Trials*, conducted by Cowan, Keane and Munro was due to report in late 2022.

New Zealand

The law governing sexual offences in New Zealand has recently undergone major legislative change. The country's law on SHE was wholly governed by the common law until the Evidence (Amendment) Act 1977 provided the original 'rape shield' limiting the admission of private sexual evidence about rape complainants in proceedings concerning sexual offences. Section 44 of the Evidence Act 2006 currently governs SHE in New Zealand. Section 44A specifies the procedure that must be followed, including form and notice requirements, but which can be dispensed with by the judge in certain broadly drafted circumstances (section 44A(6)). These sections were replaced by new provisions in December 2021.

In its prior iteration, section 44 provided that evidence of a complainant's "sexual experience" with any person other than the defendant would be inadmissible, except by leave of the court. The court would not grant permission for SHE to be admitted unless it reached a "heightened relevance threshold" (NZLC 2019, at 3.2) which required a judge to find that "the evidence or question is of such direct relevance to facts in issue in the proceeding, or the issue of the appropriate sentence, that it would be contrary to the interests of justice to exclude it" (section 44(3)). No evidence relating to the complainant's reputation in sexual matters was admissible (section 44(2)). Evidence of the complainant's sexual experience with the defendant was not governed by section 44 and was admissible subject to the general rules governing the admissibility of relevant evidence.[26]

Case law governs the boundaries of "sexual experience" in section 44(1). In some circumstances the courts have held that evidence of a prior allegation of sexual offending by the complainant (against someone other than the

25 The introduction of specialist rape courts has also been mooted in England and Wales as a way of "clearing the backlog" of rape cases (HMIC et al. 2022, Rec 4).
26 See further Evidence Act 2006 (NZ) sections 7 and 8.

defendant) falls within the meaning of "sexual experience."[27] Sexual experience will not include general sexual knowledge,[28] nor sexual activity with another person just prior to the alleged offending.[29] Sexual experience is likely to include, for example, evidence as to a complainant's virginity (NZLC 2018, at 3.25) as well as (sexually explicit) text messages, even where no physical contact takes place.[30] New Zealand's Supreme Court have commented in judicial dicta that the section may need further legislative clarification, particularly as to whether what has been termed "sexual disposition" evidence – essentially evidences which goes to the complainant's sexual preferences or propensities rather than her actual experience or behaviour – comes within the scope of section 44.[31] The concern here, which feminist commentators have repeatedly raised, is that the narrow drafting and interpretation of "sexual experience" in section 44 has allowed evidence relating to the complainant's sexual disposition to sneak into the courtroom 'through the back door' without defence counsel having to apply for leave.

Elisabeth McDonald's extensive study of the use of SHE in trials of sexual offences in New Zealand found examples of cases in which evidence of sexual orientation, use or possession of contraceptives, possession of sex toys, and prior pregnancies were admitted in evidence without reference to section 44, but in a way that clearly implicated the complainant's sexual history (2020a, 131–160). McDonald argues that a lot of "sexualised behaviour" should be included within the regulatory ambit of section 44 (for example, evidence of a complainant kissing, flirting or cuddling) because it can have the same prejudicial impact on a jury as evidence of sexual intercourse (McDonald 2020a, 149). McDonald also argues that the "heightened relevance" requirement in section 44(3) – designed to ensure an "extra check" before SHE is admitted – is applied by the courts in an inconsistent manner and cannot be relied upon as a panacea to cure various other problems arising with SHE (2020a, 160–186).

The New Zealand Law Commission reviewed the Evidence Act 2006 in 2019 and considered the operation and implementation of section 44 in some detail, making several wide-ranging recommendations for reform (NZLC 2019). These included clarifying section 44 to ensure that sexual disposition evidence fell within the scope of protection. New Zealand's Labour Government responded to the Commission's report in September 2019, accepting many of

27 See *R v Morrice* [2008] NZCA 261.

28 *R v M* (2000) 18 CRNZ 368 (CA); *M v R* [2010] NZCA 620.

29 *Jones v R* [2018] NZCA 288. This is another example of the regulatory significance of temporality in SHE: An event which has just occurred is too immediate to constitute a separate 'experience.'

30 *R v Singh* [2015] NZCA 435.

31 *B (SC12/2013) v R* [2014] 1 NZLR 261, at 56.

its findings and undertaking to initiate reform of the relevant law.[32] The Sexual Violence Legislation Act 2021 passed into law on December 21, 2021.

Among other root and branch legislative reforms to the laws governing sexual violence in New Zealand, the Sexual Violence Legislation Act 2021 extends the protection conferred by section 44 to sexual experience with the defendant and clarifies that sexual disposition evidence falls within the scope of section 44 protection.[33] Interestingly, following a Law Commission recommendation, evidence seeking to establish 'the mere fact' that the complainant and defendant had prior sexual experience (as opposed to the nature or details of that experience) is explicitly excluded from the scope of section 44. The Law Commission concluded that this was evidence of a "background or factual nature" which did not need to meet the heightened test of relevance prescribed by section 44 (NZLC 2019, 3.52).

Some commentators remain concerned that the Act does not fully address the problems to which sexual history evidence give rise, and, moreover, that the gateways for the admission of SHE will continue to be exploited (see further McDonald 2020b). Such objections notwithstanding, these newly enacted provisions represent some of the most restrictive SHE laws in the jurisdictions we consider.

Canada

Canada's first rape shield statute was passed in 1976, prior to which the use of SHE was governed by the common law. The current law is found in sections 276 and 277 of the Canadian Criminal Code (RSC 1985). Those provisions have undergone several rounds of reform since they became law in 1983. Under section 276, as it was passed, admission of evidence of 'sexual activity' (with anyone other than the defendant) was prohibited unless it fell within one of three exceptions: (a) rebuttal evidence; (b) evidence going to identity; or (c) evidence relating to consent to sexual activity on the same occasion as the trial incident. Section 277 excluded evidence of sexual reputation for the purpose of challenging or supporting the complainant's credibility.

In 1992, in the *Seaboyer*[34] case, the Canadian Supreme Court struck down section 276[35] as an unconstitutional infringement on defendants' liberty and fair trial rights because it failed to provide sufficient scope for judicial determination of the relevance and probity of the evidence sought to be submitted. In response to the decision, Bill C-49 was passed, re-enacting section 276,

32 See further: 'Sexual Violence Legislation Bill' www.parliament.nz/en/pb/bills-and-laws/bills-proposed-laws/document/BILL_93010/sexual-violence-legislation-bill. Accessed August 24, 2022.

33 See sections 4(a) and 4(b) Evidence Act 2006.

34 *Seaboyer v R, Attorney General of Canada and others intervening; Gayme v Same* [1993] 1 LRC 465.

35 Section 277 (excluding evidence of the complainant's sexual reputation) was held to be compatible with the defendant's constitutional rights.

albeit in a "weakened form" (Gotell 2006, 753). The new section 276 has been expanded to regulate the admissibility of all sexual activity, including between the complainant and the accused. Moreover, section 276(1), drawing on judicial guidelines articulated in *Seaboyer*, categorically excludes evidence of prior sexual history where its relevance is premised on one or both of the 'twin myths,' that is, to support an inference that the complainant, by virtue of her prior sexual history, is more likely to have consented to the sexual activity which forms the subject matter of the charge, and/or is less worthy of belief. Section 276(2) creates a presumption of inadmissibility unless the evidence relates to a specific instance of sexual activity, is relevant to the issue at trial, and is of "significant probative value" not outweighed by its prejudicial effect. Section 276(3) then requires the judge to perform a complex balancing act taking account of a prescribed list of factors including the defendant's right to make a full defence (section 276(3)(a)) and the potential prejudice to the complainant's personal dignity and right of privacy (section 276(3)(f)) to determine the admissibility of sexual history evidence.[36] Applications for the admission of SHE must also be heard *in camera*.

In this revised incarnation, section 276 adopts a two-stage approach to the admission of sexual history evidence, first positing a presumption of inadmissibility, followed by the structured exercise of judicial discretion. It is an approach that has met with wide approval across the common law world: In her evaluation of the Irish rape shield framework, Leahy (2014) identifies it as best practice while Gillen (2019) commends the Canadian model in his discussion of the operation of the legislative provisions governing the admissibility of SHE in Northern Ireland. A perceived strength of the Canadian approach is that it avoids the rigidity of the gateways approach adopted in England and Wales, retaining but structuring judicial discretion to direct and limit the application of the regulatory framework. An additional strength is the range of factors judges are directed to take into account, some of which extend beyond the direct interests of either the complainant or defendant. As Gotell (2006, 755) observes:

> These provisions were clearly intended to compel judges to engage in complex balancing exercise that extends beyond a narrow contest between the 'privacy' of the individual complainant and the legal rights claims of individual defendants... in effect, contemplate[ing] a contextual analysis of sexual history ... applications at trial.

36 There are eight factors listed in total, including section 276(3)(h): "any other factor that the judge ... considers relevant."

And yet, in their operationalisation, this "ideal framework" has disappointed, with feminist critics arguing that the rape shield has effectively been "rendered permeable through judicial interpretation" (Gotell 2006, 746). This is partly a failure of proper implementation – Gotell points to the continued high rates of admissibility of SHE after the 1990s reforms (2006, 757). More recently, Elaine Craig (2016), in her critical study of the role of the Canadian legal profession in sexual offences trials, argues that a general lack of understanding among trial judges of how section 276 is supposed to work, accompanied by a continued reliance on rape myths in decision making, has meant that SHE that should rightfully be excluded is often admitted in practice. However, as Gotell, in particular stresses, it is not just a problem of implementation. A stance of judicial resistance to "feminist-inspired reforms" (2006, 758) has provoked judges to carve out a series of narrow exceptions to the application of section 276, thereby avoiding the requirement to "balance" as prescribed by section 276(3).[37]

In 2018, Bill C-51 reformed section 276 further, introducing several new clauses into the statutory schema around SHE. For example, section 278.94(2) allows a complainant to appear and make submissions at rape shielding proceedings/admissibility hearings. Section 278.94(3), for the first time, also allows any participating complainants to be represented by counsel in such proceedings. Complainants must be informed by a judge of this right as soon as possible.[38] Danielle McNabb and Dennis Baker (2021) argue that, in amending the rape shield law, the disproportionate focus of the Canadian legislature on due process over problems of judicial interpretation means that the reforms introduced by Bill C-51 in 2018 are unlikely to improve the complainant's trial experience.

Recurring Themes and Patterns

Several themes and patterns emerge from our selective pan of regulatory trends and directions governing the use of sexual history evidence. First, as we have noted, in almost every jurisdiction we looked at, the law has undergone several rounds of review and revision, many in the last five years. McNabb and Baker analyse this process using a "policy cycle" framework which highlights a distinct cyclical pattern: A problem is identified and an agenda for investigation set; a policy approach is formulated and buy-in from relevant actors sought; decisions are made, legislation drafted, and policy and guidance issued; implementation is executed; and finally, the changes are evaluated against relevant criteria (2021, 26). In theory, as the policy cycle repeats, the 'best model' should reveal itself through a natural dialectic. In the case of sexual offences,

37 Craig (2016) similarly critiques judicial interpretations of section 276, calling for a more "rigorous" approach.

38 See further McCallum and Ng (2020).

this process of repetition seems to be occurring with increased regularity – often sparked by moral outrage arising from the publicity attached to watershed cases. In their analysis of the policy cycle as it has manifest in Canadian SHE law and policy, McNabb and Baker identify a trend towards the "judicialization of politics" in which policy problems with questions of social and political justice at their heart are stripped of their complexity and transformed into matters of legal doctrine that privilege due process concerns (McNabb and Baker 2021, 25). Not that due process concerns are unimportant. The problem that McNabb and Baker identify is that they attract undue legislative and policy attention (2021, 40) coming to be seen as a solution to the persistent problems of implementation of rape shield regimes. We observed this shift towards procedural norms in several jurisdictions, for example, in the enhanced elaboration of steps to be followed when leave to admit SHE is sought (New Zealand) as well as in the emergence of ILR as a key technique to countervail SHE misuse (Northern/Republic of Ireland). Yet problems of implementation continue to surface in virtually every jurisdiction we surveyed.

The review and revision of protective legislative frameworks is often the first port of call for critical attention whenever an injustice is perceived. Legislatures and policymakers interpret the need to be 'seen' to be addressing the issues raised with tangible change, measured in terms of updated directives or new procedures and enactments. Such measures often require little financial commitment, making them a palatable compromise in a context where frontline services have been ravaged by decades of austerity, and all aspects of the criminal justice apparatus back.[39] Yet, the successive introduction of new measures to improve the criminal justice response to sexual violence sits uneasily alongside continued accounts of rising rates of reporting and decreasing rates of prosecution or conviction rates for sexual offences.[40] Indeed, across many of the jurisdictions we reviewed, there is a paradoxical sense of stasis in constant change, which the frequency and strictures of the policy cycle arguably promotes.

The fact is that notwithstanding an apparent consensus about the normative foundations of modern sexual offences law, rehearsed in judicial opinions as well as in legislative and policy texts, the use of SHE in rape trials remains mired in deep contestation. Controversy was a feature of virtually every jurisdiction we explored. While academics and victims' rights advocates are largely united in the view that law and policy is failing in the area, judges and legal

39 In England and Wales, a 2019 report found that Government cuts to service provision were directly related to the fall in rape prosecutions, having left the criminal justice system "close to breaking point" https://www.justiceinspectorates.gov.uk/hmcpsi/wp-content/uploads/sites/3/2019/12/Rape-inspection-2019-1.pdf Accessed August 24, 2022.

40 In England and Wales, a Home Office inquiry was launched after successive reports found rape prosecutions to be at their lowest since records began, when the number of police-recorded rapes were at their highest ever level (Home Affairs Committee 2022).

practitioners continue to be less convinced, considering the "problem" of the (mis)use of sexual history evidence to be largely resolved (O'Malley 2020), only rarely problematic (Hoyano 2018), or subject to legislative overkill to the detriment of the interests of justice (Marsh and Dein 2021). This disagreement over the effectiveness of the relevant law mirrors a much deeper clash of worldviews as to the evidentiary significance of SHE in which 'common sense' assumptions about (female) sexual behaviour struggle to command the necessary consensus to found claims of relevance. Rape shield laws act here to trouble assumptions that have operated unchecked in courtrooms for centuries, exposing to scrutiny figurations of female sexuality which, while rooted in the patriarchal past, continue to reside in legal reasoning and decision making.[41] Cases such as *Seaboyer* and *R v A (No 2)* provide fora for working through the clash of social and legal imaginaries to which the use of SHE gives rise. This has yielded undoubted gains, including the formal rejection in legal judgments and texts of the 'twin myths': The assumptions that unchaste women are more likely to consent to sex and are less worthy of belief.[42]

One can see nevertheless the legal appeal of discretionary approaches to SHE regulation and the deep legal suspicion of 'gateway' regimes. By placing matters in the 'safe' hands of the judiciary, complexity gives way to simplicity and the conceptual structure of evidence law remains intact. A key feature of this structure is the weight traditionally given to the defendant's right to a fair trial. Indeed, in an adversarial culture, this is the predominant measure of justice. The parameters of deliberation are set within a frame in which the rights of the defendant and the interests of the complainant are conceived as "diametrically opposed," encouraging a 'winner takes all' approach to evidentiary matters rather than striving to find middle ground (Ozkin 2011, 328). The differential weighting of these apparently conflictual concerns poses real problems for 'balancing' regulatory techniques, which are often at the forefront of discussions around how to improve SHE law. Yet, the rise of victims' rights discourses and the development of human rights thinking has encouraged the articulation of rights-based groundings for rape shield laws. In Scots and Canadian law, for example, the rights of complainants to have their privacy and dignity protected is explicitly enshrined in the relevant SHE provisions.[43] Gotell characterises the relationship between a complainant's rights to privacy or dignity with the

41 Thomason's (2018) analysis of the relevance of SHE is particularly reliant on problematic tropes of female sexuality including conspiracies with secret lovers, revenge triggered by sexual rejection and "relatively young" complainants who cannot have obtained their knowledge of sexual matters other than through direct sexual experience. These figurations of femininity would not look out of place in the court of Matthew Hale.

42 See, e.g., L Steyn in *R v A (No 2)* [2002] 1 AC 45, at 27, citing the judgment of McLachlin J in *R v Seaboyer* (1991) 83 DLR (4th) 193 and the Canadian Criminal Code (RSC 1985 c C-46).

43 Criminal Procedure (Scotland) Act 1995, section 275(2)(b)(i); Canadian Criminal Code (R.S.C. 1985), section 276(3)(f).

rights of the accused to call any and all relevant evidence in their defence as a "zero-sum" game (2006, 767). The play of rights is zero-sum because the complainant's interest in the "empty" or "negative" right to privacy necessarily yields to the accused's right to a fair trial, framed in terms of broader access to justice language, which implicates the system as a whole (Gotell 2006, 753). While legislatures often prescribe that these rights be balanced, in practice, they are put into competition with each other with a hierarchical approach prevailing in which defendants' rights are seen as tangible, weightier and more urgent (Gotell 2006, 766). While an attempt to give substance to complainant rights through limited entitlement to ILR, for example, certainly challenges the inevitability of the normative schema in operation where SHE is at issue during the trial, such initiatives appear piecemeal when set against the full force of a legal and policy framework that remains otherwise unmoved.

If we look at prosecution and conviction statistics or studies of victims' experiences of the criminal justice process (see for example Gillen (2019)), we might well wonder whether rape shield regulation has in any way contributed to improving the criminal justice response to sexual violence. Some feminist commentators speculate that it has not – indeed, are concerned that it may have further entrenched the use of SHE in the trial process (Burman et al. 2007, 2009; Leahy and Fitzgerald 2018). This prompts a further question about how the success or otherwise of such legislative interventions should be measured, a question which is intimately connected to efforts to distil 'best practice,' which is of course a common goal of comparative or jurisdictional reviews. One interesting by-product of rape shield regimes is that it has created some space for the articulation of counternarratives of criminal justice. The historical conditions in which the adversarial model assumed foundational significance tilted the normative balance towards the institutional embedding of the accused's right to a fair trial (Beattie 1991; Cairns 2017), yielding a discourse in which defendants' rights became synonymous with criminal justice. Within this frame of reference, advancing the interests of complainants is perceived to be in competition with justice itself. The development of rape shield regimes, however, has compelled the articulation of additional justice concerns, such as the interest in ensuring that crimes are reported, and citizens protected from harms which the state is committed to guard against. These and other concerns are expressly enshrined in section 276 of the Canadian Criminal Charter and even in *R v A (No 2)*, Lord Slynn acknowledges that the unfair harassment of rape victims in court is "bad for society in that women will be afraid to complain and as a result men who ought to be prosecuted will escape" (at 1).

Therefore, while it may be that rape shield laws do not yet conform to conventional measures of success, whether understood in terms of prosecution/conviction rates or victims' experience of the trial process, that does not mean that there is not something interesting – and possibly progressive – going on. It may be that rape shield legislation is slowly opening a space for a more expansive conception of criminal 'justice,' one which does not compete with a defendant's fair trial rights but locates those rights within a more capacious justice imaginary. Moreover, legislative initiatives are also contributing to the development of a new language of rights centred on the harmful and exclusionary effects of the trial process on vulnerable witnesses. A range of potential rights infringements are now implicated in the misuse of SHE, including the complainant's right to have her dignity respected, her privacy not unnecessarily intruded upon, as well as her rights to physical autonomy and security and, in some contexts, her equality rights (as, for example, in Heureux-Dubé's partial dissent in *Seaboyer*). The promotion of ILR has prompted a discourse of participation rights which problematises the traditional marginalisation of witnesses in the adversarial criminal trial. Again, while the current tendency is still to view these concerns in terms of a clash of rights which, in the interests of justice, courts and legislatures are required to 'balance,' the idea of rights in inevitable conflict holds far less water once fairness is recalibrated to align with a continually evolving criminal justice imaginary.

Of marked importance in this context is the growing policy attention accorded to the notion of secondary victimisation, often referred to as a 'second rape.' This theme was present throughout the jurisdictions we reviewed with reformatory energies increasingly attached to efforts to mitigate or cure the harms to the complainant occasioned by the trial process. We particularly noted the legislative enshrinement of the concept of secondary victimisation in Irish law.[44] Strikingly too, this provision applies beyond the context of sexual offences, serving as an example of the wider discursive impact of rape shield legislation on criminal justice norms. At the heart of the concern to avoid secondary victimisation is the disturbing idea that the justice process is itself actively implicated in the perpetration of sexual violence. This is an extraordinarily strong indictment of the legal process, and yet the impetus to improve the experience of the trial for the complainant where SHE is concerned continues to rub up against the seemingly intractable wall of evidentiary 'relevance' as the cornerstone of the accused's right to a fair trial. As we have seen, rather than confront the changing landscape of justice to which a concern with SHE has undoubtedly contributed, the trend in many jurisdictions is to channel legal anxieties into bolstering procedural rights, for example, by introducing or extending victims' access to ILR or by directing courts explicitly to consider a wider range of factors in the conduct of modified balancing exercises (as, for example, in section 276(3) of the Canadian Criminal Code).

While we have highlighted the scepticism of some commentators observing this trend towards proceduralism (McNabb and Baker 2021; Illiadis 2020; Illiadis et al. 2021), this too is indicative of efforts to reframe the schema of norms that govern the discourse around SHE. Norms for victim inclusion or

44 See note 19 above. The provision is framed within a stated concern for respecting the victim's 'private life.'

participation through ILR, for example, are posited as a way of pushing back against the inevitability of the secondary victimisation of the complainant during the trial and to better articulate what is at stake when a court is called to consider the admission of SHE. These initiatives can be read as attempts to intervene in and displace the assumption that the idea of a fair trial aligns perfectly and exclusively with defendant rights.

Conclusion

This chapter has conducted a 'state of the field' analysis of several similar common law jurisdictions. We have found that the laws and policy around SHE are subject to constant review and revision, and that discussion of the best way forward remains highly contested. We highlighted some of the recurring themes which emerged from our panoramic overview including the shared sense of stasis in change brought on by frequent calls for review and revision of a legislative framework that remains highly resistant to meaningful change. We also observed the persistent and deep disagreement between scholars, activists, criminal justice actors, and policy makers about what to 'do' about SHE, adding to the difficulties around enacting meaningful change in the area or even as to how to measure that change. We also noted attempts in many jurisdictions to give substance to the notion of 'victim's rights' through ILR. These types of measures endeavour to change the normative schema or discourse around SHE, which has historically been dominated by defendant-centred notions of a 'fair trial,' invariably the normative founding for efforts to circumvent statutory frameworks designed to prevent the admission of SHE.

What is more difficult to assess in the context of mainstream debates taking place in the jurisdictions we reviewed is the extent to which efforts to date have upset the frame and/or underlying logic which supports the use of SHE. There is a constant reassertion, consciously or unconsciously, of the need to retain the integrity and coherence of the common law evidentiary framework and as the value of a flexible framework for managing the exclusion – and by implication, admission – of SHE. There is little in the way of a direct reckoning with the normative structure which supports the SHE admission. A closer look suggests that the foundations are nevertheless under stress: The logic supporting claims of relevance is becoming increasingly strained as appeals to 'common sense' falter and criminal justice discourse slowly moves towards the contemplation of new justice imaginaries. At the same time, the strictures and timescales of the policy cycle inhibit our ability to recognise and assess these developments, diverting attention towards strategies with more immediate political appeal. We need to hone our ability to see and scrutinise the structure and logic that supports the use of sexual history evidence in the rape trial as well as to excavate and critique the barely articulated but nevertheless operative assumptions underpinning claims to relevance. Perhaps, most importantly, we need to engage directly with ideas of criminal *justice* and contemporary critiques thereof, harnessing our concerns about sexual violence to new criminal justice imaginaries emerging from the wreckage of a system whose decline appears increasingly inevitable.

Acknowledgements

Thanks to Jasmine Bundhoo and Megan Johnson for research assistance during the drafting of this chapter. Russell would like to acknowledge the support of the Leverhulme Trust (RF-2021-433).

References

Angel, Katherine. 2021. *Tomorrow Sex Will Be Good Again: Women and Desire in the Age of Consent.* London: Verso.

Beattie, John M. 1991. "Scales of Justice: Defense Counsel and the English Criminal Trial in the Eighteenth and Nineteenth Centuries." *Law and History Review* 9 (2): 221–267.

Brewis, Brian, and Adam Jackson. 2020. "Sexual Behaviour Evidence and Evidence of Bad Character in Sexual Offence Proceedings: Proposing a Combined Admissibility Framework." *The Journal of Criminal Law* 84 (1): 49–73.

Burman, Michele. 2009. "Evidencing Sexual Assault: Women in the Witness Box." *Probation Journal* 56 (4): 379–398.

Burman, Michele, Lynn Jamieson, Jan Nicholson, and Oona Brooks. 2007. *Impact of Aspects of the Law of Evidence in Sexual Offence Trials: An Evaluation Study*. Edinburgh: Scottish Government.

Cairns, Ilona. 2017. "'Access to Justice' for Complainers? The Pitfalls of the Scottish Government's Case to Abolish Corroboration." In *Scottish Criminal Evidence Law: Current Developments and Future Trends*, edited by Peter Duff and Pamela Ferguson, 41–60. Edinburgh: Edinburgh University Press.

Campbell, Liz, and Sharon Cowan. 2017. "The Relevance of Sexual History and Vulnerability in the Prosecution of Sexual Offences." In *Scottish Criminal Evidence Law: Current Developments and Future Trends*, edited by Peter Duff and Pamela Ferguson, 67–96. Edinburgh: Edinburgh University Press.

Conaghan, Joanne, and Yvette Russell. 2023. *Sexual History Evidence and the Rape Trial.* Bristol: Bristol University Press.

Cowan, Sharon. 2020. *The Use of Sexual History and Bad Character Evidence in Scottish Sexual Offences Trials.* Glasgow: Equality and Human Rights Commission.

Craig, Elaine. 2016. "Section 276 Misconstrued: The Failure to Properly Interpret and Apply Canada's Rape Shield Provisions." *Canadian Bar Review* 94: 45–84.

Gillen Review. 2019. *Gillen Report into the Law and Procedures in Serious Sexual Offences in Northern Ireland.* Accessed August 24, 2022. https://www.justice-ni.gov.uk/sites/default/files/publications/justice/gillen-report-may-2019.pdf.

Gotell, Lise. 2006. "When Privacy is Not Enough: Sexual Assault Complainants, Sexual History Evidence and the Disclosure of Personal Records." *Alberta Law Review* 43: 743.

Her Majesty's Inspectorate of Constabulary and Fire & Rescue Services and HM Crown Prosecution Service Inspectorate. 2022. *A Joint Thematic Inspection of the Police and Crown Prosecution Service's Response to Rape - Phase Two: Post-charge.* Accessed August 17, 2022.

https://www.justiceinspectorates.gov.uk/hmicfrs/wp-content/uploads/joint-thematic-inspection-of-police-and-cps-response-to-rape-phase-2.pdf.

Home Affairs Committee. 2022. "Investigation and Prosecution of Rape." *House of Commons*. Accessed August 24, 2022. https://committees.parliament.uk/publications/9600/documents/166175/default/.

Hoyano, Laura. 2018. "The Operation of YJCEA 1999 Section 41 in the Courts of England & Wales: Views from the Barristers' Row." *Criminal Bar Association*. Accessed August 17, 2022 https://ora.ox.ac.uk/objects/uuid:b20b6eab-7a41-4fa5-adc9-cf1656662f46.

Iliadis, Mary. 2020. "Victim Representation for Sexual History Evidence in Ireland: A Step Towards or Away from Meeting Victims' Procedural Justice Needs?" *Criminology & Criminal Justice* 20 (4): 416–432.

Iliadis, Mary, Olivia Smith, and Jonathan Doak. 2021. "Independent Separate Legal Representation for Rape Complainants in Adversarial Systems: Lessons from Northern Ireland." *Journal of Law and Society* 48 (2): 250–272.

Killean, Rachel. 2021. "Legal Representation for Sexual Assault Victims." In *Sexual Violence on Trial: Local and Comparative Perspectives*, edited by Rachel Killean, Eithne Dowds, and Anne-Marie McAlinden, 174–186. London: Routledge.

Killean, Rachel, Eithne Dowds, and Anne-Marie McAlinden, eds. 2021. *Sexual Violence on Trial: Local and Comparative Perspectives*. London: Routledge.

Leahy, Susan. 2014. "Whether Rules or Discretion? Developing a Best Practice Model for Controlling the Admissibility of Sexual Experience Evidence in Sexual Offence Trials." *Irish Journal of Legal Studies* 4 (1): 65–91.

Leahy, Susan. 2021. "The Realities of Rape Trials in Ireland: Perspectives from Practice Realities of Rape Trials in Ireland." *Irish Research Council*. Accessed August 17, 2022 https://www.drcc.ie/assets/files/pdf/leahyrealitiesreport.pdf.

Leahy, Susan, and Margaret Fitzgerald O'Reilly. 2018. *Sexual Offending in Ireland: Laws, Procedures and Punishment*. Dublin: Clarus Press.

Lord Justice Clerk's Review Group. 2021. "Improving the Management of Sexual Offence Cases." *Scottish Courts and Tribunal Services*. Accessed August 24, 2022. https://www.scotcourts.gov.uk/docs/default-source/default-document-library/reports-and-data/Improving-the-management-of-Sexual-Offence-Cases.pdf?sfvrsn=6.

Marsh, Luke, and Jeremy Dein. 2021. "Serious Sex Offences in England and Wales: Defending the Indefensible." In *Sexual Violence on Trial: Local and Comparative Perspectives*, edited by Rachel Killean, Eithne Dowds, and Anne-Marie McAlinden, 46–58. London: Routledge.

McCallum, Myrna, and Gloria Ng. 2020. "A Toolkit for Navigating Section 276 and 278 Criminal Code Matters as Complainant Counsel in Criminal Proceedings." *West Coast Leaf*, April. Accessed August 17, 2022 http://www.westcoastleaf.org/wp-content/uploads/2020/04/lower-res-Complainant-Counsel-Toolkit-April-22-2020-web.pdf.

McDonald, Elisabeth. 2020a. *Rape Myths as Barriers to Fair Trial Process: Comparing Adult Rape Trials with Those in the Aotearoa Sexual Violence Court Pilot*. Christchurch: Canterbury University Press.

McDonald, Elisabeth. 2020b. Submission on Sexual Violence Legislation Bill 2019. Accessed August 24, 2022. https://www.parliament.nz/en/pb/sc/submissions-and advice/document/52SCJU_EVI_93010_JU68867/elisabeth-mcdonald.

McNabb, Danielle, and Dennis Baker. 2021. "Ignoring Implementation: Defects in Canada's 'rape Shield' Policy Cycle." *Canadian Journal of Law and Society/La Revue Canadienne Droit et Société* 36 (1): 23–46.

Ministry of Justice. 2021. "End-to-End Rape Review Report on Findings and Actions." *HM Government*. Accessed August 24, 2022. https://assets.publishing.service.gov.uk/government/uploads/system/uploads/attachment_data/file/1001417/end-to-end-rape-review-report-with-correction-slip.pdf.

New Zealand Law Commission. 2018 "IP42 Second Review of the Evidence Act 2006 – Te Arotake Tuarua i te Evidence Act 2006: He Puka Kaupapa." Accessed August 24, 2022. https://www.lawcom.govt.nz/sites/default/files/projectAvailableFormats/NZLC%20IP42%20Second%20Review%20of%20the%20Evidence%20Act%20-%20FINAL.pdf.

New Zealand Law Commission. 2019. "R142 The Second Review of the Evidence Act 2006 – Te Arotake Tuarua i te Evidence Act 2006." Accessed August 24, 2022. https://www.lawcom.govt.nz/sites/default/files/projectAvailableFormats/EA2%20-%20FINAL%20REPORT%20R142%20-%20Web%20Publishing.pdf.

Northern Irish Department of Justice. 2020. "Implementation Plan: The Gillen Review into the Law and Procedures in Serious Sexual Offences in Northern Ireland." Accessed August 24, 2002. https://www.justice-ni.gov.uk/sites/default/files/publications/justice/the-gillen-review-implementation-plan.PDF.

O'Malley, Tom. 2020. "Review of Protections for Vulnerable Witnesses in the Investigation and Prosecution of Sexual Offences." Accessed August 24, 2022. https://www.justice.ie/en/JELR/Review_of_Protections_for_Vulnerable_Witnesses_in%20the_Investigation_and_Prosecution_of_Sexual_Offences.pdf/Files/Review_of_Protections_for_Vulnerable_Witnesses_in%20the_Investigation_and_Prosecution_of_Sexual_Offences.pdf.

Ozkin, Senem. 2011. "Balancing of Interests: Admissibility of Prior Sexual History under Section 276." *Criminal Law Quarterly* 57: 327.

Rape Crisis Network of Ireland. 2009. *Rape and Justice in Ireland*. Dublin: Liffey Press.

Rape Crisis Network of Ireland. 2012. "Previous Sexual History Evidence and Separate Legal Representation: RCNI Position Paper." Accessed August 24, 2022. https://www.rcni.ie/wp-content/uploads/RCNIPreviousSexualHistorySLRPositionPaperMay12.pdf.

Smith, Olivia, and Ellen Daly. 2020. *Evaluation of the Sexual Violence Complainants' Advocate Scheme*. Loughborough: Loughborough University.

Thomason, Matthew. 2018. "Previous sexual history evidence: A gloss on relevance and relationship evidence." *The International Journal of Evidence & Proof* 22(4): 342–362.

Chapter 8

Mind the Gap

Implementing 'Rape Shield' Laws in Scottish Sexual Offences Trials

Sharon Cowan

Introduction

Scottish academics, third-sector organisations and independent reviewers have long identified various systemic and practical issues as potentially impacting upon the prospects of a just outcome for sexual violence survivors who choose to engage with the criminal justice system. Concerns have been raised about, for example, the size of juries and the integrity of jury decision making; the "not proven" verdict (which is an acquittal verdict); the treatment of vulnerable witness-complainers[1] in sexual offences hearings; the use and retention of "private data" such as that taken from mobile phones; and the impact of strict evidential requirements such as corroboration on the likelihood of sexual offences convictions (see, for example, Chalmers and Leverick 2013; Ormston et al. 2019; Keane 2022; Chalmers, Leverick and Munro 2021; Munro 2023; Cowan 2020; Cowan and Hewer 2020; Callander 2014; Cairns 2017; Aspinall-Miles 2019; O'Floinn and Ormerod 2012). The Scottish government has recently put in place a number of reviews and initiatives to investigate specific features of sexual offences law and policy, such as Lady Dorrian's judicial-led review 'Improving the Management of Sexual Offence Cases,'[2] the Victims' Taskforce chaired by the Lord Advocate and the Cabinet Secretary for Justice,[3] and the Scottish Sentencing Council's commitment to propose sentencing guidelines in some sexual offences cases.[4] The first Scottish study of mock jury trials, commissioned by the Scottish government, was also recently

1 The person alleging an offence is Scotland is referred to as the complainer.

2 www.scotcourts.gov.uk/about-the-scottish-court-service/scs- news/2019/03/20/improving-the-management-of-sexual-offence-cases. The final report, published in March 2021: www.scotcourts.gov.uk/docs/default-source/default-document-library/reports-and-data/Improving-the-management-of-Sexual-Offence-Cases.pdf?sfvrsn=6, made a number of recommendations for consideration by the Scottish government including specialist sexual offences courts and piloting judge-only trials in sexual offences.

3 See www.gov.scot/groups/victims-taskforce/ for minutes and papers from the meetings.

4 See the reports produced in 2021, analysing sentencing in sexual offences and people's perceptions of sentencing in these cases: www.scottishsentencingcouncil.org.uk/media/2122/public-perceptions

DOI: 10.4324/9781003379331-12

published (Ormston et al. 2019).[5] None of these reports or reviews, useful though they are in highlighting areas for concern or reform, investigated the use of sexual history, 'bad character' or private data evidence in sexual offences proceedings, leaving a substantial gap in knowledge. In this chapter, I aim to highlight various areas for ongoing concern in this area by interrogating the aims and outcomes of 'rape shield' provisions, designed to restrict the kinds of evidence that can be introduced in sexual offences trials, to highlight where the criminal justice system fails on its own terms.

Pressing for improvements to the law on sexual offences should not be taken as support for the criminal justice system as we know it. Feminist critiques of contemporary carceral 'justice' systems, and in particular the disproportionate impact of criminal convictions and imprisonment on poor, racialised, mentally unwell and immigrant communities cannot be ignored, and it is tempting to see contemporary criminal approaches to sexual offending as a lost cause (Cowan 2015; Cowan and Munro 2021). Rather I align myself with the work of critics such as Taylor (2020), who has argued feminists should aim towards dismantling prisons and radically rethink the best way of dealing with sexual offending, and, as Srinivasen puts it, "work for the undoing of a system of domination" rather than "secure the grip of that system by relieving its most egregious symptoms" (2021, 157). Feminists who question carceral impulses have argued that prevention of, and resistance to, rape cannot and should not be reduced to a strategy of prohibitive laws (Russell 2021; Larcombe 2011), or highlighted the way that reforming sexual offences laws can allow legislators to present themselves as taking sexual violence seriously, but with little impact on the rate of sexual violence, co-opting feminist concerns and perpetuating heteronormative regulatory regimes (Phoenix and Oerton 2005).

Likewise, in this chapter, I confront the criminal justice system, not to bolster support for an unreflective punitive justice framework, or suggest that law reform can be neatly finessed in a way that fundamentally addresses structural inequalities and violence, but to highlight the need for more exploratory research into the routinised operation of what is assumed to be a system that protects the most vulnerable and that fairly balances the rights and interests of the parties involved in a sexual offences trial. This kind of scrutiny is a

-of-sentencing-qualatative-research-of-sexual-offences-final-july-2021.pdf; and www.scottishsentencingcouncil.org.uk/media/2086/20210203-sexual-offences-involving-rape-lit-review.pdf.

5 The study found that found that the number of jurors, the number of verdicts available, and the size of majority required do have an effect on verdict choice; jurors on 15 person juries (as is the case in Scotland) have lower levels of participation, and are less likely to change their minds than jurors on 12 person juries; jurors who were asked to reach a majority verdict were more likely to vote guilty, and took substantially less time to come to a verdict than jurors who were asked to come to a unanimous decision; and in juries where the not proven verdict was available, acquitting jurors were more likely to choose not proven rather than not guilty verdicts, and jurors generally were less likely to choose a guilty verdict.

necessary first step if we are to show how the legal protections against sexual violence require more than superficial reform.

In the following sections, I examine the operation of Scottish 'rape shield' laws – s274 and s275 of the Criminal Procedure (Scotland) Act 1995 – that restrict the introduction of sexual history and bad character evidence in sexual offences trials.[6] The legislation is designed to protect witness-complainers from inappropriate questions about their sexual history and character in court. I provide a contextual picture of the sexual offences statistics in Scotland, and the knowledge produced from official records, before going on to examine how the law is currently being implemented in Scotland, and to highlight a problematic 'justice gap.' I will show that more evidence is needed to fully understand the complex constellation of legal, procedural and practical barriers to proper implementation of rape shield legislation, particularly since the last study on this issue was published 14 years ago. However, the evidence we *do* have suggests that the dignity and privacy of those reporting sexual offences are not fully protected by the legislation, despite a specific statutory provision detailing that aim.

Sexual Offences in Scotland: The Official Account

Recorded Sexual Offending

To give some background context for the operation of sexual history and character evidence in Scottish sexual offences trials, it is useful to have a sense of the incidence of sexual offending. Between 2009–2010 and 2018–2019, while overall police recorded crime rates in Scotland steadily fell until 2017–2018 (when a slight increase was partly explained by the inclusion of handling offensive weapons offences), sexual crimes increased steadily: Recorded crime was at one of the lowest levels since 1974, but sexual crimes were at their highest level since records began in 1971. In particular, the category of rape/attempted rape more than doubled in that decade.[7] The most recent statistics show reported sexual crimes have risen by 15% and rape and attempted by 9% between April 2020 and April 2021.[8]

6 Much of the following analysis is based on my report commissioned by the Equality and Human Rights Commission (Cowan 2020).

7 www.gov.scot/publications/recorded-crime-scotland-2018-19/pages/8/. It is not entirely clear why this pattern has emerged. It can be partly explained by increased reporting, particularly of 'historical' offences, but it is unlikely that the rise in recorded incidences of sexual crimes can, in its entirety, be explained by increased reporting. It is reasonable to suppose that it can also be at least partially explained by an increase in offences, as well as the expansion of the *actus reus* component of rape, since after the Sexual Offences (Scotland) Act 2003 s1, oral and anal penetration by the penis was included in the definition of rape.

8 www.gov.scot/publications/recorded-crime-scotland-2021-2022/pages/6/. Apart from two small decreases in 2019–2020 and 2020–2021, recorded rape has been increasing year on year since records began.

These increases can be partly explained by increased reporting, particularly of historical offences. It can also be at least partially explained by the expansion of the *actus reus* component of rape, since after the Sexual Offences (Scotland) Act 2003 s1, oral and anal penetration by the penis was included in the definition of rape. However, it is unlikely that the rise in recorded incidences of sexual crimes can, in its entirety, be explained by increased reporting or the widening of the offence since the rise has continued well past the date of the changes to the offence parameters and continues to rise. It would be astonishing if there were not also an increase in the number of offences in this period.

Most sexual offences are not reported to the police. However, the same disparity between rates of overall crime and sexual offences is clear from the most recent Scottish Crime and Justice Survey (SCJS) figures from 2019 to 2020 show that crime has fallen by 46% since 2008–2009. However, the self-completion questions on sexual victimisation show that since 2008–2009 the proportion of adults who since aged 16 have experienced attempted forced sexual intercourse has risen from 1.5% to 2.0%, while attempted other forced sexual activity rose from 0.7% to 1.3% and unwanted sexual touching from 4.8% to 7.4% (these figures cover 2018/19 and 2019/20 combined since the sexual victimisation survey is completed biannually). The survey also found that only around 22% of those who had recounted the most recent/only rape, and 13% of those who had recounted the most recent/only attempted rape, reported the incident to the police.[9]

Only a small number of reported offences reach trial, but at the same time, the 2017 Inspectorate of Prosecutions Report found that sexual crimes made up 75% of Crown Office and Procurator Fiscal Service (COPFS) High Court work, up from 50% in 2015 (2017, 3). Although the total number of people proceeded against for all crimes and offences has been dropping steadily since 2009–2010 (from 136,303 to 89,725 in 2018–2019),[10] the number of people proceeded against for rape/attempted rape has almost trebled in the same period (from 117 in 2009–2010 to 313 in 2018–2019).[11] The most recent figures cover 2020–2021, the first full year of the COVID pandemic, and show an overall rate of 46,497 people proceeded against, a further fall, and a decrease of 46% from the previous year, and a significant drop; rape and attempted rape dropped from 299 to 152 people proceeded against, a drop of 49%.[12]

9 www.gov.scot/publications/scottish-crime-justice-survey-2019-20-main-findings/pages/21/. The true figure is likely to be even lower than that reported by the SCJS as not all of those who have experienced rape or attempted rape will have felt able to disclose it.

10 See www.gov.scot/publications/criminal-proceedings-scotland-2018-19/pages/10/. The statistical bulletin states that: "Figures for some categories dealt with by the high court - including homicide, rape and major drug cases - may be underestimated due to late recording of disposals" (Table 4(a)).

11 www.gov.scot/publications/criminal-proceedings-scotland-2018-19/pages/10/.

12 www.gov.scot/binaries/content/documents/govscot/publications/statistics/2022/06/criminal-proceedings-scotland-2020-21/documents/criminal-proceedings-scotland-2020-21/criminal

The conviction rate also remains low. In 2020–2021, for all sexual crimes, 1030 people were proceeded against, 152 of them for rape or attempted rape. For the latter, 31 were acquitted via a not guilty verdict, 42 were acquitted via a not proven verdict (NP),[13] and 78 people were found guilty.[14] This represents a conviction rate of 51% of those proceeded against, the lowest rate of any crime category (while the overall conviction rate is 90%).

In short, crime rates in Scotland have been falling for some time, but sexual offences are increasing year on year and remain at the highest level on record, while conviction rates remain the lowest for any crime group.

Legislation and Common law Rules

For the minority of sexual offences complainers who do report the incident, and whose case reaches trial, there are, in many jurisdictions, evidential restrictions on the use of information about their sexual history (and sometimes character more generally) – frequently called 'rape shield' rules.[15] Rape shield laws are designed to prevent evidence being led where it is of limited relevance and is intended to undermine the credibility of the complainer, and they were first introduced in Scotland by the Law Reform (Miscellaneous Provisions) (Scotland) Act 1985, s36, which restricted certain questioning about the sexual history or 'bad character' of the complainer. These provisions were re-enacted in revised form by s274 and s275 of the Criminal Procedure (Scotland) Act 1995; s274 limits the introduction of evidence relating either to character or sexual history in a sexual offences trial, subject to the exceptions laid out in s275.

The s274 restrictions are in line with a general common law prohibition on 'bad character' evidence in Scotland on the basis that it is understood to be 'collateral,' i.e., not sufficiently connected to the facts at issue that need to be proven. There are, of course, exceptions to this exclusionary rule, for example where the character evidence relates directly to the crime charged, and is deemed relevant because it bears directly on, or makes more probable, a fact in issue at trial. The basic rule is that s274 only applies where evidence has already been deemed relevant and admissible at common law.[16] If the evidence

-proceedings-scotland-2020-21/govscot%3Adocument/criminal-proceedings-scotland-2020-21.pdf.

13 See Chapter 10 of this volume.

14 www.gov.scot/publications/criminal-proceedings-scotland-2018-19/pages/7/.

15 Feminists across jurisdictions have long critiqued the narrowness of the protections afforded by rape shield laws, or the propensity for exceptions to the protections to be construed widely. See, for example: In the UK, McGlynn (2017) and Kelly et al. (2006); in New Zealand, McDonald and Tinsley (2011); in Canada, Craig (2016); in India, Avinash (2021).

16 The test of relevancy is whether the evidence sought to be led has "a reasonably direct bearing on the subject under investigation" (*CJM (No.2) v HM Advocate* [2013] HCJAC 22).

is inadmissible at common law, it cannot be admitted through s275 – the common law test of relevancy cannot be circumvented by the statutory provisions (*CJM (No. 2) v HM Advocate*; *Oliver v HM Advocate* [2019] HCJAC 93).

S274 of the 1995 Act has four distinct subsections. S274(1)(a) prohibits the leading of evidence or questioning that would show or tend to show that the complainer is **not of** "**good character** (whether in relation to sexual matters or otherwise)." S274(1)(b) prevents the complainer from being questioned, or evidence being led, about any **"sexual behaviour not forming part of the subject matter of the charge**." S274(1)(c) prohibits evidence that the complainer has at **any time** "**other than shortly before, at the same time as, or shortly after**" the alleged offence[17] "**engaged in behaviour, not being sexual behaviour**" which might ground an inference that the complainer consented or is not a credible or reliable witness. S274(1)(d) restricts evidence of "**any condition or predisposition**" to which the complainer is subject **which might lead to the inference being drawn that the complainer consented or is not a credible or reliable witness** (emphasis added).

However, evidence about sexual history and/or bad character *can* be presented if it is admissible at common law *and* falls within s275, which sets out a three-stage cumulative test which must be satisfied before the trial judge can allow questioning or evidence to be led about sexual history or character.

(1) First, the evidence must relate to a **specific occurrence** or occurrences of behaviour, or to **specific facts** regarding the character, condition or predisposition of the complainer (s275(1)(a)).
(2) Second, the behaviour or facts must be **relevant to establishing the accused's guilt** (s275(1)(b)).
(3) Third, the **probative value** of the material must be **significant and outweigh any risk of prejudice to the proper administration of justice** (s275(1)(c)) (emphasis added).

Importantly, the proper administration of justice includes the appropriate protection of **the complainer's dignity or privacy** (s275(2)(b)(i)). The question of how the complainer's dignity and privacy might be protected in practice has been directly at issue in some of the cases explored, in section 3, below.

How and When are s275 Applications Made?

Brown et al.'s research in Scotland in the early 1990s was the first comprehensive study of sexual history evidence in the Scottish courts. They found that

17 The courts have held that the closer in time the evidence is to the facts at issue, the more likely the court will be to allow the evidence (*Stewart v HMA*, 2014 SCCR 1).

complainers were asked about their sexual history in around half of all jury trials for sexual offences, with over half of those relating to history with a third party (1992). They also found that in many cases sexual history evidence was introduced without a formal application. As explained above, new legislation was introduced in 1995 to increase protections for complainers, and this was amended to enhance protections further by the Sexual Offences (Procedure and Evidence) (Scotland) Act 2002.

Following the 2002 reforms, Burman et al.'s study in the Scottish courts, published in 2007, found an *increase* in sexual history applications after the introduction of the restrictive provisions (in part because the new framework required what would previously have been verbal applications to be made in writing). The study found that, of 231 sexual offences cases that were indicted to the High Court over a 12-month period (2004–2005), 72% included a s275 application (with 76% of rape trials involving such applications (2007, 2, 115). Just 7% of the s275 applications were disallowed, and in all but a small number of cases, all evidence allowed in the application was introduced in the trial, usually through cross-examination of the complainer (2007, 2). Several of the interviewed practitioners considered it relatively easy to demonstrate the relevance of sexual history/bad character evidence (2007, 133). Evidence or questioning concerning the bad character of the complainer often concerned the complainer's use of alcohol or drugs (2017, 3).

These findings are both surprising and worrying, yet, unlike other jurisdictions, there has been no further empirical research in Scotland that could shed light on issues such as: Whether the success of s275 applications has remained at this level; the circumstances under which s275 applications are made and the content of applications; whether and when they are challenged by the Crown; why they are not challenged; and whether evidence related to sexual history or character is raised during the trial despite the absence of a s275 application. At least some of this quantitative data *could* be collected and published more routinely – and ideally in electronic form – by the Scottish Courts and Tribunals Service (SCTS), and/or by COPFS (neither of whom do so currently). But there would still be a need to study in-depth the more qualitative questions highlighted here to understand the complex reasons for s275 applications not being challenged, particularly since it is more than a decade since Burman et al.'s study was undertaken.

Nonetheless, there are some glimpses of what may be happening. For example, Keane and Convery (2020) have stated that, according to the response to a Freedom of Information Request made by them to the SCTS in August 2019, there were 317 s275 applications in 2018–2019, and of these, 286 were in the High Court of Justiciary, whilst 31 were in the Sheriff Courts. It is not clear how or where these records are kept, and SCTS state that no further breakdown of figures is available because data is collected – for 'operational data management' reasons – on individual case files rather than collated systematically for statistical purposes.

Table 8.1 Applications Under s275 of 1995 Act between 11 January and 11 April 2016.

	- *Applications*	*No. Accepted (Fully or in Part)*	*No. Rejected*	*No. Unopposed by Crown*	*No. Challenged by Crown*
High Court	52	47	5	48	4
Sheriff Court	5	1	4	3	2
Total	57 (100%)	48 (84%)	9 (16%)	51 (90%)	6 (10%)

Figures on s275 applications were also released by Scotland's Cabinet Secretary for Justice on June 26, 2016, as shown below in Table 8.1.[18] In a three-month period from 11 January–11 April 2016, there were 57 s275 applications (52 in the High Court and five in the Sheriff Courts). Of the 52 High Court applications, 42 were granted in full, five were granted in part, and five refused. Of the five that were rejected, four of them were not challenged by the Crown (i.e., the judge rejected the application without Crown intervention). In fact, of the 57 total applications, only six were opposed by the Crown (four in the High Court and two in the Sheriff Courts) while 51 were unopposed by the Crown (48 in the High Court and three in the Sheriff Courts). Since COPFS do not currently routinely collect data on s275 applications, the method used to collect the data presented here is unknown.

Although only a three-month snapshot, these figures show that Crown prosecutors were not challenging applications to introduce sexual history evidence. The reasons for this obviously cannot be gleaned from these statistics alone. However, the timeline roughly corresponds with a 3 month "monitoring exercise of the prosecution attitude to defence 275 applications lodged at the time of the preliminary hearing and their outcomes," undertaken by the Inspectorate of Prosecution (2017) in the period 12 December 2016–12 March 2017.[19] The Inspectorate report does not state how many cases in total there were during this period but says there were 14 applications. Of these, five were granted unopposed; in seven, also unopposed, the judge questioned the application but granted three in full or part, and in four, continued them for more information. In the remaining two, which were opposed by the prosecution, the court held them to be irrelevant. In other words, the Crown did not oppose 12 out of the 14 applications. Yet the Inspectorate concluded at para 371: "**Other than providing some re-assurance that the prosecution and court are questioning the relevance and scope of such**

18 Letter from Michael Matheson to Margaret Mitchell, MSP, available at www.parliament.scot/General%20Documents/20160624CSfJtoConvenerILR.pdf.

19 Applications made at trial (which may well be a significant proportion of all applications) were not included in the monitoring exercise.

applications, where appropriate, the exercise is of **limited value** to assess the effectiveness of the legislation" (emphasis added).

Without more detailed information, it is difficult to offer any nuanced analysis of these sorts of statistics – they are indeed of limited value. We cannot say whether the figures are higher or lower than previous years, or other three-month periods, because we have no comparative statistics, and we do not know whether a three months' sample is necessarily indicative of any particular trend or pattern. Nor do we know whether any of these statistics mirror the high rate of successful applications as seen in the Burman et al. (2007) study.

More transparency around COPFS practice and the development of more systematic processes to capture data is urgently needed to properly understand how the law is, and should be, implemented in practice. Arguably, collecting more robust and transparent data – for example the number of s275 applications, the kinds of cases in which they are made, and the number accepted or refused – that could be used for monitoring purposes is part of the courts' and COPFS public sector general equality duty, under s149 of the Equality Act 2010, to eliminate discrimination and advance the human rights of both accused and complainer.[20]

The Content of s275 Applications

There is no systematic data capture of the types of issues that are raised in s275 applications. There is also no official record of which sorts of s275 applications are refused or allowed. Therefore, there is a clear and pressing need for more sustained record keeping in this area in order to be able to properly monitor how the law on s275 is currently applied.

Moreover, since no research findings relating specifically to sexual history evidence have been available since 2007, for the proper administration of justice, it is crucial that we have a better, more up-to-date understanding of how the Scottish court processes and personnel – judges, advocates, solicitors, and potentially others such as police officers – are dealing with sexual history and bad character evidence in Scotland today. This includes examining the decisions and practices of those who make, challenge and assess s275 applications (noting that both the defence and the prosecution can both make s275 applications); whether or not advocates keep within the parameters of a s275 application that has been granted – and whether this is given appropriate scrutiny by the court; and the experiences of those complainers who go through sexual offences trials, including the question of whether further interventions, such as independent legal representation (ILR, discussed below), are required. At the time of writing, a Scottish government-funded empirical project is being

20 The Equality Act 2010 (Specific Duties) (Scotland) Regulations 2012 (as amended) imposes specific duties on listed authorities, including COPFS.

undertaken (somewhat delayed by COVID) by this author, with colleagues Vanessa Munro and Eamon Keane, which will observe rape and attempted rape trials, and scrutinise the content of s275 applications, in order to investigate how the rape shield legislation and associated procedures are understood and applied during court proceedings.

In the meantime, there are identifiable areas of concern. In the next section, I will highlight two important aspects of the Scottish process that could be further improved in order to properly protect complainers in sexual offences proceedings: The complainer's right to be heard and represented; and the protection of the complainer's dignity and privacy during sexual offences trials.

Implementing the 'Rape Shield' Laws: A Justice Gap

Various elements of the rape shield provisions have been challenged in the courts, including the compatibility of the legislation with the European Convention on Human Rights (ECHR).[21] Here, however, I will focus on two specific issues that have been contested before the courts in recent years; whether or not complainers have a right to be heard or represented in preliminary hearings where s275 applications (arguing that evidence about sexual history should be admissible) are heard; and the protection of the complainer's dignity and privacy under the s275(1)(c).

Representation for Complainers

Recent cases in Scotland have made it possible to argue for complainers to have independent legal representation (ILR) at s275 applications. This is mainly due to the 2016 landmark decision *WF*, which held that complainers can be heard during hearings for applications for recovery of sensitive records, such as medical and counselling records.[22] The court held that a complainer's ECHR Article 8 rights were engaged in a criminal case where an application has been made to recover sensitive records, that the complainer has the right to be heard before

21 See *Moir v HMA* 2005 1 JC 102; *DS v HMA* 2007 SCCR 222; *Judge v United Kingdom* 2011 SCCR 241. In the latter, the European Court of Human Rights held that the Scottish legislative scheme gave appropriate weight to protection of the public interest in excluding irrelevant evidence while protecting the accused's right to a fair trial (at 29). For similar challenges against the equivalent legislation in England and Wales see *R v A (No. 2)* [2001] UKHL 25; for discussion see McGlynn (2017), and for a feminist judgments project re-writing of *R v A* see McGlynn (2010). See also *Judge v UK* 2011 SCCR 241 (Scotland) and *R v Darrach* (2000) 191 DLR (4th) 539 (Canada), and *Doorson v the Netherlands* (1996) 22 EHRR 330 (ECtHR).

22 *WF v Scottish Ministers* 2016 SLT 359. The right to legal aid for this purpose was then legislated for by the Advice and Assistance (Proceedings for Recovery of Documents) (Scotland) Regulations 2017 (SSI 2017 No 291). See also *JC, Petitioner* 2018 HCA/2018/000013/XM. Applications for access to sensitive records is heard at a commission and diligence hearing. This is a completely separate and different process from the preliminary hearing for s275 applications.

the court determines whether to grant recovery, and that to facilitate this right to be heard, legal aid should be available. More recently, in *AR v HM Advocate* [2019] HCJ 81, the court accepted that a petition to recover the mobile phone belonging to the complainer, was analogous to a petition to recover medical records. Therefore, akin to the decision in *WF*, the complainer should be able to access legal aid to contest the application. These decisions about complainer representation apply regardless of whether or not it is a sexual offence at issue.[23]

Some have argued that by analogy this right could be extended in the future to s275 application hearings in sexual offences; as early as 2010, Fiona Raitt's research for Rape Crisis Scotland concluded that, with respect to s275 applications,

> [T]he most cogent argument for ILR in Scotland arises in response to breaches of the complainer's dignity and privacy. There is no scope for the Crown to embark on a policy of developing a coherent framework for complainers' privacy rights as the Crown are constitutionally bound to locate these interests within the wider public interest. In these conditions, as the interests of the complainer are not constitutionally embedded, they are always destined to be subordinate.
>
> (2010, at 8.08)[24]

More than a decade later, this is still a live issue. In their 2020 report, Keane and Convery argue for the right of a complainer to be heard, and to be legally represented – via legal aid – at s275 hearings in Scotland. This is necessitated, they suggest, by the especially private and intrusive nature of the questioning that follows a successful s275 application, combined with the risk of re-victimisation of sexual offence complainers. They argue that relevant Article 8 ECHR case law (domestically and at Strasbourg) supports this position,[25] and that since the complainer is a state witness undertaking a public duty to attend court and give evidence, they should not be asked to take on the cost of representation at a s275 hearing (2020, 3). Keane and Convery conclude that complainers should be notified, either by the court, or by the reporting officer in the police investigation, that an application has been made and that they are entitled to legal representation (2020, 32–33; see also Inspectorate of Prosecution (2017)).

A similar right has been introduced successfully in Ireland: s4A of the Criminal Law (Rape) Act 1989 gives the right for complainants to be heard and represented during a hearing about the introduction of sexual history evidence

23 For discussion of how digital evidence can be used to buttress existing myths and stereotypes in sexual violence cases, see Dodge (2018).

24 See also Chalmers (2014, 185-–189).

25 *WF v Scottish Ministers* 2016 SLT 359 and *Y v Slovenia*, (2016) 62 EHRR 3; *X & Y v The Netherlands* 1985 EHRR 235, respectively.

(though this right extends only to 'rape' offences and aggravated sexual assault offences). State funding for legal representation in a sexual history evidence hearing has been available in Ireland since 2001 (s34 of the Sex Offenders Act 2001). Similarly, s278.94(3) of the Canadian Criminal Code allows for the complainant in a sexual offences case to be represented at a hearing for a sexual history application (or any record relating to the complainant that is in the possession of the accused including medical, counselling or other sensitive records that the defence wishes to rely on during the proceedings) (see Gluzman 2019). A comparable right was recommended by Sir John Gillen in his review of serious sexual offences in Northern Ireland (Gillen 2019). In their report, Keane and Convery highlighted that prosecutors in Ireland recognised their submissions did not always align with submissions made on behalf of the complainer and that one of the advantages of representation for complainers in this context was "its effect on the complainer and its ability to ensure that their views were heard" (2020, 19). They point out that the words of Lord Glennie in *WF* could apply equally to complainers in s275 hearings: "If the complainer is not given the opportunity to be heard, how is the court to carry out the balancing exercise required of it?" 2020, 19, citing *WF*, at 39).

In fact, as a result of the full-bench *Nobile Officium*[26] case *RR* (*(Petitioner) v HMA* [2021] HCJAC 21). Scotland has recently taken a step towards some limited legal rights for complainers – i.e., to be told of a s275 application, and to have their views taken by the Crown Office in advance of the preliminary hearing. The court held that since section 1 of the Victims and Witnesses (Scotland) Act 2014 states that a witness should be able to obtain information about what is happening in proceedings, and, insofar as is appropriate, participate effectively in them, the Crown has a duty (on behalf of the court) to tell the complainer of the application and ascertain their views on it, including any objections as to accuracy, and then present those views to the court. The guidance produced by the Crown Office on engaging complainers for this purpose specifically mentions the need to approach the meeting in a trauma-informed and witness-centred way (though it is not clear what sort of training those who conduct the meetings have had in these matters). Complainers are also to be told of the outcome of the hearing, and re-precognosed[27] by the Crown afterwards. The legal rights of the complainer extend no further than this, thus falling far short of the sort of ILR rights introduced in Ireland and envisaged by Keane and Convery. The court in *RR* recognised that the complainer's ECHR Article 8 rights were engaged, and that she had the right as a victim to

26 The *Nobile Officium* is a residual power of the Court of Session and the High Court of Justiciary, using its 'equitable jurisdiction' to afford the petitioner a remedy when there is no other remedy available.

27 Precognition is the Scots law word for statement. This Crown Office guidance is not public but is on file with the author.

participate in proceedings; but it held that there was no right to directly participate in the trial, and only the legislature could effect IRL as it is a fundamental change to criminal procedure.

In March 2021, the Lord Justice Clerk Lady Dorrian's review group on 'Improving the Management of Sexual Offence Cases' recommended that ILR (with legal aid) be introduced for serious sexual offences complainers at s275 hearings, acknowledging that this would require the Scottish Parliament to introduce legislation (2021, 85–86; see Leverick (2021)). Despite the obvious direction of travel in other jurisdictions, and the mounting pressure on the Scottish government to introduce IRL, at the time of writing it is not evident if or when the Scottish government intend to follow Lady Dorrian's recommendation, although a 2022 consultation on improving the experiences of victims in the criminal justice system showed overwhelming support for ILR in this context.[28]

In practice, of course, there may well be difficulties with the implementation of such rights, as was found in Northern Ireland. Mary Illiadis' study found that it was common for the defence to raise late applications, which limited the amount of time the complainant had to prepare and arrange IRL (2019, 8). Also, Illiadis found at the end of the application hearing, some judges asked the representative to wait for the cross-examination to check the questions followed the spirit of what was agreed, while other judges asked the representative to leave, highlighting inconsistency in legal procedure. Illiadis suggests formally expanding the role of the representative to include being present at cross-examination, which many complainants experience as harrowing, with some experiencing it as just as traumatic as (if not more so than) the sexual assault.[29] How the Crown Office change to practice is being implemented is one of the areas being examined by the ongoing research project funded by the Scottish government, as mentioned above, but even if operating as intended, it leaves the more substantial question of IRL outstanding.[30] And the more

28 https://www.gov.scot/publications/improving-victims-experiences-justice-system-consultation-analysis/pages/8/

29 Craig, E. *Putting Trials on Trial: Sexual Assault and the Failure of the Legal Profession.* (McGill-Queen's University Press 2018); Patterson, D. (2010) 'The Linkage Between Secondary Victimization by Law Enforcement and Rape Case Outcomes' 26(2) *Journal of Interpersonal Violence* 328–347.

30 A recent amendment to the Criminal Procedure Rules *Criminal Practice Directions 2015: (Amendment No. 6)* [2018] EWCA Crim 516 (https://publications.parliament.uk/pa/bills/cbill/2016-2017/0137/17137.pdf) has made a similar change in England and Wales. It states (22A.7) that the complainant is to be made aware if a s41 application 9 the equivalent of a s275 application) has been granted before the trial though it does not state whose responsibility it is to inform the complainant. Some studies have reported that often complainants in England and Wales are not informed before the start of the trial that this sort of questioning will take place. See LimeCulture (2017). What difference the new practice directions will make remains to be seen.

radical proposal of ILR for complainers across the board in sexual offences trials has effectively been neutralised by the focus on ILR for preliminary hearings.[31]

A final, important, issue worth highlighting is that while some of the difficulties in ensuring complainers in sexual offences trials are treated with dignity and allowed to participate meaningfully in proceedings, might be alleviated if ILR were available to them in s275 applications, and even though complainers have been entitled to funded legal representation in sensitive records application since *WF* in 2016, some confusion persists.

One question is who should notify the complainer about a defence request for their private records. The 2017 Inspectorate of Prosecution Report highlighted that it may not be possible for the defence to inform the complainer of the intention to apply for sensitive records as they may not know the complainer's address – nor is it an appropriate victim-centred approach for the accused's solicitor to contact the complainer in this way; but neither is it the role of the prosecutor to do so as they are not acting on behalf of the complainer. The Inspectorate recommended that this task be undertaken by the court (2017, 72).

There is also confusion with respect to the Crown accessing sensitive data; in the *Nobile Officium* case *JC, Petitioner* 2018 HCA/2018/000013/XM, where the complainer was allowed to have representation in a commission and diligence hearing to recover her sensitive records, the court noted that the complainer's representative could not tell the court whether or not a statement taken from the complainer's doctor had been taken with or without the complainer's consent, and neither could the advocate depute appearing for the Crown. Nor could the Crown say whether or not anyone had even told the complainer that they intended to speak to her doctor. This suggests that complainers are not able to participate effectively in proceedings because they are not being given timely and correct information; and that they may not have given appropriate consent to data being accessed.

Moreover, in his research, Reed examined medical record requests made to one Scottish Health Board and found that over a six-month period, there were no cases in which Crown requests were seen by clinicians, no redaction of files took place, and records were released by managerial NHS staff (2020, 192). Healthcare professionals were often not aware when or how records had been requested, or who had sanctioned their release, until arriving in court to give evidence. Similarly, two complainers he spoke to were unaware of the extent of disclosure their consent had permitted until they were questioned in court (2020, 269–270).

COPFS officially changed its policy on sensitive records in 2020, indicating that they would ask complainers for consent, and the processes to be followed

31 ILR across the board has been introduced in some Scandinavian countries. ILR has also been considered for victims of domestic abuse – see for example Iliadis, Fitz-Gibbon and Walklate (2021).

if consent is not given, including the right to funded representation.[32] The COPFS policy makes explicit reference to the Article 8 rights of complainers to privacy. However, anecdotal evidence from Rape Crisis Scotland (RCS) suggests that the new system is not working as smoothly as it should, and that they are receiving requests from complainers for help accessing lawyers who can take on this work (who seem to be in scant supply) at a very late stage in the process. At a recent event organised by RCS, COPFS stated that they do not keep easily accessible records of the number of sensitive records applications, or the number of cases where there is legal representation for the complainer. New research is planned by RCS to investigate the implementation of the new policy.

It is difficult to see how these gaps in process can be reconciled with the legislation's professed aim of ensuring the proper administration of justice or protecting complainers' dignity and privacy. Maintaining (and monitoring) a transparent and ethical process for obtaining and disclosing sensitive records, that preserves the dignity and privacy of the complainer, is crucial. And it is to the dignity and privacy of the complainer that we now turn.

Dignity and Privacy, and Cross-examination: s275 (2)(b)(i)

Unlike the equivalent legislation in England and Wales, the rape shield provisions in Scotland specifically mention the need to protect the dignity and privacy of the complainer when weighing up the probative value of evidence. Several recent cases are worth mentioning here, where the High Court has given a welcome strong steer to lower courts, and to the Crown prosecutors and defence, on how bad practice relating to s275 applications, and the process of cross-examination on sexual history and character, can have a deleterious impact on the complainer's dignity and privacy.

The first is *Dreghorn v HM Advocate* [2015] HCJAC 69, where the accused was originally charged with 43 counts of sexual assault and assault against three different complainers, and was ultimately convicted on eight charges, including rapes, indecent assaults and assaults. The complainers in the case were clearly very vulnerable, as was noted by the court several times. There had been a s275 application in this case but it is unclear from the report what issues it pertained to. What is clear is that the defence raised questions about the credibility of one of the complainers, based on her character. The Lord President, Lord Carloway, was critical of the manner and length of cross-examination of that particular complainer at trial, and the lack of respect for her dignity or privacy. He specifically noted the duty of the trial judge to intervene where a proper balance regarding fairness to the parties is not struck by defence and Crown.

32 Available at: www.copfs.gov.uk/images/Sensitive%20Personal%20Records%20Policy%20-%2012%20Oct%202020.pdf.

Here, at first instance, neither the Crown nor the trial judge had challenged a very lengthy and problematic cross-examination. For example, the defence began questioning by saying, "you are a wicked, deceitful, malicious, vindictive liar? And you have been for twenty years?" As the High Court noted, it was "putting matters mildly, combative" (at 17). Lord Carloway went as far as to say that courts should intervene in cross-examination that is in effect a "sustained attack" that is "protracted, vexatious and unfeeling" and that "[i]f a proper balance cannot be achieved by the representatives of the Crown and defence, the court may have a duty to intervene" (at 38–40).[33]

The matter of good practice, and the dignity and privacy of the complainer, was raised in a second recent case, *HM Advocate v JG* [2019] HCJ 71, where the accused was charged with raping his partner. A s275 application was made (in part by the Crown), to adduce evidence of the complainer's previous consensual SM sexual behaviour. The case involved very long delays for complainer because of late applications from both parties delaying the trial. Lord Turnbull, hearing the application, did not think special cause had been shown for such a late application, but due to administrative and communication problems on both sides in the lengthy process, he did consider the application. However, Lord Turnbull held that the evidence met neither the common law test of relevance nor the criteria of s275, and was very clear in his judgment that the Crown had failed to challenge a substandard s275 application, that had little preparation or detail, and that did not mention any of the s275 criteria. It was found that the probative value of the evidence was therefore outweighed by the need to appropriately protect the complainer's dignity and privacy.

In *RN v HM Advocate* [2020] HCJAC 3, the accused was charged with sexual assaults against one of his sons, and his partner. He made an s275 application on the basis of an allegation that in the past the complainer had herself made false allegations and induced both his sons to make false accusations against teachers at the school. This was refused by the sheriff at first instance and the accused appealed. The opinion of the court was delivered by the Lord Justice Clerk Lady Dorrian, who referred to the accused's justifications for the admission of the evidence as "remote" and "bizarre" (at 9). She dismissed the evidence as 'collateral' in that it had no direct or indirect connection to the facts at issue, and criticised the way that the paperwork was presented by representatives to the court. Her main criticism, though, was reserved for the prosecutor and

33 Similar observations were made by Lady Dorrian, the Lord Justice Clerk, in *Donegan v HM Advocate* [2019] HCJAC 10, where she expressed surprise that there was no objection from the Crown, and noted that the trial judge also failed to intervene during lengthy questioning of one of the complainers over three days (which was described as unjustified and insulting, and wholly inappropriate) but rather engaged in behaviour more akin to cross-examination (at 54).

the sheriff – the former because she did not challenge parts of the application which were in fact inadmissible, and the sheriff for not recognising this.

Finally, in perhaps the most egregious example of this sort of problematic behaviour, in *MacDonald v HMA* [2020] HCJAC 21, the accused was convicted of sexual assault by penetration and sexual assault. The accused appealed on the ground that in referring to the complainer as a 'victim,' the sheriff's charge to the jury had constituted a miscarriage of justice. In refusing the appeal, the Lord President, Lord Carloway, commented extensively on the trial process, focusing particularly on the administration of the s275 application, the cross-examination, and the duties of the defence agent and the presiding trial judge.

Before trial, an s275 application had been made – unopposed by the Crown – to adduce evidence of the complainer's bad character – that she had sustained her injuries from two previous incidents, and that she had consumed cocaine with the accused at the time of the alleged assault. Lord Carloway noted that during cross-examination, the defence questioned the complainer on issues related to her 'bad' character. The sheriff, in his charge to the jury (which spanned 45 pages), repeated some of the defence claims about the complainer's use of cocaine and the defence agent's explanation that she had alleged rape because she was worried about what her boyfriend would say about her engaging sexually with the accused.

In his decision, Lord Carloway referred to the importance of the proper administration of justice (at 33) and emphasised the Crown's duty to oppose applications that seek to adduce inadmissible evidence, and the court's duty to carefully consider the application, and give reasons – that are minuted – for admitting the evidence. The Crown should have opposed the evidence, and the sheriff should not have admitted it – or indeed repeated it to the jury – since it related to irrelevant incidents and a gratuitous attack on the complainer's character regarding cocaine use – and supply (at 38–40): "[a]llowing evidence of this irrelevant and insulting nature into a trial of a sexual offence is a serious failure in the administration of justice" (at 37). Lord Carloway concluded that the trial had been "conducted in a manner which flew in the face of basic rules of evidence and procedure" and that "[w]ere this to be repeated, the situation in sexual offences trials would be unsustainable" (at 47).

These are strong words from Lord President, which encapsulate the High Court's recent narrowing of the interpretation of s275 exceptions; but it also indicates a level of scrutiny – and opprobrium – of the practices of lower courts on the part of the High Court, who appear to be signalling the importance of the need to protect the dignity and privacy of the complainer, and enhance good practice in preparing applications for court that adhere to the statutory framework of s275. Whether or not these messages from the bench are having an impact on practice is unknown – the practices identified as poor in these cases would not have come to light had there not been a reported appeal court decision, and so it is not evident that such practices are infrequent.

These represent only a handful of appeal court cases; there are many more sexual offences cases coming before trial in any given period. While it may be unwise to extrapolate too far from these instances, it does suggest that there is a pressing need for better administration and management of s275 applications, and systematic recording of, for example, when s275 applications are made and challenged, and why/why not. The legislation explicitly states that the dignity and privacy of the complainer must be given full consideration in weighing up whether evidence is admissible. But whether this is happening in practice, for example during cross-examination on matters relating to s275, and whether the exhortations of the High Court are filtering through to courts at first instance, are empirical questions that require close attention. These are amongst the urgent issues that the Scottish government-funded project aims to investigate.

The position of the High Court here is also supported by jurisprudence from Strasbourg. Signatory states have a positive obligation to ensure that they have in place an adequate legal framework which affords protection to individuals' physical and psychological integrity – not just in relation to sexual history, character or private evidence but also more broadly – under Article 8 of the European Convention of Human Rights (*X & Y v The Netherlands* 1985 EHRR 235). In *Y v Slovenia* (2016) 62 EHRR 3, the European Court of Human Rights said that "cross-examination should not be used as a means of humiliating a witness" (at 108), and Keane and Convery have noted that this positive obligation under Article 8 may extend to the "effective regulation of evidence given at criminal proceedings" (2020, 16) (though it is important to note that *Y v Slovenia* involved a defendant cross-examining the complainant himself, a practice no longer permitted in Scotland).

Conclusion

Recent cases in Scotland have made it possible to argue for complainers to have independent legal representation at s275 applications. Although each jurisdiction has its own particular legal, political and cultural context that will inform how best to respond to the issue of dealing with sexual history evidence, consideration of reforms introduced in other jurisdictions, such as ILR for sexual history evidence hearings in Canada and Ireland, can inform law and policy making in Scotland, while still bearing in mind the specific Scottish social and legal context (including the peculiarities of the Scottish system such as the larger jury, the not proven verdict, and the corroboration requirement amongst others), as well as the ECHR rights of the accused and the complainer in a sexual offences case.

Unlike some other jurisdictions, such as England and Wales, the Scottish "rape shield" legislation explicitly mentions the need to consider the dignity and privacy of complainers (section 275 (2)(b)(i)). This has allowed senior judges in appeal cases to censure COPFS, defence lawyers and judges in the lower courts who do not adequately protect complainers, and develop clear judicial guidance on how to interpret sections 274 and 275 correctly.

Notwithstanding some important shifts in policy and practice, there is a dearth of official recorded and publicly available statistical and other information about how sections 274 and s275 – and the new rules regarding complainer consultation, participation and representation – are implemented. Building on the Inspectorate's 2017 report, and the Equality and Human Rights Commission (Cowan 2020), a focused, in-depth root and branch review of COPFS practice in relation to s274 and s275 applications in sexual offences cases, akin to the 2019 HMCPI report[34] – was recently undertaken by the HM Inspectorate of Prosecution in Scotland who reported in November 2022.[35] However, unlike the Scottish government-funded project which analyses practices and procedures throughout the entire sexual offences proceeding, this focuses solely on Crown procedures and practices, and although useful in outlining gaps in Crown Office practice, is somewhat limited in scope.

My intention in this chapter is not to fetishise the law as the desirable tool or framework for addressing sexual violence. Rather it aims to open up legal provisions and practice to scrutiny, in order to better protect complainers who engage in Scottish sexual offences proceedings. To do so, we must also address the dearth of academic research on these issues. Scotland is behind other jurisdictions in generating rigorous research findings that illuminate the more qualitative aspects of the operation of the rules excluding sexual history and bad character, that would give context to the minimal statistical data referred to in section 2, shed light on the extent of the 'justice gap' in this area, and prompt necessary further and deeper change, at the legal, procedural – and societal – levels. The worry is that despite a fairly progressive narrowing by the High Court of the relevance of sexual history, bad character and private data evidence, patchy implementation on the ground may still reflect a 'culture lag' rooted in deeper systemic failures. There are pressing empirical questions here that remain to be answered, and it is hoped that the ongoing Scottish government-funded project will be part of a new era of research that can address this knowledge deficit.

References

Aspinall-Miles, Mary. 2019. "The Fundamentals of Mobile Phone Evidence." *Counsel Magazine*. https://www.counselmagazine.co.uk/articles/r-v-e-and-the-great-disclosure debate.

34 HM Crown Prosecution Service Inspectorate "Rape Inspection," December 2019. Available at www.justiceinspectorates.gov.uk/hmcpsi/hmcpsi-rape-inspection-2019/.

35 https://www.gov.scot/publications/inspection-copfs-practice-relation-sections-274-275-criminal-procedure-scotland-act-1995/documents/

Avinash, Shruti. 2021. "To Repair a Damaged Rape-Shield." *The RMLNLU Law Review Blog*, July 18. https://rmlnlulawreview.com/2021/07/18/india-rape-shield-laws/.

Brown, Beverley, Michele Burman, and Lynn Jamieson. 1992. *Sexual History and Sexual Character Evidence in Scottish Sexual Offence Trials*. Edinburgh: The Stationery Office.

Burman, Michele, Lynn Jamieson, Jan Nicholson, and Oona Brookes. 2007. "Impact of Aspects of the Law of Evidence in Sexual Offence Trials: An Evaluation Study." Scottish Government, Official Publication, Crime and Justice Social Research. No 41.

Cairns, Ilona. 2017. "'Access to Justice' for Complainers? The Pitfalls of the Scottish Government's Case to Abolish Corroboration." In *Scottish Criminal Evidence Law*, edited by Peter Duff and Pamela Ferguson, 41–66. Edinburgh: Edinburgh University Press.

Callander, Isla. 2014. "The Challenge of "Best Evidence" in Rape Trials: The Victims and Witnesses (Scotland) Act 2014." *Edinburgh Law Review* 18 (2): 279–284.

Chalmers, James. 2014. "Independent Legal Representation for Complainers in Sexual Offence Cases." In *Post-Corroboration Safeguards Review Report of the Academic Expert Group*, edited by Chalmers, James, Fiona Leverick, and Elizabeth Shaw, 185–189. Edinburgh: The Scottish Government.

Chalmers, James, and Fiona Leverick. 2013. "Majority Jury Verdicts." *Edinburgh Law Review* 17 (1): 90–96.

Chalmers, James, Fiona Leverick, and Vanessa E. Munro. 2021. "Beyond Doubt: The Case Against 'Not Proven'." *Modern Law Review* 85 (4): 847–878. https://doi.org/10.1111/1468-2230.12707.

Cowan, Sharon. 2015. "Sex/Gender Equality: Taking a Break from the Legal to Transform the Social." In *Exploring the Legal in Socio-Legal Studies*, edited by Dave Cowan and Daniel Wincott, 121–146. Bristol: Palgrave MacMillan.

Cowan, Sharon. 2020. *The Use of Sexual History, Bad Character Evidence and 'Private Data' in Scottish Sexual Offences Trials*. Edinburgh: Equality and Human Rights Commission.

Cowan, Sharon, and Rebecca Hewer. 2020. "Vulnerability, Victimhood and Sex Offences." In *Research Handbook on Gender, Sexuality and the Law*, edited by Chris Ashford and Alexander Maine, 341–360. Cheltenham: Edgar Elgar.

Cowan, Sharon, and Vanessa E. Munro. 2021. "Seeking Campus Justice: Challenging the 'Criminal Justice Drift' in UK University Responses to Student Sexual Violence and Misconduct." *Journal of Law and Society* 48 (3): 308–333. https://doi.org/10.1111/jols.12306.

Craig, Elaine. 2016. "Section 276 Misconstrued: The Failure to Properly Interpret and Apply Canada's Rape Shield Provisions." *Canadian Bar Review* 94: 45–84.

Craig, Elaine. 2018. *Putting Trials on Trial: Sexual Assault and the Failure of the Legal Profession*. Montreal: McGill-Queen's University Press.

Dodge, Alexa. 2018. "The Digital Witness: The Role of Digital Evidence in Criminal Justice Responses to Sexual Violence." *Feminist Theory* 19 (3): 303–321. https://doi.org/10.1177/1464700117743049.

Gillen, John. 2019. *Report into the Law and Procedures in Serious Sexual Offences in Northern Ireland*. https://www.lawsoc-ni.org/DatabaseDocs/new_8655264__gillen-review-report-into-the-law-and-procedures-in-serious-sexual-offences-in-.pdf.

Gluzman, Helena. 2019. "A Delicate Act of Judicial Balancing: Breathing New Life into Section 276 of the *Criminal Code*." Available at SSRN: https://ssrn.com/abstract=3472112.

HM Crown Prosecution Service Inspectorate. 2019. *Rape Inspection: A thematic review of rape cases by HM Crown Prosecution Service Inspectorate.* https://www.justiceinspectorates.gov.uk/hmcpsi/hmcpsi-rape-inspection-2019/.

HM Inspectorate of Prosecution in Scotland. 2022. *Inspection of COPFS Practice in relation to sections 274 and 275 of the Criminal Procedure (Scotland) Act 1995.* https://www.gov.scot/publications/inspection-copfs-practice-relation-sections-274-275-criminal-procedure-scotland-act-1995/documents/

Illiadis, Mary. 2019. "Victim Representation for Sexual History Evidence in Ireland: A Step Towards or Away from Meeting Victims' Procedural Justice Needs?" *Criminology & Criminal Justice*, 20(4): 1–17.

Iliadis, Mary, Kate Fitz-Gibbon, and Sandra Walklate. 2021. "Improving Justice Responses for Victims of Intimate Partner Violence: Examining the Merits of the Provision of Independent Legal Representation." *International Journal of Comparative and Applied Criminal Justice* 45 (1): 105–114.

Inspectorate of Prosecution in Scotland. 2017. *Thematic Review of the Investigation and Prosecution of Sexual Crimes.* Edinburgh: Inspectorate of Prosecution. https://www.gov.scot/publications/thematic-review-investigation-prosecution-sexual-crimes/.

Keane, Eamon P.H. 2023. "Scotland's Not Proven Verdict: The Nightmare of History?" In *The Ian Willock Collection on Law and Justice in the 21st Century*, edited byEamon P.H. Keane and Peter Robson. FDUP, forthcoming.

Keane, Eamon P.H., and Tony Convery. 2020. *Proposal for Independent Legal Representation for Complainers where an Application is Made to Lead Evidence of Their Sexual History or Character.* www.law.ed.ac.uk/sites/default/files/2020-06/ILR%20Report%20Final%20Version%20June%20_0.pdf.

Kelly, Liz, Jennifer Temkin, and Sue Griffiths. 2006. *Section 41: An Evaluation of New Legislation Limiting Sexual History Evidence in Rape Trials.* London: Home Office.

Larcombe, Wendy. 2011. "Falling Rape Conviction Rates: (Some) Feminist Aims and Measures for Rape Law." *Feminist Legal Studies* 19 (1): 27–45.

Leverick, Fiona. 2021. "Improving the Management of Sexual Offence Cases in Scotland: The Dorrian Review." *Edinburgh Law Review* 25 (3): 385–393.

LimeCulture. 2017. *Application of Section 41 Youth Justice and Criminal Evidence Act 1999: A Survey of Independent Sexual Violence Advisers (ISVAs).* Cheshire: LimeCulture.

McDonald, Elizabeth, and Yvette Tinsley. 2011. "Reforming the Rules of Evidence in Cases of Sexual Offending: Thoughts from Aotearoa/New Zealand." *The International Journal of Evidence & Proof* 15 (4): 311–337.

McGlynn, Clare. 2010. "*Regina v A (No. 2)* [2001] UKHL 25." In *Feminist Judgments: From Theory to Practice*, edited by Rosemary Hunter, Clare McGlynn, and Erica Rackley, 211–227. Oxford: Hart Publishing.

McGlynn, Clare. 2017. "Rape Trials and Sexual History Evidence: Reforming the Law on Third-Party Evidence." *The Journal of Criminal Law* 81 (5): 367–392.

Munro, Vanessa E. 2023. "'It Felt Like a Comma, Not a Full Stop'. Complainers' Experiences of the Not Proven Verdict within Scottish Rape Trials" (this volume,).

O'Floinn, Micheal, and David Ormerod. 2012. "Social Networking Material as Criminal Evidence." *Criminal Law Review* 7 (7): 486–512.

Ormston, Rachel, James Chalmers, Fiona Leverick, Vanessa E. Munro, and Lorraine Murray. 2019. *Scottish Jury Research: Findings from a Large-Scale Mock Jury Study.* Scottish Government. https://www.gov.scot/publications/scottish-jury-research-fingings-large-mock-jury-study-2/.

Patterson, D. 2010. "The Linkage Between Secondary Victimization by Law Enforcement and Rape Case Outcomes." *Journal of Interpersonal Violence* 26 (2): 328–347.

Phoenix, Jo and Sarah Oerton. 2005. *Illicit And Illegal: Sex, Regulation And Social Control.* Cullompten: Willan.

Raitt, Fiona. 2010. *Independent Legal Representation for Complainers in Sexual Offence Trials.* Edinburgh: Rape Crisis Scotland.

Reed, Dominic. 2020. *Medical Confidentiality and Domestic Abuse*. PhD Thesis for University of Glasgow, on file with author.

Russell, Yvette. 2021. "Theorizing Feminist Anti-Rape Praxis and The Problem of Resistance." *Signs* 46 (2): 465–488.

Srinivasan, Amia. 2021. *The Right to Sex*. London: Bloomsbury Publishing.

Taylor, Chloe. 2020. *Foucault, Feminism and Sex Crimes: An Anti-Carceral Analysis*. London: Routledge.

Chapter 9

Complainant Intoxication Evidence and Proof of Non-Consent in Australian Rape Trials

Insights from Appellate Court Decisions[1]

Julia Quilter and Luke McNamara

Introduction

Despite four decades of progressive legislative reforms in Australia designed to deliver justice to victims of sexual violence through prosecutions in the criminal justice system, rape case attrition rates remain high, and conviction rates are still low (Australian Bureau of Statistics (ABS) 2021; NSW Bureau of Crime Statistics and Research (BOCSAR) 2020, 2017; Fitzgerald 2006; Judicial Commission of NSW 2011). Similar (though not universal) patterns have been identified in many other countries (Lovett and Kelly 2009; Triggs et al. 2009; Daly and Bouhours 2010; Rotenberg 2017; Office for National Statistics (UK) 2018). A large body of research – in Australia and internationally – has attempted to explain the gap between reform objectives and both outcomes and the experience of complainants (Daly and Bouhours 2010; Lonsway and Archambault 2012; Australian Women Against Violence Alliance (AWAVA) 2017; McDonald 2014; Burgin 2018, Temkin et al. 2018; Larcombe 2011, 2017; Quilter 2011; Powell et al. 2013; Mason & Monaghan 2019).

Studies have identified the continuing influence of 'rape myths' as a cause of the failure to deliver justice to victim-survivors (Australian Institute of Family Studies 2017; Angiolini 2015; Smith 2018; Haskell and Randall 2019; McDonald et al. 2020; Leverick 2020; Chalmers, Leverick and Munro 2021; cf Thomas 2020). Rape myths are deeply embedded in how dominant gender norms construct a set of common-sense assumptions about heterosexual negotiations (Gavey 2008, 2019; Ellison and Munro 2009). In courtrooms, legal actors (particularly defence lawyers), mobilise discriminatory gender norms and actively resist the potential of progressive reforms including definitions of consent (McDonald et al. 2020; Craig 2018; Lazar 2010).

A powerful myth is that a woman who has consumed alcohol or other drugs (AOD) shares responsibility if she is raped, and that the culpability of the perpetrator is reduced (Taylor 2007; Croskery-Hewitt 2015; Carline, Gunby

1 The law as stated in this chapter is as at November 2021.

DOI: 10.4324/9781003379331-13

and Taylor 2018). This also contributes to self-blame for victims (Flowe and Maltby 2018). The prevalence of such attitudes has significant implications in practice because AOD consumption – by victims, offenders or both – is commonly associated with rape. Studies have estimated that AOD consumption is a factor in some 50-80% of rapes (Zawacki et al. 2003; Finney 2004; Lievore 2005; Triggs et al. 2009; Stern 2010; Abbey 2011, 2014; Graham et al. 2014; McDonald et al. 2020). Intoxication is also a major factor in low reporting, high attrition, and low conviction rates (Lievore 2003; Kelly, Lovett and Regan 2005; Taylor 2007; Flowe and Maltby 2018).

In Australia, most jurisdictions have introduced legislative provisions to overcome the tendency for complainant intoxication evidence to operate as a barrier to successful prosecution. Most jurisdictions have added a provision to the statutory definition of rape that seeks, to a greater or lesser extent, to re-orient complainant intoxication away from carrying an assumption of consent, and towards being characterised as evidence of *non-consent*. For example, in Victoria, s 36(2)(e) of the *Crimes Act 1958* (Vic) provides that a person does not consent if "the person is so affected by alcohol or another drug as to be incapable of consenting …." In NSW, s 61HE(8) states: "The grounds on which it may be established that a person does not consent to sexual intercourse include: (a) if the person consents to the sexual activity while substantially intoxicated by alcohol or any drug …."[2]

Internationally, there is a body of literature on the relationship between intoxication and consent in the context of rape trials (for example, Finch and Munro 2004; Cowan 2008; Rumney and Fenton 2008; Croskery-Hewitt 2015; Clough 2019). Other work has focused on how complainant intoxication evidence impacts on earlier criminal justice system decisions, such as police decisions and practices (Finney 2004; Tasca et al. 2013; Flowe et al. 2016; Shaw et al. 2017) and prosecution decisions pre-trial (Lievore 2005; Gunby, Carline and Beynon 2010; Topping 2016). In addition, a number of studies have attempted to simulate a jury trial by an experimental design that uses 'mock' juries to understand how jurors understand the relevance of intoxication evidence (Finch and Munro 2005, 2006, 2007, 2009; Taylor 2007; Dinos et al. 2015; Nitschke et al. 2021).

Little is known about the operation of Australian legislation introduced to guide how evidence of complainant intoxication is applied in rape trials and whether it is having the effect intended by law makers (Henderson and

2 Other Australian jurisdictions (except Queensland and Western Australia) have also adopted provisions on the relationship between complainant intoxication and consent: *Crimes Act 1900* (ACT), s 67(1)(e); *Criminal Code 1924* (Tas), s 2A(2)(h); *Criminal Code* (NT), s 192(2)(c); *Criminal Law Consolidation Act 1935* (SA), s 46(3)(d).

Duncan 2016). In this chapter, we report on the initial findings of a study that attempts to contribute to filling this gap.[3]

In previous research (Quilter et al. 2018; Quilter and McNamara 2018; McNamara et al. 2017) we have shown that, in criminal trials in Australia, decisions about the relevance of a person's intoxication (specifically, accused persons and, in the context of rape trials, complainants) are often made on the basis of "common knowledge" (Valverde 2003). In Valverde's terms, common knowledge "is not some kind of average of what people know. It is not descriptive but imperative; it is the knowledge we all ought to have" (Valverde 2003, 224). It is akin to the things we are all *assumed* to know about a subject. 'Common knowledge' about the relationship between alcohol and drug consumption and 'availability' for sex may be especially dangerous in the rape trial context, given the long and entrenched history, and resilience, of myths and stereotypes about rape complainants. It is important to understand whether progressive legislative reforms designed to debunk or neutralise them are having the intended effect.

In this chapter we report on the findings of the first phase of an Australian study of intoxication evidence in rape trials: a study of appellate court decisions. After explaining the research design for this study, we summarise the main findings on what the cases reveal about: whether and how complainant intoxication evidence is engaged to prove non-consent; and the relationship between a complainant's intoxication and assessment of her reliability and credibility as a witness. The final part of the chapter offers a general discussion of the project's findings, and of recent amendments to the NSW legislation governing complainant intoxication in sexual assault trials.

Research Design

We analysed all decisions of the highest criminal appellate court in each Australian state and territory[4] and the High Court of Australia in the decade 2010–2019, involving an appeal against conviction on a rape charge,[5] in which

3 J Quilter and L McNamara, 'Intoxication Evidence in Rape Trials: A Double-Edged Sword?' Australian Research Council Discovery Project (DP200100101) (2020–2023). This project responds to the call for "greater and more systematic" empirical research "[g]iven the discrepancy between community attitudes about sexual offending and sexual offences legislation" (Hanley et al 2016, 560).

4 Australian Capital Territory Court of Appeal, New South Wales Court of Criminal Appeal, Northern Territory Court of Criminal Appeal, Queensland Court of Appeal, South Australian Court of Criminal Appeal, Tasmanian Court of Criminal Appeal, Victorian Court of Appeal, Western Australian Court of Appeal.

5 Rape charges for the purpose of this study relates to the primary rape offence (or its aggravated version) in each Australian State/Territory. *Crimes Act 1900* (NSW), s 61I; *Crimes Act 1958* (Vic), s 38; *Crimes Act 1900* (ACT), s 54; *Criminal Code Act 1924* (Tas), s 185; *Criminal Code Act 1983* (NT), s 192; *Criminal Law Consolidation Act 1935* (SA), s 48; *Criminal Code Act 1899* (Qld), s 48; *Criminal Code Act Compilation Act 1913* (WA), s 325. We included one case, even though it is not technically

the intoxication of the victim (complainant) formed part of the evidence in the case (n = 102). The collected cases were then subjected to qualitative content analysis focusing on claims made – by appellate judges, trial judges, and prosecution and defence counsel – about the significance that should be attached to evidence regarding the complainant's intoxication. The sample size does not support quantitative analysis, but provides a robust basis for qualitative analysis, noting that it represents all conviction appeals during the review period that met the criteria for inclusion in the study.

We recognise the limitation of a study based on appellate decisions. Appellate court decisions are not representative of criminal trials generally. Further, conviction appeals are, by definition, cases in which the defendant was found guilty at trial and so our sample does not include cases in which the accused was acquitted at trial. Despite these limitations, appellate court decisions are an accessible and valuable data source. In their own right they are an "authoritative voice of 'knowledge' on the nature and relevance of intoxication for criminal law purposes" (McNamara et al. 2017, 150), and they also offer a window into the conduct of rape trials, noting that these trials are rarely the subject of first-hand observation and analysis.[6]

Complainant Intoxication and Non-consent

As noted above, the general intent or spirit of legislative provisions on complainant intoxication (that operates in all Australian jurisdictions except Queensland and Western Australia) is to break the nexus between intoxication and assumed consent. The Crown's obligation to prove the element of non-consent has been notoriously challenging – in a cultural context which has tended to assume a woman's 'availability' for sex, all the more so where she has consumed alcohol or other drugs. To the extent that statutory provisions on complainant intoxication are designed to overcome this barrier – to write this assumption out of the criminal law concept of consent – one way of thinking about these provisions is that they are designed to 'assist' the Crown to prove the element of non-consent. It might be said that the statutory language employed is more qualified than this account suggests, but we stand by our characterisation of the spirit of legislative reform in this area. Our analysis of appellate decisions did not yield strong evidence that this goal is being achieved on a consistent basis.

a conviction appeal, because of its importance, including as a catalyst for the NSW Law Reform Commission's recent inquiry into consent (NSWLRC 2020). *Lazarus* [2017] NSWCCA 279 was a Crown appeal from an acquittal – permitted under the special rules that apply to judge-alone trials in NSW (*Crimes (Appeal and Review) Act 2001* (NSW), s 107).

6 We note that analysis of appellate court decisions is only the first stage of our three-stage ARC study noted above (n 3) which includes qualitative analysis of transcripts from a sample of rape trials and interviews with prosecutors and defence lawyers.

Our dataset contains instances of express judicial recognition that a complainant's intoxication (even at high levels) is not necessarily synonymous with non-consent. In *Mitic v R*[7], at 24, the Victorian Court of Appeal cited the following statement from *R v Francis*[8]:

> It is not correct as a matter of law that it is rape to have [sexual intercourse with] a woman who is drunk who does not resist because her submission is due to the fact that she is drunk. The reason why it is not is that that at least includes the case where the [intercourse] is consensual notwithstanding that the consent is induced by excessive consumption of alcohol. The critical question in this case was whether the complainant had, by reason of sleep or a drunken stupor, been rendered incapable of deciding whether to consent or not.[9]

Other cases revealed judicial scepticism about the credibility of the defendant's assertion that a highly intoxicated woman had consented to having sex with him (*Makary*[10]; *Tabbah*[11]; and *Ewen*[12]) or a defendant's assertion that a complainant could have been mistaken that she did not consent due to her intoxication (*Paite v Tasmania*[13]).

Assumptions about the intoxication/consent relationship were still evident in the cases we examined, and these took a variety of forms. In some cases, the defence attempted to turn the complainant's intoxication to advantage. For example, to support an assertion that it lowered inhibitions resulting in consensual sex: the defendant submitted that "[t]he complainant's intoxication 'has removed the complainant's inhibitions, or inflamed her passion, or reduced her power of self-control'" (*Makary*).[14] In another case, the defendant complained that there was a misdirection on intoxication as

> at no stage … did the [trial] Judge address the critical question on the defence case which was whether the complainant had lost her inhibitions and was now either unwilling or unable, as a result of intoxication or some other reason, to positively admit her conduct.
>
> (*R v Crafter*[15])

7 [2011] VSCA 373, at 24.
8 [1993] 2 Qd R 300, at 305.
9 See also *Jones* [2010] NSWCCA 117.
10 [2018] QCA 258, at 71.
11 [2017] NSWCCA 55, at 170.
12 [2015] NSWCCA 117, at 164.
13 [2019] TASCCA 5, at 118.
14 [2018] QCA 258, at 31. See also *Ewen* [2015] NSWCCA 117, at 164; *Collins* [2018] HCA 18, at 14.
15 [2019] SASCFC 25, at 71.

At other times, the submission was that "that if the complaint could not remember other aspects of the evening, then it was reasonably possible that she had in a waking state, consented to the sexual encounter with the applicant but had subsequently forgotten it" (*Cordeiro v R*[16]).

At times, generalised assumptions were engaged by the trial judge when directing the jury, in a way that suggested or implied that they were relevant to the complainant in this instance:

> It is a *common experience* that intoxication may reduce a person's inhibitions, may cause them to be more relaxed and outgoing and, in certain circumstances, it may cause them to do things they would not do if they were not intoxicated.
>
> (*R v Crafter*[17])

In other cases, such arguments were rejected:

> What is implicit in the appellant's contentions is the suggestion that, perhaps affected by alcohol, the complainant agreed to sexual intercourse, but then quickly regretted her actions and made, and persisted with, a false complaint of rape. In our respectful opinion, it would be wrong to doubt the credibility of the complainant's account based on a generalised notion that alcohol has such an effect. There was no evidence that alcohol may have affected the complainant in that way and, because of the way in which the trial was conducted, it was not a proposition which was put to her so as to give her an opportunity to respond to it.
>
> (*Paite v Tasmania*[18])

Yet, we note that the dissenting judge in this matter considered that the intoxication evidence should have caused reasonable doubt in the jury:

> Even making due allowance for the possibility that a combination of intoxication and distress could account for the complainant's behaviour and demeanour as she arrived at her residence and subsequently, the possibility of initial alcohol induced euphoria turning into ex post facto regret for her conduct looms in my mind sufficiently to raise a reasonable doubt as to her assertion of lack of consent.
>
> (*Paite v Tasmania*[19])

16 [2019] NSWCCA 308, at 71; the submission was rejected on appeal, at 72.
17 [2019] SASCFC 25, at 72; emphasis added.
18 [2019] TASCCA 5, at 124.
19 [2019] TASCCA 5, at 59.

Occasionally, other rape myths were engaged to *support* the Crown case that the complainant had not consented. In *Tabbah*[20]: "[t]he complainant gave evidence that, due to her level of intoxication, she was unable to *'fight'*, and simply leant back in the seat [of the taxi where she was sexually assaulted]." Similarly, in *Hofer v R*[21] the Crown relied on the level of the complainant's intoxication to prove non-consent: as "incontestable evidence that the applicant had plied each of these young women with alcohol evinced his intent, from the outset, to reduce their capacity for resistance."

One of the most striking (and disturbing) features of our dataset was that the cases in which intoxication was accepted as strong evidence of non-consent were instances in which the complainant was intoxicated to the point of being unconscious or asleep, or very nearly so. For example, in *Bevinetto*[22], the complainant "was asleep through the whole event and only awoke when the [defendant] moved away from her body in response to [the defendant's girlfriend's] loud and violent intrusion." (The girlfriend's 'intrusion' involved shouting at the complainant to wake up, punching the defendant in the face and saying to him, "Are you fucking kidding me?")[23] In *R v Crafter*[24] the Crown argued that she was "unconscious, either asleep or passed out from the alcohol" (at 82) when the rape commenced, and therefore was "incapable of freely and voluntarily" consenting (at 86). In *Cordeiro v R*[25] the Crown's position was that the complainant was unconscious, "asleep and not alert and responding … and was therefore unable to give consent." In other cases, the complainant was described in terms which suggested she was nearly unconscious or asleep: for example, "lolling back in the car seat with her eyes half-closed in a state of grossly compromised consciousness" (*Tabbah*).[26]

In cases where the complainant's intoxication 'fell short' of the point described in these examples, there was more contestation about the significance that should be attached to the intoxication. For example, in *R v Teece*[27], the implication was that consent was likely given as she had not "passed out":

> While the complainant gave evidence of having consumed six drinks during the night and feeling tipsy, there was no evidence that her intoxication was such that she passed out or could not control her actions. Her

20 [2017] NSWCCA 55, at 26.
21 [2019] NSWCCA 244, at 191.
22 [2018] QCA 219, at 26.
23 See also *Fuller* [2015] SASFC 71, at 5; *Di Giorgio* [2016] VSCA 335, at 6; *Day* [2017] NSWCCA 192; *De Silva* [2018] QCA 274.
24 [2019] SASCFC 25.
25 [2019] NSWCCA 308, at 55.
26 [2017] NSWCCA 55, at 166. See also *Makary* [2018] QCA 258, at 68; *Rosenburg* [2016] NSWCCA 292.
27 [2019] QCA 246, at 24.

> evidence was that she decided to go to bed because she was tipsy, demonstrating, as the respondent submitted, an awareness of her state and level of comprehension.

This leads us to question the utility of statutory provisions on complainant intoxication (like s 61HE(8) of the *Crimes Act 1900* (NSW) and equivalents in other jurisdictions, discussed above). Note that in most Australian jurisdictions, evidence that the complainant was asleep or unconscious is a separately listed statutory factor negating consent (*Crimes Act 1900* (NSW), s 61HE(5)(b); *Crimes Act 1958* (Vic), s 36(2)(d); *Criminal Code* (Tas), s 2A(2)(h); *Criminal Law Consolidation Act 1935* (SA), s 46(3)(c); *Criminal Code* (NT), s 192(2)(c)). Our analysis suggests that, in practice the 'intoxication' provision may be being blurred with the 'asleep or unconscious' provision, such as to make the former largely redundant and ineffective for the large number of victims of sexual violence who were intoxicated – but not asleep or unconscious – at the time of their rape.[28]

A further risk, to which we now turn, is that, having led evidence of the complainant's intoxication to support proof of the actus reus element of non-consent, the Crown (and the complainant) may face the challenge that the defence will seek to rely on the complainant's intoxication to raise doubt about the complainant's reliability and credibility as a witness.

Complainant Intoxication and Credibility/Reliability

In a number of cases in our dataset, the implications of the complainant's intoxication for her/his credibility and reliability as a witness were scrutinised. Our analysis focused on how judges approached the relationship between intoxication and credibility/reliability. There was consistent recognition across the cases that the fact of a person's intoxication is relevant to assessing the veracity of her/his account of what occurred. More surprising was that we found variation as to how that relevance was conceived.

In some cases, it appeared to be accepted that intoxication necessarily diminishes the reliability of a complainant's evidence. For example:

> In my view, the direction failed to adequately instruct the jury that, in considering the reliability of the complainant's evidence, and whether they could be satisfied beyond reasonable doubt of the appellant's guilt upon her evidence, her state of intoxication was relevant. It was relevant to

28 Our analysis has focused on the relationship between complainant intoxication and the actus reus element of non-consent. We acknowledge that complainant intoxication evidence may also be engaged in relation to the mens rea element of knowledge, but this did feature prominently in the appellate decisions in this study.

> her perception, and to her recall of the events. It was also relevant, when considering her credibility. In restricting his direction to the question of whether the complainant might have lost her inhibitions, but has now forgotten, or is now unwilling to admit her conduct, the trial judge failed to give a sufficient direction about the relevance of the complainant's state of intoxication.
>
> (*Daniel*)[29]

In *Bakshi*[30] the Court characterised the fact that the complainant was "obviously affected by alcohol on the night in question" as evidence "that might be thought to cast some doubt upon the complainant's credibility," but pointed to other "significant features of the complainant's account which gave her evidence a ring of truth." In *Costa v The State of Western Australia*[31]; *Costa v The State of Western Australia*[32] it was submitted for the appellant that the allegation was an alcohol induced fabrication or something that she just thought happened when she woke up in the middle of the night (*Costa v The State of Western Australia*[33]). The Court of Appeal found that her intoxication went to her credibility/reliability:

> The complainant's limited recollection of the events after dinner on 7 March 2015, and her memory being in 'pictures,' provides grounds for approaching the complainant's evidence with some caution. That is so despite the evidence of recent complaint and the complainant's distressed state when collected ....[34]

Some judges displayed a more sensitive and sophisticated understanding of the relationship between intoxication, memory and the ability to recall details. In fact, in some cases, evidence of the complainant's intoxication was regarded as making them *more* credible and their account *more* reliable. For example:

> ... although cross-examination of the complainant was firm and extensive, no 'knock-out blow' was landed. In particular, many of the inconsistencies and gaps in recollection on her part could be amply explained by her gross intoxication, the evidence for which came from many sources: the

29 (2010) 207 A Crim R 449, at 50-51. See also *R v Crafter* [2019] SASCFC 25, at 72.
30 [2018] VSCA 83, at 84.
31 [2019] WASCA 3.
32 [2019] WASCA 200.
33 [2019] WASCA 3, at 75.
34 [213]. See also *Omot* [2016] VSCA 24; *Roberts* (2012) 225 A Crim R 452; and *Cook* [2010] WASCA 241, at 213.

> complainant herself, Ms Hart, the second taxi driver, the finding of the shoe on the garbage bin, and the CCTV from the second taxi.
>
> (*Tabbah*)[35]

In other cases, evidence of the complainant's intoxication was identified as just one of the factors relevant to the veracity of their account (*Rosenburg*[36]; *Duckworth*[37]; *Keogh*[38]; *Fuller*[39]).

General Discussion

The findings reported in this chapter tend to confirm that there is reason to be concerned by the fact that, in rape trials, critical decisions about whether a complainant was relevantly intoxicated are often made on the basis of imprecise evidence and 'common knowledge.' Such common knowledge can easily slip into 'rape myths' and other generalised assumptions about the significance of a person's intoxication. Where there was evidence that the complainant was very intoxicated, our analysis revealed two things. First, tribunals of fact (whether juries, or judges in judge-alone trials) face a formidable exercise in translation. It is often the case that jurors are given little guidance in deciding how to use evidence from the complainant about their level of intoxication – for example, that s/he felt 'wobbly' or 'out of it,' or had consumed 8–12 drinks, or was 'a nine' on a one-to-ten scale – and apply it to the critical decisions they are required to make in a rape trial. Second, complainant intoxication evidence can be a 'double-edged sword.' It *can* strengthen the Crown case – although the strongest examples of this effect were in cases where the complainant was so intoxicated as to be asleep or unconscious. We did not discern significant differences in the approaches adopted across Australian jurisdictions – including those states and territories with variously worded complainant intoxication provisions as part of their legislation on consent/non-consent, and those states without (Queensland and Western Australia). The nature of this study (of appellate decisions) does not allow us to reach firm conclusions on whether (and, if so, why) Crown prosecutors actively avoid attempting to engage statutory provisions on complainant intoxication, but we believe this will be an important avenue for further research.

This study further suggests that, despite legislative reform, it is still the case that complainant intoxication evidence can *impede* conviction, and this can

35 [2017] NSWCCA 55, at 169. See also *MCS and AAZ* [2018] QCA 184, at 169; *Compton and Barratt* (2013) 237 A Crim R 177; *Bray* [2014] VSCA 276; *O'Loughlin* [2011] QCA 123; *Hofer v R* [2019] NSWCCA 244.

36 [2016] NSWCCA 292, at 47.

37 [2016] QCA 30.

38 [2018] VSCA 145.

39 [2015] SASCFC 71.

occur in two ways. First, it can be engaged by the defence to assert that the complainant was 'disinhibited' and consenting – suggesting that cultural assumptions and generalisations about AOD consumption and sex (and women) may still be perceived, by some at least, as valid.

The second technique of defence engagement of complainant intoxication evidence observed in this study was to challenge the complainant's credibility as a witness and the reliability of their account of events. In this respect, we were struck by the diversity of approaches evident in the appellate decisions we examined. Certainly, the traditional (and problematic) view that intoxication inevitably diminishes credibility and reliability is still in circulation. However, more positively, we did detect some appellate court awareness of the fact that scientific knowledge on the relationship between intoxication and memory/recall is not static, and that a more nuanced approach should be taken. For example, in *Keogh*[40], the Victorian Court of Appeal held that the complainant's intoxication did not compel the jury to conclude that her evidence, regarding absence of consent, was unreliable, and in *Roberts*[41], the same Court recognised the difference between core issues and peripheral details, when it came to the recall of a complainant who was intoxicated at the time of the alleged rape.

As the body of research on intoxication, rape, memory and recall continues to grow (Flowe et al. 2016, 2019; Jores et al. 2019; Kloft et al. 2021; Flowe and Carline 2021), it is important that rape trials have the benefits of the latest scientific knowledge. Our study suggests that there is a need to improve the quality and consistency of courtroom knowledge about the effects of AOD. The provision of such information should be routine rather than occasional in rape trials, so that 'common knowledge' about intoxication – including problematic assumptions and myths about AOD use and consent – are no longer the dominant frame for adjudication in rape trials. Expert opinion evidence may be a viable mechanism for achieving the goal of better educated lawyers, judges and juries.

Conclusion

The findings reported in this chapter suggest that current legislative provisions in Australian states and territories on complainant intoxication operate unevenly, at best, and are relatively ineffective in transforming the ways in which complainant intoxication evidence operates in rape trials. It is anticipated that future phases of our larger study of intoxication evidence in Australian rape trials, including trial transcript analysis and interviews with lawyers, will shed greater light on why legislative reform appears to have failed to seriously

40 [2018] VSCA 145, at 93.
41 [2012] VSCA 313, at 52.

disrupt long-held cultural assumptions about intoxication, consent and credibility. In the meantime, this chapter provides yet another reminder that statutory change is not self-executing, and that in the setting of the adversarial trial, the attitudes and practices of defence lawyers, prosecutors and judges – as well as juries – exert powerful influence on the experience of complainants and trial outcomes.

Postscript

On 23 November 2021, the NSW Parliament passed the *Crimes Legislation Amendment (Sexual Consent Reforms) Act 2021* (NSW), based largely on recommendations of the NSWLRC (2020). The amendments will commence on a date appointed by proclamation which is likely to be in six months. Relevantly, in the context of a new section on non-consent (*Crimes Act 1900* (NSW), s 61HJ), the former complainant intoxication provision (based on a "substantially intoxicated" formula) has been replaced with: "A person does not consent … if the person is so affected by alcohol or another drug as to be incapable of consenting ….".[42] Our cross-jurisdictional analysis in this chapter suggests that such a change will do little to address one of the main problems we have highlighted in this chapter: the tendency to regard the level of intoxication required to vitiate consent as synonymous with being asleep or unconscious (or very nearly so). The Commission had suggested that the proposed approach focuses on the "key issue" being "the effect of the intoxication on the complainant's capacity to consent, and not the circumstances in which the complainant came to be intoxicated" (NSWLRC 2020, at 6.86). However, in light of our findings, it is possible that the new focus in NSW on '*incapable* of consenting' may be worse than the 'substantially intoxicated' formulations it replaced. Centring the inquiry on incapacity may serve only to consolidate the problematic practice of equating relevant intoxication with being asleep or unconscious.[43]

References

Abbey, A. 2011. "Alcohol's Role in Sexual Violence Perpetration: Theoretical Explanations, Existing Evidence, and Future Directions." *Drug & Alcohol Review* 30: 481–489.

42 *Crimes Act 1900* (NSW), s 61HJ(1)(c). The new formulation is based on the language in the *Crimes Act 1958* (Vic), s 36(2)(e); and the *Criminal Code* (NT), s 192(2)(c).

43 Nor do we endorse the alternative formulation found in s 67(1)(e) of the *Crimes Act 1900* (ACT): "… the consent of a person to sexual intercourse with another person … is negated if that consent is *caused* by the effect of intoxicating liquor, a drug or an anaesthetic …" (emphasis added). One of the cases in our dataset – *Agresti* [2017] ACTCA 20 – illustrates the problems created by the causation inquiry that this formulation demands.

Abbey, A., R. Wegner, J. Woerner, S.E. Pegram, and J. Pierce. 2014. "Review of Survey and Experimental Research That Examines the Relationship Between Alcohol Consumption and Men's Sexual Aggression Perpetration." *Trauma, Violence & Abuse* 15 (4): 265–282.

Angiolini, E. 2015. *Report of the Independent Review into the Investigation and Prosecution of Rape in London.*

Australian Bureau of Statistics. 2021. *Recorded Crime – Victims, 2020.* ABS.

Australian Women Against Violence Alliance. 2017. *Sexual Violence: Law Reform & Access to Justice.* Issues Paper, May 17. AWAVA.

Australian Institute of Family Studies. 2017. *Challenging Misconceptions About Sexual Offending: Creating an Evidence-Based Resource for Police and Legal Practitioners.* Canberrra: AIFS.

Burgin, R. 2018. "Persistent Narratives of Force & Resistance: Affirmative Consent." *British Journal of Criminology* 59 (2): 294–314.

Carline, A., C. Gunby, and S. Taylor. 2018. "Too Drunk to Consent? Exploring the Contestations and Disruptions in Male-focused Sexual Violence Prevention Interventions." *Social & Legal Studies* 27 (3): 299–322.

Chalmers, J., F. Leverick, and V. Munro. 2021. "Why the Jury Is, and Should Still be, out on Rape Deliberation." *Criminal Law Review* 9: 753–771.

Clough, A. 2019. "Finding the Balance: Intoxication and Consent." *Liverpool Law Review* 40: 49–64.

Cowan, S. 2008. "The Trouble With Drink: Intoxication, (In)capacity, and the Evaporation of Consent to Sex." *Akron Law Review* 41: 899–922.

Craig, E. 2018. *Putting Trials on Trial: Sexual Assault and the Failure of the Legal Profession.* Montreal and Kigston, London, Chicago: McGill-Queen's University Press.

Croskery-Hewitt, S. 2015. "Rethinking Sexual Consent: Voluntary Intoxication and Affirmative Consent to Sex." *New Zealand Universities Law Review* 26: 614–641.

Daly, K., and B. Bouhours. 2010. "Rape and Attrition in the Legal Process: A Comparative Analysis of Five Countries." In *Crime & Justice: A Review of Research*, Vol. 39, edited by M. Tonry, 565–650. Chicago: University of Chicago Press.

Dinos, S., N. Burrowes, K. Hammond, and C. Cunliffe. 2015. "A Systematic Review of Juries' Assessment of Rape Victims: Do Rape Myths Impact on Juror Decision-Making?" *International Journal of Law, Crime and Justice* 43: 36–49.

Ellison, L., and V. Munro. 2009. "Of "Normal Sex" and "Real Rape": Exploring the Use of Socio-Sexual Scripts in (Mock) Jury Deliberation." *Social & Legal Studies* 18: 291–312.

Finch, E., and V. Munro. 2004. "The Sexual Offences Act 2003: Intoxicated Consent and Drug Assisted Rape Revisited." *Criminal Law Review* October: 789–802.

Finch, E., and V. Munro. 2005. "Juror Stereotypes and Blame Attribution in Rape Cases Involving Intoxicants: The Findings of a Pilot Study." *British Journal of Criminology* 45: 25–38.

Finch, E., and V. Munro. 2006. "Breaking Boundaries? Sexual Consent in the Jury Room." *Legal Studies* 26 (3): 303–320.

Finch, E., and V. Munro. 2007. "The Demon Drink and the Demonized Woman: Socio-Sexual Stereotypes and Responsibility Attribution in Rape Trials Involving Intoxicants." *Social & Legal Studies* 16: 591–614.

Finch, E., and V. Munro. 2009. "Reacting to Rape: Exploring Mock Jurors' Assessments of Complainant Credibility." *British Journal of Criminology* 49: 202–219.

Finney, A. 2004. *Alcohol and Sexual Violence: Key Findings From the Research*. London: Home Office.

Fitzgerald, J. 2006. "The Attrition of Sexual Offences From the New South Wales Criminal Justice System." *Contemporary Issues in Criminal Justice* No. 92. Sydney: NSW BOCSAR.

Flowe, H.D., M.K.T. Takarangi, J.E. Humphries, and D.S. Wright. 2016. "Alcohol and Remembering a Hypothetical Sexual Assault: Can People who Were Under the Influence of Alcohol During the Event Provide Accurate Testimony." *Memory* 24 (8): 1042–1061.

Flowe, H., and A. Carline (eds.). 2021. *Alcohol and Remembering Rape New Evidence for Practice*. London: Palgrave MacMillan.

Flowe, H., and J. Maltby. 2018. "An Experimental Examination of Alcohol Consumption, Alcohol Expectancy, and Self-blame on Willingness to Report a Hypothetical Rape." *Aggressive Behavior* 44 (3): 225–234.

Flowe, H.D., J.E. Humphries, M.K. Takarangi, K. Zelek, N. Karoğlu, F. Gabbert, and L. Hope. 2019. "An Experimental Examination of the Effects of Alcohol Consumption and Exposure to Misleading Postevent Information on Remembering a Hypothetical Rape Scenario." *Applied Cognitive Psychology* 33 (3): 393–413.

Gavey, N. 2008. *Just Sex? The Cultural Scaffolding of Rape*. London and New York: Routledge.

Gavey, N. 2019. "The Persistence of a Masculine Point of View in Public Narratives About Rape." In *Rape Narratives in Motion*, edited by U. Andersson et al., 247–255. London: Palgrave MacMillan.

Graham, K., S. Bernards, D. Wayne Osgood, A. Abbey, M. Parks, A. Flynn, T. Dumas, and S. Wells. 2014. "'Blurred Lines?' Sexual Aggression and Barroom Culture." *Alcoholism Clinical & Experimental Research* 38: 1416–1424.

Gunby, C., A. Carline, and C. Beynon. 2010. "Alcohol-related Rape Cases: Barristers' Perspectives on the Sexual Offences Act 2003 and its Impact on Practice." *Journal of Criminal Law* 74(6): 579–600.

Hanley, N., B. Fileborn, W. Larcombe, N. Henry, and A. Powell. 2016. "Improving the law Reform Process: Opportunities for Empirical Qualitative Research?" *ANZ Journal of Criminology* 49 (6): 546–563.

Haskell, L., and M. Randall. 2019. *The Impact of Trauma on Adult Sexual Assault Victims*. Ottawa: Department of Justice.

Henderson, E., and K. Duncanson. 2016. "A Little Judicial Direction: Can Jury Directions Challenge Traditional Consent" *UNSW Law Journal* 39 (2): 750–778.

Jores, T., M.F. Colloff, L. Kloft, H. Smailes, and H.D. Flowe. 2019. "A Meta-analysis of the Effects of Acute Alcohol Intoxication on Witness Recall." *Applied Cognitive Psychology* 33 (3): 334–343.

Judicial Commission of NSW. 2011. *Conviction Appeals in NSW, Ch 13 'Sexual Assault Appeals'*. Sydney: Judicial Commission NSW.

Kelly, L., J. Lovett, and L. Regan. 2005. *A Gap or a Chasm? Attrition in Reported Rape Cases*. Research Study No. 293. London: Home Office.

Kloft, L., L.A. Monds, A. Blokland, J.G. Ramaekers, and H. Otgaar. 2021. "Hazy Memories in the Courtroom: A Review of Alcohol and Other Drug Effects on False Memory and Suggestibility." *Neuroscience & Biobehavioral Reviews* 124: 291–307.

Larcombe, W, 2011. "Falling Rape Conviction Rates: (Some) Feminist Aims and Measures for Rape law." *Feminist Legal Studies* 19: 27–45.

Larcombe, W. 2017. "Rethinking Rape Law Reform: Challenges & Possibilities." In *New Directions for Law in Australia: Essays in Contemporary Law Reform*, edited by R. Levy et al. Canberra: ANU Press.

Lazar, R. 2010. "Negotiating Sex: The Legal Construct of Consent in Cases of Wife Rape in Ontario." *Canadian Journal of Women and the Law* 22 (3): 329–363.

Leverick, F. 2020. "What Do We Know About Rape Myths and Juror Decision Making?" *The International Journal of Evidence & Proof* 24 (3): 255–279.

Lievore, D. 2003. *Non-reporting and Hidden Reporting of Sexual Assault: An International Literature Review*. Canberra: Commonwealth Office of Women.

Lievore, D. 2005. "Prosecutorial Decisions in Adult Sexual Assault Cases." *Trends & Issues in Crime & Criminal Justice* No. 291. Canberra: Australian Institute of Criminology.

Lonsway, K., and J. Archambault. 2012. "The 'Justice Gap' for Sexual Assault Cases: Future Directions for Research and Reform." *Violence Against Women* 18 (2): 145–168.

Lovett, J., and L. Kelly. 2009. *Different Systems, Similar Outcomes? Tracking Attrition in Reported Rape Cases Across Europe*. London: Child and Woman Abuse Studies Unit, London Metropolitan University.

Mason, G., and J. Monaghan. 2019. "Autonomy and Responsibility in Sexual Assault law in NSW: The *Lazarus* Case." *Current Issues in Criminal Justice* 31 (1): 24–39.

McDonald, E. 2014. "From 'real rape' to Real Justice? Reflections on the Efficacy of More Than 35 Years of Feminism, Activism and law Reform." *Victoria University of Wellington Law Review* 45 (3): 487–508.

McDonald, E. et al. 2020. *Rape Myths as Barriers to Fair Trial Process*. Canterbury: Canterbury University Press.

McNamara, L., J. Quilter, K. Seear, and R. Room. 2017. "Evidence of Intoxication in Australian Criminal Courts: A Complex Variable With Multiple Effects." *Monash University Law Review* 43 (1): 148–194.

Nitschke, F.T., B.M. Masser, B.M. McKimmie, and M. Riachi. 2021. "Intoxicated But Not Incapacitated: Are There Effective Methods to Assist Juries in Interpreting Evidence of Voluntary Complainant Intoxication in Cases of Rape?" *Journal of Interpersonal Violence* 36 (9–10): 4335–4359.

NSW Bureau of Crimes Statistics and Research. 2017. *The Progress of Sexual Offences Through the NSW Criminal Justice System, 2017*. Sydney: BOCSAR.

NSW Bureau of Crimes Statistics and Research. 2020. *Criminal Court Statistics 2019*. Sydney: BOCSAR.

NSW Law Reform Commission. 2020. *Consent in Relation to Sexual Offences: Report 148*. Sydney: NSW Law Reform Commission

Office for National Statistics (UK). 2018. *Sexual Offending: Victimisation and the Path Through the Criminal Justice System*. London: Office for National Statistics.

Powell, A. et al. 2013. "Meanings of 'sex' and 'consent': The Persistence of rape myths in Victorian rape law." *Griffith Law Review* 22 (3): 456–480.

Quilter, J. 2011. "Re-Framing the Rape Trial: Insights From Critical Theory Limitations of Legislative Reform." *Australian Feminist Law Journal* 35: 23–56.

Quilter, J., and L. McNamara. 2018. "The Meaning of 'Intoxication' Australian Criminal Cases: Origins & Operation." *New Criminal Law Review* 21: 170–207.

Quilter, J., L. McNamara, K. Seear, and R. Room. 2018. *'Intoxication' and Australian Criminal Law: Implications for Addressing Alcohol and Other Drug-Related Harms and Risks*. Report to the Criminology Research Advisory Council. Grant: CRG 20/14-15.

Rotenberg, C. 2017. *From Arrest to Conviction: Court Outcomes of Police-reported Sexual Assaults in Canada, 2009 to 2014*. Ottawa: Statistics Canada.

Rumney, P., and R. Fenton. 2008. "Intoxicated Consent in Rape: *Bree* and Juror Decision-Making." *The Modern Law Review* 71: 279–290.

Shaw, J., R. Campbell, D. Cain, and H. Feeney. 2017. "Beyond Surveys and Scales: How Rape Myths Manifest in Sexual Assault Police Records." *Psychology of Violence* 7 (4): 602–614.

Smith, O. 2018. *Rape Trials in England and Wales: Observing Justice and Rethinking Rape Myths*. London: Palgrave Macmillan.

Stern, V. 2010. *Report by Baroness Vivien Stern CBE of an Independent Review into How Rape Complaints Are Handled by Public Authorities in England and Wales*. London: Home Office.

Tasca, M., N. Rodriguez, C. Spohn, and M.P. Koss. 2013. "Police Decision Making in Sexual Assault Cases: Predictors of Suspect Identification and Arrest." *Journal of Interpersonal Violence* 28 (6): 1157–1177.

Taylor, N. 2007. "Juror Attitudes and Biases in Sexual Assault Cases." *AIC Trends & Issues in Crime & Criminal Justice No. 344*. Canberra: Australian Institute of Criminology.

Temkin, J., J. Gray, and L. Barrett. 2018. "Different Functions of Rape Myth Use in Court: Findings From a Trial Observation Study." *Feminist Criminology* 13 (2): 205–226.

Thomas, C. 2020. "The 21st Century Jury: Contempt, Bias and the Impact of Jury Service." *Criminal Law Review* 11: 987–1011.

Topping, A. 2016. "The 'Blurred Lines' of Capacity to Consent in Rape." *North East Law Review* 4 (1): 72–96.

Triggs, S., E. Mossman, J. Jordan, and V. Kingi. 2009. *Responding to Sexual Violence: Attrition in the New Zealand Criminal Justice System*. Wellington: NZ Ministry of Women's Affairs.

Valverde, M. 2003. *Law's Dream of a Common Knowledge*. Princeton: Princeton University Press.

Zawacki, T. et al. 2003. "Perpetrators of Alcohol-involved Sexual Assaults." *Aggressive Behavior* 29 (4): 366–380.

Chapter 10

"It Felt Like a Comma, Not a Full Stop"[1]

Complainers' Experiences of the 'Not Proven' Verdict within Scottish Rape Trials

Vanessa E. Munro

The strength of Scotland's constitutional connection to its adjoining southernly neighbour has fluctuated substantially over time. Yet, through seismic ruptures, including the Acts of Union in 1707 and establishment of its devolved Parliament in 1999, Scotland has retained its own distinctive laws (at least in respect of many key areas), civil and criminal justice processes, and court and tribunal systems. Amongst the distinguishing characteristics of the Scottish criminal process, which have a particular bearing on the pursuit and achievement of justice for rape complainers, are not only a distinctive doctrinal context (now largely set out in the Sexual Offences (Scotland) Act 2009), but an evidential requirement for corroboration retained despite its steady retraction across other jurisdictions, and a jury arrangement that is unique amongst its common law counterparts in involving 15 members, required to reach decisions by simple majority[2] from a choice of 'guilty,' 'not guilty' and 'not proven' verdicts, with the latter two existing as alternative forms of acquittal with identical consequences for the accused.

In Scotland, as elsewhere, the patterns of attrition that mark the trajectories of sexual offence complaints give rise to ongoing concern (Scottish Government

1 Miss M, quoted in Murty (2021). The author would like to thank, first and foremost, the complainers who generously shared their time and experience as part of this research, and Rape Crisis Scotland for their assistance. Though a separate strand of research activity, this exploration of complainers' experiences followed from work conducted as part of the 'Scottish Jury Study' which explored the use and understanding of the 'not proven' verdict amongst members of the public acting as jurors. I am very grateful to the colleagues with whom I conducted that study – Rachel Ormston and Lorraine Murray (Ipsos MORI Scotland) and Professors James Chalmers and Fiona Leverick (Glasgow University) – and to the Scottish Government for funding it. While any errors here are my own, I have benefitted greatly from ongoing work on the history, and future, of the 'not proven' verdict, undertaken with James Chalmers and Fiona Leverick, and I am indebted to them for the many discussions we have had on the topic. I am also very grateful to them, and to Julia Quilter (University of Wollongong), for comments on an earlier draft of this chapter.

2 That is to say that a minimum of eight votes is required for conviction, but there is no requirement for the jury to reach, or even a direction for them to make any attempt to reach, a unanimous or near-unanimous decision.

DOI: 10.4324/9781003379331-14

2021). While the requirement for corroborated evidence has often been identified as a particular barrier that diminishes the prospects for complaints being taken forward to prosecution (see, further, Brindley and Burman 2011; Cowan 2010; Cairns 2017; Cairns 2019), it is also apparent that, amongst those cases that proceed to trial – where the Crown clearly feels that corroboration has been secured – sexual offence complaints are still far less likely to result in convictions. In 2019–2020, for example, against an overall acquittal rate at trial of 6% across all crimes and offences, rape and attempted rape had an acquittal rate (via 'not guilty' or 'not proven') of 56% at trial, whilst 33% of sexual assault trials resulted in acquittal (Scottish Government 2021, Chart 3). Research focused upon police, prosecutor and jury decision-making, as well as survivors' justice journeys, in Scotland attests to the existence of obstacles, shared in other jurisdictions, regarding complainer-rather-than-suspect-focused investigations, reliance upon – or predictions of others' reliance upon – myths and stereotypes about rape, and suspicions grounded in a concern about the prospect of false allegations (Brooks-Hay et al. 2019; SCTS 2021). In previous work, I have explored the ways in which such myths and misconceptions, particularly in respect of levels of victim resistance and injury, timing of complaints to police (or others) and emotional reactions in the immediate and subsequent aftermath of an attack, as well as conservative views about 'appropriate' gendered behaviours and scope for 'miscommunication' of sexual signals, might influence the tone, content and outcome of jury decision-making in Scottish rape trials (Chalmers et al 2021a; Munro 2019). Related research has also explored the impact on mock jurors and juries of the unique features of the Scottish criminal process, in respect of the number of jurors, decision-making rules and range of verdict choices (Chalmers et al. 2020; Ormston et al. 2019).

The ways in which these features of the jury system interact with one another, and with evidential requirements for corroboration as well as tenacious stereotypes about 'real' rape and 'genuine' victims, are complicated, and beyond the scope of this chapter to explore in detail. Evidence suggests, however, that there has been a disproportionate reliance on the 'not proven' verdict by juries in sexual offence cases in Scotland.[3] In a context in which there is no legal definition available by which to direct jurors on the difference between the two acquittals at their disposal, Scottish trial judges have been cautious about offering any instruction above and beyond the fact that jurors have a

3 In 2019–2020, 'not proven' verdicts accounted for 20% of all acquittals at trial across all trial types; but it accounted for 44% of acquittals in rape and attempted rape trials and 38% in sexual assault trials. As a percentage of all the rape and attempted rape trials that proceeded in 2019–2020, this means that 25% resulted in acquittal via 'not proven' (and a further 32% via 'not guilty'); 13% of all sexual assault cases proceeded against resulted in 'not proven' verdicts (and 20% in 'not guilty'). Most offences had rates of 'not proven' acquittal in the range of 1–4% of all cases proceeded against, with the only exceptions being homicide (6%) and attempted murder or serious assault (7%) (Scottish Government 2021).

choice and both verdicts have the same effect (Chalmers et al. 2021b). In the absence of more specific guidance, recent findings with mock jurors suggest that they tend to understand 'not proven' as the appropriate verdict to be used when they suspect the accused *may* be 'guilty' but lack sufficient certainty to convict, when they want to communicate a level of belief to the complainer or suspicion to the accused, or when they are struggling – individually or collectively – to reach a clear decision (Chalmers et al. 2022; Scottish Government 2022). Though tied to the trial scenarios that were presented to participants within that study (one involving a rape charge where consent was contested, and the other a physical assault), this mock jury research has also found a preference amongst jurors for acquittal via 'not proven', where that verdict was available to them. Thus, while translation to the real courtroom is never simple, with the specifics of each trial and the composition of each jury likely to have an impact, this research has indicated that, at least in finely balanced scenarios, removal of the 'not proven' verdict might incline jurors more to conviction rather than acquittal via the alternative 'not guilty' verdict (Ormston et al. 2019).

Debate in Scotland continues over the retention or abolition of 'not proven', and indeed it was a prominent feature in the manifestos of most political parties ahead of the 2021 Holyrood elections. While the parameters of that debate have shifted over time, in recent periods, it has been framed in particular by concern regarding the aforementioned substantial use of 'not proven' in sexual offence cases, and anxiety regarding the differential meanings that might be attributed to it by jurors in the context of their deliberations, with the attendant implications this might generate in terms of transparency, due process and stigma (Chalmers et al. 2021b; Chalmers et al. 2022). There has, however, been less sustained consideration given to the lived experiences of trial parties who receive a 'not proven' verdict. Miss M Justice, whose words are foregrounded in the title of this chapter, has been a high-profile voice in this context, having successfully brought a civil claim against her attacker after the criminal trial against him resulted in a 'not proven' acquittal.[4] Working with Rape Crisis Scotland and its wider Survivors Reference Group, Miss M's campaigning to #EndNotProven has secured growing attention. But the wider range and ramifications of complainers' experiences has not to date been adequately represented in existing research. The aim of the study that informs this chapter was thus to bring those perspectives more clearly to the fore. To do so, I draw here on a series of semi-structured interviews and a focus group discussion conducted with complainers, in which I explored their levels of preparedness for and access to support in the aftermath of the verdict, understandings of what 'not proven' means and why it might have been returned in their

4 *AR v Coxen* 2018 SLT (Sh Ct) 335. For further information, see https://www.rapecrisisscotland.org.uk/campaigns-end-not-proven/.

case, and the immediate and longer-term impacts of the verdict in terms of their pursuit of justice and closure (Munro 2020; see also Chalmers et al. 2022).

While my aim in this study was not to second-guess the outcome of the court process nor to endorse the veracity of the allegations at issue in the criminal trial, it is important to be clear here that the fact of return of a 'not proven' verdict at trial does not entail that claims of victimisation were untrue. Nor does it mean that complainers' justice interests in being treated with dignity, and in being afforded a voice and a space for participation throughout the process, as well as in having the harms that were perpetrated upon them recognised in a meaningful way, are not still appropriately engaged. Indeed, the ways in which participants reconciled their experiences of reporting, giving evidence at trial, and receiving and learning to live with the resultant verdict in their cases provide important lessons that are relevant to improving the justice journeys – both in and beyond the criminal process – for a wide range of victim-survivors. With this in mind, in the following discussion, I situate the themes arising from discussions with my participants within a wider literature, invoking in particular McGlynn and Westmarland's (2019) notion of the complex, fluctuating and multi-faceted dimensions of kaleidoscopic justice for survivors of sexual violence. The aim in doing so is to highlight not only the ways in which the 'not proven' verdict provided specific challenges, but to reflect on how those challenges are apt to be echoed in the experiences of other victim-survivors, regardless often of case progression and outcomes.

Conversations with Complainers: The Data

This chapter draws on findings from a series of ten one-to-one semi-structured interviews, lasting approximately an hour, which were conducted by the author with participants (either by phone or video-call) during February to March 2020. It also draws on the content of a two-hour focus group discussion convened by Rape Crisis Scotland and held at the end of January 2020, which the author had permission to participate in and record. In that focus group, five complainers discussed with representatives from the Scottish Government their experiences of making a complaint through the criminal justice process in Scotland, with the 'not proven' verdict being a prominent but not exclusive focus of discussion. Four of the one-to-one interviews that I went on to conduct were with participants from that focus group, and the remaining six were recruited through pre-existing contacts, or via a Rape Crisis social media call.

The remit for the study was not specifically limited to sexual offences, since it was open to anyone who had experienced the return of a 'not proven' verdict in respect of their reported victimisation. Nonetheless, high-profile campaigning around the use of the 'not proven' verdict specifically in sexual offence trials, together with the collaboration with Rape Crisis Scotland in the recruitment phase for this study, entailed that the vast majority of respondents were rape complainers. Of the eleven individuals who shared experiences with me (whether via interview, focus group discussion or both), nine had made complaints of rape (in some cases amongst other sexual and violent offences). Of the remaining two, one had made a complaint in respect of physical assaults experienced in the context of a domestic relationship and the other was a bereaved family member of a victim of homicide. All the participants were female, other than the family member who was a male relative of the deceased female.

Nine of these participants had received 'not proven' verdicts at the end of their trials. One participant – who contributed to the focus group but not interview – saw her rape case collapse at court stage. A final participant, whose complaint involved historical sexual abuse against herself and a sibling, received a 'guilty' verdict. This participant was nonetheless included in the cohort for follow-up interview after the focus group discussion because she had participated actively in the Survivors' Reference Group that liaised with and had advocated on behalf of complainers who received 'not proven' verdicts. Her contributions offered powerful insights about the wider process of reporting and participating in a criminal trial, but her reflections specifically in relation to 'not proven' were inevitably based not on her own personal experience but on views and experiences recounted to her by, or witnessed of, others.

The rape allegations at issue arose in a variety of contexts and involved a wide spectrum of types and levels of corroborating evidence. Complaints ranged from sexual violence within intimate relationships, to assaults perpetrated by acquaintances at social gatherings, to attacks in public places. They were supported – variously – by DNA evidence, CCTV footage, audio recordings of the incident, physical injuries inflicted upon the complainer, and text messages after the event. In all but one case, the incident was a relatively recent one. In two of the cases, the accused had been charged with sexual offences not only against the participant but also against their family members (specifically, a sibling or child). Nine of the ten verdicts returned were delivered by a jury (eight 'not proven', one 'guilty'); in respect of the assault charge, the 'not proven' verdict was returned by a judge in a specialist domestic abuse court.

All discussions with participants were recorded, transcribed and analysed qualitatively using Nvivo, on the basis of an open and grounded thematic coding frame. Reflecting in part the challenges involved in recruiting in an ethical manner to survivor-focused studies, as well as various pragmatic constraints, it is important to bear in mind that the sample here is a small one. That said, other influential studies that have qualitatively explored survivors' experiences of justice processes have also often relied on relatively small samples, particularly where their inclusion criteria require engagement with and through a criminal trial.[5] In the present study, that recruitment pool was reduced further

5 In respect of UK studies, McGlynn and Westmarland (2019) relied on data from 20 victim-survivors, only 11 of whom had ever reported an experience of sexual violence to the police. Meanwhile, Brooks-Hay et al.'s study (2019) of Scottish victim-survivors' "justice journeys" drew from 17

by a small jurisdiction and the focus on a specific – 'not proven' – verdict outcome. In this context, and particularly given, as I explore further below, the themes that emerged resounded strongly and repeatedly across all the participants, this small sample still yields robust substantive findings that merit careful attention.

In the following discussion, I will focus on two key themes that emerged from these complainer conversations, reflecting both on the ways in which their experiences echo findings of previous research regarding complainers' aspirations for, and experiences of, the criminal justice process, as well as on how the specific variable of the 'not proven' verdict in Scotland appeared to intersect to produce its own distinctive, and often damaging, effects. The themes in question relate, first, to participants' preparation for, receipt of and immediate reactions to the verdict in the wider context of their participation in and experience of rape prosecution; and second, to longer-term impacts on participants of having had the jury return a 'not proven' as distinct from 'not guilty' acquittal, including in terms of their faith in the justice process. As I explore, participants' contributions across these themes support and in important ways extend existing theories regarding victim-survivors' interests, including in particular in respect of the interaction between their interests in participation, recognition and collective forms of redress.

Of course, the contributions discussed here are limited to one cohort whose justice interests and lived experiences are engaged acutely by the presence and return of a 'not proven' verdict. Alongside extended families and criminal justice professionals, who may be impacted, the most obvious other category of person whose experiences would be relevant is those who are accused and acquitted through this route. To date, no research has considered the meaning and effects of the verdict for this cohort: learning more about any perceived or actual impact on their lives, relationships, or views about justice, and considering how that unfolds beyond the immediate moment of acquittal, would be a valuable addition to the evidence, which could inform discussion about

complainers, all of whom reported to police, but only five participants saw the sexual offence charges in question proceed through to the end of the trial process (with one further case resulting in a 'guilty' plea). Most recently, 'A Joint Thematic Inspection' Report also relied on interviews with 26 survivors, all of whom reported to the police but only one had seen her case go to trial (with another securing conviction following a 'guilty' plea) (CJJI 2021). As McGlynn and Westmarland note, though these sample sizes are modest, this is broadly in line with international studies. Herman (2005) relied on interviews with 20 US victim-survivors of domestic and sexual violence while Jülich's study in New Zealand (2006) involved 21 adult survivors of child sexual abuse. More recently, in Australia, Holder's (2015) research with survivors of domestic abuse extended to 27 participants, and Clark's work (2015) involved 22 sexual assault victim-survivors, approximately two-thirds of whom had experienced the criminal justice system. In England and Wales, data recently released from the Victims' Commissioner Office (2020) has offered a larger dataset, comprised of survey response from just under 500 survivors. Though this was analysed primarily quantitatively, free-text responses that supplemented survey measures confirmed findings in previous qualitative studies (see Munro 2022).

the verdict's future. It is, however, beyond the scope of the present study. So too, recent research has explored legal professionals' views of the verdict and the case for or against its abolition, but consideration of it is largely beyond the scope of this chapter (Curley et al. 2021; Scottish Government 2022).

Long Roads and Abrupt Stops: Receiving a 'Not Proven' Verdict

One of the most commonly reported reactions in the immediate aftermath of receiving a 'not proven' verdict recounted by participants was surprise. Interviewees reported that, despite the journey from complaint to trial being a very long one, they were not prepared for a 'not proven' verdict and did not feel that they had been properly alerted to this as a possibility during the investigative process. Participants remarked that not only were they not expecting this verdict in the sense of thinking it unlikely to be returned in their case, but they "didn't really think it was a possibility" (Participant 6). In some cases, that was because the verdict's existence, or its availability to the jury in their case, was not something that they had previously been made aware of by anyone involved in their case. As Participant 1 put it, "it wasn't explained to me at all," whilst Participant 7 observed that "I didn't even know it existed, to be honest .... I didn't even know that that was a possibility." For Participant 6, this mapped onto a wider and "really underwhelming experience from the point of view of just basically being part of the evidence." She recalled that "the process and the outcome wasn't explained to me at all, and the first time I really heard of 'not proven' was when she told me that was the verdict." In other cases, while participants were aware of the verdict and its potential applicability to their case *in theory*, they reported there had been no discussion with those involved in their case to suggest that it was a realistic prospect.

For many participants, this resulted in immediate feelings of confusion and frustration upon receipt of the verdict, though this was often combined in complicated ways with a sense of relief that the trial, which had dominated their lives and demanded so much of them for such a long time, was finally over. As Participant 2 put it, "at first, it was just kind of indifferent, and I'd waited a really long time for it to be over." That initial sense of relief quickly transitioned for many into a sense of resignation, however. Participant 7 spoke of how she came to feel that she had "wasted her time" and that the 'not proven' verdict in particular felt "very un-final, like in limbo....as if it was all just for nothing"; a view echoed by Participant 9 who commented that, in this moment, she felt that "the whole thing had been pointless."

Several participants lamented the lack of support available to them, both throughout the investigation and trial process and once the verdict had been returned. Participant 10 described it as "absolutely negligible," for example, while Participants 4 and 5 said communications with criminal justice professionals had been "just pitiful" and "exceptionally poor," resulting in "long periods of emptiness" (Participant 5) and "a very isolating process where you …had to fight them every step of the way for any bit of information" (Participant 4). Some participants spoke of not being informed prior to the trial about matters as fundamental as what charges were being brought against the accused, whilst others reported being actively dissuaded from attending the trial, other than for the duration of their testimony, for fear of how it might appear to the jury or judge, especially where special measures had been used. Indeed, Participant 8, who had been cautioned against court attendance, reported that she nonetheless felt it important to be proximate, so spent the duration of the trial sitting in a café near the courthouse.

In respect of the return of the verdict specifically, Participant 4 recounted that she only found out about it "accidentally" as a result of an email from the lead police officer, and then had to chase her court liaison officer for formal notice. Meanwhile, Participant 7 observed that at the court "they just leave you: nobody explains what it [the verdict] means and it's as if you're invisible, or you don't matter."

After participants in the present study had adjusted to the shock of the cessation of the trial and its outcome, they all recounted a growing desire to find meaning in the process and to make sense of the verdict. Whether or not they were aware of it in advance, complainers were unanimous in reporting that they did not really have any clear grasp on what the 'not proven' verdict meant or when it would be used. In the hopes of finding answers to those questions, many had taken steps to request meetings with the criminal justice personnel involved in their case or asked for court transcripts. Access restrictions and the prohibitive costs involved in obtaining transcripts prevented the latter route, but a number secured meetings with police officers or prosecutors. All who attended such meetings found them unsatisfactory, however. Many continued to be confused about the meaning of the 'not proven' verdict; this was reflected in the fact that most asked at some point during their interview with me for clarification, for example, as to whether the verdict could be taken into account in any future case against the accused. Moreover, the majority perceived officials' responses in those meetings to be evasive and reflective of either a lack of sympathy or discomfort at having to engage in this difficult conversation. Participant 1, whose prosecutor had been so confident about her case in the run up to trial that she had "almost laughed" when the complainer expressed worry about the outcome, reflected that in the post-verdict meeting, "I was bombarding them with questions but they felt like very political answers" and "it was almost as if, if there was an eject button in that room, she would have pressed it."

Of course, in the specific context of the 'not proven' verdict, there is a sense in which these meetings were always apt to be somewhat disappointing. As one participant acknowledged – for justice professionals as well as for complainers – it is "a process of piecing together puzzles that don't even exist" (Participant 2).

Providing an explanation for any verdict returned by a jury is inevitably based on conjecture, and since there is no legal definition of 'not proven', it would have been impossible for justice personnel to provide the authoritative explanations that complainers were seeking. Still, participants recounted frustration that, when asking for an explanation of the meaning of the verdict, what they received instead were generic statements about its implications, i.e. acquittal. As Participant 7 put it, "I knew what the consequence was. I knew that he was walking. I knew that he was off the register, but what is 'not proven', what is it?" Meanwhile, Participant 8 explained that she was told by a senior prosecutor that "no one really knows what 'not proven' means and it's quite misunderstood by different organisations, so it is not very helpful for me to give you a different interpretation of what 'not proven' means." As noted above, while this may be true, it does little to redress a sense amongst rape complainers, documented in previous research and articulated by Brooks-Hay et al., that their "interests were marginal to a process that was mundane or habitual to those working within the system" (2019, 23).

These experiences also resonate with existing research that has highlighted the importance of – yet ongoing challenges in achieving – procedural justice for rape complainers (Kelly et al. 2005). In particular, participants' reflections here correspond to previous findings, in Scotland and elsewhere, which have highlighted both the importance of effective and reliable communication with complainers regarding the progress (or otherwise) of the rape investigation, and the fact that this is often lacking (Brooks-Hay et al. 2019). In the survey commissioned by the Victims' Commissioner, for example, 82% of responding rape victim-survivors who had reported their complaint to the police agreed or strongly agreed that there were long periods where they heard nothing at all regarding case progression, and 70% reported that they felt the onus was on them to chase for any updates throughout the process (VCO 2020). These concerns are taken further by McGlynn and Westmarland in their conceptualisation of victim-survivors' justice interests in *dignity* – that is, in being treated as an end rather than means to an end – and *voice*, which encompasses active participation in the decisions and directions of justice processes as well as an opportunity to speak out and make sense of harms in a way that is meaningful to a range of audiences (2019, 189–193). The experiences recounted by participants in this study indicated a substantial falling short of basic good practice demands in terms of communication, let alone the deeper forms of participation required to sustain such dignity and voice. Moreover, participants' contributions also underscored acutely the longevity of the journeys through which that dignity and voice was pursued: And the fact that these are justice journeys that do not terminate when a verdict is returned, but that instead continue to wind in unmapped paths, requiring navigation by complainers with often depleted reserves and diminishing access to support.

Indeed, participants' contributions highlighted the damaging and long-lasting effects that their lack of dignity and voice within the justice process had upon them. Participant 5, for example, who felt that "information is power" reflected on the fact it is a "difficult" process:

> to put faith in these officials and then to be let down again and again and again, you know, you really do just have to spill your beans and then slap a blindfold on and just be led the whole way, and it is really, really not good enough.

Meanwhile, Participant 6 discussed the impact on her of being let down at a point of heightened vulnerability:

> it was just basically explained as don't get your hopes up and we could be here forever, like there is no timescale, this can go on and on and on. And that's probably what stuck with me the most, when I was giving evidence, is like 'this is never going to end, I'm going to be standing here for the rest of my fucking life' … it was that traumatic in the sense where it just felt like you couldn't escape.

Reflecting on the feeling that she was "abandoned" by the court process, she said: "that's their level of care and all you're worth…when you're at your most fragile, being exposed to the system is just toppling on the trauma." Linking this specifically to 'not proven', she also recounted how "down the line and with loads of counselling … there's still this confusion and lack of understanding, and a bit of frustration … what does it even mean, why has nobody explained it," while Participant 8 said that "confusion" about the verdict had created ongoing trauma "when people ask you what does that mean?"

While some participants felt that they were thus given no help with understanding and interpreting the verdict outcome, others indicated that they were offered a somewhat informal steer on its meaning and likely reasons for its return. But for those complainers, it was evident that this rarely provided the kind of resolution and clarity that had been hoped for. To the contrary, it served in all cases to provoke more, and more challenging, questions. For example, Participant 6 recounted how the prosecutor who called her to relay the verdict, when she asked what 'not proven' meant, said "it means that they know he's guilty, they just don't want to say it." This was the interpretation most frequently alluded to by others with whom participants discussed the verdict in its aftermath, and it is one that was certainly prevalent in mock jury discussions where its meaning and correct application was expressly considered. For those mock jurors, as noted above, 'not proven' often provided a middle-ground through which they intended to communicate a level of belief in the veracity of the complainer's account, even where they felt they lacked sufficient certainty to convict, doubted the adequacy of corroboration available or otherwise were disinclined to return a conviction, for example, because of the weighty consequences (Chalmers et al. 2021b; Chalmers et al. 2022).

However, as is discussed further in the next section, to the extent that the assumption here is that 'not proven' offered some kind of comfort to complainers, their lived experience strongly indicated to the contrary. What is more, it often generated more confusion and prompted greater retrospective agonising over what complainers might have done differently to tip what was perceived to be a marginal balance in the jury toward conviction. Several participants analogised this to the experience of passing or failing a test. As Participant 1 put it,

> it's like finding out you've failed a test with a 50% pass mark at 49% ... I'd rather have failed it at 10 because it's easier .... they've been able to pass on this message that we believed you a little bit and it's like, well, wait a minute, what more did you need from me?

Similarly, Participant 2 reflected:

> I can actually get over that I was beaten and raped, I can heal from that, I can understand he's a monster, and I can understand the best thing for me now is the fact that he is out of my life. But what eats away at me every day is that 'not proven' verdict. That's the thing that traumatises me, that's the thing I think about on a daily basis; and I can't get my questions answered from that.

Leaving complainers to grapple at the end of an often distressing and traumatic trial process with such intractable and ultimately unanswerable questions, with little sense of meaningful support from the system, radically undermined what McGlynn and Westmarland have identified as their justice interests in being treated as more than a piece of evidence (*dignity*) and as an agentic participant within their own justice journey (*voice*). In this respect, it was clear that, alongside a range of experiences shared with complainers in other jurisdictions – for example, regarding a lack of communication during, and support after, the trial process – participants in this study were confronted with unique challenges as a consequence of Scotland's third verdict, which compounded their sense of procedural disempowerment, institutional instrumentality and re-traumatisation. Indeed, for many respondents, as I discuss below, this profoundly undermined their faith in the ability – indeed, the interest – of those tasked with helping and protecting them to perform that role; and the legacy of 'not proven' was one in which that collapse of faith became more, rather than less, pronounced over time, with lasting and inter-generational effects.

A Tale of Two Acquittals: Confusing Consolation with Consequences

The period following the 'not proven' outcome was apparently marked for many of the participants, then, by a fluctuating mixture of relief at the trial being over, combined with intrusive and impossible questions over how to make sense of the verdict. It was also clear, nonetheless, that some complainers did feel – at least in this initial period – that it was an easier verdict to receive than 'not guilty' might have been. The reason for this mapped onto the consolatory connotations of the verdict alluded to and anticipated by mock jurors. Participant 9 reflected, for example, on how "momentarily, it did help in the sense that there is a bit more belief there in you." However, she observed that this initial feeling that "I got something from it" proved to be short-lived since "at the end of the day, it actually meant nothing because it had no impact" on the life of the accused: "it was only me saying 'not proven' and him more saying acquitted…it didn't really make any difference because his narrative was still stronger."

Of course, this participant could not know for sure what impact, if any, the 'not proven' verdict *did* have on their accused; and more broadly – as noted above – research on the ways in which those acquitted via 'not proven' verdicts process and experience that, both in the short and long-term, is lacking. Certainly, though, the participants in this study who retained connections to the accused, either because he remained in the local community, was a family member or co-parent, or had shared acquaintances in common, were confident that all external signs indicated that his 'normal life' had resumed. Participant 6 observed, for example, that, while her life had been turned upside down by the assault, trial and verdict, "he walks free … he can be whatever he wants" and Participant 7 noted that the verdict "sends him no message, no message, he walked straight back into his job, straight back into his life."

Being confronted with evidence or assumptions about the accused's return to normal life post-acquittal, combined with their unsuccessful attempts to discover answers that could explain the meaning of and reasons for the verdict in their case, appeared to take an incremental toll on several of the participants over time. As a consequence, this depleted altogether any lingering sense they may have had that the 'not proven' outcome could offer any consolation. As Participant 9 came to conclude, for example, the 'not proven' verdict is "just meaningless…it's sort of limbo" and the only reason to think that a 'not guilty' verdict would feel worse is if "you're still clinging on to a false hope that 'not proven' means something."

No doubt, there is a significant counter-factual at play here in that these participants did not receive a 'not guilty' verdict and so can only hypothesise as to how they would have experienced that, and whether it would have been harder or easier for them to process and move beyond over time. Nonetheless, it was clear that participants had often reflected carefully on this counter-factual and all were insistent that the 'not proven' verdict had introduced an additional layer of trauma that further impeded their recovery. Participant 4 reflected: "I know that some part of them [the jury] believed me and that hurts," whilst Participant 1 observed that "they're trying to be nice by saying we kind of believe you, but I feel like that just makes it so much worse." More specifically, other participants explained that what made this difficult was not only the lack of clarity and finality associated with the 'not proven' verdict, but also the profound sense of being let down by the return of a verdict that, on the one hand tokened belief that an assault took place against them, but on the other nonetheless failed to hold the assailant to account.

As Participant 2 put it:

> with the 'not proven' verdict, people are saying, well, it is better to receive that because you get an acknowledgement that the jury believed you, but I would argue no, not really, because at least if I thought that everyone was wildly not believing ... I would at least be able to sort of trust life ... I know what happened ... Being told that it did, but that no one is going to get convicted for it just leaves me thinking what sort of society do you live in.

She went on to discuss how, over the course of the trial – which she attended in person throughout, despite being specifically advised by justice professionals not to do so, and despite reporting that she felt "awkward" and "just sat at the side" – she felt she had seen the law "being manipulated so that people didn't have to make a decision." She reflected that this had made her "feel very unsafe" in the world, with "no faith in the justice system."

This profound injury to one's sense of safety and trust was also underscored by other participants. Participant 7, for example, observed that the 'not proven' verdict had, in her mind, "made the system look hollow," whilst Participant 8 concluded that "the 'not proven' verdict probably ruined my life more than the rape itself" because it caused her to "lose trust in services and organisations, and a court system that is supposed to uphold the law." Relatedly, Participant 3 shared how agonisingly difficult this had been to deal with when the perceived denial of responsibility to protect extended not only to herself but to her child; and Participant 7 was clear that, following her own experience, "if my daughter came to me and said she'd been raped, there is absolutely no way in this world I'd get her to report it."

Again, complainers' experiences here can be seen to resonate with the findings of previous research, in particular that by McGlynn and Westmarland which highlighted, amongst the justice interests of victim-survivors, the desire and need for 'recognition.' Such recognition, they explain, extends beyond 'being believed' to encompassing a deeper appreciation of the significance of the victimisation and its consequences. While it might be argued that the return of a 'not proven' rather than 'not guilty' acquittal communicates, at least in some cases and to some degree, a level of belief in the complainer's account, it was clear from the narratives of participants in the present study that this fell substantially short of affording the deeper dimensions of recognition that McGlynn and Westmarland identify. Indeed, such a deeper recognition would require exposing and scrutinising the logic, identified as influential in mock jury deliberations, that although a violation is perceived as likely to have occurred and there is no dispute as to the identity of the perpetrator, there is nonetheless insufficient certainty, confidence or commitment to return a conviction, with 'not proven' being seen to offer an acceptable compromise. It is in this space between the consolation and consequences of 'not proven' that the injustice to complainers' interests in recognition is located, and it is this which enables us to better understand what might otherwise appear as counter-intuitive, namely that this verdict is often a more damaging form of acquittal, since its superficially sympathetic tones are undermined by contradictions and derelictions.

Despite all of this, for many of the participants, there was clearly little mystery behind the appeal of the 'not proven' verdict and its apparently preferred status in sexual offences cases in Scotland. Interviewees acknowledged in particular the "massive responsibility" (Participant 7) facing jurors in rape cases, and the ways in which this could impose "a heavy moral duty" (Participant 10). In this context, they appreciated how 'not proven' could offer a welcome mechanism by which jurors could "ease their conscience" by "standing on the sidelines" or "sitting on the fence" (Participant 7). However, they also underscored that this outcome was "damaging" for all trial parties, and fundamentally "not what justice is about, whether you are the attacker or the survivor" (Participant 6). Participants were unanimous in the view, then, that 'not proven' ought to be abolished. Notwithstanding that it ultimately had the same consequences as 'not guilty', they felt that jurors being compelled to make a choice only between 'guilty' and 'not guilty' would encourage a more clear-sighted engagement with the evidence. As Participant 7 put it, jurors "instead of having this cushion, this safety net .... might look at it more authentically."

The adequacy of jurors' approach to evaluating the evidence and determining verdicts within Scottish rape trials remains the subject of debate, and was given renewed prominence by the recent suggestion in a Review conducted by the Lord Justice Clerk, Lady Dorrian, that consideration be given to a pilot of judge-only rape trials (SCTS 2021). In relation to the views expressed by participants in the present study, while there was some disagreement as to whether removal of the jury was necessarily the best approach, there was clear consensus that more had to be done in order to support jurors in performing their task adequately, and that this prospect was severely hampered by retention of the 'not proven' verdict. In this respect, then, participants were also clear on the need to think beyond the immediate implications for their own trial to the wider context in which other complaints might be approached in the future. This in turn resonates with McGlynn and Westmarland's idea of 'justice as connectedness' which involves victim-survivors each holding an interest in "justice beyond individual interactions or perpetrator consequences." As McGlynn and Westmarland explain, justice as connectedness "is about society's material expression of empathy, support and dignity, with the aim of enabling a victim-survivor to regain a sense of belonging and connection with society and feel a sense of justice"

(2019, 194). More than that, it is "also an end in itself: it is the material expression, and recognition, of society's commitment to ensuring victim-survivors are full members of society and feel a sense of justice" (McGlynn and Westmarland 2019, 195). In a context in which – as discussed above – complainers' lack of preparation for, and inability to find adequate explanations of, the 'not proven' verdict undermined their interests in dignity and voice, and the encouragements they received to give the verdict a consolatory gloss were progressively hollowed out in ways that undermined any illusion of recognition, participants still continued to seek collective redress. As Participant 8 put it,

> if it was a slim chance that it might mean they [the jury] would think about it a bit more, I would risk that any day, so that another survivor might get a guilty … I would much rather take a 'not guilty', which is essentially what a 'not proven' means, in the hope that someone else on the jury might actually think about what these two verdicts mean.

Meanwhile, Participant 7, reflecting on how the operation, impact and future of 'not proven' is intimately bound up with wider questions about what the justice system, and society in general, owes to those who make a claim, noted: "[returning a 'not proven' verdict] might put a wee plaster on the wound, but it doesn't stitch the wound shut, it doesn't repair it" …. and while jurors might think "the wound is not my responsibility," when you are in that courtroom "it is your responsibility, because it is my life and it is a defendant's life."

Concluding Remarks

The justice journeys of each rape complainer are inevitably mapped and navigated in their own distinctive ways. However, in a context in which, to date, there has been little academic attention afforded to the lived experiences of victim-survivors in Scotland who receive a 'not proven' verdict, this study provided important insights. In particular, it highlighted the commonalities that are shared with fellow-travellers in other jurisdictions in terms of poor communication, traumatic testimony-giving, instrumentalised evidential status and a paucity of support at the end of the trial process. But it also shed light on the ways in which the sense of "limbo" uniquely imposed by the return of a 'not proven' verdict, which cannot be adequately defined or explained, compounded trauma, amplified disempowerment, reduced the prospects for closure and undermined faith in the justice system. Framed through the lens of victim-survivors' multi-faceted justice interests – including specifically of voice, dignity, recognition and connectedness – it becomes ever clearer, then, that retention of this third verdict is apt to undermine trauma-informed responses in the criminal justice system, and to generate case outcomes that risk purchasing comfort for lay decision-makers at the cost of clarity for the trial parties.

References

Brindley, Sandy, and Michelle Burman. 2011. "Meeting the Challenge? Responding to Rape in Scotland." In *International Approaches to Rape*, edited by Nicole Westmarland and Geetanjali Gangoli, 147–168. Bristol: Policy Press.

Brooks-Hay, Oona, Michelle Burman, and Lisa Bradley. 2019. *Justice Journeys: Informing Policy and Practice Through Lived Experience of Victim-Survivors of Rape and Serious Sexual Assault*. Glasgow: Scottish Cetnre for Crime & Justice Research. https://www.sccjr.ac.uk/wp-content/uploads/2019/08/Justice-Journeys-Report_Aug-2019_FINAL.pdf.

Cairns, Ilona. 2017. "Access to Justice for Complainers? The Pitfalls of the Scottish Government's Case to Abolish Corroboration." In *Scottish Criminal Evidence Law*, edited by Peter Duff and Pamela Ferguson, 41–66. Edinburgh: Edinburgh University Press.

Cairns, Ilona. 2019. "Smith v Lees: Judgment & Reflective Statement" [with commentary by Isla]. In *Scottish Feminist Judgments: (Re)Creating the Law from the Outside in*, edited by Sharon Cowan, Chloë Kennedy, and Vanessa E. Munro, 39–53. London: Bloomsbury.

Chalmers, James, Fiona Leverick, and Vanessa E. Munro. 2020. "Three Distinctive Features, But What is the Difference? Key Findings from the Scottish Jury Project." *Criminal Law Review* 11: 1012–1033.

Chalmers, James, Fiona Leverick, and Vanessa E. Munro. 2021a. "The Provenance of What Is Proven: Exploring (Mock) Jury Deliberation in Scottish Rape Trials." *Journal of Law and Society* 48 (2): 226–249.

Chalmers, James, Fiona Leverick, and Vanessa E. Munro. 2021b. "A Modern History of the Not Proven Verdict." *Edinburgh Law Review* 25 (2): 151–172.

Chalmers, James, Fiona Leverick, and Vanessa E. Munro. 2022. "Beyond Doubt: The Case Against Not Proven." *Modern Law Review* 48 (4): 847–878.

Clark, Hayley. 2015. "A Fair Way to Go: Justice for Victim-Survivors of Sexual Violence." In *Rape Justice - Beyond the Criminal Law*, edited by Anastasia Powell, Nicola Henry, and Asher Flynn, 18–35. London: Palgrave MacMillan.

Cowan, Sharon. 2010. "All Change or Business as Usual? Reforming the Law of Rape in Scotland." In *Rethinking Rape Law: International and Comparative Perspectives*, edited by Clare McGlynn and Vanessa E. Munro, 154–169. London: Routledge.

Criminal Justice Joint Inspection (CCJI). 2021. "A Joint Thematic Inspection of the Police and Crown Prosecution Service's Response to Rape: Phase One – From Report to Police or CPS Decision to Take No Further Action." https://www.justiceinspectorates.gov.uk/hmicfrs/wp-content/uploads/joint-thematic-inspection-of-police-and-cps-response-to-rape-phase-one.pdf.

Curley, Lee, James Munro, Lara A. Frumkin, and Jim Turner. 2021. "Informing Reform: The Views of Legal Professionals on the Unique Aspects of Scottish Law." *Medicine, Science and the Law* 61 (4): 256–265.

Herman, Judith. 2005. "Justice for the Victim's Perspective." *Violence Against Women* 11 (5): 571–602.

Holder, Robyn. 2015. "Satisfied? Exploring Victims' Justice Judgments." In *Crime, Victims and Police: International Contexts, Local Experiences*, edited by Dean Wilson and Stuart Ross, 184–213. London: Palgrave Macmillan.

Jülich, Shirley. 2006. "Views of Justice Among Survivors of Historical Child Sexual Abuse." *Theoretical Criminology* 10 (1): 125–138.

Kelly, Liz, Jo Lovett, and Regan L. Linda 2005. *A Gap or a Chasm? Attrition in Reported Rape Cases*. London: Home Office. https://webarchive.nationalarchives.gov.uk/ukgwa/20110218135832/rds.homeoffice.gov.uk/rds/pdfs05/hors293.pdf.

McGlynn, Clare, and Nicole Westmarland. 2019. "Kaleidoscopic Justice: Sexual Violence and Victim-Survivors' Perceptions of Justice." *Social and Legal Studies* 28 (2): 179–201.

Munro, Vanessa E. 2019. "Judging Juries: The "Common Sense" Conundrums of Prosecuting Violence Against Women." *New Zealand Women's Law Journal* 3: 13–34.

Munro, Vanessa E. 2020. "Piecing Together Puzzles: Complainers' Experiences of the Not Proven Verdict." http://wrap.warwick.ac.uk/137857/1/WRAP-91104-Law-Research-Report-Munro-2020.pdf.

Munro, Vanessa E. 2022. "A Circle that Cannot Be Squared? Survivor Confidence in an Adversarial Justice System." In *Rape: Challenging Contemporary Thinking*, 2nd ed., edited by Miranda Horvath and Jennifer Brown. Cullompton: Willan Publishing: 203–217.

Murty, Jim. 2021. "Not Proven Verdict: Miss M Speaks Out on Proposed Scots Law Change." *The National*, April 18. https://www.thenational.scot/news/19240741.not-proven-verdict-woman-speaks-night-changed-life/.

Ormston, Rachel, James Chalmers, Fiona Leverick, Vanessa E. Munro, and Lorraine Murray. 2019. *Scottish Jury Research: Findings From a Large Scale Mock Jury Study*. Edinburgh: Scottish Government. https://www.gov.scot/binaries/content/documents/govscot/publications/research-and-analysis/2019/10/scottish-jury-research-fingings-large-mock-jury-study-2/documents/scottish-jury-research-findings-large-scale-mock-jury-study/scottish-jury-research-findings-large-scale-mock-jury-study/govscot%3Adocument/scottish-jury-research-findings-large-scale-mock-jury-study.pdf.

Scottish Government. 2021. "Criminal Proceedings in Scotland, 2019–20." https://www.gov.scot/publications/criminal-proceedings-scotland-2019-20/.

Scottish Government. 2022. *The Not Proven Verdict and Related Reforms: Analysis of Responses to Consultation*. Edinburgh: Scottish Government. https://www.gov.scot/publications/not-proven-verdict-related-reforms-consultation-analysis/.

SCTS. 2021. *Improving the Management of Sexual Offence Cases: Final Report from the Lord Justice Clerk's Review Group*. Edinburgh: Scottish Courts and Tribunals Service. https://www.scotcourts.gov.uk/docs/default-source/default-document-library/reports-and data/Improving the management-of-Sexual-Offence-Cases pdf?sfvrsn=6

Victims' Commissioner Office (VCO). 2020. *Rape Survivors and the Criminal Justice System*. London: Victims' Commissioner Office. https://victimscommissioner.org.uk/document/rape-survivors-and-the-criminal-justice-system/.

Part Four

Speaking Truth to Power

Chapter 11

Beyond Speaking Out

#MeToo and the Limits of Narrative Politics

Tanya Serisier

In late 2017, a global outpouring of speech occurred under the hashtag #MeToo as millions shared their stories of surviving sexual violence or implied them by tweeting 'Me Too.' The movement was widely hailed in media commentary as a watershed that irrevocably altered the cultural and political terrain around sexual violence. Not long afterwards, however, this presumption began to appear less certain. In the aftermath of #MeToo, criminal justice systems globally continue to fail survivors of sexual violence, women's testimony continues to be subject to disbelief and denial, and widespread cultures of impunity, especially for rich and powerful men, continue to exist. It is clear that lasting and systemic change in the aftermath of #MeToo cannot be taken for granted.

As I trace in my book, *Speaking Out: Rape, Feminism and Narrative Politics*, this was not the first time that a public outpouring of speech had produced widespread conviction about inevitable changes in the political landscape surrounding sexual violence (Serisier 2018). Following the first speak-outs about rape in the 1970s, early feminist activists like Susan Brownmiller (1976) wrote of their sense of the inevitability of change. In the late 1980s, celebrities like the actor Kelly McGillis, began to speak publicly alongside 'ordinary' women about their experiences of sexual violence, prompting a sense that change was both necessary and inevitable (Serisier 2018). In 2014, responding to the hashtag #YesAllWomen, feminist commentators like Rebecca Solnit (2014) spoke of a seismic cultural shift in public understandings of and responses to sexual violence. Each time, these outpourings of speech were accompanied by optimistic assessments of their long-term consequences, but also by a similarly strong sense that such a change had not previously occurred.

I have come to describe those moments through the analogy of throwing a rock into a pond (Serisier 2018). The immediate effect is dramatic, and the pond appears to be completely different to a moment ago. Immersed in that moment of instability, it is easy to imagine the pond will never return to its previous state. However, in the absence of anything else happening, this is precisely, gradually, what the pond does, until there is no lasting trace of the disruption. As #MeToo progressed, and the hashtag returned periodically, I

DOI: 10.4324/9781003379331-16

began to rethink the metaphor. It is perhaps a boulder, or an avalanche of rocks, but still the pond continues to settle, even if it is not identical to how it was before. It is in this sense that I would argue #MeToo can be seen as a *limit point* of speaking out as a political strategy. It is the most successful and consequential example of this kind of politics and, as such, the most complete demonstration of its limits. Perhaps after throwing the biggest or most rocks you can, it is time to do something new. In this chapter, I expand on the need to think beyond speech about sexual violence as an end in itself, and about the need to engage sexual violence politically. This means, I argue, exploring how sexual violence interacts with, and is determined by, systemic power relations such as gender, race, and class, and how a politics that seeks to confront and end sexual violence must also grapple with those power relations. I first recap the history of which #MeToo is a part and then articulate more fully my sense of it as a limit case. In the final two sections, I look at two ways of moving 'beyond' speaking out through changing the stories that we tell or thinking more carefully about how the politics of speech might relate to other forms of activism against sexual violence.

#MeToo and the Limits of Speaking Out

At the close of 2017, there seemed to be few limits to what media pundits, at least, saw as the potential of #MeToo and associated acts of speaking out. Epitomised in the *Time* magazine 'person of the year' issue, devoted to the 'Silence Breakers,' #MeToo was described as a "watershed" or "revolution" and presented as a decisive blow to the male entitlement and an end to the deliberate blindness to violence and harassment that characterises the experience of women and many others in the workplace and elsewhere (Zacharek, Dockterman and Sweetland Edwards 2017). It is undeniable that #MeToo was massive in scope, with approximately 500,000 tweets and 12 million Facebook posts recorded in the days following the hashtag's eruption (Santiago and Criss 2017). Multiple columns and personal disclosures by celebrities, politicians and other public figures and literally uncountable numbers of personal discussions and disclosures were generated in its aftermath. Consequently, numerous updatings, introductions and reviews of sexual harassment policies and procedures were initiated in a number of industries. Additionally, a number of high-profile men, particularly but not only in the entertainment industry, faced serious professional consequences while Harvey Weinstein, of course, faced trial and was convicted (Boyle 2019). This sense of limitless possibility has, however, dimmed over time, with many seeing the confirmation of Brett Kavanaugh to the United States Supreme Court, despite the compelling testimony of Christine Blasey Ford alleging to have been sexually assaulted by Kavanaugh decades earlier, as a significant turning point (Serisier 2023). As others have noted, the damage to prominent men's careers has on the whole been temporary, and many alleged to have committed sexual misconduct, such as Jian Ghomeshi and Louis C. K. have not only made come-backs but incorporated their status as "victims" of an overzealously feminist, anti-male public culture into their celebrity identities (Srinivasan 2021). It is my contention here that, considered in the context of a history of speaking out, this oscillation between hope and disappointment is not new, and that it tells us something important about speaking out as a political strategy, and particularly about its political limits.

The feminist project of 'speaking out' might be seen to have begun in 1972, when the New York Radical Feminists organised the first public 'speak-out' against rape, organised around the theme that 'Rape is a Political Crime Against Women.' This conference was a key moment in sexual violence, and especially rape, becoming one of the central issues for the second-wave feminists of the 1970s, and the generations of feminist activists that followed. It was also the inauguration of speaking out, women publicly discussing their experiences of victimisation, as a key tactic in feminist efforts to transform sexual violence from a subject that was both taboo and normalised into a political issue and a key marker of gendered power and women's oppression (Serisier 2018). The politics of speaking out is constituted by a belief in the transformative potential of survivor narratives to change cultural understandings of rape, reduce the shame and stigma faced by survivors, and, ultimately, challenge the cultural norms that allow this violence to be so ubiquitous and unexceptional. This strategy arose from feminists' sense, when they began to share stories of rape and sexual violence in consciousness-raising groups, that their pre-existing understandings of rape, taken from law, medicine and other powerful social institutions, were profoundly belied by their experience. Taught that rape was rare, the product of individual psychopathy, and explicable through notions of individual criminality, feminists in these groups found that their experiences were common, that many had been assaulted by 'normal' men, including friends, partners, and family members, and that the responses of police, friends, family, and others were frequently to deny and dismiss the reality of their experience or to place the blame on them.

Following the conference, 'breaking the silence' to 'end the violence' became one of the most distinguishing features of the feminist movement up to and including in #MeToo. The commitment to speaking out has continued over the following half-century, with survivors speaking publicly at feminist protests, through media from magazines to talk shows, publishing autobiographical accounts and, more recently, producing podcasts and documentaries. Fundamental tenets of 'speaking out' about sexual violence have come to seem like common sense truisms. Not only feminists and progressives, but many conservatives and anti-feminists, take for granted the assumption that combatting sexual violence requires listening to the voices of survivors.

The approximately 40 women who took the stage in 1972, were, however, by no means the first women to speak publicly about sexual violence as a political act, even in the USA. In the context of the civil rights movement,

Black women had been speaking publicly for decades about sexual violence as a tool of both gendered and racial terror, exercised against Black women and, through them, against entire Black communities (McGuire 2010). The lack of reference to this history at the 1972 conference reflected a wider tendency among feminists to neglect the links between rape and other forms of structural violence, and the connections between gender and other forms of oppression. The tensions between seeing rape as a singular form of gendered violence and analysing it within wider structures of gender, race, class and other forms of power, also continued to play a central role in feminist politics. These tensions are reflected in the differential treatment that continues to face women who speak publicly about sexual violence. While feminist scholars have documented that all survivors risk shame, stigma, and disbelief when they speak about rape, the disproportionate "tainting" of women of colour, poor women and others like sex workers who are seen as lacking "respectability" continues to mark public reception of survivor stories (Gilmore 2017). Where feminists hoped that women speaking out would gradually and inevitably lead to more public acceptance of survivor narratives, the pool of stories that are able to be heard and believed remains limited and marked by class, race, and other dynamics of social power. It is telling that the only actor whose story of victimisation was immediately publicly contested by Harvey Weinstein was Lupita Nyong'o, the only Black actor to speak out against him (Serisier 2018). These dynamics cannot be understood through a politics that assumes all survivors and their stories face the same or equal barriers to speech, or that all survivors face the same consequences for speaking.

Another question increasingly raised by feminist commentators is whether a politics formed around the presumption that rape is a topic shrouded in silence and taboo adequately address what Tanya Horeck (2004) has described as the public "volubility" around rape. Early feminist speak-outs were designed to insert survivor voices into a public sphere from which they were excluded. However, from at least the 1980s onwards, there has been an expanded interest in, and market for, mediated stories of at least some women's suffering, particularly in relation to sexual violence (Serisier 2018). This has, in part, resulted from feminist and survivor success in insisting on the importance of these narratives being heard, producing what Linda Alcoff and Laura Gray-Rosendale (1996) describe as an ongoing tension between "transgression" and "recuperation" in the public dissemination and consumption of these narratives. As they, and other, more stringent critics such as Louise Armstrong (1994) have argued, commodified and re-packaged survivor narratives can be sold as spectacles of suffering, casting survivors as damaged victims to be pitied, or as "neoliberal life narratives" of individual overcoming which deny the need for systemic change (Gilmore 2017).

These narratives limit survivors to one-dimensional characters whose ability to tell their stories is restricted by norms of gender, race and class, so that, for instance, stories of respectable white women victimised by criminal others may be told through carceral and "penal populist" lenses while women of colour, sex workers and others are largely barred from speaking as victims at all, let alone expressing the ways in which experiences of sexual violence are connected to wider patterns of state based violence, or the violence of racial exclusion and poverty (Serisier 2018). Indeed, so-called 'carceral feminist' responses to sexual violence are argued by many to rely on a particular white and middle-class speaking position which does not see the state as a potential agent of violence, and views sexual violence as a uniquely political or structural harm (Bernstein 2010). In contrast, Black feminists in the US and Indigenous feminists in countries such as Australia have written extensively about experiencing sexual violence as connected to wider structural harms associated with poverty and racism, and seeing state violence as a central element of these harms (e.g., Davis 2020, Ryan 2019). In this context, more policing and harsher sentencing makes no sense as a solution for narratives of harm and victimisation, and feminist politics that call for these things as responses to survivor narratives, work, in effect, to extend the harms experienced by women whose lives are marked by racial exclusion and poverty as well as gender-based oppression.

These issues tie into broader feminist debates about co-optation, and particularly the way that feminist demands for more serious measures against violence against women can become realised in ways that distort their original intentions, through massive investment in the carceral state as opposed to women's services. The need for feminists to recognise and respond effectively to this process has become a key argument of many contemporary critical theorists (e.g., Fraser 2009). An adequate response, I suggest, drawing on Wendy Brown (1995), must involve a shift to seeing feminist mobilisations such as speaking out through the lens of politics and strategy rather than morality. Many feminist discussions around speaking out are framed in terms of moral imperatives, that to listen to survivors is right and to fail to do so is wrong. While this may be true, Brown suggests that there are two problems with this. First, it claims authority for women's speech on the basis of wounded identities and fosters an attachment to woundedness as a feminist virtue, seeing survivor speech not as a claim for the right to a political subjectivity that can speak to the harms of sexual violence, but for a privileged moral status because of woundedness. This source of authority not only forecloses political agency but is inherently more available to those able to access a privileged politics of femininity due to their racial and class positioning. Second, it is a perspective that loses sight of the reason for speaking out, which was to contribute to ending sexual violence. Where speaking out becomes moral rather than political it becomes untethered from the promise that society could be different, or as I put it in my own work, that the goal of a world in "which we do not have to speak of rape so much, or, perhaps, one day, even at all" (Serisier 2018, 196).

The other effect is that it obscures and flattens the political element to survivor speech, inferring that survivor speech comprises a singular narrative with a shared and obvious moral. A more politicised understanding would see the experience of sexual violence as producing particular kinds of knowledge in interaction with existing social discourses and broader life experiences to produce different meanings in different contexts (Naples 2003). For instance, an experience of attempting to achieve justice through the criminal justice system may lead a survivor to call for the strengthening of prosecution and policing measures to improve conviction rates or to call for abandonment of the criminal justice system as itself a site of structural gendered and racialised violence. Neither of these perspectives arises naturally from the experience of sexual violence, although they are, as Angela Davis (2020) argues, likely to be influenced by the ways that racial and class positions affect whether women see the criminal justice system as a source of protection or violence. The point is that these are political perspectives, which demand debate, discussion, and assessment between and among survivors and feminists, and they may involve differences that are ultimately unresolvable.

What both of these points tell us is that stories do not have inherent meanings. Rather, these meanings are produced within and through cultural contexts and discourses. Speaking out does not simply tell unheard stories but attempt to give those stories new meanings. The discussions reported in early consciousness-raising groups around rape were sometimes about stories that had never been told before but often included descriptions of telling the story of being sexually assaulted to friends, family or partners only to have them refuse the meaning given to it by the survivor. The continued contested meaning of stories is similarly attested to by Chanel Miller (2019, 47) in her memoir, as she describes reading the comments section below a news article describing her rape, with multiple commentators insisting that the story told was either one of consensual sex or where an older woman had manipulated a younger and vulnerable man. Feminist critique has tended to focus on the fact that stories of sexual violence are minimised and not taken seriously. However, in the 50 years since early feminists speak-outs, it has become clear that we need to think what taking sexual violence seriously means in different contexts. Taking sexual violence seriously can, for instance, be incorporated into racist and "femonationalist" discourses that define non-Western cultures as especially oppressive to women justifying Western military projects and stoking fears around immigration (Farris 2017). They also frequently are taken as unquestionably supporting criminalisation and increased sentencing (Gruber 2009; Davis 2020). As Indigenous women in Australia have argued in debates around 'coercive control' legislation, the call for more policing in colonial societies such as Australia ignores the ongoing violent histories of policing of Indigenous communities and the fact that Indigenous women particularly are not made safer by increasingly carceral regimes of policing, but face increased risk of criminalisation and incarceration (Watego et al. 2021). Many dominant feminist responses to narratives of sexual violence tend to reify understandings of rape as a problem of exceptional criminality that exists in opposition and clear distinction to "normal" heterosex, and cast marginalised communities as outside the domain of acceptable and protected sexual practices (Serisier 2005). All narrative framings prioritise certain responses and solutions and exclude others by prioritising certain perspectives. It is part of the political challenge of feminism to contest framings that increase the harm suffered by marginalised women particularly.

As #MeToo has become an increasingly accepted touchstone for the existence of ongoing and widespread harassment and assault in our society and workplaces, an undisputed effect of the hashtag is that it is no longer possible, at least in the near future, to say that as a society we 'do not know' what passes for normal in many industries and workplaces, homes, and public settings. The question, as I have indicated here, that remains undetermined is what forms of action will be taken on the basis of this knowledge. Tarana Burke, founder of the original 'Me Too' movement, a community organisation aimed primarily at, supporting, in Burke's words, 'Black and Brown girls,' has repeatedly made this point in her discussions about the impacts and aftermath of the #MeToo hashtag. In what now seems a highly prescient comment made in early 2018, Burke raised the hypothetical possibility of "an outbreak of some communicable disease that 12 million people got in a 24-hour time period," noting that in such an event, the US "would be focused solely on the cure" (Wagmeister 2018). Speaking elsewhere about next steps, Burke has repeatedly referenced "strategy" and "organising," noting explicitly and pointedly that if "we keep on 'making statements' and not really doing the work, we are going to be in trouble" (Walden 2018). What is doing the work, however? In the following two sections I suggest that this involves both thinking differently about narrative practice and not relying solely on stories of sexual suffering in our politics.

Telling New Stories

Although Burke's statements might be taken as asserting the relative unimportance of narrative for politics, I would insist that developing new social narratives is a key part of feminism or any social movement that seeks to change society (Polletta 2006). However, this project must go beyond faith that experiential narratives have an obvious or automatic meaning that will automatically produce desirable change. As I have argued elsewhere, a straightforward and undifferentiated reliance on the power of stories of rape means that those narratives that are easiest to tell and be heard dominate the stories in the public sphere. This ultimately means those stories that are most compatible with the criminal justice and medical/psychiatric discourses, and stories told by those women who are granted the most credibility and respectability, generally white, middle-class women with respectable jobs and heteronormative lifestyles (Serisier 2018). In other words, it is easier to find a reception for stories that are already legible, or, as close as possible to legible, within existing discourses and norms.

More fundamentally, experience itself is understood and interpreted through available discourses. As Naples (2003) argues, even where survivors have full control over their stories and their interpretation, they must still draw on existing discourses to make them legible. They also have little control over the way in which audiences will read and rewrite their experiences using these discourses. example of these processes can be seen in the case of Chanel Miller, originally known as 'Emily Doe.' Miller's story of being raped while unconscious at a fraternity party was able to draw on long-standing tropes around incapacity but also cultural concerns about sexual violence at elite universities. While her account spoke of the trauma of her experience of rape it was also an excoriation of her treatment by the criminal justice system and, ultimately, her disappointment at the sentence given to the student who assaulted her, BrockTurner (Baker 2016). There are a number of possible meanings to be drawn from this experience, including challenging or contesting the role of the criminal justice system in adjudicating sexual violence. However, public campaigns focused solely on punitive measures such as the recall of the trial judge on the grounds that he had been too lenient, and to increase sentences for sexual assault (Serisier 2018).

To be heard, stories must fit within wider narrative conventions as well as engage with the specific generic expectations that audiences increasingly have about the structure of survivor narratives. In this sense, narrating experience is more than simple recounting. It must author the experience of sexual violence into a recognisable narrative, or in the words of survivor-author Patricia Weaver Francisco (1999a), give it the "shape of a story." This can be experienced as a pressure by survivors because their experience of trauma does not always fit with conventions of narrative. As Jamie Kalven (1999, 291–292) writes in his account of his family following the rape of his wife: "The conventions by which we recognise and understand stories – dramatic conflict and defining moments, reversals of expectations and denouements – are poorly adapted to the task of rendering that which is strenuously ongoing." But creating narrative from experience can also be an opportunity to bring politics to bear on the meaning of the story. The potential of authorship is related by Francisco when she talks about her decision to engage her rapist in conversation as a survival strategy. She acknowledges there are other ways of telling the story: "The conversation that I believed saved my life may also have given him confidence. He'd sized me up, too, found me desperate to live, willing to bargain" (1999, 28). However, acknowledging this possibility, Francisco deliberately authors her story differently: "I like this part of the story. In fact, I have become committed to it. In this part, I look cagey and victorious and well worth saving" (1999, 17–18). Rather than pondering whether her account is accurate, Francisco claims the right to author the meaning of the story. Similarly, at a pivotal point in her account of her recovery, author Martha Ramsey (1995, 202) asks herself, "In my story, what did I want to say the rape had really meant?" In asking this question, she, like Francisco, transforms the meaning of her experience from a 'truth' that must be uncovered to a conclusion that she is in the process of writing.

This possibility has been recognised by feminist advocates of survivor writing, such as Toni McNaron and Morgan Yarrow (1982, 55). They write in their collection of writing by survivors of incest:

> To tell orally is the first step... To write these same stories as narrative is a second and huge step because we put form around what has seemed so chaotic, we make public to strangers the most intimate truths about ourselves... When we write a poem or letter or story about the impact or centre of that narrative, we take a third leaping step – we dare to make art out of our female experience – to fly in the face of all expectations for what is acceptable in such forms.

What this suggests is that it is precisely the ability of survivors to mould that experience narratively and artistically that allows them to engage in individual acts of control. It also, I would suggest, is what allows them to render their experiences politically and artistically significant.

This commitment to the political potential of style is, as the McNaron and Yarrow quotation above demonstrates, itself a part of the heritage of feminist and survivor politics. It can be found in influential but politically opposed feminist writers from the 1980s, for example. Andrea Dworkin (1997, 16), for instance, demonstrated a consciousness around the necessity of style to communicate the truth of feminism effectively:

> My only chance to be believed is to find a way of writing bolder and stronger than woman hating itself – smarter, deeper, colder. This might mean that I would have to write a prose more terrifying than rape, more abject than torture, more insistent and destabilizing than battery, more desolate than prostitution, more invasive than incest, more filled with threat and aggression than pornography.

Similarly, Dorothy Allison (1996, 3), a feminist writer with different politics than Dworkin who blended autobiographic writing, fiction and non-fiction:

> I'm a storyteller. I'll work to make you believe me. Throw in some real stuff, change a few details, add the certainty of outrage. I know the use of fiction in a world of hard truth, the way fiction can be a harder piece of truth. The story of what happened, or what did not happen but should have – that story can become a curtain drawn shut, a piece of insulation, a disguise, a razor, a tool that changes every time it is used and sometimes becomes something other than we intended.

For both of these feminist writers, making use of words as weapons required more than content, but also a grappling with style. For Dworkin, this primarily entailed a register of the terrifying, abject and invasive, while for Allison, the methods were more bound in uses of fiction to insulate, disguise, or like a razor, slip in between the cracks. Regardless of their different styles, however, they both ask us to think about what is necessary to shape truth into a form that will give it political efficacy.

Leigh Gilmore (1994), writing in part about Dorothy Allison, suggests that stylistic experimentation can make visible aspects of experience that a commitment to transparent referentiality may not, and that this can be particularly useful for more marginalised subjects who have been denied automatic access to the authority of the autobiographical 'I.' Describing this style of writing as "autobiographic," Gilmore would include autofiction, memoir, poetry, essays and generic blends, as well as the use of tools from fiction and experimental writing within autobiography. In Gilmore's reading, an easy or transparent relationship between narrative, truth and politics is forestalled, and a more experimental form of autobiographical storytelling necessitated, by the social tropes that have marginalised some stories and their tellers from the realm of autobiography. This analysis also applies within and among survivor texts and narratives, so that survivors whose stories have historically failed to be heard, due to racial marginality, poverty, disability, sexuality, or other axes of oppression, are responsible for producing some of the most creative and challenging work around sexual violence. As a lesbian who had grown up in an impoverished and violent family in the American South, Allison exemplifies this. In grappling with complicated questions of the boundaries between sex and violence, the allures of the speaking position of survivorhood, and the possibility of self-authoring, more experimental texts may pose different political questions and open up further voices.

One of the most prominent recent examples of this is the 2020 BBC television series, *I May Destroy You* (2020), written and starred in by Ghanian-British artist and writer, Michaela Coel. The series tells the story of Arabella, a character based on Coel's experience, but who is also not simply a stand-in for Coel herself. Coel's series both is and is not autobiographical and uses experimental techniques, such as including fantastical elements and offering multiple endings to the story, to explore intersections between gender, race and sexuality to question the ways in which survivor stories are and aren't heard, and to challenge reductive or simple tellings. The series concludes with three alternative versions of Arabella's confrontation with the man who sexually assaulted her after spiking her drink. These range from a case of rape-revenge where Arabella kills her assailant to one where she forces or helps him to confront his own emotional damage. In doing so, Coel offers ambivalence and uncertainty as part of what she chooses to make her rape mean, answering Ramsey's question (1995, 2) about "what did I want to say the rape had really meant?" with the fact that the rape, and recovery from it, might look like any or none of the alternative scenarios presented. In challenging the generic boundaries of autobiography, Coel's series offers a narrative that asks more questions than it answers but refuses to deny agency to its heroine and never allows her subjectivity to be fully subsumed or defined by the experience of rape. Perhaps most importantly, the series allows for Arabella to experience significant ambivalence about what role she wants the experience of sexual violence to play in her life and how it impacts upon her sense of self.

Another way in which stylistic experimentation occurs in these narratives is through the use of metaphor and particularly metaphors that draw on fictional genres such as horror or fairy tales. For instance, Chanel Miller's memoir, *Know My Name*, makes extensive use of metaphor to navigate her experience of sexual violence and the legal and medical encounters that flow from it, as well as the way she navigates the relationship between this violence, her previous experiences of structural violence, including teen suicides at her school and a mass shooting, as well as her experiences of racial difference and exclusion as an Asian woman living in California. For instance, she evokes the ambience of a horror film in her discussion of her experience of the medical examination following her rape, as like being alone in a "still, dark ocean, flat and vast":

> Horror was present, I could feel it moving, shifting my insides, wet and murky and weighted, but on the surface, I saw only a ripple. Panic would arrive like a fish, briefly breaking the surface, flicking into the air, then slipping back in, returning everything to stillness.
>
> (Miller 2019, 7)

South African author, Charlene Smith (2001, 176) uses fairy tales both as a contrasting trope to demonstrate how her life exceeds linear narrative conventions, but also myth to signify this: "If this were a fairy story I would end the book with my testimony, but it is not. In some ways the rape survivor's testimony is the opening of Pandora's box, and so it was in my case." In Smith's case, this Pandora's box includes navigating the racial politics of sexual violence as a white woman raped by a Black man as well as the intersecting debates between medical care for rape victims and HIV prevention and treatment efforts in a period when much mainstream politics in the country was marked by explicit denial of the significance and epidemic nature of both sexual violence and HIV.

Reflecting on her own use of fairy tales to describe the experience of rape, Patricia Weaver Francisco (1999b, 3) writes that there is "in all stories relished by the teller… the alchemy we are promised in fairy tales." It is this alchemy, both in terms of personal and social transformation, that these survivor-authors seek to harness through drawing on well-known or evocative fictional tropes. Following Gilmore, it is important to note that, perhaps counter-intuitively, a further alchemical function of stylistic variation is that it opens up the possibility of increased diversity in survivors who tell their stories of sexual violence. While one of the promises of speaking out as a movement was that it would replace dominant myths and misconceptions of rape with a vision more reflective of women's experiences, speaking out narratives that reach the public sphere tend to be those that most easily accrue authority; stories of stranger rape told by respectable white, middle-class, cis-gender, heterosexual women with high levels of formal education (Serisier, 2018). In contrast, as Gilmore has shown, traditions of speaking about sexual violence among marginalised communities such as Indigenous or colonised communities, tend to make use of practices of collective storytelling, myth and metaphor. Traditions of African-American storytelling have tended to tell stories of sexual violence as part of wider narratives of oppression, for example slave testimonies and in the personal testimonies which fuelled the civil rights movement (McGuire, 2010). In this sense, shifting boundaries around the types of stories that are recognised as part of a political tradition of confronting sexual violence would also involve shifting boundaries around who we recognise as participating in this tradition and what kinds of politics it produces.

Speaking Out vs Doing 'the Work' – What Does this Mean in the Current Era?

Although #MeToo is frequently represented as a singular manifestation of feminist politics, it clearly contains at least two distinct political and cultural trajectories, described by Karen Boyle (2019, 5) as "Me Too" and "#MeToo." The former references the community campaign begun by African-American activist Tarana Burke which has been running from 2006 while the latter refers to the hashtag begun by actor Alyssa Milano and the movements and campaigns that have emerged from that. While much commentary tends to operate on the assumption that the two are politically aligned, this generally means assuming that Burke's campaigning work has been incorporated within and subsumed by the hashtag and its cultural ramifications. However, as I've argued elsewhere, Burke's "Me Too" is not merely the "back story" to Milano's "#MeToo" (Serisier 2018). They represent different conceptions of feminism and political change. In Burke's vision, #MeToo is not the culmination or outcome of the work of "Me Too." For Burke, instead, the discursive activism associated with "#MeToo" is best seen as a form of "amplification" that enables organising and strategy work to occur. Burke warns, however, that "if we keep on 'making statements'and not really doing the work, we are going to be in trouble," even to the extent that the momentum built up around "#MeToo" will simply disappear in (Walden 2018).

For decades, as Kaitlyn Mendes (2015) notes, feminist activism in relation to sexual violence might be best described as "discursive," both in that it seeks to alter dominant discourses around violence and in the sense that it is a primarily discursive form of activism, focused on the dissemination and production of new and different types of speech. So even rallies like 'Reclaim the Night' are about bringing participants together to share stories. Or, in the case of 'slutwalk,' Mendes' prime object of analysis, the action was focused on performatively responding to victim-blaming and "slut-shaming," reclaiming the rights of all women to both be free from violence and dress how they want to.

The questions posed by Burke are whether it is sufficient to engage purely or primarily in discursive activism and what are the costs of focusing on that activism to the extent of other forms of political intervention? Or, returning to Boyle's distinction, how might we rebalance feminist politics against sexual violence towards the community campaigning of 'Me Too' and away from the discursive spectacle of '#MeToo'? This is not to devalue the work of the latter but to think about what kinds of grassroots movements are needed and appropriate in the current era. The forerunners for 'Me Too' include the development of rape crisis centres, as well as law reform, and efforts to reform policing and medical responses to survivors. It includes the history of community transformative justice efforts in relation to sexual violence such as those of Incite! and Critical Resistance, as well as the histories of political organising around feminism but also anti-racism and for social services rather than increased funding to criminal justice (see, for instance, Incite! and Resistance 2001). This kind of work is often slower and less immediately rewarding, but it is also often more connected to the complex social dynamics surrounding sexual violence, and the way these dynamics are determined by questions of race and class as well as gender. Rather than simply drawing attention to sexual violence as a problem it raises questions such as whether it is better to ameliorate immediate harms or focus on the harder and less immediate work of shifting the structures that enable sexual violence and excuse it, and indeed, also questions the extent and nature of these structures.

Wendy Brown (1995) has written about a preference in feminist politics for the moral and narrative terrains over the terrain of politics. She criticises the lure of asserting that one has been wronged without focusing on how things might be different and on claiming the power to change things. Speaking out is at core a drawing attention to a problem and a lack, testifying to a harm and, at best, demanding that things be different. But it does not work through the how of that difference, both in terms of what needs to happen to address the cause of the harm and how that might be achieved. It is undoubtedly important to make a claim about the unacceptability of harm and wrongdoing. For Brown, as for Burke, however, politics cannot stop there, but must entail a working towards the desired state. Doing so entails abandoning the speaking position of victim or survivor, at least to an extent, and instead adopting the position of political agent or activist.

This is a terrain on which the political schisms within and among feminists become clearer, or at least play out differently. It also demonstrates the extent to which 'listening to' or being led by survivors is not a replacement for political disagreement and debate. While many survivors continue to believe it is important and necessary, for instance, to reform and engage the criminal justice system (e.g., Miller 2019), others are declared abolitionists and speak of wanting something other than prosecutions and convictions (e.g., Leo 2011). These preferences also speak to the location of survivors within different strands and trajectories of feminist and anti-rape politics, from the transformative visions of organisations like Incite! and Critical Resistance to ongoing work around law reform within the criminal justice system. At times, these different strands of feminism are about different emphases or priorities. But they can also signify political disagreements and speak to long-standing political tensions between Black and Indigenous organising and that of historically white-dominated organisations. Research, policy work or activism with survivors requires working through these complexities and divergences. It requires political debates and judgements around whether hearing and responding to survivor experiences of secondary trauma in the criminal justice system should lead to attempts at reform or efforts to decentre this system as a response to sexual violence. It is possible to make a survivor led argument for both, and equally possible to accuse those who take a different path of either a kind of unhelpful utopianism or encouraging survivors to invest false hope in a system that will not fulfil their needs.

In other words, speaking out is an activity that occurs within, alongside and in parallel with debates among feminists about issues such as the root cause of sexual violence and the role of criminal justice in responding to it, and survivors are both actors and symbols within these debates. The problem with this is not the political mobilisation of speech or authorisation and authority. Rather, the problem lies in the attempt to claim that only one political position represents the authentic wishes and speech of survivors, and in corresponding attempts to delegitimate those with different views. For Brown (1995), this is the dead end of a moral politics that refuses to call for what it wants or think about how to get it. In contrast, a properly political feminist politics would acknowledge the disparities between work to reform law and criminal justice systems and abolitionist projects that seek to dismantle the carceral state through building better and less harmful alternatives that render it obsolete. It means revealing counter-posed positions and political priorities that are not so evident in the project of speaking out. This is because it is a project of building a world beyond endemic sexual violence, and so, as Brown argues, necessitates real, and fraught, engagements about what that world can and should look like.

Anti-Rape Politics Beyond Speaking Out

Thinking differently about feminist politics is not about disavowing or denying a legacy but asking how we might recognise and respond to the limitations of speaking out as a political strategy. To return to the metaphor of the rock in the pond, it means recognising that the rock shatters the presumption that everything was fine and normal as it was and creates the space to demand that things be different. But it is also to insist that we should not need to throw rocks forever, and indeed that our politics involves building a new world as much as disrupting this one. That project of world-building must be cognizant of, and incorporate, understandings derived from the experiences of survivors of sexual violence. But it must also exceed individual experiences by working towards a collective goal, and as I noted in the previous section, this means accepting conflict and disagreement as part of a political practice.

Responding to disagreement is one aspect of necessary shifts. Another is moving beyond the usual practices of speaking out. As I have discussed here, this is both in the realm of discourse and narrative and in the extra-discursive realm. In the former case I mean embracing the creative, artistic and imaginative power of responses to sexual violence, as well as focusing on truth in a narrow sense, and broadening our conception of what these responses look like. If narratives and creative responses to colonisation, endemic racism, ableism and other forms of systemic violence are also seen as part of the tradition of speaking, writing and other creative practices against sexual violence, the field of possible rewritings becomes so much wider, and a wider range of voices and experiences are recognised within this project.

Feminist politics beyond speaking out does not mean refuting or rejecting the political value of survivor speech. It means using the space created by speaking out but not relying on it as our sole mode of politics. It perhaps means questioning if there is a uniform or universal 'feminist' position on sexual violence or whether there are other political commitments that also shape our thinking. Ultimately, I think it means not losing focus on the desire to work towards ending sexual violence but recognising that it will require more than breaking the silence to do that.

References

Alcoff, Linda Martín and Laura Gray-Rosendale. 1996. "Survivor Discourse: Transgression or Recuperation?" In *Getting a Life: Everyday Uses of Autobiography*, edited by, S. Smith and J. Watson, 198–255. Minneapolis: University of Minnesota.

Allison, Dorothy. 1996. *Two or Three Things I Know For Sure*. London: Flamingo.

Armstrong, Louise. 1994. *Rocking the Cradle of Family Politics: What Happened When Women Said Incest*. Reading: Addison-Wesley.

Baker, Katie J.M. 2016. "Here's the Powerful Letter the Stanford Victim Read Aloud to her Attacker." *Buzzfeed* 4 June. Accessed March 23, 2018. https://www.buzzfeednews.com/article/katiejmbaker/heres-the-powerful-letter-the-stanford-victim-read-to-her-ra

Bernstein, Elizabeth. 2010. "Militarized Humanitarianism Meets Carceral Feminism: The Politics of Sex, Rights, and Freedom in Contemporary Antitrafficking Campaigns." *Signs* 36 (1): 45–71.

Boyle, Karen. 2019. *#MeToo, Weinstein and Feminism*. London and New York: Palgrave.

Brown, Wendy. 1995. *States of Injury: Power and Freedom in Late Modernity*. Princeton: Princeton University Press.

Brownmiller, Susan. 1976. *Against Our Will: Men, Women and Rape*. Melbourne: Penguin Books.

Coel, Michaela. 2020. *I May Destroy You*, edited by Sam Miller and Micaela Coel. London: BBC Studios.
Davis, Angela. 2020. "Struggle, Solidarity, and Social Change." In *The Routledge Handbook of the Politics of the #MeToo Movement*, edited by G. Chandra, Irma Erlingsdóttir, G. Chandra, and Irma Erlingsdóttir, 27–33. New York and London: Routledge.
Dworkin, Andrea. 1997. *Life and Death*. New York: The Free Press.
Farris, Sara R. 2017. *In the Name of Women's Rights' The Rise of Femonationalism*. Durham: Duke University Press.
Francisco, Patricia Weaver. 1999a. "Self Interview with Patricia Weaver Francisco." [Website]. Accessed April 14. http://www.tellingofrape.com/tellingfiles/interviews.html#anchor14868517.
Francisco, Patricia Weaver. 1999b. *Telling: A Memoir of Rape and Recovery*. New York: HarperCollins.
Fraser, Nancy. 2009. "Feminism, Capitalism and the Cunning of History." *New Left Review* 56: 97–117.
Gilmore, Leigh. 1994. *Autobiographics: A Feminist Theory of Women's Self-Representation*. Ithaca and London: Cornell University Press.
Gilmore, Leigh. 2017. *Tainted Witness: Why We Doubt What Women Say About Their Lives*. New York: Columbia University Press.
Gruber, Aya. 2009. "Rape, Feminism and the War on Crime." *Washington Law Review* 84: 581–657.
Horeck, Tanya. 2004. *Public Rape: Representing Violation in Fiction and Film*. New York: Routledge.
Incite!, and Critical Resistance. 2001. *Incite! and Critical Resistance Statement: Gender Violence and the Prison Industrial Complex*. Accessed January 10, 2023. https://incite-national.org/incite-critical-resistance-statement/.
Kalven, Jamie. 1999. *Working With Available Light: A Family's World After Violence*. New York: W. W. Norton.
Leo, Jana. 2011. *Rape New York*. New York: The Feminist Press.
McGuire, Danielle L. 2010. *At the Dark End of the Street: Black Women, Rape and Resistance - a New History of the Civil Rights Movement from Rosa Parks to the Rise of Black Power*. New York: Vintage Books.
McNaron, Toni, and Yarrow Morgan, eds. 1982. *Voices in the Night: Women Speaking About Incest*. Minneapolis: Cleis.
Mendes, Kaitlynn. 2015. *Slutwalk*. London: Palgrave Macmillan.
Miller, Chanel. 2019. *Know My Name: A Memoir*. New York: Penguin.
Naples, Nancy A. 2003. "Deconstructing and Locating Survivor Discourse: Dynamics of Narrative, Empowerment and Resistance for Survivors of Childhood Sexual Abuse." *Signs: Journal of Women in Culture and Society* 28 (4): 1151–1187.
Polletta, Francesca. 2006. *It Was Like A Fever: Storytelling in Protest and Politics*. Chicago: University of Chicago Press.
Ramsey, Martha. 1995. *Where I Stopped: Remembering An Adolescent Rape*. San Diego, New York and London: Harcourt Brace & Company.
Ryan, Tess. 2019. "This Black Body is not Yours for the Taking." In *#MeToo and the Politics of Social Change*, edited by Biance Fileborn and Rachel Loney-Howe, 117–132. New York and London: Routledge.
Santiago, Cassandra, and Doug Criss. 2017. *An Activist, a Little Girl and the Heartbreaking Origin of 'Me too'*. Accessed January 10, 2023. https://edition.cnn.com/2017/10/17/us/me-too-tarana-burke-origin-trnd/index.html.

Serisier, Tanya. 2005. "'Remembering Anita': Rape and the Politics of Commemoration." *Australian Feminist Law Journal* 23: 121–146.
Serisier, Tanya. 2018. *Speaking Out: Feminism, Rape and Narrative Politics*. London: Palgrave Macmillan.
Serisier, Tanya. 2023. "What Does it Mean to #BelieveWomen? Popular Feminism and Survivor Narratives." In *The Routledge Companion to Narrative Theory*, edited by P. Dawson and M. Mäkelä, 342–353. New York and London: Routledge.
Smith, Charlene. 2001. *Proud of Me: Speaking Out Against Sexual Violence and HIV*. Sandton: Penguin Books.
Solnit, Rebecca. 2014. Our Words Are Our Weapons. *TomDispatch*. Accessed June 11, 2018. https://tomdispatch.com/rebecca-solnit-yesallwomen-changes-the-story/.
Srinivasan, Amia. 2021. *The Right to Sex*. London: Bloomsbury.
Wagmeister, Elizabeth. 2018. "How Me Too Founder Tarana Burke Wants to Shift the Movement's Narrative." *Variety*. Accessed January 10, 2023. https://variety.com/2018/biz/news/tarana-burke-me-too-founder-sexual-violence-1202748012/.
Walden, Celia. 2018. ""It Could all Disappear": #MeToo Founder Tarana Burke on Where the Campaign is Going Wrong." *The Telegraph*. https://www.telegraph.co.uk/women/life/could-disappear-metoo-founder-tarana-burke-campaign-going-wrong/.
Watego, Chelsea, Alissa Macoun, David Singh, and Elizabeth Strakosch. 2021. "Carceral Feminism and Coercive Control: When Indigenous Women Aren't Seen as Ideal Victims, Witnesses or Women." *The Conversation*. https://theconversation.com/carceral-feminism-and-coercive-control-when-indigenous-women-arent-seen-as-ideal-victims-witnesses-or-women-161091.
Zacharek, Stephanie, Eliana Dockterman, and Haley Sweetland Edwards. 2017. "The Silence Breakers." *Time*. Accessed January 10, 2023. https://time.com/time-person-of-the-year-2017-silence-breakers/.

Chapter 12

New Materialism and Artful Interventions

Exploring the Affects of 'Let's Talk about Sexual Violence'

Anna Carline and Clare Gunby

Introduction

This chapter explores New Materialism and the 'affective turn' to develop novel insights into the development and implementation of interventions which aim to reduce and respond to sexual violence. While New Materialism and affect theory are becoming increasingly popular and utilised in the social sciences and humanities, to date there has been little engagement by socio-legal scholars and even less engagement in the area of sexual violence prevention/education. To this end, the chapter will map out the key elements of New Materialism and affects and draw upon this theoretical framework to consider the development, implementation and impacts of an educational intervention – entitled *Let's Talk About Sexual Violence*. In so doing, we draw on qualitative data from 31 participants who attended an exhibition tour and participated in a focus group designed to understand the impacts and influence of this 'artful intervention.' In the chapter, we focus on one specific aspect of the exhibition: the installation called 'A Safe Space.' The overall premise of the chapter – and the 'artful intervention' – is that an understanding of New Materialism and affects enables the development of new approaches for communicating the problem of sexual violence and working towards more effective prevention solutions. We begin by providing a brief overview of the exhibition and its aims, we then discuss New Materialism and what has been referred to as the 'affective turn,' along with the closely related concept of assemblages, before applying this approach to the focus group data.

Let's Talk About Sexual Violence: An Artful Intervention

Let's Talk About Sexual Violence is what we have called an 'artful intervention,' due to the use of creative approaches to translate research evidence about sexual violence into a more communicable form. The exhibition ran across various locations within the University of Leicester in 2019 (where the chapter authors were based at the time) to coincide with Sexual Abuse and Sexual

DOI: 10.4324/9781003379331-17

Violence Awareness Week. Twice daily walking tours took attendees around the artful intervention, where exhibition guides provided information and background about the art. The exhibition was a collaboration between colleagues at the University of Leicester, students, activists, legal and specialist practitioners working in the East Midlands (all with a detailed knowledge of sexual violence – lived, academic and practice-based), coming together with a group of local and national artists. The exhibition's aims were multiple, including to challenge and combat various myths and misconceptions surrounding rape and sexual violence and to inform and educate students and the public (academic, professional service and those from the local community), as to the reality of, and the law relating to, sexual violence. Ultimately, the hope was for the intervention to work to improve responses to sexual abuse by making visible and challenging problematic victim blaming attitudes, encourage the reporting of incidents (to the university or the police) and reduce the perpetration of assaults.[1] The resulting intervention was fundamentally cross-disciplinary and multi-sector, allowing us to challenge insidious and entrenched rape myths with a collective voice.[2]

The initial idea for the exhibition was to develop six 'crime scenes,' translated into pieces of art, which depicted the scope and breadth of rape. This included male rape, the rape of a vulnerable victim, acquaintance rape, relationship rape, rape involving intoxication and the rape and murder of an elderly woman (the case which became the installation A Safe Space). The team examined 22 legal cases that spanned these six rape types (cases where the perpetrator had been found guilty) in order to understand and foreground the key themes associated with them. Thus, the exhibition was curated thematically and drew upon the eight themes of power, consent, trial, shame, myths and misconceptions, justice, space and resistance. Each of the six sites that featured a piece of art incorporated these separate and overlapping concepts.

A Safe Space

The exhibit A Safe Space was the formative idea for the exhibition, initially conceived by the prosecutor in a local case who the authors have a history of collaborating with on research projects. This case involved an elderly woman who was raped and killed by a younger man with whom she was acquainted. The case was seen to disrupt numerous commonly held myths around stereotypical notions of 'real rape' (Estrich, 1988). That is, that the rapist is a stranger, driven by sexual desire and uses a weapon. In this script victims are primarily

1 For a broader discussion of the issues relating to the production and implementation of sexual violence interventions, see Gunby et al. 2017 and Carline et al. 2018.

2 We would like to thank Harriet Smailes, Olivia Taylor and Kajal Nisha Patel for their invaluable work in the development, implementation and evaluation of the exhibition.

Figure 12.1 A Safe Space. Photograph by Kajal Nisha Patel.

young, white, beautiful, physically resist and sustain injuries. This is typically considered the standard against which rape is deemed 'real' or legitimate by members of the public and the justice system more broadly, despite very few rape cases meeting this standard.

The final Safe Space installation was not created to physically represent the victim's bedroom. Instead, the room's composition was informed by reading around the case and discussions amongst the university-based project team (academics, students and support service staff) as to how the bedroom should look and feel. This team curated the room and included their own items – as an act of personalising, uniting and foregrounding a range of women, all of whom find themselves vulnerable to male violence. As such, the bedroom represented a collective, emergent and original piece of artwork by those who were specialists within the field, but not artists. We focus specifically on this installation in the chapter because post-tour evaluation indicated that it had the biggest 'affect' on attendees – often positive but also provocative and confronting. It was clear that the room often shifted attendees, had a visceral impact and precipitated the strongest response.

Evaluating the Exhibition: Methodology

Throughout Sexual Abuse and Sexual Violence Awareness Week, we held two daily one-hour walking tours around the exhibition, seeing 120 participants attend. We asked attendees to complete a post-tour survey which explored

Figure 12.2 A Safe Space. Photograph by Kajal Nisha Patel.

their perspectives on the intervention and asked if they would participate in a follow-on focus group discussion. Ethical approval for which was granted from the University of Leicester. Eight focus groups were conducted between six to eight weeks after the exhibition tours, with 31 individuals participating.[3] Of the 31 participants, 24 were women and seven were men. Sixteen were students, ten were practitioners in the field of sexual and domestic abuse, five were University of Leicester members of staff and three were members of the public (this total exceeds 31 due to three participants with dual roles). Focus group sizes ranged from two to six participants and runtimes were between 43 and 95 minutes. Due to the time lapse between the focus groups and the exhibition tour, facilitators used visual prompts to remind participants of the artwork from each of the sites. In addition to exploring their opinions on various pieces of artwork and the impact of the exhibition on them, participants were asked about their personal understandings of sexual violence and how the artful intervention could be improved. The qualitative data were fully transcribed and analysed thematically (Braun and Clarke 2006) using the data analysis software NVivo. Two overarching themes of 'being moved' and 'challenging stereotypes of rape and rape victims' were developed from the data. Prior to discussing these themes, we set out the key elements of New Materialism and affect theory.

3 We would like to thank Olivia Taylor for her research assistance in relation to facilitating the tours and the evaluation.

New Materialism and Affect Theory

New Materialism is a diverse, "vivid and dynamic field" (Lemke 2015, 490), encompassing a broad range of disciplines (see for example: DeLanda 1996; Braidotti 2000; Barad 2003; Clough and Halley 2007; Alaimo and Hekman 2008; Bennett 2010; Bennett and Joyce 2010; Coole and Frost 2010; Greig and Siegworth 2010; Dolphijn and Van der Tuin 2012). However, it can be broadly and briefly conceptualised as a renewed concern with the material side of life – an aspect of existence which was often ignored or eclipsed by the post-structuralist focus on representation and language – wherein matter was frequently posited as an inert and passive substance which was brought into being and constructed by discourse. As McLure notes:

> Many New Materialist writers … have been especially critical of the 'linguistic turn' in post-structural theory, detecting a pervasive 'representationalism' that has rendered material realities inaccessible behind the linguistic of discourse systems that purportedly construct or represent them.
> (2013, 659)

In contrast, New Materialism restates the importance of the material and rejects any conceptualisation of matter as a docile and reactive substance. In contrast, "new materialists routinely emphasize how matter is 'alive,' 'lively,' 'vibrant,' 'dynamic,' 'agentive,' and thus *active*" (Gamble et al. 2019, 111). Hence, there is a vitality to matter which needs to be acknowledged and can be subject to exploration (Bennett 2010). This is not to state that discourse and representation are not important or ineffectual, but rather to propose a "flattened logic," whereby "discourse and matter are mutually implicated in the unfolding emergence of the world" (MacLure 2013, 660). This in turn leads to the unsettling of binaries, such as subject/object, nature/culture, human/non-human and organic/non-organic (Deleuze and Guattari 2017; Dolphijn and Van der Tuin 2012). Indeed, and as we will detail further, we can explore the very real intensities, forces and affects which flow from non-human and inorganic bodies and importantly, while interconnected with discourse, these affects go beyond the social and cultural meanings and subjective interpretations given to such artefacts (Bennett 2010).

In positing this innately active and dynamic nature of matter, we draw upon the work of Bennett and her concept of 'Thing-Power,' which she notes "gestures to the strange ability of ordinary, man-made items to exceed their status as objects and to manifest traces of independence or aliveness constituting the outside of our own existence" (2010, xvi). Through this conceptualisation, objects such as artwork become things which have a certain liveliness and forcefulness beyond that prescribed to them by socio-cultural norms and discourses and subjective interpretations and constructions. In other words, they have a vibrancy which is in excess to that prescribed by human meaning, and which is, importantly, intrinsic to the matter. Such forces are immanent, not transcendent (Massumi 2013). In developing and applying the concept of 'Thing-Power,' Bennett explores how various objects "become vibrant things with a certain effectivity of their own, a perhaps small but irreducible degree of independence from the words, images and feelings they provoke in us" (2010, xvi). As such, we can apply this theory to the artwork (Thobo-Carlsen 2017) and recognise that the various exhibition sites and art have an autonomous existence and affective capacity of their own; one that is independent to, and cannot be completely captured and controlled by, the meanings and intentions formulated by the artists, the exhibition team and those who attended the exhibition. Thus, there is something beyond the representational function or knowledge that art emits. Furthermore, as we will explore, the concept of assemblages enables a rethinking of the exhibition, which breaks down the subject(attendee)/object(artwork) divide, and rather recognises how the relationships and processes between various diverse bodies (both human and non-human) constantly recreates anew the affectual and political potential of the exhibition (see also Thobo-Carlsen 2017).

Theory of Affects

To further explore the immanent vibrancy of the artwork, we turn to the theory of affects, a key philosophical concept within New Materialism (Massumi 2002, 2015; Ahmed 2004; Brennan 2004; Clough and Halley 2007; Gregg and Seigworth 2010; Wetherell 2012). As with the innate vitality of matter, affect is something which exceeds discourse and representation (Massumi 1995). This, in turn, renders presenting a precise definition problematic. Indeed, as Massumi notes, "the notion of affect does take many forms" and it cannot be "reduced to one thing" (2009, 1). This is because affect is "not a thing" but rather "an event or a dimension of every event" (2009, 1). Following Massumi (2009, 2015a), along with Deleuze and Guattari (2004), we can start with Spinoza (2000), who emphasises that affect can be thought of as a quality, or to be more precise, a relational capacity of bodies. Bodies, be those human or otherwise, have the ability to affect and be affected and here we can see that affects are embodied and relational (Ahmed, 2010; Burkitt 2014; Sointu, 2016). Moreover, it is a relation that brings about a change whereby "a body passes from one state of capacitation to a diminished or augmented state of capacitation" (Massumi 2009, 1–2). In this sense, affects have a political dimension as they can be normative – in that they can shore up and reaffirm various ways of living and existing – but can also be transformative in that they can bring about positive change (Mulcahy 2021). In terms of sexual violence, we can contemplate how normative or diminishing affects problematically maintain and perpetuate certain myths and stereotypes and particular patriarchal concepts of sexuality. In contrast, those which are transformative provide for a wider and more inclusive understanding of sexual behaviour, which is less constrained by ideal notions of femininity, masculinity and heterosexuality.

Thus, the concept of affect relates to an embodied change which involves the body's transition from one state of capacitation to another. This is a *felt* transition (Massumi 2009, 2), however, it is important to note that this feeling is bodily, and as such, can remain beyond cognition. Bodies are constantly in the throes of affecting and being affected, in transition and moving from different states of capacitation without the subject being consciously aware (Massumi 1995; Probyn 2005). Affects are preconscious and can be distinguished from emotions which may be reframed as the process of subjectively and discursively interpreting what becomes the conscious aftermath of a bodily felt affect. This of course makes sense. Affects are not the exclusive potential of human bodies, but rather the domain of all bodies, including non-human and inorganic bodies; hence, they are not dependent upon consciousness. Intuitively, we also understand and appreciate how our bodies can move and do things completely independently from consciously processed thought.

Another way to understand this approach to affects is through the notion of shock. Massumi explains that "affect … is inseparable from the concept of shock" but that there does not need to be "a drama" and can include "microshocks, the kind that populate every moment of our lives," such as "a change in focus or a rustle at the periphery of vision that draws the gaze towards it" (2009, 4). Further, while some affects, or aspects of affects, may escape conscious perception, this is not to assert that there is no relationship between discourse and affects. Numerous scholars illustrate how discourse – those social and cultural scripts which produce identities and meanings – and affects intertwine to produce meaning (Ahmed 2004a, 2004b; Seyfert 2012; Wetherell 2012; Sointu 2016). Hence, we frequently draw upon discourses to make sense of the affects we encounter. Indeed, language and discourse can be used to cue bodies and trigger certain affects and language itself also has an affective register – that which is beyond the signifying register (O'Sullivan 2001).

Massumi continues to explain that this affect, this felt transition, "constitutes a [bodily] memory" as it "leaves a trace" (2009, 2). On this basis, it is not possible to confine affects to a particular moment or event; but rather these felt transitions remain and reside within the body and return. The manner and the extent to which the capacities of a body are enhanced or diminished in the process of being affected are fundamentally shaped by that which has occurred previously (2009, 2). This bodily history encompasses "what we think of as subjective elements, such as habits, acquired skills, inclinations, desires, even willings, all of which come in patterns of repetition" (2009, 2). The body is bound up in processes of repetition, which alter bodily responses to affects. The body has a tendency, which flows from its lived past, and which shapes its reactions and future becomings. This is important, as ultimately, it is not possible in advance to fully determine how a particular body will respond to a particular affective event:

> Since each body will carry a different set of tendencies and capacities, there is no guarantee that they will act in unison, even if they are cued in concert. However different their eventual actions, all will have unfolded from the same suspense.
>
> (2009, 6)

Hence, even when "shocked in concert" each bodily reaction will be unique, dependent upon its history, and thus variation is a key element of affects. Massumi refers to this as "affective attunement," which he notes is "a crucial piece of the affective puzzle" (2009, 6). Herein we can see the emergent and non-linear reality of life. There is always an unknowingness which flows from how differently situated bodies may react to a certain event. When producing the exhibition, the team and artists had certain ideas and hopes with respects to the reactions the artwork may provoke, along with representational messages we wished to convey, but in reality, this is not possible to control. However, this does not need to lead to a nihilistic attitude whereby the inability to ensure certain outcomes undermines the aims and objectives of the artful intervention. Rather, it highlights the importance of reflectively engaging in the field of affects and thinking through how to effectively 'cue' differently situated bodies. This leads to developing continual processes of feedback and reflection, which consider and respond to the varieties of responses which occur. Furthermore, and as we examine below, for Massumi a political potential springs from this realm of uncertainty (2009, 2015a, 2015b).

Affective Assemblages

Focusing on the relational and affectual capacities of bodies brings us to the closely allied concept of assemblages which can be described as a "multiplicity of heterogeneous objects, whose unity comes solely from the fact that these items function together, that they 'work' together as a functional entity" (Patton 1994, 158). An assemblage emerges out of the affective relations and processes between autonomous and heterogenous components which are brought together in, and operate as, a collective of sorts. These components encompass all forms of bodies and matter, be those human, non-human, organic or non-organic and what is vital is how they relate to each other and operate together (Deleuze and Guattari 1986, 2004; Delanda 2016). Most social and cultural entities can be conceived of as an assemblage: Individuals, towns, cities, institutions and organisations, to nation states (Delanda 2006; 2016). All of these are constituted by the affective relationships and processes between various and diverse autonomous and component parts. In this bringing together of a multitude of elements, an assemblage can be understood as having an expressive and a material regime, although it is important to recognise that these two regimes are inseparably and dynamically interconnected and interacting in affects (Deleuze 1988). The former comprises language and discourse and incorporates elements such as legal instruments and the research which influenced the artwork and the details contained in the exhibition booklet. The material regime encompasses non-discursive components, this includes the physical artwork and the spaces and buildings in which it was housed. Furthermore, it also includes those who attended the exhibition.

By conceptualising the various pieces of artwork and exhibition as an assemblage, we can begin to understand and explore how those who interacted with the exhibition are a vital and inseparable element of the artful intervention and the affects that were produced (Reestorff 2015). The attendees – along with the exhibition guides – are not distinct and disconnected subjects who observe the artwork from a detached and objective viewpoint. Rather, they interact and intermingle with each other and the various exhibits to produce unique affectual encounters which cannot be pre-determined in advance and have a lifeforce beyond the temporal instance of the exhibition. As such, affects and their effects will change dependent upon the unique constitution of each tour group, as the various human bodies interact and react with, and respond to, each other and the artwork. This was particularly the case with the exhibit A Safe Space, which can be understood more as an installation, which involved attendees entering into and moving around the room.

Affectual Politics – Micropolitics

As has been outlined, there are certain key aspects to affects. They are embodied, they involve a relation and there are always variations. It is these three elements for Massumi that foreground affects' political potential (2009; 2015a). Mulcahy further unpacks the politics of affects, noting that it requires inquiries into three aspects:

> 1) the composition of bodies and their capacities to affect and be affected, 2) the role of relations between individual or collective bodies in the engagement of these capacities, and 3) the question of how to compose relations capable of sustaining individuals and communities in active and affirmative modes of existence.
>
> (2021, 3)

What is pivotal to understand is that it is possible to engage in techniques of affect which involves participating in the social field in such a way that certain affects are triggered in bodies. Indeed, Massumi notes that this is now a common feature of politics, and which he explores in relation to the politics of fear and response to the aftermath of 9/11 and terrorism, scrutinising how the production of certain affects – such as fear – enabled increased state control and surveillance of bodies (2015b). Hence, in *Ontopower*, Massumi (2015b) explores how the adoption of a colour-coded terror alert system by the Bush administration's new Homeland Security Office was designed to "modulate fear" following 9/11. At the same time, however, there will always remain the real potential for an alternative reaction and here lies hope for a more progressive politics. Massumi contemplates that within the coming forth of a body's capacitation, which proceeds the affective event, there are a number of potential reactions which stem from the body's tendencies or its lived history. While a particular response will eventually be actualised, others will remain unactualised. Nevertheless, these unactualised responses remain in the body as a potential (2009, 5). He notes that there is always a "reservoir" of untapped responses which can be tapped into and "re-cued." He notes that this alternative response is "not a mere possibility" but rather it is "an active part of the constitution of that situation" albeit one that has yet to be fully developed and actualised (2009, 6). Hence, in every situation there remains the real potential for an alternative response, which can be tapped into and brought into being (2009, 7). This, for Massumi, amounts to a "micropolitics" or an "affective politics," which he notes: "…seeks the degrees of openness of any situation, in hopes of priming an alter-accomplishment" (2009, 7).

Massumi's work on the autonomy of affect has been critiqued as a misreading of Spinoza (Gatens 2014) and as reinstituting a mind/body dualism (Leys 2011), which of course is directly antithetical to New Materialist theory. Ahmed has also critiqued the distinction between affects (as unintentional) and emotion (as intentional) (Schmitz 2014). While space does not permit a detailed discussion of these issues, it remains the case that affects can and do move bodies in unconscious as well as conscious ways. Further, Massumi's consideration of affective attunement provides an interesting framework to understand the differing reactions to the artwork.

Thus, for Massumi, power and politics have become affective. However, the point here is not to oppose this utilisation of affect, but rather to stress that alternative political action "has to learn to function itself on that same level – to meet affective modulation with affective modulation." This, he notes, "requires in some ways, a performative, theatrical or aesthetic approach to politics" (2015a, 33), which is where we situate Let's Talk About Sexual Violence. As O'Sullivan notes, the function of art is "to reconnect us with the world. Art opens us up to the non-human universe that we are part of" (O'Sullivan 2001, 128) and art can be understood as "the name for a function: a magical, aesthetic function of *transformation*" (O'Sullivan 2001, 130).

Analysis: Exploring the Affects of the Safe Space Exhibit

Being Moved

Participants described the bedroom and accompanying narrative that outlined details of the victim's case as 'massively powerful,' in and of itself, but also by comparison to some of the other pieces of exhibition art. It was described as "a different type of art" (FG3, p5), "different to what I've ever experienced" (FG6, p2) and "on a different level" (FG2, p3). Embodied language was used to denote the room's impact through expressions such as 'hard hitting,' 'hit home' and it 'really struck me.' Participants sensed the potential to be affected (Massumi 2009), and were impacted by the bedroom, in a manner that was embodied and amounted to a felt transition. The affectual capacity of the room emerged at multiple points in their engagement with the space, whether that be before they came onto the exhibition tour, when entering the bedroom, once inside the space or after they had left the tour. Thus, four sub-themes were developed to capture these pertinent timepoints.

Pre-exhibition Possibility

For some attendees, witnessing or being aware of the room being set up in the days prior to the exhibition launch created a sense of intrigue as well as assumptions around what the room would be/look like. For some, this included the perception that going on the tour and into the bedroom specifically could have "been quite an odd experience," "a bit dark touristy and a bit voyeuristic" (FG2, p5) and "sensationalising" (FG8, p2). Thus, we see how there is a 'cuing' of the body, with the expectation that certain affects and emotions would ultimately unfold. However, as we explore below, when in the bedroom these assumptions were typically not met.

For others, having friends who had attended the exhibition and spoken about the bedroom led to a feeling of 'enticement' which motivated their own attendance:

> I was ... I wasn't sure whether I was gonna go to it or not, and then two friends who had actually been to it, I asked them how it was and they said 'oh yeah, there was this really good exhibit which you go into the room of an old lady who was, um, abused.' So that actually was what enticed me to go.
>
> (FG2, p2)

Again, we see a cuing of the body's capacitation which linked to various discourses and expectations of the exhibition, priming attendees for affects. This pre-attendance expectation can be conceptualised as a shock – a minor drama – emanating from discourse and which has political potential in that it sparked intrigue and encouraged participation (Massumi 2009). We can also see how the artwork had a vibrancy and force which exceeded the four walls of the exhibition site.

Crossing the Bedroom Threshold

For many participants, a feeling of trepidation was associated with crossing the threshold from the carpark and into the room that housed the installation:

> …before we went in, the guy said 'oh, be aware, this could be triggering and this could be too much.' And I was like 'okay, let's prepare myself, I'm going in ready to be, you know, affected.'
>
> (FG4, p3)

The threshold can be conceptualised as a transition point whereby attendees enter into, and become part of, the artwork assemblage, in so doing ushering in various affectual encounters between the human bodies in attendance and the 'Thing-Power' – "the strange ability of ordinary, man-made items to exceed their status as objects" – of the bedroom (Bennett 2010, xvi). As the participant quote suggests, the trepidation was linked to the narrating of the victim's story prior to entry, as well as an explicit warning that the room may be trigging, both of which played a role in simultaneously cuing and managing participants' expectations – tendencies which are fundamentally informed by each body's lived history (Massumi 2009).

Furthermore, we can see the affectual capacity of discourses, whereby the narrating of the victim's story was recognised to produce a felt transition. Indeed, the apprehension linked to not knowing what might be behind the bedroom door and the possibility of its potential states provoking certain responses in the attendee. For some, the narrating of the victim's story precipitated an expectation of how the room would be/feel:

> When you walk into the room… we chatted outside and then you walk in, it's quite sombre and no one says that you need to be quiet, but everybody that walked in immediately became quiet. So it's … it's hearing the story and then you go into it, and then it … it … it feels quite dark and quite heavy … it was the contrast between hearing what happened and walking in and seeing this perfectly, like, not dishevelled room, and everything was in its place, and that it was an elderly woman who had been attacked.
>
> (FG7, p2)

The participant's quote speaks to the notion of affective atmospheres, which operate in a transformative manner to bring about changes to our bodies and moods. In this context, atmospheres can be understood as the "shared ground from which affect emerged" (Gherardi 2017, 349). While emerging from the collective coming together of the various bodies and artwork, it is also important to emphasise that the affective atmosphere always exceeds the sum of its parts. While radiating from and between the various components, they are not "reducible to the individual bodies" from which they spring forth (Anderson 2009, 80). For participant FG7, p2, the room's atmosphere on entry is one of sombreness, but the 'non-dishevelled' appearance sits in contrast to the dark and heavy feeling generated by the victim's story, an observation made by other participants: "I thought everything was gonna be everywhere … you know it's just … it's just gonna be a mess. But it wasn't, it was just … just set … laid out perfectly" (FG8, p3). The fact that certain expectations were not met – and the dissonance created between this anticipation and reality – linked to the response generated: "it was probably more hard-hitting, um, because I'd already made a judgement before going in… thinking it was gonna be a certain way" (FG8, p2). This dissonance sits alongside the issue of affective attunement and the reality of the emergent and non-linear affective capacity of the artwork. While bodies were cued and primed in a certain way, which led participants to anticipate certain affects, how these actually played out differed to their expectations, leading to a lasting impact of the affects. This shows the liveliness of the 'Thing-Power' that the artwork possess; its affects cannot be pre-determined in advance.

When in the Room

Being in the bedroom resulted, for many, in a sense of being "immersed" in the experience, "part of it" and operating on "a whole different level" (FG2, p3). Inhabiting a space that could have been the victim's bedroom, and in so doing reducing the distance (physically, emotionally and metaphorically) between the exhibition attendee and the victim, was also central to the capacity to generate an affect: "…you put yourself in their space […] it's a lot easier to empathise with how that person was feeling when you're in their space" (FG2, p6). The quote links to affective assemblages, whereby through the process of becoming immersed in the room the attendees can be understood as a vital component of the artwork, as opposed to a detached onlooker. This breaks down the subject/object divide and places attendees as part of the affectual potential of the exhibition (Reestorff 2015). This lack of separation can be seen in the proximity and closeness noted by participants, which had the affectual capacity to provoke empathy and establish connection with the victim. Indeed, this approach was argued to "humanise" the victim and "show that person as a person" (FG2, p4) with the use of statistics – in media reporting as well as educational interventions – being criticised by participants for acting to de-centre individual survivors: "…it was a story of something that happened, so it was so much more emotive than figures and facts" (FG2, p2). Again, seeing sexual violence and its impacts "presented in a different way, so it's not a written news article" was argued to "hit you" (FG6, p3). The importance of the non-representational aspect of the exhibition, the affective and transformative power of the aesthetic, is emphasised here. As O'Sullivan comments, art "transforms, if only for a moment, our sense of our 'selves' and our notion of the world" (O'Sullivan 2001, 128). That the case was "local," a rape and murder that had occurred in Leicestershire or in exhibition attendees "own back yards," also added to its resonance for many, giving the sense of yet further proximity to sexual violence: "a particular personal impact there knowing … coming from the same city and living in the same village" (FG2, p3).

As implicated, despite the trepidation, for the majority of participants something valuable was reported to have come from crossing the threshold and spending time in the bedroom, despite discomfort also being part of the experience (with discomfort indicating that attendees had been moved by the installation):

> And I find it hard to talk about that without like the personal element, um, in there. But… but at the same time, would I have wanted it to be any different? I… I don't… I don't think so. Um, there's something about that that was so impactful that, yeah, maybe it just needs to be [confronting], to take notice.
>
> (FG2, p3)

For many participants there was an acceptance with feeling uncomfortable in the bedroom or at least a recognition of the value associated with the difficult feelings it generated. "I mean, it was deeply upsetting but really powerful" (FG6, p3), a perspective that acknowledges the transformative and political potential of affects. Such findings are interesting to consider in the context of recent debates around removing emotive material related to rape from educational syllabuses. A debate that does not always acknowledge that whilst dialogue around sexual violence may cause distress, distress does not automatically lead to damage; a sense that was particularly evident in our data. Thus, rather than silencing the topic of sexual violence, it would likely be more appropriate to collaborate with survivors in the development of educational interventions, represent sexual violence authentically and ensure that the choice of whether to engage (or not) is available to students. Indeed, powerful messages, those which have the potential to change attitudes and behaviour, were often argued to be those that produced intense affects, that were emotive and could make you "go home and think about it and feel gross" (FG2, p4). Participants saw the value of affective messaging, as a tool for educational purposes but also as a means of honouring a survivor's experience, and did not believe such messages should be diluted:

> … We don't want you to be inspired, we want you to be fucking terrified, because it could happen to you and it's terrifying that it's happening. So I think, um, getting that across is perhaps more respectful to, er, victims than kind of taming it down a bit…
>
> (FG2, p5)

However, for one participant, the horror or "haunting" impact of rape was argued to have not been fully conveyed to them via the bedroom: "you didn't quite get the same haunting feel that really it is horrifying" (FG3, p4). For a second attendee, it was argued that the impact was minimal as a consequence of their own lived experience:

> Someone who already knows this, someone who knows this is happening… goes in, and there is no message because, you know, I'm there and I know, yeah, I know it's there, it's me practically, yeah. And that… I thought it was really, really smart, because this way it was directed to people who had no experience.
>
> (FG4, p3)

This again links to Massumi's (2009) notion of affective attunement and even when "shocked in concert," the lived history of the differently situated bodies of those who attended the exhibition means that it is not possible to bring about a uniformity of response. Indeed, the bedroom installation was not curated with the intention of directing its messages at those with no experience of sexual violence and written evaluative feedback indicated that profound affects – such as a shock, disgust and upset – were experienced by some survivors in response to the room. This nonlinearity in reaction speaks to the reality of the author being dead and the inability to control the affects, flows or interpretation – literally or bodily – of something that has been produced. Similarly, for one participant, there was more overt regret at having crossed the threshold and spent time in the bedroom: "it was really powerful but I came out feeling a bit like I shouldn't have gone in there" (FG2, p4). However, for others, assumptions held prior to tour attendance around the bedroom potentially being "a bit voyeuristic" were challenged, "…but then [after going into the room] I thought they handled it, um, really well" (FG2, p5). For participant FG2, p4, the regret stemmed from a feeling of being overly intrusive by spending time in the bedroom, linked to broader questions associated with who has the right to narrate a person's experience, particularly a rape victim's whose power and autonomy have been taken from them by the assault. Whilst the affects generated in this individual may have been too uncomfortable to sit with (as opposed to inevitably harmful), a nuanced debate arose for them in which questions of ethics and authorship were paramount. It is possible to surmise that exhibitions that produce affects, that link one's intellect and body, could also be those that encourage more nuanced engagement around sexual violence, in turn centring the political potential of the exhibition. This relates to Mulcahy's third element of the political potential of affects: "the question of how to compose relations capable of sustaining individuals and communities in active and affirmative modes of existence" (2021, 3). Those affects which shift us and stay with us are likely to bring about future and hopefully more positive changes, as attitudes and behaviours relating to sexual violence are challenged.

All the Senses

A lavender atomiser was installed in the bedroom and the impact of this on the senses was also important in terms of the rooms ability to move people. For one participant, the smell connected her to her mother and a sense of family and in so doing, helped to cut through some of the detachment she reported to have developed around sexual violence as a consequence of working in the field:

> Whatever products that were in there, it smelt like my mum, like, that's what my mum used. And I think that, you know, when you work in the field, you get a bit... you learn to get detached and go, you know, you try not to be too detached but you have to. And then sometimes when something comes back...
>
> (FG2, p4)

For other participants there was recognition of the role the senses played in the process of being affected and recommendations made around the use of music and sound in order to further help "visualise it more with the medium of noise" (FG3, p4). Thus, the immersive nature of the room, its capacity to enhance the proximity to the victim, their life and experience – or to humanise them – all helped attendees to "visualise the story" (FG2, p3), make it "tangible" (FG8, p2), be able to "feel it" (FG1, p2) and to engage all of the senses in the process of sexual violence education/prevention. This again attests to the non-representational power of the exhibition and how the art could be conceptualised as a 'Thing-Power' that had an affectual force and a vibrancy which was not reducible to the various artefacts which comprised the exhibit.

After You Leave the Room

A number of participants spoke about the feelings, thoughts and sensations provoked by the bedroom as being ones that had longevity, "that carried in my memory the longest" (FG7, p3). In the language of affects, the bedroom resulted in a longer or more apparent transition: "I think [the room] is one you keep thinking afterwards, I think, because then you start to, you know, remember it" (FG4, p2). The nature of the installation, as described, contributed to its lasting impact: "the crime scene, that was like something really, really different, so it was good to kind of see them like that, it has like more of an impact on you" (FG8, p3). The longevity was also kept alive through conversations had with friends at a later timepoint: "talking about it, it's such a ... it sparks so many more questions. Because I think afterwards we sort of ... we would talk about that" (FG8, p2). This again links to O'Sullivan's (2001) understanding of the transformative potential of art and how it opens us up to different worlds. We can see the lasting impact of affect, whereby bodies are moved and transformed in a way that has political potential and which carried the affectual capacity of the artwork beyond the instance of the exhibition and out into the wider world, through attendees' conversations with others. The forceful nature of affects here flow not from the representational dimension of the artwork, but from its aesthetic qualities. We can also see again how the exhibit had a vibrancy which cannot simply be reduced to the various artefacts. There was an excess which attendees felt and embodied.

Challenging Stereotypes of Rape and Rape Victims

As noted, something about the bedroom 'spoke' to participants in ways the other exhibits perhaps did not, and more specifically, challenged stereotypes in a way that the other pieces of art perhaps didn't quite achieve. The bedroom was argued to communicate "the truth of things" – namely, that rape is "something that happens to everyone, or can happen to everyone" (FG1, p3), irrespective of age and the location one finds themselves. Similarly, it was often argued that it "emphasised it's [rape] about violence rather than sex" (FG2, p4) and that "it just goes to show that it's not about sexual attraction, it doesn't matter how attractive you are … it's not about that, it's just about power over someone else" (FG4, p1). For many participants the fact the rape had occurred in the woman's home struck a chord, due to it jarring against their (inaccurate) assumption that home is a space of safety, or at least, a place where there 'should' be protection and refuge. In being confronted with the reality (or reminded) that for women, the private sphere is often not safe, "brings all those misconceptions together and shows you that, no, that's [the stereotype] not right" (FG1, p2). Thus, in many respects, the use of the home setting, rendered public via the installation and in turn dismantling the public/private divide, really did "hit home" (FG6, p3):

> … like the criminology exhibition, that that woman was in her room, a room where she felt safe, it was her home, and that still happened. She didn't do anything to be put in that position, it kind of impacts you in a whole different way because you realise it could happen to anyone, anywhere, anytime.
>
> (FG1, p2)

Here, the aesthetic affectual nature of the artwork had both a representational and non-representational function. The exhibit was successful in challenging various misconceptions related to sexual violence and this attests to its representational qualities. However, this was achieved by the bringing together of discourse (via the spoken word of the exhibition guides) and the 'Thing-Power' of the exhibit. Hence, art here had a representational aspect, operating on the signifying register, at the same time as having non-representational and aesthetic qualities.

Hence, the bedroom was able to deconstruct, for some, stereotypes of home being safe, rape being about sex and attraction, and rape victims not always being young women unacquainted to the perpetrator. However, the idea of the victim having not done "anything to be put in that position," captured in the above participant's quote, implicates that the sympathies afforded in this case may be more difficult to achieve in instances where the victim is considered supposedly culpable. We recognise that in many respects the rape being depicted via the installation was an ideal victim scenario, involving a woman perceived as particularly undeserving, made vulnerable by her age and isolation, and not in the 'wrong' place at the time of her attack. The capacity to have told the story of an alcohol-related rape or the rape of a woman who went back to a perpetrator's house in a similarly affective manner remains debatable.

Indeed, various normative aspects of affects relating to sexual violence continue to influence reactions to victims, maintaining various gendered stereotypes and misconceptions (Mulcahy 2021). But at the same time, as Massumi notes, in such a situation there remains an excess of unactualised reactions, which exist as a real potential and a promise for a more transformative response (2009, 2015a). The key would be to explore with a range of participants how to tell such a story so as to invoke more transformative affectual reactions. It should also be noted that whilst the bedroom was argued to underscore that rape is about violence and control as opposed to sexual attraction, and that frequently "our interactions are about power" (FG3, p3), it's difficult to disentangle whether the sense of violence and the affects generated came from the murder as opposed to the act of rape itself. These are aspects which could be explored in future artful interventions.

Conclusion

New Materialism and affect theory allow for the development of novel (and powerful) insights into the use of artwork as an intervention which aims to raise awareness of, and dispel, myths and misconceptions relating to sexual violence. Through the analysis in this chapter, we can see how the Safe Space installation had a transformative effect that stayed with attendees long after the instance of the exhibition. The focus group data showed that participants were affected by the artwork – they were moved in ways they did and did not always expect and/or feel comfortable with, albeit an uncomfortableness participants were often willing to bear. We trace these impacts back to not only the representational aspects of the installation, such as the information provided to the attendees on the case which informed the artwork, but also to the aesthetic qualities of the room which had an autonomous existence of its own. Herein we can situate the political potential of the artwork. Bodies were moved and transformed, often in a manner which produced positive change in the form of disrupting, questioning and contesting sexual violence stereotypes; undoubtedly a key objective of prevention interventions. However, as we have outlined, it is not possible to always cue the 'desired' response from attendees in advance, due to the uniquely situated history of each body. This points to the importance of engaging with a wide and diverse range of individuals in both the production and evaluation of future 'artful interventions,' including survivor groups, support workers, students, activists, academics and practitioners, to explore how best to produce exhibits which offer the potential to consistently bring about positive and progressive transformations. We feel that we have begun to make the case for the use of New Materialism and affect-based approaches within educational rape prevention work and would encourage others to continue to explore the possibilities of such an approach.

References

Ahmed, Sara. 2004a. "Collective Feelings: Or, the Impressions Left by Others." *Theory, Culture & Society* 21: 25–42.

Ahmed, Sara. 2004b. *The Cultural Politics of Emotion*. Edinburgh: Edinburgh University Press.

Ahmed, Sara. 2010. "Killing Joy: Feminism and the History of Happiness." *Signs* 35 (3): 571–594.

Alaimo, Stacey, and Susan Hekman, eds. 2008. *Material Feminisms*. Bloomington: Indiana University Press.

Anderson, Ben. 2009. "Affective Atmospheres." *Emotion, Space and Society* 2 (1): 77–81.

Barad, Karen 2003. "Posthumanist Performativity: Toward an Understanding of How Matter Comes to Matter." *Signs: Journal of Women in Culture and Society* 28 (3): 801–31.

Bennett, Jane. 2010. *Vibrant Matter: A Political Ecology of Things*. Durham and London: Duke University Press.

Bennett, Tony, and Patrick Joyce, eds. 2010. *Material Powers: Cultural Studies, History and the Material Turn*. New York: Routledge.

Braidotti, Rosi. 2000. "Teratologies." In *Deleuze and Feminist Theory*, edited by Ian Buchanan and Claire Colebrook, 156–172. Edinburgh: Edinburgh University Press.

Braun, Virginia, and Victoria Clarke. 2006. "Using Thematic Analysis in Psychology." *Qualitative Research in Psychology* 3 (2): 77–101.

Brennan, Teresa. 2004. *The Transmission of Affect*. Ithaca: Cornell University Press.

Burkitt, Ian. 2014. *Emotions and Social Relations*. London: Sage.

Carline, Anna, Clare Gunby, and Stuart Taylor. 2018. "Too Drunk to Consent? Exploring the Contestations and Disruptions in Male-Focused Sexual Violence Prevention Interventions." *Social & Legal Studies* 27 (3): 299–322.

Clough, Patricia, and Jean Halley, eds. 2007. *The Affective Turn: Theorising the Social*. Durham: Duke University Press.

Coole, Diana, and Samantha Frost. 2010. *New Materialisams: Ontology, Agency and Politics*. Durham, NC: Duke University Press.

DeLanda, Manuel. 1996. "The Geology of Morals: A Neo-Materialist Interpretation." Accessed July 13, 2021. http://www.t0.or.at/delanda/geology.htm.

Delanda, Manuel. 2006. *A New Philosophy of Society: Assemblage Theory and Social Complexity*. London: Continuum.

Delanda, Manuel. 2016. *Assemblage Theory*. Edinburgh: Edinburgh University Press.

Deleuze, Gilles. 1988. *Foucault*. London: Continuum.

Deleuze, Gilles, and Felix Guattari, 1986. *Kafka: Toward a Minor Literature*. Minneapolis: University of Minnesotta Press.

Deleuze, Gilles, and Felix Guattari. 2004. *A Thousand Plateaus*. London: Continuum.

Deleuze, Gilles, and Felix Guattari. 2017. *Anti-Oedipus*. London: Bloomsbury.

Dolphijn, Rick, and Iris van der Tuin, eds. 2012. *New Materialism: Interviews and Cartographies*. Ann Arbor: Open Humanities.

Estrich, Susan. 1988. *Real Rape*. Cambridge, MA: Harvard University Press.

Gamble, Christopher, Joshua S Hanan, and Thomas Nail. 2019. "What is New Materialism?" *Angelaki: Journal of the Theoretical Humanities* 26 (6): 111–134.

Gatens, Moria. 2014. "Affective Transitions and Spinoza's Art of Joyful Deliberation." In *Timing of Affects: Epistemologies of Affection*, edited by Marie-luise Angerer, Bernd Bosel, and Michaela Ott, 17–33. Chicago: University of Chicago Press.

Gherardi, Siliva. 2017. "One Turn ... And Now Another One: Do the Turn to Practice and the Turn to Affect have Something in Common?" *Management Learning* 48 (3): 345–358.

Gregg, Melissa and Gregory Seigworth. 2010. *The Affects Theory Reader*. Durham: Duke University Press.

Gunby, Clare, Anna Carline, and Stuart Taylor. 2017. "Location, Libation and Leisure: An Examination of the use of Licensed Venues to Help Challenge Sexual Violence." *Crime Media Culture* 13 (3): 315–333.

Lemke, Thomas. 2015. "The Varieties of Materialism." *BioSocieties* 10(4): 489–502.

Leys, Ruth. 2011. "The Turn to Affect." *Critical Inquiry* 37 (3): 434–472.

MacLure, Maggie. 2013. "Researching Without Representation? Language and Materiality in Post-Qualitative Methodology." *International Journal of Qualitative Studies in Education* 26 (6): 658–667.

Massumi, Brian. 1995. "The Autonomy of Affect." *Cultural Critique Part* 31 (II): 83–109.

Massumi, Brian. 2002. *Parables for the Virtual: Movement, Affect, Sensation*. Durham: Duke University Press.

Massumi, Brian. 2009. "Of Microperception and Micropolitics." *Inflexions: A Journal for Research-Creation* 3: 1–20.

Massumi, Brian. 2013. *Semblance and Event: Activist Philosophy and the Occurrent Arts*. Cambridge, MA: MIT Press.

Massumi, Brian. 2015a. *The Politics of Affect*. Cambridge: Polity Press.

Massumi, Brian. 2015b. *Ontopower: War, Powers, and the State of Perception*. Durham: Duke University Press.

Mulcahy, Dianne. 2021. "A Politics of Affect: Re/Assembling Relations of Class and Race at the Museum." *Emotion, Space and Society* 39: 1–7.

O'Sullivan, Simon. 2001. "The Aesthetics of Affect: Thinking Art Beyond Representation." *Angelaki: Journal of the Theoretical Humanities* 6 (3): 125–135.

Patton, Paul. 1994. "MetamorphoLogic: Bodies and Powers in a Thousand Plateaus." *Journal of the British Society for Phenomenology* 25 (2): 157–169.

Probyn, Elspeth. 2005. *Blush: Faces of Shame*. Minneapolis: University of Minnesota Press.

Reestorff, Camillia, M. 2015. "From Artwork to Net-Work: Affective Effects of Political Art." In *Affective Methodologies: Developing Research Strategies from the Study of Affect*, edited by Britta Timm Knudsen and Carsten Stage, 201–221. Basingstoke: Palgrave MacMillan.

Seyfert, Robert. 2012. "Beyond Personal Feelings and Collective Emotions: Toward a Theory of Social Affect." *Theory, Culture and Society* 29 (6): 27–46.

Schmitz, Sigrid. 2014. "Affect/Emotion: Orientation Matters. A Conversation with Sara Ahmed." *Freiburger Zeitschrift fur GeschlechterStudien* 20 (2): 97–108.e.

Sointu, Eeva, 2016. "Discourse, Affect and Affliction." *The Sociological Review* 64 (2) 312–328.
Spinoza, Baruch. 2000. *Ethics*. Oxford: Oxford University Press.
Thobo-Carlsen, Mette. 2017. "The Affects of the Art Work: On the Material Art Object and the Affective Encounter in the Art Exhibition." *ARKEN Bulletin* 7: 96–114.
Wetherell, Margaret. 2012. *Affect and Emotion: A New Social Science Understanding*. London: Sage Publications.

Chapter 13

Sex at the Workplace

Making Sexual Harassment Visible in Indonesian Businesses

Hendri Yulius Wijaya, Lany Harijanti, Maya Juwita, Nizma Fadila and Zelda Lupsita

Introduction

Women's rights activism aiming to end gender inequality is an essential part of Indonesia's cultural and political landscape. During the period of the authoritarian New Order regime (1966–1998), through religious organisations, grass root movements, and internationally-funded Non-Governmental Organisations (NGOs), feminist activism took multiple forms of political engagement. These initiatives ranged from intellectually exploring the compatibility of Islam, democracy, and gender equality, providing counselling for female victims of domestic violence, and advocating the rights of female migrant workers, among others (Rinaldo 2019, 137-38). Since Indonesia's democratic transition (1998–present), activists have been compelled to grapple with two critical events that subsequently shaped the activist trajectory: the mass rape of women of Indonesian Chinese descent in the May 1998 riots (ibid., 140; Robinson 2015, 55–56) and the expanding power of religious conservative groups in the public sphere advocating policies to control women's dress codes and public expressions, as well as queer sexualities (Allen 2007; Robinson 2015, 61; Wijaya 2020, 120–123).

To respond to these challenges, women's rights activists strategically used institutional and legal means offered by democratisation. In 1998, activists and the government established the Indonesian National Commission Against Violence Towards Women (*Komnas Perempuan*) to address violence against women, which increasingly became a prominent issue after the mass rape (Bennett and Davies 2015, 5). Further, since 1999, activists also championed the Elimination of Domestic Violence Law (*UU No. 23/ 2004 tentang Penghapusan Kekerasan Dalam Rumah Tangga*), which finally came into force in 2004, signifying "a huge victory for women's activism in Indonesia" (Rinaldo 2019, 142) that successfully united women's activists from various political sides to advocate for the legislation. Despite those achievements, women's and queer bodies continued to be the subject of public debates and controls, as evident in the Anti-Pornography Bill debates preceding its enactment in 2008 as the Pornography Law (*UU No. 44/2008 tentang Pornografi*) (see Allen 2007;

DOI: 10.4324/9781003379331-18

Barker 2015; Wijaya 2020, 121). While the initial draft proposing stringent restrictions on women's mobility and criminalisation of sex outside marriage was altered significantly in response to activist protests (Davies and Bennett 2015, 6–7), the law is still often used to criminalise queer people and sexualities (Wijaya 2020). Under this law, queer people can easily be charged because their sexual expressions can be considered as "pornographic performance" that threatens public morality (Wijaya 2021).[1]

This political development brings sexuality issues to the forefront of public discourses and debates, including issues of sexual violence and harassment. In this relatively new political, social and legal climate of Indonesian sexual politics, in this chapter we channel our analytical gaze to a non-state approach manifested in anti-sexual harassment in the workplace policies championed by an Indonesian business coalition, Indonesia Business Coalition for Women's Empowerment (IBCWE). On the one hand, this exploration is pertinent, especially in order to examine the other ways of addressing sexual violence and harassment that do not always rely on the legal and punitive mechanism. On the other hand, relatively little has been written about sexual harassment in the workplace in the Indonesian private sector. Rather than focus on critique, our purpose in this exploratory chapter is to examine the challenges and opportunities that IBCWE utilises to raise awareness of sexual harassment in the business world.

In this context, amidst the recent legislation of the Sexual Violence Crimes Law (*Undang-Undang Tindak Pidana Kekerasan Seksual*, TPKS) in April 2022 (Guzman 2022), we explore the other existing policy infrastructure, intriguingly unrelated to sexuality issues, that allows IBCWE to encourage companies to recognise sexual harassment as a serious workplace problem. In the ways that they strategically promote sexual harassment to the forefront of corporate awareness, IBCWE's manoeuvres are worth exploring, especially how the coalition formulates which types of action are considered sexual harassment and how businesses can facilitate an open discussion among their employees to draw a line between harassing and non-harassing behaviours. Such a process of defining and awareness-raising reveals a strategy to contextualise the discourse of sexual harassment in the business domain.

By looking at the interaction between IBCWE and business, we show how activism is still necessary to enable people to understand what sexual harassment is and to speak up about their personal experiences of it, if this is what they want. In business settings, to put it differently, policy-making and advocacy should also be accompanied by consciousness-raising. Within this purview, IBCWE's programme to foster open dialogue can be understood as a

1 Some local ordinances in several provinces like South Sumatra and South Kalimantan also emerged to police women's and queer sexualities (Robinson 2015, 57; UNDP and USAID 2014, 6; Wijaya and Davies 2019, 161).

preventive action for businesses and their staff. Throughout the process, run by a group of mostly women, IBCWE brings its personnel's diverse experiences into dialogue with the programme design, in turn shaping and assisting how each business approaches and defines sexual harassment. In our analysis, we aim to provide a situated account of the discourse formation and organisational processes that cannot be gleaned from either textual or legal-formalism analysis, by exploring how activism operates within existing constraints and opportunities in the example of anti-sexual harassment activism.

This chapter begins with a discussion of the activists' trials and travails to legislate against sexual violence since 2012, along with some context of the legal and activist climate in Indonesia. We highlight the connections between emerging local activism and patterns of feminist movements globally, revealing how feminist engagement with law and government shapes the ways sexual violence and harassment are made intelligible to the state and society. Next, we provide a brief historical overview of IBCWE as a business coalition and as a workplace gender equality advocate in the business sector, highlighting how IBCWE engages and localises international standards and frameworks in its activism. The following sections then examine the Indonesian policy infrastructure, followed by the processes, challenges and opportunities arising in mainstreaming awareness of workplace sexual harassment.[2] To conclude, we offer a reflection on what IBCWE has done to consider more dialogical interventions aimed at behaviour change rather than only punishment in addressing sexual harassment.

Trials and Travails: Legal and Activist Climate

Since sexuality issues have taken centre stage of public debates in Indonesia in the period of democracy, sexual violence against women has also increasingly become more visible, demanding an urgency for actions. Attempts at addressing sexual violence have driven women's rights activists to pursue legal pathways to legislate an anti-sexual violence bill. The bill was expected to make these forms of violence intelligible to the state and society, and enable victims to access justice and support from the state.

As a national organisation championing women's rights, Komnas Perempuan regularly publishes annual reports on violence against women (*Catatan Tahunan*, CATAHU) that consistently record varying forms of violence such as rape, forced marriage, and domestic violence, along with their respective figures nationwide. As a consequence of witnessing the breadth of violence and harassment faced by women, in 2012, *Komnas Perempuan* and women's rights activists began to develop the Sexual Violence Eradication Bill

2 IBCWE adopts and deploys the term 'sexual harassment' in their activism. We will describe the reason later.

(*Rancangan Undang-Undang Penghapusan Kekerasan Seksual*, RUU-PKS). The draft was completed in August 2016 and handed by Komnas Perempuan to the House of Representatives (*Dewan Perwakilan Rakyat*, DPR) for legislation (Supriyadi and Eddyono 2017, 3).

At the same time, while sexual violence issues have been central to the Indonesian women's rights movement since 1998, the swift rise of #MeToo movement in 2017 has contributed to galvanising activists to demand and campaign for the legislation of the RUU-PKS. In a similar vein, popular discourses, championed by young feminist activists, also circulate in the public sphere to highlight the prevalent rape culture in Indonesia (Asmarani 2016; Melati 2019, 109–112; Safira 2020), along with the vulnerability of women to sexual violence that is ignored by the state (Melati 2019, 132).[3] After a lengthy public debate and campaign, RUU-PKS comes into force as law, the Sexual Violence Crimes Law in April 2022 (Guzman 2022).

It is not too difficult to acknowledge that Indonesian activists' moves also coincide with patterns of feminist movements globally. Besides #MeToo, the last forty years have been marked by the entry of liberal feminist ideas into the state governance, through which "institutionalised discrimination and legal barriers" (ibid., 5) experienced by women are addressed by state-level policies. These policies focus on issues as varied as the criminalisation of domestic violence, sexual harassment, and human trafficking, as well as the introduction of gender quotas in parliaments (Ellerby 2017, 1). Famously, Janet Halley (2018, ix) introduced the notion of "governance feminism" to signify how "feminist ideas exert governing will within human affairs" (ibid.), increasing feminists' engagement with law and government to achieve their objectives. In this landscape, some critics argue that feminist engagement with the criminal justice system and law enforcement as a remedy for widespread sexual violence has unexpectedly led to the expansion of police power and the carceral state (Gruber 2020; see also Bernstein 2018).

These critique and studies are indeed valuable as a starting point for understanding contemporary global feminist sexual politics. At the same time, they also raise the question of whether addressing sexual harassment and violence always needs to engage punitive logics by legal mechanisms, thus calling for examining alternatives that may be available.

To address the concerns above, we consider activism, policy, and voluntary methods in the Indonesian contexts to address sexual harassment. In the

3 Before the legislation of the Sexual Violence Crimes Law (UU-PKS), although sexual violence is regulated through the Criminal Law (*Kitab Undang-Undang Hukum Pidana*, KUHP) and other laws including the Child Protection Law (*Undang-Undang Perlindungan Anak*) and the Elimination of Domestic Violence Law, the RUU-PKS proponents argued that such law does not provide adequate protection for the victims and still have a too narrow definition of rape (Mashabi 2020; Parhani 2020), because rape is mostly still confined to acts involved penile penetration to the vagina (Melati 2019, 146).

shadow of very strident activism for legal reforms, another way has emerged, which is no less regulatory, yet does not rely soley on state powers. To put it differently, such activism taps into the emerging international business and development frameworks, merging sexual harassment issues with sustainability, ESG (Environment, Social, and Governance) factors, and business reputation, among others. These frameworks and initiatives provide a platform for IBCWE to raise businesses' awareness and facilitate actions to address sexual harassment in the workplace.

IBCWE and Pathways to Workplace Gender Equality

Historically and internationally, gender equality in the business world has evolved through a series of policy developments, discourse formation, and normative frameworks.[4] In terms of women's economic empowerment, Vasuki Nesiah (2019, 507) shows that the 1975 International Conference on Women in Mexico contributed by foregrounding women and development in a way that centres "consciousness-raising and economic redistribution" (ibid., 509) in international development practices (see also Ellerby 2017). In the following decades, after introducing a Gender Empowerment Measure in the 1995 Human Development Index, women's economic empowerment continued to become central to international development, evident in the integration of gender equality issues in the United Nations (UN) Millennium Development Goals in 2000 and Sustainable Development Goals in 2015 (ibid., 507). Multilateral organisations, including the World Bank and the United States Agency for International Development (USAID), introduced programmes such as entrepreneurship and access to credit as central to gender equality initiatives (ibid., 517). Despite the critique of these practices as, for example, promoting neoliberalism (see, for example, Ellerby 2017; Halley 2018; Nesiah 2019), all these developments have also contributed to providing access to resources, including equal access to employment and education, initially denied to women (Halley 2018, x).

In the corporate domain, gender equality in the workplace can be traced back to various attempts at ensuring equal representation of women in management. For example, in 2003, Norway's Parliament required publicly listed companies to have "at least 40 per cent of directors be of the gender opposite the other percentage of directors" (Branson 2018, 91). Since then, quota laws have become part of public debate in the United States, the United Kingdom, New Zealand (ibid.), and France (see Malik 2019). However, progress does not always move smoothly. In its governance code, the Organisation for Economic Cooperation and Development (OECD) proposes that "countries may wish to

4 This section does not aim to provide a compherensive account on this development. For more discussions on the topic, see, among others, Ellerby (2017), Engel (2019) and Nesiah (2019).

consider measures such as voluntary targets, disclosures requirements, boardroom quotas, and private initiatives that enhance gender diversity on boards and in senior management" (cited from Branson 2018, 91). As a result, it is not difficult to see the dispersed practices of this equal gender representation in different companies and countries. Along the same lines, popular discourses, analysis, and advice to empower women in business have also circulated, from Sheryl Sanberg's *Lean In* (2013), Sophia Amuroso's *Girl Boss* (2014), to Ellen Carr and Katrina Dudley's *Undiversified* (2021).

Equally crucial within this emerging landscape is the increased prominence of the Environmental, Social, and Governance (ESG) and the Sustainable Development Goals (SDGs), which have increasingly been embraced by the business sector to demonstrate the responsible and ethical status of operations (see Eccles and Stroehle 2021, 203). Those international business and development frameworks provide norms for government, international actors, and companies to align and justify their international consensus activities. Further, they offer a formulaic means for companies to engage with pressing social and environmental issues, including gender equality, previously deemed unimportant to financial profitability. While there is indeed no shortage of normative frameworks and principles to improve gender equality in the workplace, the question arising now is how to identify specific problems and address them with practical strategies that suit specific organisational contexts and cultures. As Donna Haraway (2008, 214) puts it, "the devil is in the details, and so is the deity."

For its programmatic relationship with IBCWE, Australia provides a starting point to explore the IBCWE's work and activism that the Australian government supports. Domestically, the Australian government introduced the Workplace Gender Equality Act in 2012 to mainstream gender equality between men and women in business by requiring companies with more than one hundred employees to submit reports on gender equality policy and progress (Equal Opportunity Commission, n.d.). Since January 1, 2012, the Australian Stock Exchange (ASX) has required listed companies to "comply or explain with regard to diversity" (Branson 2018, 117), compelling them to disclose relevant equality policies (ibid.). Further, through reporting, companies must disclose policies and practices in six indicators, such as "gender composition of the workforce and governing body; equal remuneration between women and men; availability of flexible work and family/caregiving policies; employee consultations; and sexual discrimination and harassment" (Investing in Women 2020). Through its international development assistance, the Australian government has also championed gender equality in South East Asia.

Established in 2016, the program 'Investing in Women' primarily aims to "catalyse[s] inclusive economic growth through women's economic empowerment." It is understood that economic growth is not only central to achieving gender equality but also "to enhancing business competitiveness, fuelling inclusive economic growth and building equitable societies" (Investing in Women, n.d.). Implemented in the Philippines, Indonesia, Vietnam and Myanmar, the programme has three focus areas, such as "Workplace Gender Equality (WGE), Impact Investment for Women's SMEs, and Influencing Gender Norms" (ibid.). Specifically, in the context of this chapter, the Workplace Gender Equality programme has manifested in the formation of "Business Coalitions who work with influential businesses on shifting workplace cultures, practices, and policy barriers to achieve WGE" (ibid.).

Besides Vietnam and the Philippines Business Coalition for Women's Empowerment (VBCWE and PBCWE), the Indonesia Business Coalition for Women's Empowerment (IBCWE), supported by the Australian government and established in 2016, believes that "business, along with government and civil society, has a key role to play in reducing inequalities, tackling poverty and achieving the Sustainable Development Goals." (IBCWE, n.d.). In its programmatic approach, IBCWE tailors programmes to support its members in:

- Closing the gender pay gap
- Progressing women into leadership and management positions
- Improving female workplace participation
- Investing in female-friendly working conditions
- Ensuring that leaders and managers drive gender equality. (ibid.)

Mainstreaming gender equality in companies is made possible by first convincing them of the benefits of obtaining an internationally-recognised certification of their gender equality practices and excellence. In Indonesia, IBCWE[5] began its programme by assisting its member companies that wanted to obtain the EDGE (Economic Dividends for Gender Equality) Certification. It is important to note here that certification is a means for companies to showcase their regulatory compliance, and the ownership of the certification itself can help increase brand reputation as an actual benefit. In short, the EDGE certification is a "global assessment methodology and business certification standard for gender equality," thus "measur[ing] where organisations stand in terms of gender balance across their pipeline, pay equity, [the] effectiveness of policies and practices to ensure equitable career flows as well as inclusiveness of their culture" (the Global Business Certification Standard for Gender Equality, n.d.).[6] Since a third-party organisation will audit the company in the process of obtaining this certificate, IBCWE helps advise and assist companies in

5 Around 90% of IBCWE's team members are female.

6 For a comprehensive information on the EDGE certification, see the website of the Global Business Certification Standard for Gender Equality, https://edge-cert.org/.

meeting the EDGE criteria. A public display of the EDGE Certification Seals can "enhance the brand's credibility" (ibid.).[7]

Since normative frameworks or tools are necessary to identify the key improvement areas alongside the precise indicators to be fulfilled, IBCWE and other business coalitions have also worked with the 'Investing in Women' core staff members based in the Phillippines to develop a diagnostic tool relevant to local contexts, in addition to the EDGE certification. This tool is called "Gender Equality Assessment, Results, and Strategies" (GEARS). Initially, GEARS was developed by Australia's Workplace Gender Equality Agency (WGEA) established by the Workplace Gender Equality Act 2012[8] (WGEA, 2019).

For South East Asia, business coalitions have contextualised GEARS's key focus areas, along with its indicators, to render them relevant to the local context and allow companies to start their improvement plans, instead of merely imposing indicators that do not always resonate locally. This application of the GEARS tool aims to track and treat improvements as a journey rather than a tick-a-box exercise. Now, consisting of ten focus areas that include equal representation and preventing gender-based discrimination and sexual harassment, the company must answer 77 questions about gender-related practices under this tool. Based on the data, IBCWE will provide advice to improve the company's practices and policies, and identify possible improvement strategies. As of writing, IBCWE has 28 corporate members, and around half of them have been diagnosed by using the GEARS tool. For those that score high in the GEARS, IBCWE can assist them in obtaining the EDGE certification since those companies are considered to already have sufficient policies and practices to be assessed by the EDGE, if they want.

The inclusion of issues of anti-sexual harassment into women's economic empowerment is associated with an increase in international attention to this issue. The flood of people joining the #MeToo movement sends a clear signal about "just how widespread sexual assault and harassment actually are; that most victim-survivors know the offender; and, significantly, these experiences are *routine* and *normalised*" (Filerborn and Loney-Howes 2019, 2). As a response, available reports also highlight that many organisations have started to create or update their anti-harassment policies, complaint procedures, and training programmes (see, for example, Edelman 2018; Bolden-Barret 2019; Buchwald 2018), promoting sexual harassment to the forefront of corporate awareness. Nowadays, it seems almost impossible to discuss gender equality in the workplace without considering sexual harassment.

7 In 2018, there were five Indonesian companies that successfully obtained the EDGE certification (IBCWE 2018).

8 In Australia, the tool is often called 'Gender Equality Diagnostic Tool' (Workplace Gender Equality Agency 2019).

Overall, the above accounts showcase the trajectory of institutionalisation of gender equality in the business sector and the various forms of policies and frameworks providing the norms for particular aspects of gender equality to be achieved by companies. However, norms are not permanently fixed or stable, and are subject to recalibration in local practices. Equally important, indicators are not merely tick-boxes but often offer opportunities and capacities to transform a corporation. It depends on how the actors make use of them. The following sections attend to the ways IBCWE strategically utilises policies and frameworks, often unrelated to gender issues, to mainstream awareness of sexual harassment, followed by their attempts at defining and contextualising sexual harassment that dynamically involved individual staff members' reflections of their situated experiences.

Policy Infrastructure: Setting the Agenda and Utilising Policy

IBCWE began its programme on sexual harassment in the workplace by investigating the existing policies and guidelines on sexual violence or harassment for businesses in Indonesia. Importantly, this exploration stage was not treated separately from the GEARS tool. This tool enables IBCWE to evaluate the needs and measure what companies already have, what they can and should do in the future, and equally, what kinds of existing state and non-state policies, programmes, and initiatives can be used as a basis or inspiration to prompt companies to improve their policies and practices.

Interestingly, several non-state initiatives and guidelines on sexual harassment are already in place. Following the introduction of the Circular Letter of Ministry of Labour and Transmigration in 2011, Indonesia's Employer Association (*Asosasi Pengusaha Indonesia*, APINDO) released a guideline to prevent and address workplace sexual harassment for employers in 2012 (APINDO 2012). In brief, the guidelines provide the definition, forms, preventive actions and recommendations on victims' grievance mechanisms and proper case-handling and investigations to ensure fairness. Additionally, since 2007, the 'Better Work' programme, a partnership programme between the International Labour Organisation (ILO) and International Finance Corporation (IFC), has not only "promote[d] humane working conditions in apparel factories in developing and emerging countries [including Indonesia]" (Djaya, Brown and Lupo 2019, 4) but also in "foster[ing] gender equality, reduc[ing] sexual harassment, and clos[ing] the gender pay gap in the global garment industry" (ibid.). The 'Better Work' programme evaluation report released in 2019 shows that "women become vocal about sexual harassment … suggesting that participation in the Better Work programme may have a positive impact on their awareness and capacity to voice concerns" (ibid., 5). Reportedly, the Indonesian Stock Exchange (IDX), as an institution, already has a provision against sexual harassment stated in the Code of Conduct or Employee Handbook and Work

Agreement (*Kode Etik/Pedoman Perilaku Karyawan dan Perjanjian Kerja Bersama*) (IBCWE, n.d.). Of course, the above list is not exhaustive, but the activities signal various workplace initiatives – though still dispersed – to curb sexual harassment. However, this overall progress calls for interrogation as to how far and how effective companies have implemented the guidelines and responded to cases. Written rules must be accompanied by concrete actions and an enabling environment, to allow people to engage with those policies.

Attempts at producing social change often utilise the opportunities and resources made available to them within the existing systems. Such efforts also depend on the actors merging their goals and interests with what the system offers. In this context, IBCWE taps into the emerging discourse, framework and policy of 'Sustainable Finance' and 'Sustainable Development Goals.' In principle, sustainability, often historically traced back to the 1987 report of the Brundtland Commission, consists of "three co-equal parts or elements...wi th the letter e: environment, economy, and equity" (Portney 2015, 6). This means that "sustainability can be achieved only by simultaneously protecting the environment, preserving economic growth and development, and promoting equity" (ibid.). Similarly, Gender Equality is one of the UN's Sustainable Development Goals (UN SDGs).

In response to this emerging landscape, the Indonesian government, through the Financial Service Authority (*Otoritas Jasa Keuangan*, OJK), has introduced specific regulations requiring banks, financial institutions and publicly listed companies to disclose their environmental, social and governance (popularly termed ESG) performance and data annually in their sustainability report[9] (KPMG 2020) to demonstrate corporate contributions to the achievement of UN SDGs. This sustainability reporting regulation requires all businesses to report their efforts to support environmental conservation, including water and energy efficiency and biodiversity protection. It also requires that companies explicitly state their anti-discrimination policies/practices in the workplace, no child labour, compliance with minimum wage, and equally, decent and safe work environment policies. While the regulation does not specify in detail how the companies should present the information, it is not rare to find those companies also learn to adopt the internationally-recognised standards of sustainability reporting to answer all the required aspects, making their reports comply with the global sustainability reporting standards.

To IBCWE, this state policy, which is built upon the state's commitment to the UN SDGs, offers a strategic entrance to convince companies to tackle sexual harassment (see also Investing in Women 2020). Referring to this policy as a basis, IBCWE encourages its members to showcase their policies or practices of addressing workplace harassment in their sustainability reports, describing

9 For a comprehensive discussion on sustainability reporting, see, among others, Bini and Belluci (2020).

them under the aspects of anti-discrimination or decent work environment. This approach can also be considered as a means to apply a gender perspective, showing how a decent work environment must also consider policies and practices to address sexual harassment often experienced by female workers. Maya Juwita, IBCWE Executive Director, optimistically believes that sustainability reporting can be a means to disclose companies' attempts at ensuring gender equality in Indonesia, similar to what the Australia Stock Exchange (ASX) does for listed companies (explained earlier).

Nevertheless, the extent to which the gender policies and practices can be described in the report is contingent on the companies' commitment and level of understanding, not to mention the current state of their gender policy's implementation that determines what the companies could and would disclose in the reports. These challenges drove IBCWE to apply the GEARS tool to assess the current state of the companies' practices on workplace sexual harassment, which would be followed by recommendations for improvement from IBCWE. Among the ten key focus areas identified by GEARS, including gender pay equity, workplace gender composition, recruitment, selection and promotion, focus area six specifically highlights gender-based harassment and discrimination. Within this aspect, IBCWE would examine whether or not the member companies have particular policies, have applied them in practice, and finally, have monitored a policy's implementation and continuously improved their results over time. Based on this assessment, IBCWE then provides some recommendations, for instance, to encourage the companies to conduct employee consultations, organise regular mandatory training, or develop a grievance or complaint handling mechanism on sexual harassment. Combined, the companies can then report the results of their assessment and any future improvement plans in their sustainability reports to demonstrate their commitment to ensuring a decent and safe workplace for employees, particularly for women.

Interestingly, while the IBCWE's scoping assessment of the companies' practices in early 2020 shows that a large portion of them already have a clear policy to tackle sexual harassment (and hence can already be written in their sustainability reports), three main concerns have come to IBCWE's attention. First, companies do not always have a reliable mechanism to respond to complaints, evident in how they refer the victims to a third-party, such as a psychologist. In other words, this mechanism is not yet embedded in the human resources management structure. Second, companies often tend not to monitor progress when the case is handed to the third-party. Finally, employees do not always feel comfortable or are not always willing to report the harassment.

Some other notes are arising from such an evaluation as well. On the one hand, it is essential to acknowledge that these findings do not offer a generalised account of workplace sexual harassment in Indonesian companies. On the other hand, the points above also reveal an interesting point about the inadequacy of simply having a policy in place. For the policy to be enacted with proper practices, it requires highly-capable actors to tackle the case and assist the victim-survivors during and after the grievance is received and being investigated. Additionally, it is also necessary to increase the employees' awareness of the existing policy and provide an enabling environment that would not hinder them from reporting the harassment.

With these challenges identified, IBCWE agrees to work on awareness-raising as the first step. Working to set up a clear grievance mechanism and increase the organisation's human resources capacity might take a longer time. In contrast, preventive action can be taken immediately to halt potential harassment from happening. Said differently, activism is often carried out in gradual steps, and prevention can be effective when people understand what harassment means and build a consensus in the workplace about what is allowed and what is not. The strategy of IBCWE to convince companies to open their doors and facilitate awareness-raising training is the focus of the next section.

Programmatic Design: Defining Scope and Identifying Problems

There were at least two principal concerns for IBCWE when developing the design of the awareness-raising programme. Besides defining sexual harassment in the workplace, another main challenge is how to convince companies to facilitate internal discussions or seminars on the topic. Activists highlighted that companies might still think that tackling sexual harassment and/or violence is not a priority (Jumisih and Asmawaty 2020). Moreover, data on the prevalence of sexual harassment and/or violence in the corporate world is scattered (Ford 2018, 13). There was an urgency to at least have basic information about the prevailing types of workplace sexual harassment and/or violence to understand the current state of the matter. Another concern is deeply related to the awareness-raising programme design and its impacts. Said differently, how far would the company be able and willing to handle and solve the employees' complaints, if they arise after the training? This question guided IBCWE to develop the scope of training and the potential apparatus to be engaged if employees file complaints as they become more aware of the harassment issue.

To begin with, available data on sexual harassment and/or violence mostly demonstrate the upward trend of registered cases over the last five years, reaching over 431,471 cases in 2019 (Gerlach 2020). It is also reported that "in almost all settings, the majority had been perpetrated by their intimate partner," while segregated cases occurring in corporate workplaces were not always easily located (see Ford 2018, 13). One possible explanation is that sexual harassment and/or violence in the workplace is not always disclosed to actors outside of the company due to the protection of business' reputation. Another explanation might be related to the victims' unwillingness to report for various reasons, the absence of a clear grievance mechanism, or the lack of awareness of the existing policy.

To convince companies to seriously address sexual harassment, from February to March 2019, IBCWE worked together with the Never Okay Project to conduct a snapshot survey on sexual harassment in the workplace. Never Okay Project (neverokayproject.org) is an anonymous online platform aiming to facilitate a safe space for victims of sexual harassment at work to share their experiences. By administering an online survey to companies across different industry sectors, both organisations reached out to 6,616 respondents. Most of them were women from the manufacturing sector. One of the important findings from the survey that influenced IBCWE's programmatic design is the fact that most respondents had limited knowledge on how to respond to any of the types of sexual harassment they experienced as victims and bystanders, and believed both men and women can be victims, as well as perpetrators of sexual harassment and/or violence.

Equally important, based on the survey results, sexual violence, like rape, can be more readily identified by the respondents compared to sexual harassment which, ranging from an unwanted gaze and catcalling to physical touching, often occurs in a 'grey area.' The term 'grey area' here refers to the multivarious meanings that might arise and thus might be differently perceived by both senders and recipients in particular social and cultural contexts, meaning that the experiences of such actions cannot always be predetermined. For example, calling each other 'dear' or 'darling' between two long-term colleagues might simply mean a kind gesture signalling close friendship, whereas in another case involving a manager and a subordinate, it might cause discomfort for the subordinate or vice versa.

Not only does the above understanding drive IBCWE to focus first on sexual harassment instead of sexual violence, but IBCWE also believes that this scope is a strategic step to begin the program. Again, activism is about gradual moves, and change does not happen overnight. Starting the awareness of issues of sexual violence would potentially deter companies from continuing the program. Companies are wary that sexual violence will involve the Criminal Code and the Court, which will quickly affect, and subsequently damage, the business's reputation. At the same time, IBCWE is also fully aware that they cannot handle sexual violence cases independently, especially if they involve a lawsuit. Besides the Sexual Violence Crimes Law coming into force recently, it is necessary to note here that the Criminal Code includes a few general provisions that can be used as a basis to prosecute cases of sexual violence and/or harassment (see also Ford 2018, 5).

Eventually, having considered the organisational capacity, policy infrastructure, and programmatic scope, IBCWE's awareness-raising training is then positioned as a means to open dialogue within the company about sexual harassment. Through this dialogue, employees are facilitated to establish consensus about what is permissible and non-permissible behaviour in the workplace, in order to prevent future misconduct. Far from the intention to quickly punish people, the following section will describe IBCWE's attempts to develop training materials that take into account the social contexts of intimate encounters between people, preventing us from quickly collapsing all of them under the rubric of 'harassment' and empowering people to speak up about their experiences.

Awareness Development: Recognising Messiness and Trudging Ambiguity

In tailoring the awareness-raising materials, the question arising now is how does IBCWE best define and understand sexual harassment in a manner that takes into account not only "*what* happened and *who* it happened to" (Fileborn and Phillips 2019, 102) but also the social circumstances of where it happened. All these considerations would help conceptualise a definition of sexual harassment that does not always associate it with misconducts of "men-versus-women" (Gruber 2020, 16) and, importantly, considers multivarious meanings of intimate actions between two or more people in the workplace.

When first developing the training materials, IBCWE adopted the sexual harassment definition widely deployed internationally; it primarily consists of two forms: 'quid-pro-quo' and 'hostile working environment.' The first refers to "a situation when a job benefit is tied to an employee submitting to unwelcome sexual advances" (American Bar Association 2013), while the latter highlights sexually-animated behaviours or attitudes that generate an intimidating environment and are offensive to the workers" (APINDO 2012, 8). Examining this definition and other training resources available on various international websites made IBCWE realise that although there is no shortage of clear examples, discourses, and explanations of sexual harassment on the Internet, all these examples must be situated in the workplace's social contexts to make them resonate with the employees' complex experiences. No wonder, then, if most of the IBCWE team members brought their past working experiences to the table, revealing that developing training materials is a dynamic process in which subjective experiences inform the ways the materials are shaped, assembled, highlighted and delivered.

Despite the high prevalence of harassment by men towards women, the first issue coming to the discussion during the training material development among the IBCWE team members was how to convince people that sexual harassment can also occur the other way around. Attention to this possibility helps detach women's stereotype as always a victim and passive, and equally, persuade the workplace that this is everyone's issue. Lola (not her real name), previously holding a human resources manager position, contributed to the discussion by telling of her experience a few decades ago when she deliberately touched and called her white American male colleague 'darling' in the workplace. After participating in human resources training, she realised that this was a form of harassment, consequently prompting her to apologise to him. Her white male colleague then replied that he believed that harassing him was not

Lola's *intention* (italics added). Intriguingly, he also said that what could be put him at serious risk was if his female spouse heard about Lola calling him 'darling' as this it would make her suspicious of his relationship with Lola.

Lola's experience helped the IBCWE team highlight the centrality of 'intention' and 'impacts' in debates and discussions on sexual harassment. In terms of impacts, the above anecdote presents an example of sexual harassment that is distinct from narratives of trauma, emotional or physical injury, or hostile environment. Illustrating the effect of potentially debilitating one's relationship with their spouse could help obtain male employees' commitment to addressing the issue, when they otherwise often consider themselves to be immune from sexual harassment. However, when stumbling into the aspect of 'intention,' the team felt that the issue could be contentious since it is not always possible to ascertain the intention behind an action. In one discussion during the training material development, some IBCWE team members also raised the issue of 'flirting' in the workplace. One member raised her objection to permitting flirting at work, because people could easily argue that what they were doing was 'just flirting,' to conceal their actual intention to harass a person. Here, we saw the debate as productive and constructive, calling for a more precise boundary to define 'harassment' vis-à-vis 'flirting' when the intention is not explicitly apparent. What is no less intriguing was the realisation that 'intimate encounters' or 'closeness' between colleagues – particularly when they become close friends, lovers or married – is not necessarily rare in the workplace. Said differently, it is not unusual for opposite-sex colleagues to form a close relationship in the workplace as friends and express their closeness by calling each other using terms of endearment, like 'dear,' 'babe' or 'darling.' In fact, the IBCWE team members even realised that a male adviser of the company, aged around 70 years old, often kissed their cheeks in a friendly manner when visiting the office. Should such an action be classified as sexual harassment? In some instances, it should be. But in the above case, the team did not think it was harassment because not only they could 'feel' that the intention was not to harass them, but also because kissing cheeks is part of the daily manner to express closeness. For the team, that adviser's act is symbolised as a 'fatherly' gesture (*kebapakan*) that does not carry any sexual intention.

Since intention is not always identifiable, defining harassment is reliant on how the receiver reacts to such action, and how the perpetrator responds to any reaction from the receiver. To illustrate, if the receiver is angry, says no, or expresses discomfort to the flirting attempts and the alleged perpetrator then ceases their actions, it would likely not quickly morph into harassment. Nevertheless, harassment does occur when such 'flirting' attempts are carried out continuously despite the receiver's negative responses, making the situation hostile and antagonistic. Similar logic can also be applied to two opposite-sex colleagues, who become close to each other and call each other endearment terms while engaging in a long-term work relationship. When neither of them expresses discomfort and each responds positively, it is difficult to classify this as harassment. Resolving the contention about 'intention,' the team, therefore, proposed to carefully consider the action's repetitiveness and the perpetrator's response to rejection from the receiver to determine whether an action is harassment or not.

The above illustrations are not meant to be exhaustive. Instead, they highlight that in specific social circumstances where an action can have multiple meanings, whether or not something is harassment will depend on social contexts and interactions between the receiver and the perpetrator that cannot be easily predetermined. Having recognised this complexity, IBCWE's training materials are intended not only to present definitions and examples of harassment, together with the statistics of women who experience harassment in the workplace cited from many available resources. They also aim to equip participants to be aware of the 'grey area' and genuinely evaluate their actions based on the above considerations that IBCWE introduces. Particular meanings of any actions cannot always be predicted before they unfold in a particular situation involving specific individuals.

As of the time of writing, the IBCWE awareness-raising session is designed for two hours for all company members. Within that limited amount of time, IBCWE presents the definition, statistical data, and the impacts of harassment on companies and employees from available resources. But more importantly, IBCWE includes discussions and case studies to incite the participants' evaluative faculty to be more sensitive to contexts and a potential receiver's responses. By doing so, IBCWE wishes to foster open dialogue among employees, equipping them with awareness to continuously consider the responses to their actions in the workplace. What is also important to note from this approach is that this awareness-raising is not a means to apply punishment to people, but instead a preventive strategy to create a comfortable workplace. Ultimately, preventive action can only be effective when an open discussion about boundaries is allowed, enabling people to know their actions' limits and risks. Thus, IBCWE has not yet developed specific training for any Human Resources department to handle complaints. As a mitigation strategy, IBCWE provides some referee contacts (i.e. non-profit organisations handling trauma for rape victims) for employees who might experience trauma or want to consult with experts during or after the training.

Last, IBCWE understands that this approach is not always perfect. At the time of writing, the awareness-raising has been rolled out online to three companies (due to the COVID pandemic restrictions), the organisation has been monitoring what worked and what did not, to improve its training materials. As a reminder again, activism is often an experimental practice, subject to continuous recalibration.

Reflection

This chapter does not aim to offer a generalised and complete account of activism addressing sexual harassment and/or violence in Indonesia's workplaces.

Instead, it attempts to open up conversations about the complexity and challenges and opportunities involved, enabling this activism to be carried out within the business world. A more situated and grounded exploration of activist strategies is essential to properly understand how activism involves attempts at trudging the lack of data, navigating ambiguity, and defining the focus to succeed in obtaining commitment from companies. In this initial programme, we have not integrated issues of sexual orientation and/or gender identity beyond the category male and female due to the anti-LGBT backlash in the country a few years ago (see Wijaya 2020). By recognising such intricacies, we wish to offer key learnings from the field that might help other activists who share the same mission.

Connecting IBCWE's activism with current debates in feminist engagements with legal order and state powers (see, among others, Bernstein 2018; Halley 2018; Gruber 2020), we also hope this chapter can provide a practical case study on the current debates about the heightened use of punishment and legal means to address sexual harassment. As described in the introduction, there is an increase in awareness of sexual harassment and/or violence in Indonesia, accompanied by activists' pathways to address this issue through law. This chapter does not intend to engage in the debates above. Rather, IBCWE's activism demonstrates more dialogical interventions aimed at behaviour change, which provide a space for employees and their employers to build on the consensus and boundaries of permissible and non-permissible behaviour in the workplace. IBCWE will continue assessing and recalibrating their approaches, depending on what worked and what did not work in the field.

Bibliography

Allen, P. 2007. "Challenging Diversity? Indonesia's Anti-Pornography Bill." *Asian Studies Review* 31 (2): 101–115.

American Bar Association. 2013. *The Law and Your Job: Sexual Harassment.* American Bar Association Website. Accessed May 10, 2021. https://www.americanbar.org/groups/public_education/resources/law_issues_for_consumers/sexualharassment_quidproquo/.

Amuroso, S. 2014. *Girl Boss.* New York: Portfolio/Penguin.

Asosasi Pengusaha Indonesia (APINDO). 2012. *Pencegahan dan Penanganan Pelecehan Seksual di Tempat Kerja: Panduan Bagi Para Pemberi Kerja*, edited by I.R. Noor and I.M. Hidayana. Jakarta: APINDO.

Asmarani, D. 2016. *Ending Rape Culture in Indonesia.* Magdalene. Accessed May 10, 2021. https://www.magdalene.co/story/ending-rape-culture-in-indonesia.

Barker, T. 2015. "Sex on Indonesia's Screens." In *Sex and Sexualities in Contemporary Indonesia*, edited by L.R. Bennett and S.G. Davies, 253–272. London and New York: Routledge.

Bernstein, Elizabeth. 2018. *Brokered Subjects : Sex, Trafficking, and the Politics of Freedom.* Chicago: The University of Chicago Press.

Bini, L., and M. Bellucci. 2020. *Integrated Sustainability Reporting.* Cham: Switzerland: Springer International.

Bolden-Barrett, V. 2019. *New Report Compiles Sexual Harassment Policy Reforms Made Since #MeToo*. HRDive Website. Accessed May 10, 2021. https://www.hrdive.com/news/new-report-compiles-sexual-harassment-policy-reforms-made-since-metoo/560675/.

Branson, D.M. 2018. *The Future of Tech Is Female : How to Achieve Gender Diversity*. New York: New York University Press.

Buchwald, E. 2018. *In the Wake of #MeToo, More U.S. Companies Reviewed Their Sexual Harassment Policies*. Market Watch Website. Accessed May 10, 2021. https://www.marketwatch.com/story/in-the-wake-of-metoo-more-than-half-of-companies-have-reviewed-their-sexual-harassment-policies-2018-07-10.

Carr E., and K. Dudley. 2021. *Undiversified: The Big Gender Short in Investment Management*. Columbia: Columbia University Press.

Davies, S.G., and L.R. Bennett. 2015. "Introduction: Mapping Sex and Sexualities in Contemporary Indonesia." In *Sex and Sexualities in Contemporary Indonesia*, edited by L.R. Bennett and S.G. Davies, 1–25. London and New York: Routledge.

Djaya D., D. Brown, and L. Lupo. 2019. *An Impacy Evaluation of Better Work from a Gender Perspective, Discussion Paper, International Labour Organisation (ILO) and International Finance Cooperation (IFC)*. Accessed May 10, 2021. https://betterwork.org/wp-content/uploads/2020/01/Discussion-Paper-30.pdf.

Eccles, R.G., and J.C. Stroehle. 2021. "The Impact on Mutual Profit on Business Behaviour." In *Putting Purpose Into Practice: The Economics of Mutuality*, edited by C. Mayer and B. Roche, 199–210. Oxford: Oxford University Press.

Edelman, L.B. 2018. *How HR and Judges Made It Almost Impossible for Victims of Sexual Harassment to Win in Court*. Harvard Business Review Website. Accessed May 10, 2021. https://hbr.org/2018/08/how-hr-and-judges-made-it-almost-impossible-for-victims-of-sexual-harassment-to-win-in-court.

Ellerby, K. 2017. *No Shortcut to Change: An Unlikely Path to a More Gender Equitable World*. New York: New York University Press.

Engel, K. 2019. "Feminist Governance and International Law: From Liberal to Carceral Feminism." In *Governance Feminism: Notes from the Field*, edited by J. Halley, P. Kotiswaran, R. Rebouche, and H. Samir, 3–30. Minneapolis and London: University of Minnesota Press.

Equal Opportunity Commission. *Workplace Gender Equality Act*. Equal Opportunity Commision Website. Accessed May 10, 2021. https://eoc.sa.gov.au/resources/discrimination-laws/australian-laws/workplace-gender-equality-act#:~:text=The%20Workplace%20Gender%20Equality%20Act,and%20men%20in%20the%20workplace.&text=support%20employers%20to%20remove%20barriers,in%20relation%20to%20employment%20matters.

Fileborn, B., and R. Loney-Howes. 2019. "Introduction: Mapping the Emergence of #MeToo." In *#MeToo and The Politics of Social Change*, edited by B. Fileborn and R. Loney-Howes, 1–18. Cham: Palgrave Macmillan.

Fileborn, B., and N. Phillips. 2019. "From 'Me Too' to 'Too Far'? Contesting the Boundaries of Sexual Violence in Contemporary Activism." In *#MeToo and The Politics of Social Change*, edited by B. Fileborn and R. Loney-Howes, 99–116. Cham: Palgrave Macmillan.

Ford, M. 2018. *Investing in Women: Indonesia Country Context Paper*. Sydney: Sydney Southeast Asia Centre – The University of Sydney.

Gerlach, R. 2020. *The Fight to Outlaw Sexual Violence in Indonesia*. Inside Indonesia. Accessed May 10, 2021. https://www.insideindonesia.org/the-fight-to-outlaw-sexual-violence-in-indonesia.

Gruber, A. 2020. *The Feminist War on Crime : The Unexpected Role of Women's Liberation in Mass Incarceration*. Berkeley: University of California Press.

Guzman, Chad de. 2022. "After a Teacher Was Convicted of Raping 13 Girls, Indonesia Finally Passed Sexual Violence Reform." *Time*. Accessed April 21, 2022. https://time.com/6166853/indonesia-sexual-violence-law/.

Halley, J. 2018. "Preface: Introducing Governance Feminism." In *Governance Feminism*, edited by J. Halley, P. Kotiswaran, R. Rebouche, and H. Samir, ix–xxi. Minneapolis and London: University of Minnesota Press.

Haraway, D. 2008. *When Species Meet*. Minneapolis and London: University of Minnesota Press.

Indonesia Business Coalition for Women Empowerment (IBCWE). n.d. *About Us*. IBCWE Website. Accessed May 10, 2021. https://www.ibcwe.id/eng/about.

Indonesia Business Coalition for Women Empowerment (IBCWE). n.d. *Tanya Jawab: Bagaimana Kontribusi Bisnis Dalam Pencapaian Sustainable Development Goals No. 5?* IBCWE Website. Accessed May 10, 2021. https://www.ibcwe.id/event/dets/193.

Indonesia Business Coalition for Women Empowerment (IBCWE). 2018. *Strengthening Women's Economic Empowerment*. Accessed May 10, 2021. https://www.ibcwe.id/event/dets/64.

Investing in Women. n.d. *About Us*. Investing in Women Website. Accessed May 10, 2021. https://investinginwomen.asia/about/.

Investing in Women. 2020. *WGEA Director Libby Lyons Discusses the Business Case for WGE at IW Partner Events*. Investing in Women Website. Accessed May 10, 2021. https://investinginwomen.asia/posts/wgea-director-libby-lyons-business-case-wge-iw-partner-events/.

Jumisih, and A.C. Asmawaty. 2020. *Sexual Violence and Women Workers*. Inside Indonesia. Accessed May 10, 2021. https://www.insideindonesia.org/sexual-violence-and-women-workers.

KPMG. 2020. *Sustainable Finance in Indonesia*. Jakarta: KPMG.

Malik, M. 2019. "Governance Feminism in the French Republic: Veils, *Parité*, and Feminists." In *Governance Feminism: Notes from the Field*, edited by J. Halley, P. Kotiswaran, R. Rebouche, and H. Samir, 317–343. Minneapolis and London: University of Minnesota Press.

Mashabi, S. 2020. "Indonesia Darurat Kekerasan Seksual, Kenapa RUU PKS Tak Kunjung Disahkan?" *Kompas.com*. Accessed May 10, 2020. https://nasional.kompas.com/read/2020/08/13/09403501/indonesia-darurat-kekerasan-seksual-kenapa-ruu-pks-tak-kunjung-disahkan?page=all.

Melati, Nadya Karima. 2019. *Membicarakan Feminisme*. Yogyakarta: EA Books.

Nesiah, Vasuki. 2019. "Indebted: The Cruel Optimism of Leaning-in to Empowerment." In *Governance Feminism: Notes from the Field*, edited by J. Halley, P. Kotiswaran, R. Rebouche, and H. Samir, 505–554. Minneapolis and London: University of Minnesota Press.

Parhani, S. 2020. "5 Hal yang Perlu Kamu Ketahui tentang RUU PKS, Magdalene." Accessed May 10, 2020. https://magdalene.co/story/5-hal-yang-harus-kamu-ketahui-tentang-ruu-pks.

Portney, K.E. 2015. *Sustainability*. Cambridge, MA: MIT Press.

Rinaldo, R. 2019. "The Women's Movement and Indonesia's Transition to Democracy." In *Activists in Transition: Progressive Politics in Democratic Indonesia*, edited by T. Dibley and M. Ford, 135–152. Ithaca and London: Cornell University Press.

Robinson, K. 2015. "Masculinity, Sexuality, and Islam." In *Sex and Sexualities in Contemporary Indonesia*, edited by L.R. Bennett and S.G. Davies, 51–68. London and New York: Routledge.

Safira, D. 2020. *Sekarang, Kita seperti Hidup dengan Pasangan yang Posesif. Voxpop Indonesia.* Accessed May 10, 2021. https://voxpop.id/sekarang-kita-seperti-hidup-dengan-pasangan-yang-posesif/.

Sanberg, S. 2013. *Lean In: Women, Work, and The Will to Lead.* New York: Alfred A. Knopf.

Supriyadi, M.R., and W. Eddyono. 2017. *Menuju Penguatan Hak Korban dalam RUU Penghapusan Kekerasan Seksual.* Jakarta: Institute for Criminal Justice Reform.

The Global Business Certification Standard for Gender Equality. n.d. *What is EDGE Certification?* The Global Business Certification Standard for Gender Equality Website. Accessed May 10, 2021. https://edge-cert.org/certifications/#intro.

UNDP (United Nations Development Programme) and USAID (United Nations Development Programme and United States Agency for International Development). 2014. *Being LGBT in Asia: Indonesia Country Report.* Bangkok: UNDP.

Wijaya, Hendri Y. 2020. *Intimate Assemblages: The Politics of Queer Identities and Sexualities in Indonesia.* Singapore: Palgrave Macmillan.

Wijaya, Hendri Y. 2021. "Privacy, Porn, and Gay Sex Parties: The Carceral Governance of Homosexuality in Indonesia." *Laws* 10 (4): 87. https://doi.org/10.3390/laws10040087.

Wijaya, Hendri Y., and S.G. Davies. 2019. "The Unfulfilled Promise of Democracy: Lesbian and Gay Activism and Indonesia." In *Activists in Transition: Progressive Politics in Democratic Indonesia*, edited by T. Dibley and M. Ford, 153–170. Ithaca and London: Cornell University Press.

Workplace Gender Equality Agency. 2019. *Gender Strategy Toolkit.* Workplace Gender Equality Agency Website. Accessed May 10, 2021. https://www.wgea.gov.au/tools/gender-strategy-toolkit.

Index

For Product Safety Concerns and Information please contact our EU
representative GPSR@taylorandfrancis.com
Taylor & Francis Verlag GmbH, Kaufingerstraße 24, 80331 München, Germany

www.ingramcontent.com/pod-product-compliance
Ingram Content Group UK Ltd.
Pitfield, Milton Keynes, MK11 3LW, UK
UKHW022317250926
475702UK00046B/897
* 9 7 8 1 0 3 2 0 5 1 4 6 8 *